NICHOLAS II

Other books by the author

Russia and the Origins of the First World War
Russia's Rulers under the Old Regime
The Aristocracy in Europe, 1815–1914

NICHOLAS II

Twilight of the Empire

DOMINIC LIEVEN

St. Martin's Press
New York

Library of Congress Cataloging-in-Publication Data

Lieven, D. C. B.
Nicholas II : twilight of the Empire / Dominic Lieven.
p.   cm.
ISBN 0-312-10510-X
1. Nicholas II, Emperor of Russia, 1868-1918.   2. Russia—Kings
and rulers—Biography.   3. Russia—History—Nicholas II, 1894-1917.
I. Title.
DK258.L46   1994
947.08′3′092—dc20   [B]   93-37269   CIP

First published in Great Britain by John Murray (Publishers) Ltd.

First U.S. Edition : January 1994
10 9 8 7 6 5 4 3 2 1

For Maxie

Contents

Illustrations

The author and publishers would like to thank the Hulton Deutsch Collection for permission to reproduce Plates 1 and 28.

Preface

In recent years there have been a number of biographies of Nicholas II. Why then is another one necessary? The answer is that this book has aims very different to those of its predecessors. The latter have concentrated their attention on Nicholas as family man, father of a haemophiliac heir, protector of Rasputin, or victim of the tragedy at Ekaterinburg in July 1918. Some of these books have fulfilled the tasks set by their authors admirably. Robert Massie's work, *Nicholas and Alexandra* (London, 1968), was a sensitive and moving study of Nicholas and Alexandra's marriage and, above all, of their fate as parents of a haemophiliac child. In *The Last Tsar* (London and New York, 1992), Edvard Radzinsky unearthed a great deal of fascinating new material on the murder of the imperial family. But neither Massie nor Radzinsky ever claimed to be writing a study of Nicholas not just as a man but also as Emperor, politician and head of government, which is the main task of this book.

The closest equivalent to my book is the work of Andrew Verner, published in 1990 and entitled *The Crisis of Russian Autocracy*. As its sub-title, *Nicholas II and the 1905 Revolution*, suggests, the subject of Verner's book is much narrower than this one. Verner's work is an interesting and intelligent study, and it includes useful material from the former Soviet archives. But, quite apart from its narrower scope, both Verner's premises and his conclusions are rather different to mine.

The basic premise of this book is that it is worth presenting to the public a view of the life and reign of Nicholas II very different to the one commonly held either in the West or in Soviet Russia. To say that this book is more sympathetic than most to Russia's last monarch does not mean that it is an attempt to whitewash Nicholas II or to deny that he was by personality and temperament in many ways ill-suited to the task which fate called upon him to perform. Still less does it attempt to absolve the last Romanov sovereign from responsibility for a number of important errors committed during his reign. What I do intend is to attack the trivialization of Nicholas and his regime, and to question the unthinking imposition of Western liberal or socialist assumptions and values on the history of late Imperial Russia.

This book is very much a study of the reign as well as the man. It attempts to understand Nicholas's personality but also the system of government over which he presided and the empire which he ruled. Russia in the last decades of the empire was a fascinating, vibrant but by no means happy society. Unless one understands its problems and the political context in which Nicholas II operated, his ideas and actions are bound to seem incomprehensible, trivial and absurd to the Western observer. In fact, there was rather more sense and logic behind them than is usually imagined.

One basic aim of this book is to explain just how difficult and contradictory were the problems facing Russia's rulers in this era. Another is to illustrate how Russian government actually functioned, in the process showing what were the limits of a tsar's power and why in particular Nicholas II found it so difficult to use that power effectively. Throughout this book I have tried to make wide-ranging comparisons between Nicholas II and the Russian monarchy on the one hand, and monarchs and monarchical systems of government elsewhere in the nineteenth and twentieth centuries on the other. Like the history of other nations, that of Russia can benefit greatly from international comparisons. One can understand quite a lot about the personality, dilemmas and options of Nicholas II by looking, for instance, at Imperial Germany, Japan or Iran. These comparisons will seldom provide definitive answers to questions concerning Nicholas's personality or reign. But they may well challenge assumptions, open up new visions, and simply give a shake to historians locked into the traditional debates of a particular nation's history or obsessed by issues or approaches which seem 'relevant' to their generation of scholars. Putting in an international, comparative perspective some of the major issues of Nicholas's reign – the Rasputin affair, for instance – is one way in which I have tried to challenge some traditional views of Nicholas and his regime. Even well-trodden territory can look different when viewed from a balloon rather than from the traditional national hill-top. Indeed, in my view the only way to say something genuinely interesting and new about Nicholas's political role is by resorting on frequent occasions to the comparative approach.

In recent years Russia has, to put things mildly, been in the news. The Soviet regime, seemingly so immovable, has disintegrated in peacetime in the course of a crisis lasting only a handful of years. The entire Soviet era has come and gone during a single lifetime. Having spent much time in the last decade teaching and writing on contemporary Soviet politics, the parallels between the decline and fall of the imperial and Soviet regimes have always struck me powerfully. The last chapter of this book is devoted in part to drawing these parallels and judging their validity and usefulness. In addition, I have attempted to place both contemporary events and the reign of Nicholas II within a broader interpretation of the whole of Russian history.

This book has been written by someone who has spent most of his scholarly career ferreting in libraries and archives in order to understand the history of late Imperial Russia. But for the last few years this task has been supplemented by the requirement to explain to students and, largely through the press, to a bewildered public the events surrounding the collapse of Soviet Communism. Liberated for the last eight months from Britain's besieged university system, I have been able to pause for reflection and to indulge an interest in subjects seemingly remote from the history of Imperial Russia or the collapsing Soviet regime. This book, written in one of Tokyo's quietest corners, is the product of these months.

I could not have written the book without my wife's encouragement or the support provided to me in her country. I owe great thanks first and foremost to Caroline Knox, Grant McIntyre, Gail Pirkis and my British publishers, John Murray, but also to Mr Tsuneo Taguchi and my Japanese publishers, Nihon Keizai Shimbun. I am very grateful for support from Hambros Bank (London), IDS International (Minneapolis), the Fair Foundation (Tokyo), the Government of Japan (Ministry of Finance) and Kampo (Tokyo). Professors K. Hirano and K. Nakai, together with the whole International Relations Department of the University of Tokyo, provided me with an office, as well as other help. The staff at Tokyo University's many libraries and at Harvard University's Widener Library were also friendly and very helpful. Dr Michael Hughes, formerly of the London School of Economics and now of Brunel University, was an invaluable ally and research assistant in this and other projects. The Director of the LSE, Dr John Ashworth, kindly permitted my escape to Japan, and Professor Gordon Smith, on top of his other sorrows as Convenor of the Government Department, had to busy himself with even more chores in order to find a replacement for me. Claire Wilkinson, Ros Tucker and Vanessa Sulch typed the book. And, thanks to the inventor of the fax machine, I was able to persecute and exploit my own secretary, Mrs Marion Osborne, almost as effectively from Tokyo as I had always done when in London.

Last, but anything but least, my thanks are due to other historians of Imperial Russia, on whose wisdom and scholarship I have drawn heavily for this book. In the endnotes I have done no more than provide references for direct quotations and one or at most two hints about further reading in the English language on topics I have been discussing. Having worked in this field for fifteen years, comprehensive notes covering every book or article I have read on the subject would be longer than the text itself. Since these sources may not be well known to Russian specialists, I have cited in rather more detail works on countries other than Russia which I have found useful for comparative purposes. All dates in this book are rendered according to the Western calendar, which was twelve days ahead of the Russian calendar in the nineteenth century and thirteen days in the twentieth.

CHAPTER 1

The Inheritance

Nicholas Romanov, the last of Russia's emperors, was born on 18 May 1868. As the eldest son of the heir apparent to the Russian throne his destiny was clear from the moment of his birth. Among his contemporaries in the 1870s only two men faced an inheritance as awesome as his own. One was the young Emperor of China, heir to the terrifying Dowager Empress. He was murdered before he could take up the reins of government. The other was the Austrian Crown Prince, Rudolf von Habsburg, who committed suicide with his mistress at Mayerling in 1889. Nicholas II lived longer than either of his peers but in the end his fate was to be no happier.

The empire over which Nicholas II was to reign had been many centuries in the making. Its earliest origins went back to the tiny principality of Moscow in the thirteenth century. At that time Moscow was ruled by a minor branch of the Russian royal dynasty, all members of which traced their ancestry to the ninth-century Viking chieftain, Rurik, who had founded the royal house.

The original home of the Rurikid dynasty was Kiev, today the capital of the Ukraine. It was there that the dynasty's grand princes lived and there that the Orthodox Church established its headquarters. By the twelfth century, however, the power of Kiev's grand princes was in sharp decline. Their inheritance had been splintered by divisions between heirs, and the rival branches of the royal family were in constant conflict with each other. The Rurikid principalities of southern and western Russia were shattered by the Tatars in the thirteenth century. In the next two hundred years their remnants were collected into the Polish-Lithuanian Empire which grew up on Russia's western borderlands.

Already in the twelfth century a new centre of Russian power had arisen amidst the snow and forests of the north-east. As Kiev declined, the grand princes of Vladimir, a town founded in 1108, emerged as the most powerful of Rurik's descendants. Moscow was their creation but for the first century and a half of its existence it was a relatively minor possession, ruled over by a junior descendant of its founder, Grand Prince Yuri Dolgoruky of Vladimir. Only in the fourteenth century did Moscow become the leading power of the Russian north-east, ultimately uniting not only the possessions of the principality of Vladimir but also the whole Rurikid inheritance and much else besides. But by then Russian life and politics had been transformed by the Tatar invasions.

Sweeping into Russia in the early thirteenth century, the Tatars defeated all the Russian princes and devastated their lands. But whereas the southern and western Russian territories were then absorbed by Lithuania, in north-eastern Russia descendants of Rurik continued to rule semi-autonomous principalities under Tatar sovereignty. For two centuries north-eastern Russia lived under the Tatar yoke, and Tatar approval was the *sine qua non* of any Russian principality's survival. Moscow's princes rose to prominence in north-eastern Russia in this era with Tatar consent and even, at times, outright support. This Moscow won by absolute obedience, cunning diplomacy and the ruthless collection of taxes to ensure prompt and generous subsidies to the Tatar khans. In addition, Moscow out-fought and outwitted its Russian rivals, above all the princes of Tver, and won for itself the support of the Russian Orthodox Church, whose patriarchs established themselves in Moscow in the fourteenth century. The Church came to see the Muscovite princes as the most powerful available protectors of Orthodoxy and as potential unifiers of Russia's territories and her Orthodox flock.

The Muscovite principality was military and despotic. It was not feudal in the Western sense of the word. In feudal Europe the king and his barons were linked by a legal contract binding on both sides. England's Magna Carta proclaimed that barons had rights *vis-à-vis* the king and that if these rights were infringed resistance was legitimate. The ancestors of modern parliaments were feudal assemblies in which the estates of the realm gathered to debate whether to grant the king taxes from their own pockets. In Muscovy neither contracts nor estates bound the rulers' hands. Princely power was absolute. Faced by the murderous and increasingly insane policies of Ivan the Terrible in the sixteenth century, Moscow's aristocracy had no legal protection. More important, modern liberalism and democracy had few roots in ancient Muscovite soil.

In terms, however, of its own priorities the Muscovite political system was very successful. The prince, who from the mid-fifteenth century called himself the Tsar, ruled Moscow with the aid of a small group of aristocratic families, whose heads were in general his kinsmen by marriage. In tribal fashion, relationships within the ruling group were defined not by law but by face-to-face contacts and family ties. Moscow politics had something of the air of Al Capone. To outwit rival princely gangs in north-eastern Russia, not to mention the Tatars, it was vital for Moscow's rulers to stick together and for the prince's absolute authority to be recognized. Life was unpleasant for any lieutenant who aroused the boss's ire. On the other hand the princely boss could not rule without his lieutenants. The rewards of unity and ruthlessness were enormous. In six centuries the tiny principality of Moscow expanded to cover one-sixth of the world's land surface. Though individual aristocrats suffered at the hands of Moscow's tsars, the leading aristocratic clans survived and were over the centuries the greatest beneficiaries of tsarist power and Moscow's expansion. On this brilliantly successful example of gangster politics the Orthodox Church put a religious and patriotic stamp of approval and nineteenth-century nationalist historians scattered phrases about Russia's unity, power and world-historical destiny. In a sense, of course, they were right. In the wake of the Tatar invasions the north-east was the only conceivable base from which a powerful Russian state could have emerged. In the conditions of medieval north-eastern Russia only the ruthless and cunning despot had any chance of success.

Without the monarchy Moscow's rise would have been inconceivable. In Moscow as elsewhere in medieval Christendom the idea reigned that earthly order reflected divine providence and that the powers-that-be derived their authority from God. For aristocrat, priest and peasant alike it was difficult to envisage a form of political authority other than monarchy. More pragmatically, a powerful monarchy was the only force capable of preventing rival aristocratic families from unleashing anarchy and civil war.[1]

The lesson was made clear in Moscow's case by the Time of Troubles of the early seventeenth century. When the reigning dynasty died out in the 1590s aristocratic claimants to the throne fought each other and encouraged foreign intervention in Russian affairs. Anarchy reigned, borderlands were lost to Swedes and Poles, and a Polish prince was crowned in Moscow. A Russian revolt expelled the foreigners and in 1613 elected a new Tsar, Michael Romanov. The Romanovs were not part of the old royal clan, descended from Rurik, unlike some of the great aristocratic families who were to throng their court right down to 1917. They were an old Moscow aristocratic family, one of whose members had married Ivan the Terrible. Throughout the three centuries of Romanov rule conservative and nationalist propagandists were to recall the Time of Troubles as an era of anarchy and national humiliation, reminding their listeners that such was the inevitable fate of a Russia in which autocratic power was weakened. Faced with doubters, they pointed to the example of neighbouring Poland, a once great empire laid low by the lack of a strong monarchy capable of disciplining aristocratic magnates and deterring foreign intervention in domestic affairs.

The first two hundred years of their rule were a triumphant period for the Romanovs. Inheriting a weak country on Europe's borderlands, by 1814 they had turned it into the continent's most formidable military power. Admittedly Russia's expansion had begun before the Romanovs acquired the throne. The conquest of Siberia was nearing completion by 1613 and Ivan IV had already broken Tatar power on the river Volga and opened up the route to the Caspian Sea half a century before Michael Romanov was crowned. In the seventeenth century, however, the Romanovs recaptured Smolensk from the Poles and began Russia's absorption of the Ukraine. The Russian frontier was pushed further and further south across the Steppe in the teeth of Tatar raiders from the Crimea, in the process providing vast and fertile agricultural lands on which Russians from the barren north-east could settle. In the next century Peter I ('the Great') established Russia as the leading power in the Baltic region and Catherine II smashed the Ottoman armies and brought Russia's border to the Black Sea. With the conquest of southern Siberia and the Caucasus already well under way by 1800, the Romanovs had created one of the most formidable expansionist empires the world had ever seen. In 1812, having subjugated the Hohenzollerns and the Habsburgs, Napoleon invaded Russia in an effort to cement his hold over all Europe by destroying the continent's last great independent military power. Two years later, on 31 March 1814, the Emperor Alexander I rode down the Champs-Elysées in the French capital as the arbiter of Europe, followed by the superb regiments of the Russian Guard.[2]

The Romanovs' empire was based on the principle that every subject must serve the state and its military power. Peter the Great proclaimed that the monarch himself was the state's first servant and devoted his life to fulfilling this role. Some of his successors, most notably Nicholas I, shared his sense of duty and dedication. Russian society was divided by law into a number of 'estates', each of which was largely hereditary and was defined by the type of service it performed. Nobles dominated the army and upper bureaucracy. The labours of peasant serfs supported the nobility, and peasants also paid the state's taxes and were recruited into its armies. Priests prayed to God and upheld public morals and the people's loyalty to the crown. The urban population created wealth, traded, paid taxes and helped the state to rule the towns.[3]

By the early eighteenth century some men from ordinary gentry backgrounds, and a sprinkling of complete outsiders, had risen through state service and imperial favour into the ranks of the wealthy court aristocracy. By the 1860s the state's bureaucracy was increasingly displacing the aristocratic landowning magnates as Russia's true ruling class. In twentieth-century urban Russia rapid economic development made the old estate divisions meaningless. In the countryside, however, nobles, priests and peasants still lived entirely distinct lives and remained largely hereditary social groups. Right down to 1917, moreover, the traditional legal 'estate' categories were carried in every Russian subject's passport and shaped the way in which conservative Russians thought about their society.

The system of 'estates' was one aspect of the Russian government's attempt to control Russian society, turning the latter into a mere instrument of the state and its goals. In Russian history a great tension existed between, on the one hand, the all-devouring and all-controlling state and, on the other, the freedom of a vast and open frontier. Traditionally, people were the state's scarcest and most valuable resource. Unless subjects could be controlled, taxed and recruited, the state could never compete with its great-power rivals. Even European Russia, let alone Siberia, was huge and empty: Russia's population in 1750 was less than that of Louis XV's France. The open frontier was a haven to which Russian peasants could flee from state and landlord, an area beyond the government's control from which vast insurrections erupted in the seventeenth and eighteenth centuries. Russia's empty plains, thick forests and open borders help to explain the traditional obsession of her rulers with order and control. To outsiders indeed it sometimes seemed that not only Russian politics but the Russian personality itself was the seat of an unremitting conflict between the anarchical freedom of the open frontier and the harsh, authoritarian, externally imposed order of the state. If in the end, at least in the political sphere, the state always seemed to win, that had much to do with the fact that the Russian frontier was very different to the American one. Even the eighteenth-century conquest of the Bashkirs in southern Siberia required large military forces. Pushing out Russia's frontiers against Swedes, Poles and Turks was a formidable military task. The state and its needs could never be avoided for long on the frontiers. In time even the cossacks ceased to be free-living communities on Russia's boundaries and became the Tsar's auxiliary cavalry, bulwarks not just of the state's external military glory but also of its authoritarian domestic political order.

The forty years between Napoleon's abdication in 1814 and Russia's entry into the Crimean War in 1854 were a period of political stability and conservatism in the Romanov empire. Countries which win great wars are seldom likely to question the foundations of their society and government. Nicholas I, who ruled from 1825 to 1855, believed that serfdom was immoral and inefficient but, confident in Russia's external security and her great-power status, he lacked the motivation to risk radical domestic reform. Old fears of peasant anarchy if the serf-owners' power was abolished were reinforced by new worries about the influence of French revolutionary doctrines, in whose name military radicals (the so-called Decembrists) had attempted a *coup d'état* in the first days of Nicholas's reign. Gradual, cautious though sometimes intelligent reform was the watchword of Nicholas's reign. The Tsar's chief ideologue was his Minister of Education, Count Serge Uvarov, who coined the trinity of 'orthodoxy, autocracy and nationality' as Russia's answer to liberty, equality and fraternity. Yet Uvarov was not a blind or thoughtless reactionary. Like many contemporaries he disliked some of the values which underlay capitalist development in Western Europe and feared the social and political instability it would bring. Like many statesmen in post-war Third World countries he wanted to borrow Western ideas and technology while preserving as much as possible of the traditions, self-esteem and cohesiveness of his own society. But Uvarov's vision of balanced progress based on a mix of Russian and European principles was blown apart in 1854–6 during the Crimean War.[4]

Not only Russians but also many foreigners had regarded Nicholas I's empire as Europe's leading military power. Defeat in the Crimea undermined the regime's prestige and its leaders' self-confidence. During the war Russian artillery had often been outranged by English and French rifles. Russian reinforcements took longer to reach the Crimea on foot from the Russian heartland than British and French reserves travelling from Western Europe by rail and steamship. Administration and medical services collapsed under the strain of war and, once deprived of senior commanders, Russian troops lacked energy and initiative, proving easy targets for the more mobile allied armies. Underlying all these facts was one basic point. When a pre-industrial society like Nicholas's Russia confronted more modern, educated and industrialized countries like Britain and France a war's outcome could not be in doubt. In the wake of the war few intelligent members of the ruling class could doubt that if Russia was to remain a European great power it had to modernize itself quickly. The Tsar's own son, the Grand Duke Constantine, commented that 'we cannot deceive ourselves any longer; we must say that we are both weaker and poorer than the first-class powers, and furthermore poorer not only in material but in mental resources, especially in matters of administration'.[5]

In 1855, in the middle of the Crimean War, Nicholas I died and was succeeded by his son, Alexander II. In the sixty-two years that separated Alexander II's succession and the fall of the monarchy in 1917 the basic problem facing Russia's rulers never changed. For both international and domestic reasons it was clear that if the empire was to survive it had to modernize itself rapidly and move into the ranks of the urban and industrial world. Equally obvious was the fact that rapid modernization would create grave threats to domestic political stability and the regime's continued existence. Like politicians and ruling classes throughout history Russia's rulers attached a very high priority to their own survival. The basic dilemma facing Alexander II, Alexander III and Nicholas II was that it was impossible to ignore the demands either of external military security or of internal political stability and that these demands pulled hard in opposite directions. This helps to explain why the policies and governments of the last three Romanov monarchs so often seemed crisis-ridden and at cross purposes.

In its broad outline the dilemma facing the Russian old regime was sometimes similar to that encountered by many Third World monarchies since 1945. Of course Russia did not have the vast wealth and tiny populations which together enabled many Arab monarchies, at least temporarily, to buy off opposition. But the domestic pressures for rapid modernization were at least as great in the post-1945 Third World as in old Russia. A regime which was seen to be hesitant about modernization would quickly forfeit the sympathy of most elements of educated and urban society. Attempts to insulate a country from foreign ideas seldom work for long and destroy any hope of economic and military competitiveness in the international arena. Even the Soviet regime, despite its formidable industrial and military technology, experienced this truth in the end. Moreover in the Russian case the educated classes, and above all the aristocracy, were extremely cosmopolitan, and enforced national isolation was never a remotely feasible policy for the imperial regime.

Rapid modernization, then as now, was inevitable. But the monarchy which instigated radical changes in society was itself a highly conservative institution, whose existence was rooted in the totally un-modern idea that power and status in society came by divine right and heredity. This was as true for Nicholas II as it was for Haile Selassie or is for King Hassan of Morocco. Traditionally monarchies enjoy support from the clergy, the aristocracy and the peasantry. As a secular society develops, the clergy is weakened, and the same fate awaits a landowning aristocracy in an increasingly urban and industrial world. Both priests and aristocrats may oppose the monarchy's reforms as attacks on their vested interests, but aristocrats in particular will often wrap up this opposition in liberal and constitutionalist phrases. After all, European liberalism's oldest roots lie in the opposition of the feudal aristocracy to the power and pretensions of royal despots. Meanwhile the awe with which an illiterate, religious and tradition-bound peasantry regard their monarch may well be dissipated by the spread of education and exposure to the world outside the village.

At the same time as the monarchy weakens and annoys its traditional supporters, its policies will create new classes on whose loyalty it cannot count. Urban and industrial workers, particularly in the first phase of industrialization, are far less reliable monarchists than are tradition-bound peasants. Still worse are the growing intellectual, professional and commercial classes. In the eighteenth century enlightened royal despotism was intellectually fashionable. Since 1789 this has ceased to be true. Particularly in a poor country conscious of its backwardness, radical and socialist doctrines are much more likely to appeal to the new middle classes than are conservative and royalist ones. The Russian intelligentsia's attitude to the Romanovs found many equivalents in the post-war Third World. A king may well tremble for his dynasty as he watches the growth of this new middle class. Perhaps the ruler understands that the crown's only hope for survival is to abandon its power and take shelter in a contemporary European version of constitutional monarchy. But his country is much poorer and less stable than those over which modern European monarchs reign. Will the new political forces which move into the power vacuum left by the monarchy's retreat respect and preserve the dynasty? Will they prove capable of creating stable, coherent government able to carry forward the programme of modernization? In a state or empire made up of many different peoples, will not the demise of an absolute monarchy bring about the disintegration of the country itself? These questions were as relevant for the rulers of Imperial Russia as for many monarchs in today's developing world.[6]

Unlike contemporary monarchs, however, Russia's emperors were the rulers of a great power. For the Russian old regime it was impossible to resign from the club of great powers. The struggle to join the club had been intense and costly: membership was vital to the Romanovs' self-esteem and their regime's prestige in Russia. But even had such considerations counted for nothing, resignation would still not have been an option. In the wicked world of imperialism, great powers that weakened went to the wall. In 1900 a number of once great empires were near or even in the grave and the future appeared to belong to a small club of great powers which dominated, directly or otherwise, the rest of mankind. The Americas, South-east Asia, Africa, India and Australasia had fallen to European armies and colonists. The ancient Ottoman, Persian and Chinese empires were on the verge of dissolution, their final collapse postponed less by their own strength than by disputes between their would-be imperialist predators over the division of the spoils. Russia was a great power controlling one-sixth of the world's land surface but by English, French, German or American standards it was still backward. Would it remain one of the club of world leaders or decline into the ranks of disintegrating empires? During the 1905 revolution, as Russia was threatened with bankruptcy and the collapse of government, the Tsar's ambassador in London, Alexander Benckendorff, was terrified lest the Romanovs' empire go the way of Peking and Tehran. The road began with international control over a bankrupt country's debts and finances but it ended in national humiliation and disintegration.[7]

Russia was not Spain or Japan, insulated against the full impact of great-power rivalries by huge distances or a Pyrenean mountain chain along its frontiers. In the late nineteenth century Russia was a full member of the great-power club with huge indefensible frontiers in an era when the European balance of power was collapsing and the threat of all-out war between the continent's leading powers was becoming more and more real.

For two centuries before 1914 a rough balance of power existed between Europe's leading capitals: London, Paris, Petersburg, Vienna and Berlin. In the Americas the United States was dominant and in East Asia the same was traditionally true of China. But in Europe the attempts of any one state or dynasty to dominate the whole continent had always been beaten off. First the Spanish Habsburgs, then Louis XIV and finally Napoleon had tried and failed. By the nineteenth century the balance of power was not merely a fact but also a theory about how international stability should be preserved. Most European statesmen believed that the balance preserved peace and stability because it ensured that any power that sought to dominate the continent would almost automatically be deterred by a coalition of other powers determined to stop it. Britain was to the fore in promoting balance-of-power diplomacy, but there was an element of hypocrisy in its advocacy. As Europe's greatest power in the nineteenth century, it sought sovereignty of the seas and colonial pre-eminence while checking potential rivals through the pursuit of a balance-of-power policy on the continent. Nevertheless, the fact that the world's richest country supported a balance of power rather than attempting to dominate the continent contributed greatly to international stability in Victorian Europe.

In 1871 many of Europe's German-speaking communities were united into a single state. In the next four decades the German economy boomed and Germany supplanted Great Britain as Europe's leading economic power. Germany also had Europe's finest army, its second-largest navy, its best educational system and its most efficient administration. As its economic and political interests grew, Germany began to compete with other countries in areas which previously the latter had regarded as their special sphere. With Britain this competition was colonial and maritime. With Russia it occurred in the Ottoman Empire and Persia. The fact that, for all its might, the Kaiser's Reich contained less than half the world's Germans gave food for thought about Germany's ultimate potential for expansion. [8]

The threat to the European balance of power was serious. Combined with the ideas that dominated pre-war Europe it was lethal. In the decades before 1914 European society had been turned upside down. Peasants flooded into towns. Mass education and the growth of industry greatly widened horizons while destroying the old certainties of a village-bound existence. For many inhabitants of this bewildering new world the nation replaced God as a focus for their ideals and values, while providing them with a sorely needed sense of community. Governments and ruling classes in general encouraged nationalism in order to unite communities, provide them with common values, and defeat radical and socialist movements. To speak of the 'sacred egoism of the nation' and of 'my country right or wrong' was intellectually respectable, for nationalism appeared to be the wave of the future. The belief was widespread that a vigorous and self-respecting nation must assert itself aggressively and must compete, by war if necessary, to be the standard-bearer of progress and history.[9]

Nowhere were such ideas held more strongly than in Germany. Russian visitors to Wilhelm II's empire often came back horrified and terrified by the confident chauvinism they had encountered there. However, not only did virulent nationalism encourage the aggression of powerful nation-states, it also threatened the existence of the great multi-ethnic empires that dominated most of Eastern and Central Europe and the Middle East. The Romanovs' own empire, only 46 per cent of whose people were Russians, was vulnerable. Still more so were the Ottoman and Habsburg empires. By the 1880s it seemed clear that the Ottoman Empire was slowly but inexorably disintegrating. The Ottoman retreat from the Balkans turned this region into the most unstable area in Europe, with rivalries between the Balkan peoples being exacerbated by great powers competing for clients and influence. When and if the Ottomans collapsed altogether, the whole Middle East would be up for grabs. If, as many predicted, the Habsburg Empire also began to totter, the chances of Russo-German conflict would further increase. The Habsburg Empire was largely composed of German-Austrians and Slavs, to whose fate neither Petersburg nor Berlin could afford to be indifferent for domestic political reasons. In addition, even a cursory knowledge of European geopolitics taught that if either Germany or Russia came to dominate the people and resources of the former Habsburg Empire their power would grow to such an extent that they would inevitably become Europe's masters. Thus in the decades before 1914, on top of an increasingly strident worldwide competition for territory and influence, a new phase seemed to be beginning in the old story of great-power rivalry to dominate Europe. No study of the life or reign of Nicholas II makes much sense unless it recognizes that such was the alarming international context in which the Russian Emperor and his regime were forced to operate.

In the longer term, the grave risk existed that great-power conflict would drag Russia into a war which would stretch her society and government beyond endurance. The everyday result of international military competition was that the Russian budget was put under enormous strain, for a developing country was attempting to hold its own with the world's leading military powers. The problem was not merely that Russia was poorer than Britain, Germany and France but also that it was far more difficult to tax effectively a predominantly rural population of smallholders scattered across a vast country. In 1900 the central government spent more even on the navy than on agriculture and education combined. The army cost more than all local government expenditure, but it was the latter which bore almost the whole burden of providing the huge rural population with schools, hospitals, roads, bridges and a range of agricultural services. In a countryside of almost 100 million peasants there were less than 10,000 state policemen in 1900 and even most of these were paid far less than the average factory worker. The clergy were potentially a powerful conservative force in the countryside but, despite having seized the Church's lands in the eighteenth century, the state was too poor to pay them. Largely dependent on handouts from peasant parishioners, the village priest's authority and independence inevitably suffered.

Russia lacked private capital and its huge distances greatly increased the cost of bringing schools, hospitals, roads, agronomists and vets to its peasant villages. The irony was that in the last two decades of the nineteenth century the armed forces' share of the state budget was actually decreasing quite sharply as the government sought to pour its resources into railway construction and industrial development. The Ministry of War complained bitterly, and with justice, that the army was lagging dangerously behind its competitors. There was simply not enough money to go round. The result was an impoverished army, a lack of modern sanitation and street-lighting in towns, bitterness among underpaid teachers, and clerics humiliated by the need to beg from their parishioners. Maladministration worsened Russia's problems but poverty was very often at their core. One result of this poverty was ferocious conflict between ministries, not to mention between central and local government, over the division of Russia's inadequate budgetary cake.[10]

Backwardness was not just a fiscal and economic problem but also a political and psychological one. Nineteenth-century Russia often had a chip on its shoulder about Europe. In Great Britain or Germany a citizen could take pride in belonging to one of the world's most admired countries. Not only the psychological but also the economic benefits of citizenship could reconcile the Scotsman or Bavarian to rule from London or Berlin. Something of this existed in Russia. Newly literate Russians often took pride in being the leading people of a huge empire, and even Polish businessmen acknowledged the benefits of access to the imperial market. But on the whole it was difficult to be very enthusiastic about belonging to Europe's most backward and 'Asiatic' great power, whose record in war and diplomacy between 1854 and 1914 was less than glorious. Bismarck had won tremendous prestige for the Hohenzollern dynasty and the Prussian upper classes by uniting Germany in two spectacularly successful wars between 1866 and 1871. The Russian old regime was unlikely to emulate him partly because the Russian army was a good deal less efficient than that of the Prussians but also because its great-power rivals were much more formidable than Austria and France had been in the 1860s.

The Japanese example illustrates how much the Russian old regime lost by its failures in war and diplomacy. From the 1860s the Japanese too had a chip on their shoulder about Europe, and Japanese intellectuals often tended to worship all things Western. The nationalist and conservative reaction which gathered pace from the 1880s was greatly strengthened by Japan's success in war and diplomacy in the 1890s and 1900s. Tokutomi Soho and Fukuzawa Yukichi were famous liberal and Westernizing intellectuals of the Meiji era. After Japan's victory over China in 1894–5 Tokutomi wrote, 'now we are no longer ashamed to stand before the world as Japanese . . . now that we have tested our strength, we know ourselves and we are known by the world. Moreover, we know we are known by the world.' Fukuzawa commented, 'one can scarcely enumerate all our civilised undertakings since the Restoration . . . Yet among all these enterprises, the one thing none of us Western scholars ever expected, thirty or forty years ago, was the establishment of Japan's imperial prestige in a great war . . . When I think of our marvellous fortune, I feel as though I'm in a dream and can only weep tears of joy.'[11]

During the nineteenth century, nationalism in Europe tended to move from the left of the political spectrum towards the right. Disraeli in England and Bismarck in Germany both went far to capture the nationalist vote for conservatism. As the mass of the population became more educated and more independent, the old appeal for loyalty to church and dynasty was no longer sufficient. Faced by liberal and socialist doctrines, the right needed an idea with mass appeal, and nationalism came closest to fitting the bill. Even in Russia Alexander III, convinced autocrat though he was, believed strongly that his regime must satisfy Russian nationalist aspirations. Since the Russian imperial government suspected any independent political activity, however, its relationship with nationalist writers and newspaper editors was always difficult. Remembering the late 1870s, when nationalist agitation in the press and society had forced Russia into a costly war with the Ottoman Empire, attempts by nationalist spokesmen to influence the state's foreign policy caused particular alarm.[12]

But the problem with nationalism went much deeper than this. Britain and Germany came close to being nations as well as states. Japan was even more homogeneous. The Romanovs, however, ruled an empire less than half of whose population were Russians. Even if, like most members of the ruling class, one regarded Belorussians and Ukrainians as mere offshoots of the Russian tribe, one was still left with more than one-third of the population who were unequivocally not Russian. Loyalty to the Tsar alone was no doubt inadequate and anachronistic as a guarantee of imperial unity in the modern age but at least the dynasty could be a supra-national symbol to which non-Russians could give their loyalty. The more the imperial regime stressed its allegiance to Russian national aspirations and cultural values, the likelier it became that non-Russian subjects would feel neglected, and increasingly persecuted, second-class citizens.

In 1900, however, non-Russian nationalism was not yet a major threat to the Romanovs' empire. The great majority of the Tsar's non-Russian subjects were peasants or nomads. These people's village and clan horizons and loyalties made them largely invulnerable to the appeals of nationalist intellectuals, even to the extent that these could penetrate government censorship. The Tsar's Muslim subjects, especially in Central Asia and the Caucasus, often greatly resented his rule but they were held in check by recent and painful memories of Russian power and ruthlessness. In an imperialist age the chances for small peoples to enjoy genuine independence seemed slim, and Latvians and Estonians – to take but two examples – had no desire to swop the Tsar's rule for that of the German Kaiser. Still less did Christian Armenians or Georgians wish to fall under Ottoman Muslim control. Enormously diverse and scattered around the empire's periphery, the non-Russians had no opportunity to co-ordinate their opposition to the Romanovs. On the contrary, a government which controlled the Russian heartland could stamp out rebellion in the various borderlands one after another, as the imperial regime indeed did after the revolution of 1905. In the long term the growing resentment and nationalism of the non-Russians were a great danger to Petersburg. In the short term, however, they would only become really dangerous if the government was weakened by war, opposition within Russia or its own bungled efforts at domestic liberalization.[13]

In the early twentieth century, the main threat to the Romanovs came less from the minorities than from the Russian population itself. In the cities the problem was on the whole a familiar one in societies in the throes of early industrial development. Rural labour poured into the towns in search of work, swamping municipal services and living in overcrowded, insanitary, wretched conditions. Its anger could lead to attacks on property and privilege, as happened in 1905 and 1917, but in many cities it also frequently exploded in anti-Semitic pogroms. On a day-to-day level, drunkenness and hooliganism were outlets for frustration. It is doubtful whether conditions were worse than in the Liverpool of the 1820s or Berlin of the 1840s, though in Petersburg the city's awful climate and high cost of living added an extra twist to life's misery.

In the factories class hatreds ran high. The conditions of early industrial development seldom leave much room for generosity or compromise on the side of either capital or labour. By Western and Central European standards Russian workers in 1900 were underpaid and worked excessive hours in conditions which were often unhealthy and sometimes dangerous. Management was always authoritarian, often insulting and usually arbitrary in its treatment of workers. From management's perspective labour was very unproductive by European standards. Theft and absenteeism were endemic. Imposing the regular rhythms and disciplines of factory labour on a semi-peasant workforce used to a quite different tempo was a gruelling task. In the Russian case it was particularly difficult. The Tsar's peasant subjects were not Chinese or Japanese farmers, trained over centuries in the careful, intensive year-round cultivation of tiny rice fields. The Russian peasant in old Muscovy had learned the careless and migratory habits which tend to exist in countries where the land is poor but abundant, and labour is scarce. The harsh Russian climate imposed an agrarian regime which combined months of inactivity in the winter with back-breaking work in the short growing season. This was not a good preparation for the rhythms and requirements of the capitalist factory. In addition, the Russian peasant had become accustomed to frequent movement over a huge and empty plain. There existed an age-old tradition, celebrated in peasant and Cossack folklore, of flight to the country's borderlands beyond the reach of any authority which might seek to control and discipline the peasant's life.

The complaints of foreign capital that profit margins in Russia were often small, overheads excessive and uncertainties great were truer than Russian public opinion liked to admit. The government itself was divided over economic and labour policy. The Ministry of Finance tended to stress that, if a growing population was to be employed and Russia was to become a great economic power, as few obstacles as possible must be placed in the way of capitalist development. The Ministry of Internal Affairs, responsible for public order and obsessed by the danger of socialist revolution, combined repression of strikes with welfare legislation as generous as Russia could afford, and even attempts to set up its own trade unions for workers.[14]

In comparison to earlier European experience it was not the ban on strikes or free trade unions which was unusual but rather the range of action taken to avert working class discontent. Russia did not go quite as far as Japan, whose government began to study foreign factory laws in 1882 when 'there were fewer than fifty factories using steam power in all of Japan'. The Russian government, like its Japanese equivalent, had, however, studied the history of Europe's labour movement and well understood the connection between industrialization, the emergence of a working class and socialism. During the early decades of the English, and even the German, industrial revolutions liberal ideas in both economics and politics ruled supreme. No coherent socialist ideology existed to oppose them. The Russian government, intensely alive to the threat of revolution, knew that this was no longer the case by the 1880s and 1890s, when Russian industrial development really began to take off.[15]

Even more alarming was the fact that from the 1860s Russia had possessed an underground socialist revolutionary movement committed to the destruction not only of tsarism but also of private property and all other vestiges of European bourgeois life. In the 1870s revolutionary terrorism combined with attempts to incite peasant uprisings had panicked the imperial government and persuaded even as sober an onlooker as Bismarck that the overthrow of the Romanovs and socialist revolution were distinct possibilities. In the event, the rural population in the 1870s proved largely invulnerable to the socialist propaganda of city intellectuals. Whether the same would be true of a literate urban working class uprooted from the influences of village life caused intense concern to the Russian police from the moment Russia's industrial revolution began.

Even in 1914, however, Russia was still largely a rural society with more than four-fifths of the population in the countryside. Thus the Romanovs' survival depended above all else on developments in rural Russia. This was indeed the normal pattern as regards European monarchies and conservatism in the nineteenth century. No European old regime drew its major support from the cities, least of all in the early decades of industrial development. On the contrary, in France and Prussia urban revolutions had overthrown conservative regimes in 1848 and 1871, only themselves to be suppressed by rural conservatism and armies conscripted largely from the peasant population. The greatest single weakness of the Russian old regime in 1900 was that this type of rural conservatism could not be relied upon. This did not mean that the Russian peasants themselves would take the lead in overthrowing the Romanovs. It did mean that if government was weakened or destroyed by urban revolution, the Russian peasantry was unlikely to join the ranks of counter-revolution but rather would seize the opportunity to settle scores with the landowning nobility and destroy government authority in the countryside.

One reason why Russia was different was that its landowning aristocracy was weak by the standards of England or Prussia. In nineteenth-century England 7,000 individuals, almost all of them from the aristocracy or gentry, owned over 80 per cent of the land. Prussian landowning was never this aristocratic but its rural nobility owned a much larger share of the land than its Russian counterpart. In Russia even before the abolition of serfdom in 1861 just over half the peasantry lived on lands belonging not to the nobility but to the state. Typically, whereas in England or Prussia the Church's lands had largely fallen into aristocratic hands after the Reformation, the Russian state had held on to them for itself. In 1861 the

emancipation settlement divided aristocratic estates between noble landowners and their former serfs. Between 1863 and 1915 the nobles sold over
60 per cent even of the land that remained to them, above all because in
many areas of Russia it was extremely difficult to make profits from large-
scale agriculture, a fact that Soviet collective farming was later to confront
as well.

In a sense the Russian landowning nobility in 1900 was either too weak
or not weak enough. It could not control the countryside in English or
Prussian style but in many districts it still owned quite enough land to be
very unpopular. In addition, as nobles attempted to exploit their farms and
forests in modern capitalist fashion rents shot up, many customary peasant
rights were infringed and peasant anger mounted. In the European perspective there was nothing particularly unusual about these sorts of rural
tensions in the early decades of capitalist agriculture. The English countryside, for instance, had witnessed similar tensions in the Tudor era when
'sheep ate men' and rural capitalism took root. The strange thing about
Russia was that the rural nobility was relatively weak, and government
authority in the cities collapsed both in 1905 and 1917 in the midst of this
period of rural change. Seen in the longer perspective, the Russian countryside may well have been heading in the same direction as that of western
and southern Germany. In 1848 these regions of Germany had witnessed
violent disturbances in the countryside, which forced many landowners to
flee their estates. In the second half of the nineteenth century, however,
with all remnants of serfdom gone and nobles seldom owning more than
about 5 per cent of the land in western or southern Germany, peasant
antagonism decreased sharply. Peasant and noble farmers could often unite
in defence of agrarian interests and in dislike of modern, secular, urban
culture. Rich aristocrats, most of whose wealth now came from stocks and
bonds, could become generous and welcome patrons of the local community. In the countryside as elsewhere for the Russian old regime, longer-
term perspectives were not entirely black. The worst problem was to
survive an era of transition.[16]

Even in 1900 it was evident to those with eyes to see that what really
mattered in Russian agriculture and the Russian countryside was not the
nobility but the peasantry. The Russian farming community was, however, totally different from its English or Prussian counterpart. In England
aristocrats owned the land but it was actually farmed by tenants, most of
whom were rich by continental standards. These big tenant farmers exercised a tight control over their agricultural labourers, stamping firmly on
any manifestations of socialist or trade union sympathies. Beside the tenant
farmers in the ranks of order and property stood the Anglican clergy,
whose wealth and status were also extremely high by European standards.

In Prussia, too, the rural clergy were solidly conservative and relatively well-off. Unlike Russia, many middle-class tenant farmers existed on the extensive Prussian royal domains even in the eighteenth century, and their descendants subsequently became doughty allies of the gentry in defence of property and 'order'. What really distinguished Prussia from Russia was, however, its peasants. Even in the days of serfdom, at a time when capitalist agriculture had not yet developed, there were great differences both in the wealth and the legal status of Prussian peasants. In 1800 the Prussian countryside contained many landless agricultural labourers. As agriculture developed in the nineteenth century, peasant society increasingly split into relatively rich peasant farmers on the one hand and impoverished landless labourers on the other. Though the terms on which serfdom was abolished caused conflict between noble and peasant, in time peasant farmers and gentry landowners came to share a common interest in reducing labourers' wages and 'insubordination', and defending agrarian interests against the growing urban population and its demands. Meanwhile both the law and economic realities made landless labourers very dependent on the goodwill of their employers.

The situation in the Russian countryside was entirely different. The picture usually drawn is of an increasingly poverty-stricken peasantry crushed by excessive taxation and growing over-population. The reality was not this simple. In 1904 peasants paid less than a quarter of the state's taxes though they generated between 40 and 50 per cent of the country's income. The Russian population was growing rapidly but agricultural production, most of it from peasant farms, was outpacing it. By 1914 Russia was not merely feeding itself, it had also just replaced the United States as the world's leading grain exporter. Although Russian peasant agriculture was less efficient than that of Central or Western Europe, the Russian peasant's farm was usually much bigger than that of his French or German counterpart and he was much more likely to own a horse. Russian peasants had more ample and healthier diets than a large proportion of the German population in 1900. Indeed even under serfdom the Russian peasantry in the early nineteenth century was much better fed than agricultural labourers in southern England at that time. The latest, immensely thorough, German study of the Russian peasantry in 1900 concludes that its diet was roughly comparable to that of the West German population in the early to mid-1950s.[17]

Although some Russian villagers were poor, even by the undemanding standards of pre-1914 rural Europe, and many more were vulnerable to cholera epidemics, drought and occasional but dramatic crop failures, the basic reason why the old regime was shaky in the countryside was not peasant poverty. Rather it had to do with the nature of Russian village society and the way it looked on the outside world.

By European standards the Russian peasant village was a very egalitarian world. Most land was owned collectively by the village commune and periodically redistributed to match the number of adult workers in a family. Peasant farms were at the disposal not of the head of the household but of the family as a whole. When sons grew up and married, the farm was divided among all male heirs. Very few Russian peasants employed hired labour on their farms. The Russian word for village society was *mir*, which also meant 'peace' and 'the world'. As this suggests, a sharp distinction existed between members of the village community and outsiders. The community stuck together and woe betide a peasant who flouted its values or decisions. Intense hostility often existed between neighbouring villages but the greatest suspicion was reserved for complete outsiders, in other words members of Russian educated society. Educated Russia was European in its culture, values, dress and even, in some aristocratic circles, in its preference for using foreign languages. In addition, since the traditional reason for educated Russians to involve themselves in village affairs was to exploit the peasantry in one way or another, this hostility was unsurprising.

The village had its own values and moral code which did not correspond to those of educated or propertied Russia. Peasants, for instance, tended to believe that the land belonged by right only to those who farmed it themselves, which was not at all the view either of the landowning nobility or of the imperial legal code. Though the traditionalist patriarchal landowner might be tolerated, the noble capitalist who sought to extract maximum profits from his estate would be deeply disliked since he would either raise rents or remove estate land from peasant use and try to farm it himself. The spread of education and increased contact with the cities tended in any case to make the younger peasant generation more radical than its elders and less tolerant of private landowning. In strictly economic terms peasant agriculture had proved more viable than the big estates in most regions of Russia between 1861 and 1905. Given the political opportunity, most peasants would resort to strikes, riots and arson to give noble agriculture a further push. Since the Romanov regime traditionally rested on the support of the landowning class but could not survive without at least the acquiescence of the peasantry the growing hostility between noble and peasant was a major threat to the rulers in Petersburg.[18]

Given its problems with peasant and worker Russia, it was important for the regime that it possess the united support of upper and middle-class citizens both for itself and for its programme of modernization. This was, however, far from being the case. The entrepreneurial class, natural bearer of capitalist values, was still quite small in 1900, and the fact that capitalists were very often foreigners or from despised non-Russian minorities such as Jews, Poles or Armenians further weakened their prestige. The landowning nobility and state bureaucracy were equivocal about capitalism. Most of the professional middle class and almost all intellectuals were hostile.[19]

The rift between the Romanovs' regime and many educated Russians can be traced back to the years after 1815. By 1860 a still small but nevertheless important number of educated young Russians were wedded to radical and socialist ideas. These were derived largely from French and German political writers but found fertile soil in Russia among intelligent and impatient young people angry at the constraints of life under an absolutist regime and ashamed at Russian backwardness and poverty in comparison to Western Europe. Initially enthusiastic about the string of liberal reforms introduced by Alexander II in the late 1850s and early 1860s, young radicals were inevitably soon disillusioned, for the imperial government, even in its most liberal mood, was not going to satisfy their aspirations. Disillusion led some to conspiracy and even terror.

Within eight years of the demise of Nicholas I's very conservative regime in 1855 a radical counter-culture had emerged, drawing some sections of Russian educated youth into a separate world, isolated from their parents, the state and the masses. Here they preached the abolition of monarchy, property and marriage. By 1863 a number of underground revolutionary groups were plotting to incite peasant rebellion and mutiny in the army, as well as to assassinate the Tsar. The first actual attempt to kill Alexander II occurred in 1866. Three years before this, the government's efforts to reduce repression in Poland and find a *modus vivendi* with moderate Polish public opinion had led to full-scale revolution in much of Russian Poland, which was crushed with great difficulty and brutality after the deployment of tens of thousands of Russian troops. Inevitably these developments scared the government and were grist to the mill of conservatives and authoritarians who argued that reform had gone too far and that the country was slipping beyond control. Repression became the order of the day and from the mid-1860s down to the monarchy's fall in 1917 the war between the government and the various branches of the revolutionary socialist movement never ceased. Over the decades revolutionary and socialist ideas gained a considerable following among urban workers. In the twentieth century they even began to make converts among the peasantry. Most Russian intellectuals were firmly on the left, detesting the old regime and all its works. Public opinion and instincts were much more hostile to government than was the case in most of Central and Western Europe. The regime's own response to conspiracy and terror led to wholesale infringements of the population's civil rights and further contributed to the alienation of much of educated society.[20]

By 1900 both the business and the professional middle class were much larger and more solidly established than had been the case four decades before. In the Marxist schema, it should have been the capitalists who put the most pressure on the regime for a share in political power. There were signs of discontent among industrialists in the run-up to the 1905 revolution, partly in response to the regime's own efforts to patronize and protect labour unions, but on the whole the capitalists caused the imperial government little trouble. The professional middle class was more of a problem, partly because it was closer to the intellectuals and partly because the government stood in the way of its desire to run its own professional activities autonomously and to have a commanding voice in all matters pertaining to its own sphere of interest and expertise.

Between 1861 and 1905, however, the landowning nobility, traditionally the Tsar's most loyal ally, caused the government as many headaches as any other section of educated society. The difficulties facing agriculture on the big estates, especially during the Europe-wide agricultural depression of the 1870s and 1880s, led to attacks on government economic policy. These reached a crescendo in the 1890s when government-sponsored industrialization began to have spectacular results. Since the landowning nobility controlled the elected local government councils (*zemstvos*) in the countryside, arguments between the landowners and Petersburg over economic policy quickly turned into conflicts between central and local government. One element in these battles was the aristocracy's contempt for and resentment of a bureaucracy which had pushed aside Russia's traditional noble ruling class and taken control of government policy. Moreover, like all sections of Russian educated society, the Russian aristocracy compared itself to its peers in the rest of Europe and resented its lack of the civil and political rights which they enjoyed.

For many educated Russians it was self-evident that the regime was responsible for blocking Russia's entry into Europe. It denied them the freedoms and rights to which, as civilized Europeans, they were entitled. As a result – in their view – it isolated itself from the most educated and competent sections of Russian society and systematically dug its own grave. This interpretation of events, initially created by the pre-revolutionary liberal and radical intelligentsia, became after 1917 the guiding orthodoxy of Russian history whether written in the Soviet Union or the West. It remains the generally accepted interpretation of Nicholas II's reign and the causes of the monarchy's fall. In this interpretation the role and opinions of Russia's last tsar get much attention and are trivialized. If Nicholas II had been a pragmatic, constitutionalist Englishman like his cousin George V, rather than an ignorant and reactionary mystic, revolution could have been averted and his life and throne preserved.

In reality, however, matters were more complicated and difficult. The wealth, skills and European culture of upper and middle-class Russia set them well apart from the mass of the population. If the divide was not as great as that between European and native in many colonies of the Victorian era, it was nevertheless greater than the gap between rulers and ruled in Europe. Nor were there yet in Russia large and relatively comfortable layers of middle- and lower-middle-class citizens bridging the divide between top and bottom in society. In the last decades of the old regime these layers were growing quickly and the booming capitalist economy was making Russia much more European. But the rapid growth of industry, cities and education itself caused much conflict and instability. Capitalism was not yet popular among either élites or masses. By 1905 most educated Russians were demanding a liberal or even democratic political system. But it was far from certain that a liberal or democratic government would be sufficiently strong to defend the interests of Russia's Westernized, property-owning minority or of its developing, but still weak, capitalist economy.

In the 1860s and 1870s a young revolutionary called Peter Tkachev had prophesied tsarism's fall. Tkachev was in some ways a lunatic. His fanatical egalitarianism terrified even Marx and Engels. But as a tactician Tkachev was very clever and in many ways foreshadowed Lenin. Tkachev's slogan as regards revolution was 'now or never'. At present, he argued, tsarism was weak. The old order – rural and serf-owning – had gone but a new capitalist Russia had yet to be born. In an era of transition, capitalists were relatively few and weak, and the landowning nobility was not merely in decline but also increasingly angry at government policy. The peasants were as yet far from being capitalist farmers. The regime hung in mid-air, unsupported by society and relying on its bureaucracy and army alone. If these were weakened or destroyed, perhaps by a major war, revolution was more than possible. And once a revolutionary élite was in power, socialism could be created in Russia.[21]

Tkachev was an accurate prophet. It was the misfortune of Nicholas II that fate made him responsible for guiding his country through one of the most difficult periods in its history.

CHAPTER 2

Childhood and Youth

Nicholas's father, the Emperor Alexander III, acended the throne in 1881 and reigned for thirteen years. He looked like a Russian tsar. All the Romanov men in Alexander's generation were tall but the Emperor stood out even among his brothers. His niece, the Grand Duchess Marie Pavlovna, recalled her only meeting with Alexander, who died when she was still very young. 'Once when we were having our bread and milk our father . . . came into the nursery accompanying a giant with a light beard. I looked at him with open mouth as we were bidden to tell him goodbye. They explained that this was my uncle Sasha (my father's eldest brother), the Emperor Alexander III.'[1]

Alexander was neither elegant nor handsome. By the 1880s he was balding rapidly and his face was dominated by a high forehead and a sizeable beard. The baggy uniforms he favoured sometimes seemed to hang on his enormous figure like sacks. But his height, his huge shoulders and his girth gave an impression of strength and resolution which his conversation and manner confirmed. Fifteen years after Alexander's death, a statue of him was unveiled on Petersburg's Znamenskaya Square, opposite the capital's main railway station. A huge, determined-looking Tsar bestrides a horse of almost rhinoceros-like dimensions. The statue was a political statement. It expressed the massive immovable resolution that a Russian autocrat was expected to embody. Reminiscent in style 'of representations of the *bogatyri*, the warrior heroes of ancient Russia', it reminded onlookers that Alexander III had been a great Russian patriot, opposed to the spread of Western liberal ideas. At a time when the regime was shaken by the revolution of 1905 and coming under increasing pressure from liberals and socialists, such reminders of Russian tradition and monarchical resolution were timely. But for Nicholas II, much smaller and less authoritative than his father, the statue might almost have seemed a reproach for not being a tsar in the true autocratic tradition.[2]

Alexander III was immensely strong. His daughter, the Grand Duchess

Olga, commented that 'my father had the strength of a Hercules' and remembered how 'once in the study he bent an iron poker and then straightened it out'. When the imperial train crashed at Borki in 1888 Alexander lifted the carriage roof so that his wife and children could crawl to safety. The Tsar was formidable and terrifying when angry. His language could be blunt and even crude. Ministers did not disobey his orders or hide things from him lightly. No one argued with him. Combined with the aura that surrounded an absolute monarch, the Tsar's personality and size were all the more impressive. D.N. Lyubimov, later a senior official under Nicholas II, recalled the awe he felt on first encountering Alexander III and commented that the Tsar radiated power and majesty. Although the Emperor was not an easy person, on the whole ministers liked working for him. Once chosen and trusted, they were neither quickly nor lightly discarded and Alexander would back their policies in the teeth of opposition from both within the government and in society. Serge Witte, who began his career as Minister of Finance under Alexander, commented that the Emperor 'was a man of stature who could go against prevailing attitudes and opinions . . . If he made a decision on the basis of a minister's report, he would never rescind the decision. Or, to put it another way, he never betrayed a minister on the basis of whose report he authorised some measure.'[3]

Alexander III was hated by Russian liberals, and their condemnation has been echoed by virtually all subsequent historians, Soviet and Western. By stopping, even to some extent reversing, the programme of liberal reforms initiated under his father, Alexander II, the Tsar is blamed for fatally widening the gap between his regime and Russian educated society, thereby contributing mightily to the later revolutionary overthrow of his dynasty. This was not how matters were seen by all Russians at the time and least of all, of course, by Alexander III's own family and the officials, courtiers and aristocrats with whom they came into contact. In these circles the Tsar was widely praised for restoring the government's prestige and self-confidence after the crisis of 1878–81, as well as for instilling greater order in Russian society. In the last years of Alexander II's reign the government had been bankrupted by the Russo-Turkish War of 1877–8 and shaken by a terrorist campaign that culminated in the Emperor's own assassination in March 1881. Alexander III smashed the terrorist and revolutionary underground, tightened government control over the universities and elected local government bodies (*zemstvos*), and created a new official, the Land Commandant, to supervise justice and administration among the peasant population in the villages. He cut expenditure, especially on defence, avoided confrontations with foreign powers and thereby managed both to salvage the state's finances and to restore Russia's international prestige. The last years of his reign witnessed unprecedented industrial growth in his empire. To those who had the ear of Nicholas II when he ascended the throne in 1894 it seemed clear that Russia was much more stable and prosperous than had been the case in 1881, and the government's authority much more secure. From the perspective of 1894, it was not at all difficult to paint Alexander III's reign as a triumphant success. Returning from the Tsar's funeral in November 1894, General A.A. Kireev wrote in his diary: 'A good, honest heart, a Tsar who loved peace and was a very hard worker; a man who could serve as an example to every one of his subjects both in his private and his public life.' Russian prestige in Europe 'was not so great even in the reign of the Emperor Nicholas I'. With Russia beginning at last to develop her huge economic potential and Western society increasingly decadent, 'time is on our side, the same time which is against the West'.[4]

In his personal tastes Alexander III was extremely simple and frugal. Quite unlike his father, who had installed his mistress and their children over his wife's head in the Winter Palace, Alexander III was a faithful and devoted husband. He loathed corruption, dishonesty and loose morals. Not averse to vodka, he was as indifferent to *haute cuisine* as to most other worldly refinements. In his day the imperial kitchens were notorious for the awful food they produced. Surrounded by beautiful palaces, his favourite was the ugliest of them, Gatchina, in which he lived and worked on the rather cramped and low-ceilinged second floor. The Tsar carried out his ceremonial duties with his usual conscientiousness but he did not enjoy life in high society, was no great conversationalist and felt rather ill-at-ease in large gatherings. Personal experience of the Russo-Turkish War had bred in him a positive distaste for flashy militarism with its gorgeous uniforms and grandiose parades. Though Alexander enjoyed playing the trumpet, neither books nor paintings meant much to him.

The Grand Duchess Olga recalled that her father 'loved purely family occasions, but how he grudged even a few hours given up to formal entertainment'. For him, Gatchina's great attraction was its enormous park. The Tsar liked to be out of doors, particularly in the company of his children. Of his five children it was the youngest two, Olga and Michael, who tended to be his favourites. 'We would set out for the deer park', recalled the Grand Duchess Olga,

> just the three of us – like the three bears in the fairy tale. My father always carried a big spade, Michael had a smaller one, and I had a tiny one of my own. Each of us also carried a hatchet, a lantern and an apple. If it was winter he taught us how to clear a tidy path through the snow, and how to fell a dead tree. He taught Michael and me how to build up a fire. Finally we roasted the apples, damped down the fire, and the lanterns helped us find our way home. In summer he taught us how to distinguish one animal spoor from another.

We often ended up near a lake, and he taught us how to row. He so wanted us to read the book of nature as easily as he read it himself.[5]

Alexander's other great opportunity to relax was during visits to his father-in-law, the King of Denmark. Once the doors were closed to outside observers, the Danish royal family and their numerous cousins revelled in a totally unintellectual, bourgeois existence, which included a good deal of horseplay and practical jokes. Courtiers, English as well as Russian, who caught a glimpse of the private world of Danish royalty were very often either bored to death or scandalized. In London, for instance, even after she became Queen, Alexandra of Denmark, the sister-in-law of Tsar Alexander III,

did not give up her family's passion for practical jokes and on one occasion made her nephew, Prince Christopher of Greece, dress up in the outfit Queen Victoria had worn in the days of her youth to open the Great Exhibition in Paris under Napoleon III. Arrayed in this with a feathered bonnet on his head, and equipped with a lace parasol, 'Christo' was trooped by the Queen through the corridors of Buckingham Palace, past scandalized servants, to entertain his sick aunt, the Dowager Empress of Russia.[6]

Alexander III, quite unlike his more sophisticated and sybaritic brother-in-law, Edward VII of England, flourished in Copenhagen.

He loved getting into mischief. He'd lead us into muddy ponds to look for tadpoles, and into orchards to steal Apapa's apples. Once he stumbled on a hose and turned it on the King of Sweden, whom we all disliked. My father joined us in all the games and made us late for meals, and nobody seemed to mind. I remember that couriers sometimes came with despatches but there was no telephone to St Petersburg, and the three weeks in Denmark meant such a refreshment to him. I always felt that the boy had never really died in the man.[7]

Alexander's simple, blunt personality did not endear him to the more sophisticated, refined and cosmopolitan members of Petersburg high society. Count Vladimir Lambsdorff, who later served as Foreign Minister under Nicholas II, commented in his diary that Alexander III and his family were rather commonplace and ill-bred, lacking either intellectual interests or refinement. Their entourage was made up of unintelligent people incapable of providing useful information or advice. Count Aleksei Bobrinsky, a well-known amateur genealogist and archaeologist of great wealth, who was descended from Catherine II's illegitimate son, filled his diary with gloomy comments after spending two evenings with Alexander and his brothers in January 1881. Behind the ridiculous etiquette which fenced them off even from members of the high aristocracy, the younger generation of Romanovs were, in Bobrinsky's view, uneducated and without any depth. Not one serious or sensible word had been spoken all evening. The atmosphere had even been somewhat crude, rather heavy jokes being greeted with loud laughter. Alexander was a decent, well-meaning young man and his brothers were lively, but the touch of vulgarity reminded Bobrinsky of 'Peter the Great at the court of Louis XV'.[8]

Alexander III's aunt, Queen Olga of Württemburg, agreed with Lambsdorff and Bobrinsky's judgements. Visiting Russia in 1891, she confided to Lambsdorff her dismay that the tone of the Romanov family had deteriorated sharply since the days of her father, Nicholas I, and of her brother, Alexander II. 'She remembered about meals at the court of her father, the Emperor Nicholas, and recalled the glorious memory of the Emperor Alexander II. Many interesting guests were present at these meals who could talk about serious or political matters. ''I'm accustomed to this and don't like watching while people throw pellets of bread across the table,'' ' the Queen said to Lambsdorff, commenting sourly about the table manners of her imperial nephew and his children.[9]

Sometimes it was not just the personality and behaviour of Alexander but also the activities of his government which caused sophisticated aristocrats to cringe. Themselves cultured Europeans, they shuddered at the Tsar's crude anti-Semitism and his policemen's widespread disregard for legality or civil rights. They were concerned for their own prestige, and that of Russia, in Europe, whose educated classes were much inclined to dismiss the Romanovs' empire as barbaric and Asian. Alexander II's favourite minister, P.A. Valuev, pondered: 'Where are we? In Europe? No. In Asia? No. Somewhere between the two in half-Europe, in Belgrade or Bucharest.' Surveying the methods used to crush Polish nationalism in the western borderlands in the wake of the Polish revolution of 1863, Valuev commented to Alexander II: 'Permit me to say that I feel that I love my country less . . . I despise my compatriots.' To which the Emperor nodded assent, adding: 'I also feel the same; I don't say so to others but to you I admit that I feel the same as you.' No minister would have dared to speak in these liberal and European terms to Alexander III. Had they done so, they would have received a crude and forceful response.[10]

Not even Alexander III's most fervent admirers pretended that he was very intelligent. In addition, until the death of his elder brother in 1865 he had not been heir and had therefore reached adulthood with the mediocre education of an emperor's younger son. For many high officials, however, particularly those of conservative and nationalist views, Alexander's intellectual weakness was more than offset by his 'great and noble personality', his 'high morality', his love for his country and his deep awareness of the responsibility that came with his position. Alexander Mosolov, for instance, wrote of the Tsar in his memoirs that 'my respect for his personality, poorly gifted but morally high and sensible, grew all the time. With his calm and firm mind and his deep patriotism he did Russia invaluable service. He showed the need and the possibility of broad intellectual and economic development in full agreement with the basic, historically-created special conditions of our national life.' Serge Witte, himself a statesman of great intelligence and forcefulness, would have agreed with every word written by Mosolov.[11]

Beside her enormous husband, the Empress Marie Feodorovna appeared tiny. Not so beautiful as her elder sister, Queen Alexandra of England, the Empress was nevertheless a very attractive woman who for long maintained her family's tradition of appearing eternally youthful. Her superb, luminous eyes, which her son Nicholas II inherited, were her most striking feature. In many ways the Empress was the perfect consort to a monarch. She thoroughly enjoyed her role as leader of society, revelling in great balls and ceremonies, superb clothes and fine jewellery. Her sociability offset her husband's taciturnity and she was on the whole very popular in the world of Petersburg's aristocracy. She had great charm and the royal knack that, 'when she smiles she seems to single one out of the crowd, and each separate individual appropriates her smile as personally intended'. After fifteen years as wife to the heir before ascending the throne, Marie Feodorovna knew the Petersburg aristocracy very well. She did her homework before great events and, 'gifted with a retentive memory for faces, she is particularly gracious at presentations, and puts such pertinent questions to the ladies who are being presented as to show the interest she takes in the circumstances of everyone's life. She sympathises with people's grief and rejoices in their gladness.' In addition, 'in all emergencies the . . . Empress seems to know by intuition what is the right thing to be said'.[12]

The Empress Marie was born Princess Dagmar of Denmark, changing not only her title but also her name upon conversion to Russian Orthodoxy when she married the heir to the throne. Though her parents ultimately became King and Queen of Denmark, in their early married life they were neither well-off nor in direct line of succession to the throne. Their lifestyle was homely and bourgeois, and it remained so even after they inherited the Danish crown. Neither they nor most of their children had any intellectual or aesthetic interests. 'Among the Danish royal family and their offshoots, the Greeks, the special joke was to make funny noises and yell if they saw anyone trying to write a letter. There were no "in" jokes to play on anyone bold enough to read a book since none of them did.'[13]

Queen Mary of England once commented that 'the women of that Danish family make good wives. They have the art of marriage.' This was quite true in Marie Feodorovna's case. Natural kindness and generosity were allied to strict moral principles, a simple Christian faith and great devotion to her children. But, as was often true in the Danish royal family, strong maternal instincts were also linked to intense possessiveness and the attempt to keep her children young for as long as possible. Even her brother, King George of Greece, refused to understand that his sons were grown-up, causing much misery and trouble as a result. Kenneth Rose, King George V of England's biographer, describes Queen Alexandra as 'that most possessive of mothers' and quotes her comment – *vis-à-vis* her son's marriage – that 'nobody can, or ever shall, come between me and my darling Georgie boy'. Aged 21, the Prince still described himself in letters to his mother as 'your little Georgie dear'.[14]

In the end sons could usually escape their mothers to some extent. Daughters sometimes could not. Queen Alexandra turned her daughter Victoria into an unmarried slave. Her sister, the Empress Marie, caused great trouble when her elder daughter, the Grand Duchess Xenia, married; and she pushed her younger daughter Olga into marriage with her dreadful homosexual cousin, Peter of Oldenburg, in order to keep her firmly under her mother's thumb in Petersburg. Even in 1905, Marie's youngest son, the Grand Duke Michael, already 27 years old, could accurately be described by his sister-in-law as a 'darling child still'. Ten years later, an intelligent and worldly man who became a good friend of the Grand Duke commented: 'I have never met another man so uncorrupted and noble in nature; it was enough to look into his clear blue eyes to be ashamed of any bad thought or insincere feeling. In many ways he was a grown-up child who had been taught only what was good and moral.' By universal consent the 26-year-old Nicholas II was not only inexperienced when he ascended the throne in 1894 but also very innocent and immature for his age. To some extent this was the natural consequence of life in a secure and happy family, especially one as cloistered from the outside world as that of the Romanovs. But it is hard to doubt that, unwittingly, the Empress Marie's influence contributed greatly to her son's unreadiness for the task thrust upon him by his father's death.[15]

Contemporaries frequently noted the extraordinary physical similarity between Nicholas II and his first cousin, George V. In fact the cousins were alike in more than looks, though George was no doubt much more peppery and outspoken than Nicholas, whose reticence and self-restraint were legendary. Because he was a second son the English prince had an academically inferior but much less cloistered naval education than his Russian cousin, who was taught by tutors in his father's palaces. In time too, inevitably, the very different traditions of the English and Russian monarchies influenced the two men in contrasting ways.

Yet, even in trivial matters, great similarities existed. Nicholas II's diary is the despair of his biographers. The time he awoke, the party he attended and the anniversary to be noted are seldom forgotten. Meanwhile earth-shattering political events are passed over in silence or granted a laconic mention. George V was no different. Kenneth Rose comments that 'after a false start in 1878 which lasted less than two weeks', Prince George began his journal again

> on 3 May 1880 and continued a sparse but unbroken record until three days before his death. Written in a clear schoolboy hand that hardly changed in half a century, it reveals the methodical pattern which governed his leisure as well as his work. He breathed little life and no colour into his discreet daily chronicle. The perspectives of history failed to move him; he was enthralled less by events than by their anniversaries, which he noted again and again . . . Each morning, whether on land or at sea, he recorded the direction of the wind and other meteorological detail. It is idle for his biographer to sigh for the richer fare of a Pepys or a Creevey.[16]

Similarities, however, went well beyond the trivial and were due in part to the two monarchs' mothers. Both George V and Nicholas were at heart country gentlemen. They revelled in outdoor life and rural sports. Because his father and grandmother were alive in the 1890s, the English prince could still indulge this passion to the full, pushing governmental issues to the margin of his life. Nicholas II was less fortunate. Both cousins had served as junior officers in the armed forces, absorbing the simple patriotic military code of command and obedience. Neither found the ambiguities and subtleties of politics easy. Nicholas and George inherited from their mothers a simple Christian faith that steered them through life. Both men loved their wives, preferred family to social life, and thoroughly distrusted the 'smart set' in high society. In aesthetic terms both were blind, deaf and dumb. Possessing some of the finest paintings and buildings on earth they lived amidst Victorian monstrosities. Many Russian aristocrats, heirs to a fine cultural tradition, quailed before the Victorian furnishings of Nicholas II's family's rooms at Tsarskoe Selo or the Gothic cottage, Alexandria, whose ugliness was buried in the grounds of the superb palace of Peterhof. Yet not even these could compare in awfulness with George V's beloved York Cottage, its walls decorated with the same red cloth as was used for the trousers of the French army.

Whereas the Empress Marie's influence on her son is relatively easy to define, that of his father is more difficult and contentious. Inevitably, Alexander was a role-model for his son as both man and monarch. Indeed he was Nicholas's only possible role-model – Alexander II had died when Nicholas was 13. Alexander III died before his heir had sufficient experience of politics and administration to build up an independent conception

of an autocrat's role. Had Alexander lived even for another ten years
Nicholas would have come to know many senior officials and some of their
brighter would-be successors of the younger generation. Both through
acquaintance with their views and as a result of his own experience he
would have better grasped the realities of autocratic power and how these
could be fitted to his own personality and goals. As it was, however,
particularly in the first years of his reign, he was fated not merely to
attempt to emulate his father's role but also to know that he was doing so
very inadequately. He lacked Alexander's experience, his authoritative
manner and, very important given the symbolic nature of the Tsar's position, his majestic physical stature. Through gossip and tale-telling at court
he know only too well that unfavourable comparisons between his father
and himself were rife in Petersburg. Nicholas loved and admired his father,
firmly believing those who told him that Alexander had brought tranquill-
ity and progress to Russia. In his heart too there may have lurked the
suspicion that his father himself had had doubts as to whether his heir had
the toughness and maturity required for the job. Vladimir Ollongren,
who studied and played with Nicholas for three years in the 1870s, later
remarked that the small prince had at times seemed to him rather girlish in
his looks and behaviour. Alexander III agreed and feared lest his son should
turn into a hot-house plant, shying away from straight and honest fights
with other boys, unable to cope with a tough world. On one occasion
when, after a piece of mischief, Ollongren took all responsibility and
Nicholas denied it, his father grew angry. 'Volodya is a boy and you are a
little girl.' Many years later, when Nicholas was already 23 years old,
Alexander described him to one of his ministers as 'nothing but a boy,
whose judgements are childish'. Subsequently Nicholas's sister-in-law was
to comment that 'his father's dominating personality had stunted any gifts
for initiative in Nicky'.[17]

There were perhaps some similarities between the last Emperor of
Russia and Mohammed Reza Pahlavi, Iran's last shah. The Shah's father,
Reza, was a large and extremely tough man whose reign brought Iran a
degree of order and unity unprecedented for generations. Reza was known
to express fears about his son's manliness and whether he had the necessary
maturity and strength to rule. In 1941 Reza abruptly departed the political
scene, his 22-year-old son being catapulted unexpectedly on to the throne.
Some historians have explained the Shah's personality in terms of the
attempts of a sensitive and rather feminine man to live up to the tough
model set by his father. Though the Shah's public image, boastful and
grandiose, was totally different to that of the modest and gentlemanly
Nicholas II, those who knew him well realized that when faced by hard
decisions he was weak and vacillating. With somewhat less justice, the
same view of Nicholas was widespread in Russian aristocratic and govern-

ment circles. Still more current were the accusations of shiftiness and duplicity levelled against the Tsar. The monarch, so it was said, would never confront a minister but would appear to agree with him and then undermine him when his back was turned. High officials would be greeted warmly by the Emperor at audiences only to find a letter of dismissal awaiting them in their office the next day. Almost identical accusations were frequently raised against the Shah who, 'because of his extraordinary shyness . . . never sacked anyone personally' and always left 'the task of conveying the bad news . . . to court officials'.[18]

Attempts at comparative psychoanalysis need, however, to be handled with an element of caution. Mohammed Reza Pahlavi's parents quarrelled bitterly and separated. The Crown Prince was removed from his mother's house at the age of 6 and spent most of his childhood under military tutors before being dispatched to a boys' boarding school in Switzerland at the age of 12. His sister, Princess Ashraf, comments that Reza Shah was 'an awesome and frightening father. Whenever I saw a trouser leg with a red stripe approaching, I would run, on the theory that the best way to avoid my father's displeasure was to stay out of his way.' This was a far cry from Alexander III, whose daughter Olga used to sit under his desk as he worked, on occasion affixing the imperial seal to documents, and whose son Michael could get away with emptying buckets of water on the Tsar's head as a practical joke. Alexander III was a devoted and warm-hearted father, extremely close to all his children. Vladimir Ollongren's memoirs are good testimony on this point, since as a 10-year-old he lived alongside the heir in the bosom of the imperial family. He described Alexander III as 'a quite exceptionally cheerful and simple man; he played with us children at snowballs, taught us to saw wood and helped us to build snowmen'. If Alexander sought to toughen his sons a little and pulled their ears when they got up to pranks this was scarcely wicked or unusual. The Tsar no doubt reflected on the fact that when he was gone and his son was an adult no human being would ever argue with him or tell him he was wrong. Given the challenges and temptations that would face a future tsar, a father had good reason to fear any weakness or lack of discipline in his heir.[19]

By the standards of European royalty the extraordinary thing about Nicholas's childhood was the atmosphere of love, security and attention in which he lived as a boy. Since most royal marriages were made for dynastic reasons few monarchs were as devoted and faithful to their consorts as Alexander III. Relations between fathers and sons were very often cold and distant, on occasion being shot through with jealousy and fear lest the heir become a focus for opposition to his royal father. This was, for instance, the pattern in the eighteenth-century Hanoverian dynasty in Britain and in the nineteenth-century house of Savoy, rulers of Italy after 1861.

The Savoy dynasty was traditionally so distrustful of each new generation that the heir to the throne was given no training in government and allowed no serious experience of public life . . . To a quite extraordinary extent [princes] were kept austerely in a state of personal subjection where in private and public they had to kiss their father's hand and stand to attention in his presence. Often they were shown little affection, with results that can be imagined.[20]

Nicholas was spared the fate of his almost exact contemporary, King Victor Emmanuel III of Italy, who, 'reticent and taciturn by nature . . . evidently resented [the fact] that neither parent showed him much attention, and a solitary, introverted childhood was further embittered by physical disabilities . . . As a boy, he had been forced to wear a variety of orthopaedic instruments to strengthen his legs, and his stunted growth no doubt explains much of his shyness and lack of self-assurance.' Nor was the future tsar like his cousin Wilhelm II of Germany, also a victim of physical disability, but in addition born into a family riven by the conflict between the Prussian militarist values of his grandfather and the Anglophile liberal court of his father and mother, Queen Victoria's eldest daughter. Admittedly Nicholas's grandfather, Alexander II, with whom the imperial grandchildren had close and affectionate ties, was assassinated in 1881, but this was an occupational hazard common to most of European royalty. By their often rather bleak standards, Nicholas's childhood was one of innocent happiness.[21]

From the age of 7 to the age of 10 Nicholas was taught all subjects by his governess, Alexandra Ollongren. He studied the normal syllabus for entry into Russian middle schools, passing the entrance examination with ease in 1879. His only companions in the schoolroom were his younger brother, the Grand Duke George, and Alexandra Ollongren's son, Vladimir. From the latter's recollections come the fullest description of the young prince's life as a child, though in view of the way Ollongren's memoirs were written down, they have to be treated with some suspicion.

As an old man, Ollongren recalled Nicholas's 'happy, always laughing eyes, velvet and radiant' and his 'charming, playful almost girlish laugh'. The young prince loved hopscotch and watching birds fly. Already it was clear that Nicholas had an excellent memory. 'He adored his mother' and envied Ollongren because the latter's mother was always with him. The young grand dukes in the late 1870s, at least when living in Petersburg, saw their mother twice a day, once at 11 a.m. and again at bedtime. The morning meeting was the longer one, with both parents asking about their sons' days and their mother giving them rides on the train of her dress. It was typical of Marie Feodorovna's tact and kindness that Ollongren, a nobody and an outsider, was always given the first ride. Nicholas was enormously impressed by religious services, which all the children attended regularly. The superb theatre and music of the Orthodox mass gripped the young Grand Duke, and he and his companions used later to act out the roles of priest and deacon when they were on their own. But Nicholas was also deeply excited and impressed by the story of the Passion and the Resurrection.[22]

Ollongren comments that the palace servants 'loved the family'. Many of them came from veritable dynasties of court servants who had worked for the Romanovs for generations. 'The old-timers were great grumblers, like Chekhov's Firs, who were not shy to tell the imperial family home truths directly to their faces.' Not all these servants were Russians. The Grand Duchess Olga, for instance, recalled 'old Jim Hercules, a negro, who spent his annual holiday in the States and brought back jars of guava jelly as presents for us children'. In her recollection, the servants 'were all friends', as indeed were many of the soldiers and sailors guarding the imperial palaces, who 'used to play games with us and toss us in the air'.[23]

An enormous gulf separated the Romanovs from ordinary soldiers, peasants or servants. The latter were also in general simpler and less questioning than members of Russian educated society. For these reasons natural, friendly and human relationships were generally easier with them than was the case when the Romanovs came face to face with members of the upper and middle classes. Former peasant wetnurses would address their old imperial charges in the most friendly and intimate manner which no educated Russian would have dared to use to a tsar or his children. Peasant soldiers bathing in the streams near Peterhof would thunder their cheers, standing stark naked, as the Tsar's carriage passed. In contrast a wall of etiquette divided the Romanovs from educated Russians.[24]

The son of Nicholas II's court doctor recalled his mother's first meeting with the heir to the throne in 1908:

> My mother when leaving the palace after her first presentation to the Empress, met at the entrance the little Alexis who was then a tot of four years. She bowed to him according to all rules, and said: 'How do you do, Your Imperial Highness?' But to my mother's dismay the Imperial Highness, instead of acknowledging her greeting, frowned angrily and turned away his head. When my mother returned home and told of this incident to my father, he began to laugh and said: 'Of course the Heir was angry with you. You should have bowed to him in silence, for you have no right to say anything before he himself has started to talk to you.'[25]

As an adult Nicholas II tended to idealize the Russian peasantry. His attitude towards Russian educated society was much more equivocal. The same was true of his younger sister, Olga. For this there were many reasons, some of which were well-established elements in the Russian tradition of autocratic monarchy while others had more to do with the personal difficulties that Nicholas and his wife had with Petersburg society. But one factor in the Tsar's attitude may simply have been a childhood memory of a life in which human relations were much easier with peasants, soldiers and servants than with educated Russians.

Aged 10, Nicholas was handed over to a military governor, General G.G. Danilovich, a man 'better known for his military discipline and plodding uprightness than for the brilliance of his mind or breadth and tolerance of his views'. Danilovich himself invited specialists to come to the palace to teach the heir a range of subjects including four modern languages (Russian, French, English and German), mathematics, history, geography and chemistry. Of the subjects Nicholas was taught, history was much the closest to his heart. His membership of the Imperial Historical Society from the age of 16 was more than merely honorary. Many years later, in the enforced leisure of his Siberian exile, he returned to reading works of history. He commented to his son's English teacher, Sydney Gibbs, that 'his favourite subject was history' and that he 'had read a good deal when he was young, but had no time for it later'. In his youth and adolescence Nicholas had, however, also read fiction in English, French and Russian. Someone capable of mastering four languages and coping with Dostoevsky and the historians Karamzin and Solovyov at this age cannot have been without brains.[26]

The young Grand Duke does not appzar to have been very fond of his governor, referring to him on one occasion as 'cholera'. Of his tutors, Charles Heath seems to have been closest to the heir. Heath was not an intellectual and had never been to university. He had the late Victorian English schoolmaster's love of the open air and manly sports. Heath had been a tutor at the Alexander Lycée, Russia's most prestigious civilian school, where he enjoyed an excellent reputation. Whereas comments of old boys about some of the other tutors at the Lycée were distinctly ambivalent, Heath was remembered as the Lycée's model teacher, a man with a warm heart, great energy and a respectable brain who trusted his pupils and had a deep sense of decency and fairness. Heath neither spied on his charges at the Lycée, all of whom came from upper-class families, nor made up to them or sought to curry favour with the school's director. Nicholas liked Heath and, when he visited Britain in 1894 with his fiancée, reported to his mother that 'I was very glad to see Mr Heath, whom I presented to Granny', in other words to Queen Victoria. Mr Heath was initially not overly impressed by the royal children, whom he found ill-disciplined, with table manners akin to those of a country bumpkin. His life as a tutor was not made easier by a green parrot, Popka, which belonged to the Grand Duke George, Nicholas's younger brother and his constant companion until he developed tuberculosis and was forced to decamp to the warm climate of the Caucasus. 'Popka . . . hated Mr Heath. Every time the poor English master entered Georgie's room the bird would fly into a rage and then imitate Mr Heath with the most exaggerated British accent. Mr Heath finally became so exasperated that he refused to enter Georgie's room until Popka had been removed.' It was partly under Charles Heath's guidance that Nicholas developed a calm and self-control far more characteristic of an Englishman than of a member of the pre-revolutionary Russian ruling class. General V.N. Voeykov, the last Commandant of the Imperial Palaces in Nicholas's reign, knew the monarch well. He commented that 'one of the Emperor's outstanding qualities was his self-control. Being by nature very quick tempered, he had worked hard on himself from his childhood under the direction of his tutor, the English Mister Heath, and had achieved a tremendous degree of self-possession. Mister Heath frequently reminded his imperial pupil of the English saying that aristocrats are born but gentlemen are made.'[27]

At the age of 17 the heir began his instruction in the art of government, for the first time coming into close contact with some of the leading political, military and academic figures in his father's realm. Peter Bark, who served as Minister of Finance from 1914 to the monarchy's fall, made the following comment in his memoirs about Nicholas's education:

As heir, from a young age he had a thorough training under the direction of the best teachers in Russia. His professor in political economy, who introduced him to financial questions, was Bunge, an outstanding man who served as Minister of Finance for five years. Zamyslovsky was his professor of history and Kaustin his teacher in international law. Generals Mehr and Dragomirov taught him military sciences and Beketov taught chemistry. Among his teachers, the one who exerted the greatest influence on him was undoubtedly Pobedonostsev, a professor of civil and political law. Pobedonostsev was Chief Procurator of the Holy Synod [lay administrator of the Orthodox Church] in the reigns of Alexander III and Nicholas II. He was a convinced and extreme conservative and thanks to his powerful character had great influence on both emperors.[28]

Whether Pobedonostsev's influence on Alexander III and Nicholas II was actually quite as great as Peter Bark imagined is a moot point. Nevertheless, he certainly did have some impact in shaping their views as young men. Pobedonostsev was highly intelligent, widely read and very hardworking. He had a typically conservative disbelief in the power of legislation to change morals. His view of human nature was even gloomier than that of most European conservatives: the majority of human beings were weak, selfish, gullible and largely immune to the call of reason. Given this reality, democracy was likely to turn into a chaotic sham, with professional politicians, plutocrats and press barons pandering to the prejudices and short-sighted greed of the electorate. In the Anglo-Saxon and Scandinavian countries, with their centuries-old tradition of individualism, an educated and self-disciplined citizenry had emerged which might just be able to sustain democratic politics, especially in a land of plentiful resources like the United States. Russian traditions were different, however, and the country was both more primitive and multi-national. In consequence, liberalism and democracy would bring disaster in their wake. Only the power and symbolism of an autocratic monarchy, advised by an élite of rational expert officials, could run the country effectively. Russia was built on communities – the peasant village, the Church and the nation – and these must be preserved and protected from the attacks of Western-style individualism. The educated classes, including the aristocracy, were bearers of this bacillus and were therefore dangerous. The religious and patriotic instincts of the peasantry were a firmer basis for political stability and Russian power, but the simple people must be protected from outside influences which would sow doubts among them about values and loyalties, thereby undermining the Russian national solidarity between ruler and people on which the empire's future depended.[29]

Apart from Pobedonostsev, Nicholas's best-known teacher was Nicholas Bunge. As both a professor of economics and a former Minister of Finance, Bunge was uniquely fitted to the task of teaching the heir about the history of economic thought and of Russia's economy. These two themes were the subject of the lectures which he gave to the Tsarevich in 1888 and 1889. Nicholas did not simply listen to the lectures but also took tests. Nevertheless, it is questionable how much of Bunge's lectures on economics the heir really understood. Years later, faced by the collapse of the Russian economy in 1916, Nicholas was to write to his wife, 'I never was a businessman and simply do not understand anything in these questions of supplying and provisioning.'[30]

When in 1893 Nicholas was appointed chairman of the committee which was responsible for all matters linked to the construction of the Siberian railway, Bunge was appointed the committee's vice-chairman. He was thus in a position to supplement his earlier theoretical guidance in economic affairs with practical advice and support on an issue which was very important for Russia's future and in which the heir took a great interest. In Bunge Nicholas encountered a high official who stood at the opposite pole of the spectrum, both politically and personally, to Pobedonostsev. A more humane, selfless and warm-hearted man than the Chief Procurator of the Synod, Bunge was also much more liberal and much more *au fait* with the new capitalist world of banks and industry which was beginning to develop rapidly in Russia in the late nineteenth century.

At the age of 19, Nicholas was commissioned into the Preobrazhensky Guards, the senior regiment of the Russian army. Subsequently, to give him some insight into other branches of the army, he also served in the Guards Hussars and in the Horse Artillery. This was not, and probably was not expected to be, a real training in the military art. Not only in Russia but everywhere in Europe, the most exclusive regiments of the Guards came closer to being a pleasant and sociable finishing school for wealthy young aristocrats than a serious professional training for a military career. In the great majority of cases the rich young lieutenants and captains who officered these regiments had neither the need nor the inclination to forge careers. The officers' mess was a pleasant club, duties were light and the lieutenant's relationship with his soldiers was akin to that of the heir to a great estate and his father's labourers. Neither professional, political nor other serious matters were often discussed in the mess, and much time was given over to amusements. Having never been to school or lived outside his father's palaces, all of this represented great excitement and liberation for the young heir. Nicholas had always loved the army, its traditions, uniforms and values. In later life, the officers' messes of the Guards regiments were almost the only environment where he felt at ease and at home among educated Russians. To the extent that he truly trusted anyone or had personal friends, they tended to come from this milieu. As for many other people, the time between leaving school and taking up the responsibilities of work and adulthood was more fun than any other period of Nicholas's life. Comradeship, hunting, carousals, visits to Petersburg's 'gipsy ladies' – these were all part and parcel of the heir's life, as of those of other aristocratic young men in the Guards. The heir's famous affair with the ballerina Mathilde Ksheshinskaya was also a normal rite of passage. There is no reason to think that Nicholas's parents looked on any of this with great disfavour. Soon enough the life of the Tsarevich would be burdened with obligations, constraints and hard work. A few years of carefree amusement in the very safe and loyal company of Guards officers would do him no harm.[31]

If service in the Guards was one traditional stage in a young nobleman's upbringing, the Grand Tour was another. It was designed to widen horizons, to add culture and polish, and to allow a young man to gain worldly experience away from his parents while still under the supervision of trusted older men. In the past the Grand Tour had usually taken a young man to courts, museums and galleries in Italy and France. Making use of the Victorian revolution in communications, Nicholas's parents decided to send him round the world by railway and steamship.

The heir left Gatchina in October 1890 and did not return until August 1891. His expedition began with a stop in Vienna and the customary reception at the Hofburg. It continued through Greece, Egypt, India,

Ceylon, the East Indies, Siam, parts of China and Japan. Returning across Siberia, Nicholas became the first heir ever to visit this part of his father's dominions, in which he thereafter always retained a tremendous interest. On occasion during his journey, Nicholas complained that he was seeing nothing of value, because his time was taken up with receptions and meetings with colonial officials. This was, however, the inevitable consequence of such an expedition. For reasons of both security and protocol, the heir to the Russian throne could not travel incognito through foreign countries and their empires. Nevertheless, in the course of his ten-month journey Nicholas saw some of the world's most splendid sights, visited scores of museums and galleries, and came into contact with a wide range of societies and people often quite different to anything that he had previously encountered. Even meetings with colonial officialdom were not always without interest. In India, for instance, the heir was accompanied by Sir Donald Mackenzie Wallace, the secretary to a former Viceroy but also fluent in Russian and Britain's leading expert on the Russian Empire. This was to be an acquaintance subsequently renewed when Wallace visited the Emperor at Tsarskoe Selo.[32]

Moreover, if Nicholas's entourage, like that of any other European crown prince, was largely made up of aristocratic Guards officers, some of its members were interesting men, knowledgeable about the areas they were visiting. M.K. Onu, an intelligent man and an expert on Middle Eastern and Asiatic affairs, travelled with Nicholas in Egypt and India. Prince E. Ukhtomsky, an authority on Asian religion and culture, accompanied him on the whole journey. Ukhtomsky believed, then and afterwards, that Russia's future lay in Asia. He argued that, unlike Western and Central Europeans, Russians had a spiritual affinity with Asians. 'There seems', he wrote, 'to be nothing easier for Russians than to get on with Asiatics. We agree so well with one another in our views of the most important and vital questions, that a certain close spiritual kinship soon comes to the front.' Asking rhetorically, 'when will the Christian nations of the West acknowledge the right of Asia to equality and really humane treatment', Ukhtomsky claimed, with little historic justice, that 'the idea of invading a complex foreign life, of using Asia as a tool for the selfish advancement of modern, so-called civilised, mankind, was repugnant to us'. Ukhtomsky's particular *bête noire* was the British colonial empire, and he may have encouraged Nicholas in his irritation with the red coats by which the Tsarevich was continually surrounded in India. But although Ukhtomsky was in some ways a misguided and prejudiced man he was not an unintelligent one, and his views were a novel and refreshing antidote to the conventional stereotypes about European cultural supremacy by which Nicholas was surrounded not just in his father's palaces but also when he visited his European relatives.[33]

Back in Petersburg, having narrowly escaped assassination at the hands of a policeman during his tour of Japan, Nicholas began to take a more active role in affairs of state, while still spending as much time as possible on regimental duties and living a free and easy bachelor life. Like all heirs to the throne, he was appointed a member of the State Council and the Committee of Ministers, the empire's highest legislative and executive bodies, on his twenty-first birthday. As one might expect of a young member of the 'leisured class' enjoying the first fling of freedom, Nicholas was less than enthralled at the idea of ploughing through the vast mounds of paperwork which were the day-to-day reality of Russian government in the highest echelons. In November 1891 he was appointed to chair the Special Committee on Famine Relief and in February 1893 the Siberian Railway Committee. Both of these committees were much closer to Nicholas's heart than the day-to-day business of the State Council and the Committee of Ministers. He began to express independent views in both committees, read their papers conscientiously and came to know some of his father's leading officials. It was through the famine committee, for instance, that he first encountered Vyacheslav Plehve, later to serve as his Minister of Internal Affairs. Nicholas's indoctrination into the treadmill of administration was beginning but it had not got far before his father's sudden and totally unexpected death, at the age of 49, in 1894 pushed his horrified heir into a role for which he felt himself to be thoroughly unprepared.[34]

No one either before or since has ever doubted Nicholas's assessment of his own lack of preparedness. Even his sister, the Grand Duchess Olga, deeply loyal to the memory of Alexander III, wrote 'it was my father's fault'. On ascending the throne, Nicholas was, in her words,

> in despair. He kept saying that he did not know what would become of us all, that he was wholly unfit to reign. Even at that time I felt instinctively that sensitivity and kindness on their own were not enough for a sovereign to have. And yet Nicky's unfitness was by no means his fault. He had intelligence, he had faith and courage – and he was wholly ignorant about governmental matters. Nicky had been trained as a soldier. He should have been taught statesmanship, and he was not.[35]

To what extent is the judgement of Nicholas's sister correct? As regards her brother's intelligence, she was right. The myth is widespread that Nicholas was a stupid man. This was far from true. Peter Bark, who knew the Emperor quite well, wrote that he possessed 'remarkable intelligence'. V.I. Mamantov, who worked very closely with the Emperor for two decades, remembered the speed with which he grasped complicated issues, the sharpness of his memory, and the elegance and clarity with which he expressed his written views. Admittedly, both Bark and Mamantov were loyal servants of the crown, writing their memoirs after their master's terrible death, and almost universal disparagement gave them much encouragement to defend his memory. Serge Witte, however, wrote before the revolution, much disliked Nicholas II and compared him very unfavourably with Alexander III. Nevertheless Witte commented in his memoirs that Nicholas 'has a quick mind and learns easily. In this respect he is far superior to his father.'[36]

Alexander Izvolsky, who later served as Foreign Minister under Nicholas, claimed that the Tsar's education 'was really that of a lieutenant of cavalry in one of the regiments of the Imperial Guard'. This is unfair. Guards cavalry officers were not taught by some of the empire's leading statesmen and professors. But it is true that the heir's education was inferior to that of his grandfather, Alexander II, whose tutor was the poet Zhukovsky, and to that of some of the eighteenth-century Romanovs. Here, however, one is encountering a cultural and intellectual decline common to late nineteenth-century royalty and aristocracy as a whole. In the eighteenth century some monarchs could converse comfortably with the leading thinkers of their day and could patronize some of the best artists and musicians. By 1900 the middle class dominated the intellectual and cultural world, with the aristocracy and royalty abandoning these fields and stressing instead the virtues of character, piety and proper behaviour. The world of Stravinsky and Freud was alien and incomprehensible not just to Nicholas II but also to Franz Josef, Wilhelm II and George V. As Countess Dönhoff recalls, 'not only did the landed aristocrats lay no claim to being part of the world of the poets and intellectuals, but they took pride in rejecting it . . . To the very end, this [upper-class] society remained a private, hermetically sealed world confident of the validity of its mores.'[37]

If Alexander III and his wife cannot fairly be blamed for falling victim to the 'spirit' of their age and class, for some failings in their son's education they can be held responsible. Nicholas's problem was not really that he was badly taught, still less that he was stupid. Much more to the point was the fact that the heir was naïve and immature for his age, which made it difficult for him to absorb the full value of his lectures and meant that even in his twenties he had an adolescent's view of the world. This was due in part to the fact that he was educated, together with his brother George, without outside companions of his own age. He grew up within the confines of the imperial palaces in a devoted but very cloistered family circle.

Many years later Nicholas's only son, the Tsarevich Aleksei, was brought up in a similar manner. His tutor, Pierre Gilliard, commented that a child educated in such isolation is deprived of that basic principle which plays the main role in developing judgement. He will always feel the lack of that knowledge which is obtained independently of study through life itself, by means of free relationships with his peers, exposure to various influences – sometimes contrary to the views by which he is surrounded, and by the possibility of regular contact and direct observation of people and things. In a word he will be deprived of everything that in the course of time develops intellectual horizons and provides essential knowledge. In such circumstances one needs to be an exceptionally capable person to acquire correct views, a normal way of thinking and the ability to express one's will at the opportune moment. An impenetrable barrier separates such a person from real life and makes it impossible to understand what is happening on the other side of the wall, on which people draw false pictures to amuse and occupy the person in question.[38]

Nicholas's isolated education was unlike that enjoyed by his cousins, George V or Wilhelm II, who as adolescents were dispatched to a naval college and a high school (gymnasium) respectively. Even the Emperor Hirohito, despite the divine status of the Japanese monarchy, was educated with other boys at a special class at the Peer's School, Gakushuin. In Nicholas's case considerations of both tradition and security would never have allowed him to attend a school but it would not have been impossible to select boys to be taught alongside him at the palace. Failure to do this contributed to the fact that in his twenties the heir to the throne was extraordinarily innocent in many ways. This suited some strands of the ideology of Russian autocratic monarchy. The Emperor, it was asserted, must stand not merely above all classes and factions but almost above the human condition itself. Not prey to normal human temptations, interests or frailties, he ruled on the basis of a pure heart and an Orthodox Christian conscience. But though Nicholas's immature innocence might match this saint-like vision of kingship, it was very far removed from the day-to-day business of politics in any country, let alone the bitter realities of ruling Russia in an era of acute tension and difficulty.[39]

A harsh critic might add that Alexander III and Marie Feodorovna did not approach their son's education with the same intense seriousness of purpose as, for instance, Prince Albert or his daughter Victoria, the German Empress and the mother of Wilhelm II. Popka the parrot would have been banished very speedily from anywhere near the classroom of the Prince of Wales or one of Victoria's sons. But, in Alexander and Marie's defence, educating an heir to the throne was a very difficult business. A boy had to be trained for a position for which his character might be unsuited. Even a constitutional monarch benefits from a wide range of knowledge and absolutely requires a great sense of responsibility, tact and self-discipline. The requirements for educating a young man to be head of state and head of government for life are terrifying. Too rigorous and joyless an education could backfire badly. Edward VII, a Hanoverian at heart, revolted against the austere Coburg training imposed by his father and turned into a pleasure-loving, self-indulgent but rather human adult. His nephew Wilhelm II was not merely irresponsible and notoriously incapable of consistent self-disciplined work, he also turned against the liberal values which, together with an austere Protestant work ethic, his parents had tried to inculcate into him. By these standards Nicholas II's education was quite well-balanced and successful. Nor, until the age of 18, was it in any sense military.[40]

It remains true, of course, that when he became Emperor in 1894 Nicholas was unprepared either psychologically or technically for the job. He exaggerated a little when he said to his Foreign Minister, Nicholas Giers, 'I know nothing. The late emperor did not foresee his death and did not let me in on any government business.' But it was certainly the case that he knew nothing of state secrets (such as the Franco-Russian alliance) and had little overall grasp of policy. In addition, he had a thoroughly inadequate grounding in the workings of the machinery of government. The main reason for this was obvious enough. An enormously strong and seemingly healthy man does not expect to die suddenly at the age of 49. In his early years as Emperor, Nicholas undoubtedly suffered seriously from his father's oversight. Even so, it is possible at least to understand Alexander's position. There is no evidence that, unlike the kings of Italy or some earlier Romanovs, he saw his heir as a threat or rival. There seemed every reason to believe that Alexander would live for many years. He knew better than anyone the endless chores and responsibilities of a tsar's life. Loving his son, he no doubt wished him to have at least a few carefree years before his future role engulfed him. Talking about his heir, Crown Prince Reza, the last Shah of Iran once commented that 'at his age too much responsibility might put him off administrative work for life'. Perhaps Alexander III was too much influenced for too long by similar thoughts.[41]

In one sense, moreover, it is wrong to say that Nicholas was psychologically ill-equipped to rule. No doubt he was appalled that responsibility had been thrust on to his shoulders so soon and so unexpectedly. As has been said, as an autocrat he had no other role-model than his father and yet both was, and felt himself to be, unable to meet his father's standard. Certainly he quaked, as any rational man would, before the immense burden and responsibility of ruling Russia for the rest of his life. Much of the routine even of a constitutional monarch is utterly tedious and demands inhuman self-discipline. Maybe in his heart Nicholas cursed fate for imposing on him these duties rather than allowing him the far easier life of one of his cousins or even of an ordinary member of the leisured class. That would have been very natural. But fate, interpreted as God's will, was something that

Nicholas not only accepted but positively believed in. The old European order did not glorify the individual or believe in one's right to choose one's own path in life. Nicholas belonged in his innermost values entirely to that order. Human beings served God's purpose in the role to which He assigned them. Nicholas was furious with other Romanovs who, in marrying commoners or divorcees, thereby put individual happiness before loyalty to the family collective and their inherited God-given responsibilities. If he could not easily cope with the task of being an effective autocrat there were good down-to-earth reasons for this, beginning with the immense difficulty of the job. But the young man who ascended the Russian throne certainly identified with his role, believed in its worth and necessity, and proved obstinately determined not to shed the responsibility which, in his view, God Himself had placed upon him.[42]

CHAPTER 3

Tsar and Family Man

On 1 January 1894 the Tsarevich Nicholas wrote in his diary, 'Please God that the coming year will pass as happily and quietly as the last one.' In fact 1894 was to transform Nicholas's existence. At the beginning of the year the heir was first and foremost a young Guards officer, much of whose life was devoted to reading, dancing, skating, the opera and his mistress, Mathilde Ksheshinskaya. Twelve months later he was Emperor of all the Russias, the bearer of theoretically absolute power over a vast empire. He was also a married man.[1]

Nicholas's bride was Princess Alix of Hesse, the youngest daughter of Grand Duke Louis IV of Hesse and his wife Alice, who was herself Queen Victoria's second daughter. In 1884 Alix's elder sister, Elizabeth, had married the Grand Duke Serge, younger brother of Alexander III. Alix had her first experience of Russia, aged 12, when she attended her sister's wedding. There she met the 16-year-old Tsarevich Nicholas for the first time. Subsequently they met again, both in Russia and abroad. In December 1891 Nicholas confided to his diary that it was his 'dream – to get married one day to Alix of Hesse'.[2]

The heir's choice was eminently suitable. Many of Nicholas's Romanov relations were to marry a bewildering collection of ballerinas, commoners and divorcees in the quarter century before the 1917 revolution. By contrast the heir's eye had lighted on a very beautiful young woman closely connected to many of the greatest royal families in Europe. There is no evidence that Alexander III or the Empress Marie opposed their son's choice of bride. On the contrary, almost Nicholas's first thought after his engagement was that the news would delight his parents. The problem with Alix was quite different. A Russian Empress had to be of the Orthodox faith. Therefore any foreign princess marrying the heir to the throne must convert to Orthodoxy. This the young Princess of Hesse was not prepared to do.

Not until April 1894 did Alix change her mind. On 2 April Nicholas had set off with a large contingent of Romanovs to attend the wedding of Alix's brother, Grand Duke Ernest Louis of Hesse, to another grandchild of Queen Victoria, Princess Victoria ('Ducky') of Edinburgh and Saxe-Coburg-Gotha. Much of Europe's Protestant royalty descended on Darmstadt for the occasion, including Queen Victoria herself and the Emperor Wilhelm II of Germany. On 5 April Nicholas was left alone with Alix for a time. 'She has grown wonderfully more beautiful', wrote the Tsarevich in his diary, 'but was looking very sad. They left us alone and then began between us the conversation which I had long since greatly wanted and yet very much feared. We talked until twelve but without success, she is very opposed to a change in religion.'[3]

Three days later the young princess gave in. 'A wonderful unforgettable day in my life,' wrote Nicholas,

> the day of my betrothal to my beloved Alix. After 10 o'clock she came to Aunt Miechen and, after a conversation with her, we sorted things out together. God what a mountain has fallen from my shoulders; how this joy will make dear Mama and Papa rejoice! I walked around as if in a dream all day, not fully understanding what had happened to me! Wilhelm [the Kaiser] sat in a neighbouring room and awaited the end of our conversation with the aunts and uncles.[4]

No one can be sure what caused Princess Alix to change her mind. It was certainly not overt pressure from her relatives nor a simple desire to wear a crown, for not long before she had stoutly resisted attempts to marry her to the eldest son of the Prince of Wales, 'Eddie', the Duke of Clarence. Perhaps the atmosphere surrounding her brother's wedding and the ill-suppressed hopes of many of her relatives influenced her. Perhaps she felt a little insecure at the thought of losing her position as leading lady in Hesse-Darmstadt to her brother's bride. The advice of her sister, Elizabeth, who became a voluntary and passionate convert to Orthodoxy in 1891 may have been important. When staying on her sister's estate at Ilinskoe, near Moscow, Alix seems to have conceived that romantic love for the Russian peasantry and village life which was so strongly to mark her thinking as Empress. But probably the simplest answer is the best one. Not even Alix's worst enemies ever denied that she loved her husband devotedly. And if love for a handsome, sensitive man with high ideals was allied to a romantic excitement at the prospect of life in Russia and the challenge of a throne, no young woman could fairly be blamed for that.[5]

Alix's father, Grand Duke Louis IV, had died in 1892. Though she loved her father and was greatly upset by his death, it does not seem that Alix inherited much of his personality. The Grand Duke was a rather amiable, easy-going and unintellectual man. He was a professional soldier, and in later life Alix used to take pride in calling herself a soldier's daughter. She shared her husband's liking for military pageantry and the officer's code of values and behaviour. Perhaps her love of flowers was also inherited from her father, an enthusiastic gardener. Darmstadt in the broader sense did, however, influence the young princess in ways that mattered later in Russia. The Grand Duchy and its royal family were not rich, especially after the wars of 1866 and 1870–1. Managing the household first of her father and then of her brother, the young princess learned habits of thrift and careful accounting which were to contribute to her unpopularity among the extravagant, generous and often reckless aristocracy of Petersburg.[6]

Alix was in some respects very similar to her English mother, Princess Alice. Alice was an intelligent woman, who shared the intellectual interests and the seriousness of purpose of her father, the Prince Consort, and her elder sister, Victoria, the mother of Wilhelm II of Germany. Like Victoria she encountered much criticism from German courtiers because of her English ways and sympathies, but Alice was more tactful than her elder sister and Darmstadt a less difficult place for an English princess than the intrigue-ridden and arrogant Prussian capital.

Alice was a deeply serious and thoughtful Christian.

> The princess's absorption with religion began in the period of nervous strain after the death of her father. She read Professor Jowett's *Esssays and Reviews* and F.W. Robertson's *Sermons*, starting her along the path to spiritual freedom. She conversed with the leading churchmen, who were among the few visitors to the Queen in the initial mourning period, and before she was twenty had engaged Dean Stanley in an earnest discussion of the Apocalypse and the Psalms.

In Darmstadt Princess Alice became a great friend and admirer of David Strauss, the author of *Life of Jesus* and a biblical scholar of worldwide renown and radical views. The two used to discuss not merely religious questions but also Voltaire. Strauss read lectures on religious topics to the Princess, and when these were published he dedicated them to her. Strauss did this unwillingly, knowing that in parochial and God-fearing Darmstadt the association of Princess Alice with unorthodox religious ideas would cause a stir. But where her personal friendships and her religious convictions were concerned, Princess Alice was prepared to scorn public opinion. Later, in the much wider, crueller and more important context of Russia, her daughter Alix was to do the same.

An intelligent and well-informed friend wrote of Princess Alice that 'Christianity to her was not a profession to be made lightly. If she could not embrace its essential doctrines with her whole soul and without reservation it became a meaningless lip-service which it was her clear duty to abandon.' Like her mother, Alix was a fervent Christian. She abandoned Protestantism only after a great struggle. In her bedroom at Tsarskoe Selo 'was a little door in the wall, leading to a tiny dark chapel lighted by hanging lamps, where the Empress was wont to pray'. When in Petersburg, the Empress used to go to the Kazan Cathedral, kneeling in the shadow of a pillar, unrecognized by anyone and attended by a single lady-in-waiting. For Alix life on earth was in the most literal sense a trial, in which human beings were tested to see whether they were worthy of heavenly bliss. The sufferings God inflicted on one were a test of one's faith and a punishment for one's wrongdoings. The Empress was a deeply serious person who came to have great interest in Orthodox theology and religious literature. She loved discussing abstract, and especially religious, issues, and her later friendship with the Grand Duchesses Militza and Anastasia owed much to their knowledge of Persian, Indian and Chinese religion and philosophy. Alix 'zealously studied the intricate works of the old Fathers of the Church. Besides these she read many French and English philosophical books.'[7]

As Empress, Alix held to an intensely emotional and mystical Orthodox faith. The superb ritual and singing of the Orthodox liturgy moved her deeply, as did her sense that through Orthodoxy she stood in spiritual brotherhood and communion with her husband's simplest subjects. But alongside this strain of Christian belief, Alix was also a born organizer, an efficient administrator and a passionate Christian philanthropist. Though her interests included famine and unemployment relief, and professional training for girls, her charitable work was above all concerned with help for the sick and the world of medicine. Typically, even on holiday in the Crimea, Alix toured the hospitals and sanatoria in the neighbourhood, taking her young daughters with her because 'they should understand the sadness underneath all this beauty'. Setting up medical rehabilitation centres for the wounded, busying herself with training young women, and organizing hospitals and medical services in war-time – all of this was very reminiscent too of the activities of Alix's mother. Like her daughter, Alice was an efficient, practical, down-to-earth administrator who loved organizing a range of charitable activities. Also like Alix, the world of nursing and care for the sick was closest to her heart. Princess Victoria of Hesse recalled the Franco-Prussian War in her memoirs, when 'my mother was very busy with Red Cross work and regularly visited the wounded, both German and French, and I often accompanied her'.[8]

In both mother and daughter the spirit was a good deal stronger than the flesh. Both were exhausted by numerous pregnancies. Already tired and ill by her late thirties, Alix once wrote that 'Darling Mama also lost her health at an early age.' Devoted mothers, both women insisted on nursing their own children whenever they were sick. When Nicholas II contracted typhoid in 1900 Alix nursed him herself, day and night. 'I rebelled at a nurse being taken and we managed perfectly ourselves.' Unfortunately, she added, 'now I suffer from head and heartache, the latter from nerves and many sleepless nights'. When her children went down with diphtheria in 1878 Princess Alice exhausted herself looking after them. When she too contracted the disease she was unable to resist it and died on 14 December 1878, aged only 35.

Alix and her mother were similar not only in their physical frailty but also in their highly strung, passionate temperaments. Princess Alix was a proud, strong-minded, very emotional woman who fought to control her anger and nerves. Her mother once complained to Queen Victoria that 'people with strong feelings and of nervous temperament, for which one is no more responsible than for the colour of one's eyes, have things to fight against and put up with, unknown to those of quiet, equable dispositions, who are free from violent emotions, and have consequently no feeling of nerves . . . One can overcome a great deal – but *alter* oneself one cannot.'[9]

When her mother died Alix was 6 years old. Simultaneously she lost her sister and playmate, May, also to diphtheria. One can only guess at the impact of these deaths on the small child, though Baroness Buxhoeveden may well be right in suggesting that they 'probably laid the foundations of seriousness that lay at the bottom of her character'. The gap in the children's lives left by their mother's death was to some extent filled by Queen Victoria. The Queen frequently visited Darmstadt, and the Hesse family took a long annual holiday in England. As the youngest and most vulnerable of the Hesse children, Alix was the Queen's favourite. Grandmother and granddaughter always adored each other. As Empress, the only time when Alix was seen to weep in public was at the memorial service for Queen Victoria at the English church in Petersburg. Lili Dehn, who knew Alix very well, believed that she owed a good deal to Victoria's influence.

The Empress inherited much of her illustrious grandmother's tenacity of purpose, and she refused to be dictated to . . . her morals were the ultra-strict morals of her grandmother . . . in many ways she was a typical Victorian; she shared her grandmother's love of law and order, her faithful adherence to family duty, her dislike of modernity, and she also possessed the 'homeliness' of the Coburgs, which annoyed Society so much . . . Queen Victoria had instilled in the mind of her granddaughter the entire duties of a *Hausfrau*. In her persistent regard for these Martha-like cares, the Empress was entirely German and entirely English – certainly not Russian.

In the first days of the 1917 revolution, when all the imperial children were ill with measles, Lili Dehn discovered to her surprise that the Empress not only knew how to make a bed, but was also 'especially expert in changing sheets and nightclothes in a few minutes without disturbing the patients'. Alix commented, 'Lili . . . you Russian ladies don't know how to be useful. When I was a girl, my grandmother, Queen Victoria, showed me how to make a bed . . . I learnt to do useful things in England.'[10]

It may well be partly true that Alix's 'English point of view on many questions in later life was . . . due to her many visits to England at this most impressionable age', in other words during childhood and adolescence. In any case, Princess Alice had always remained 'intensely English', and 'life in the Palace was organised on English lines, and was so carried on after the Princess's death'. The nursery, ruled over by Mrs Orchard, operated according to the English system of fresh air, simple food and a strictly observed timetable. Thence, Alix graduated to an English governess, Miss Jackson, an intelligent woman under whose direction 'the princesses were trained to talk on abstract subjects'. Not surprisingly, 'English was, of course, her natural language' and England the focus for many of her loyalties. During the First World War, Alix was to be deeply reviled in Russia as a 'German', whose sympathies lay with Russia's enemies. There was no justice whatever in this, for Alix never had the remotest loyalty to the Prussian-dominated German Reich or to its ruler, Wilhelm II. Had war broken out between Russia and Britain, however, as was entirely possible at any time between 1894 and 1906, Alix would most certainly, and more justifiably, have been denounced as an Englishwoman. Such was the inevitable fate of a foreign consort amidst the nationalist passions of late Victorian Europe. In later life Queen Victoria became doubtful of the wisdom of dynastic marriages through which her daughters and granddaughters were exposed to the strains and perils that faced foreign queens at European courts. It was Alix, for whom the Queen had particular affection, who was to confront these perils in their most cruel form. Not surprisingly, Victoria's joy at her granddaughter's love for Nicholas and her splendid marriage was tempered by fear for her fate on such a great, but also such a dangerous, throne.[11]

The most tragic inheritance Alix received from her mother and grandmother was, however, the disease of haemophilia. This hereditary ailment is generally transmitted through females but strikes only males. Its effect is to stop the blood from clotting which, in the era before blood transfusions, was a certain recipe for prolonged suffering and offered the probability of an early death. Queen Victoria's son, Leopold, was killed by this disease, from which Princess Alice's younger son also appears to have suffered. At first glance, therefore, it might seem extraordinary that the Romanovs could allow the heir to the throne to run the medical risks that marriage to Alix entailed.

In fact, Alexander III and his wife clearly knew nothing about the disease or the risks involved. Although Alix's elder sister had married the Grand Duke Serge the couple were childless, so the Russian imperial family had had no reason to confront the issue of haemophilia. Of course, having seen the disease destroy one of her sons, Queen Victoria herself must have known something about it. But the Queen can hardly be accused of deceiving the Romanovs or exposing them deliberately to danger, since she had done her utmost to persuade Alix to marry the Duke of Clarence, who stood in the direct line of succession to the British throne. The issue of haemophilia was 'a highly delicate matter rarely discussed in royal circles . . . The whole subject was more or less taboo while Queen Victoria was alive.' The question was in any case complicated by the random nature of the disease. Of Queen Victoria's four sons only one was affected. Nor was haemophilia transmitted through her eldest daughter, Victoria, to Kaiser Wilhelm II, as could very easily have happened. Instead it was the descendants of her second and fourth daughters, Alice and Beatrice, who were affected.

Even had the risks been better understood, however, it is by no means certain how Nicholas and his parents would have reacted. In Japan in 1920 a huge political storm was caused by revelations that the intended bride of Crown Prince Hirohito came from a family in which colour blindness was a common affliction. The idea that any kind of hereditary ailment might be introduced by marriage into the imperial family caused justified consternation. By contrast European royalty appears to have been extraordinarily careless about such matters. To preserve royalty's status, cousins intermarried with no regard to eugenics. Haemophilia was treated no differently. In 1914, for instance, the possibility of a marriage between the Romanian Crown Prince and Nicholas II's eldest daughter was widely canvassed without anyone, seemingly, raising the issue of haemophilia. Unlike in Nicholas II's case, when in 1905 King Alfonso XIII of Spain proposed to marry Princess Victoria Eugénie of Battenburg, another of Queen Victoria's granddaughters, the Spanish court does appear to have been warned of the risks involved. Alfonso seems, however, to have shrugged off these warnings, subsequently never forgiving his wife for the fact that two of his four sons were haemophiliacs. Nicholas II's case was more tragic than that of Alfonso in the sense that his only son, born at the end of his wife's child-bearing days, was struck by the disease. It is a measure of the Tsar's sensitive and chivalrous nature, not to mention his deep love for Alix, that never once did he blame her for 'the fact that', in Alfonso's words, 'my heir has contracted an infirmity which was carried by my wife's family and not mine'. Haemophilia helped to destroy Alfonso's marriage, causing him to turn away from his wife in bitterness and even revulsion. If it were possible, their son's disease seemed to bring Nicholas and Alix closer together than ever.[12]

In the summer of 1894, however, all thoughts of tragedy and disease were far from Nicholas's mind. The Tsarevich and his fiancée were deeply in love. In June he received his parents' permission to visit Alix in England. The day after his arrival he wrote in his diary, 'What happiness I felt, waking up this morning, when I remembered that I was living under one roof with my dear Alix.' The next few weeks passed blissfully, though not even the claims of his fiancée could stop Nicholas from visiting the barracks of the British Guards and revelling in the drill and horsemanship of the troops. From the moment of his departure every day that passed without a letter from Alix was torment. To guard against such misadventures Alix had carefully inserted loving messages in his diary for weeks in advance. Told by Nicholas of his affair with Ksheshinskaya, Alix wrote, 'God forgives us. If we confess our sins, he is faithful and just to forgive us . . . your confidence in me touched me, oh, so deeply and I pray to God that I may always show myself worthy of it.'[13]

The Tsarevich's idyllic mood was, however, to be destroyed in the early autumn of 1894 by his father's illness. In January 1894 Alexander had been very unwell, his doctors stating that the problem was influenza. Alarm spread in court and government circles, where it was recognized, in the words of General Kireev, that for all his 26 years the heir was still a child, with little training to take over the reins of government. By early March fears for Alexander's life had passed, but Lambsdorff reported that 'our monarch appears thinner, above all in the face; his skin has become flabby and he has aged greatly'. By late summer the Tsar's increasing tiredness was again causing worry, though not yet alarm. Professor Zakharin, brought in for consultations from Moscow, calmed the imperial family by saying that Alexander's life was not at risk. Nevertheless, he and Dr Leyden agreed on a diagnosis of nephritis, complicated by 'exhaustion from huge and never-ending mental work'. The Tsar stuck to his autumn routine of visiting his hunting lodge at Spala in Poland, but on 30 September he was forced to decamp to the Crimea, whose warm climate would, it was hoped, help him to recover. Although in early October Alexander was still travelling in the Crimea, by the middle of the month he was sometimes confined to bed all day and the Tsarevich had begun to read state documents on his father's behalf. On 20 October the Tsar's brothers, Serge and Paul, arrived at Alexander's bedside from Moscow. Two days later Alix arrived, Nicholas commenting, 'what joy to meet her in my own country and to have her so close – half my cares and sorrow seem to fall from my shoulders'. The Tsarevich was to need all the support he could get, for on 1 November Alexander III died. His appalled heir commented in his diary: 'My God, my God, what a day. The Lord has called to himself our adored, dear, deeply loved Papa . . . This was the death of a Saint! God help us in these sad days! Poor dear Mama.'[14]

The weeks that followed his father's death were a nightmare for the young Emperor. Together with the numbing shock of the loss came awareness of the new and enormous responsibilities which he was ill-equipped to face. The day-to-day business of government, including audiences with ministers and receptions for other officials, bore down upon him. The endless series of religious services following the death of an Orthodox monarch took up much of his time. Still worse were the many receptions for Russian and foreign delegations who arrived for Alexander's funeral and to pay their respects to the new monarch. Frequently Nicholas had to make speeches at these receptions, something to which he was little accustomed and which caused him great strain. Worst of all in a way were the innumerable members of foreign royal families who descended on Petersburg for the funeral and who had to be met at railway stations, accommodated in the imperial palaces and treated with due deference and attention. On 18 December, the eve of the funeral, Nicholas received so many delegations that 'my head was dizzy'. Two days later, after greeting and dining with two hundred guests, 'I almost howled'. On 26 November court mourning was lifted for a day and Nicholas and Alix were married. Two days later the Tsar was so busy that he only saw his wife for one hour. Not surprisingly, the strain told on him. Alix (who was her husband's aunt by marriage) wrote in Nicholas's diary, 'it's not good to grind your teeth at night, your aunt can't sleep'.[15]

The new monarch appeared rather lost in his role. On 13 November Lambsdorff commented that 'the young emperor, evidently, was shy about taking his proper place; he is lost in the mass of foreign royalties and grand dukes who surround him'. On 27 January 1895 Lambsdorff again noted that 'His Majesty still lacks the external appearance and manner of an emperor.' In February 1896 he described an incident at a ball where Nicholas waited his turn to ask Princess Yusupov to dance because others stood in the queue before him. Lambsdorff remarked that 'His Majesty goes too far in his modesty.' Not all members of high society were as kindly in their comments. Comparing the appearance of Nicholas II at his coronation with that of his father thirteen years before, Princess Radzivill remarked that, 'there, where a mighty monarch had presented himself to the cheers and acclamations of his subjects, one saw a frail, small, almost insignificant youth, whose Imperial crown seemed to crush him to the ground, and whose helplessness gave an appearance of unreality to the whole scene'. The Minister of War, General Vannovsky, complained that Nicholas 'takes counsel from everyone: with grandparents, aunts, mummy and anyone else; he is young and accedes to the view of the last person to whom he talks'.[16]

Petersburg high society was constitutionally incapable of keeping its mouth shut. The Emperor and Empress were surrounded by people only too happy to score off a rival by repeating an incautious or critical remark. It took no time for Petersburg's opinion about the monarch's lack of will or stature to reach the ears of the imperial couple. The main problem was that both Nicholas and Alix were themselves only too well aware of the Tsar's lack of experience and self-confidence. From her very first days in Russia Alix had tried to boost her husband's determination to assert himself. Together with reminders of her and God's love came the call to show who was in charge. As Alexander III lay dying, Alix advised her fiancé not to be pushed aside. 'Be firm and make the doctors . . . come alone to you and tell you how they find him, and exactly what they wish him to do, so that you are the first always to know . . . Don't let others be put first and you left out. You are [your] father's dear son and must be told all and be asked about everything. Show your own mind and don't let others forget who you are. Forgive me lovey.'[17]

At the same time as she was attempting to support her husband in his unaccustomed role as Russia's autocrat, Alix was also having to adapt herself to the enormous changes that had taken place in her own life. It helped her greatly that her marriage was, and always remained, very happy. For any young woman, however, the first months of married life can be difficult and few would relish a wedding which occurred one week after their father-in-law's funeral. In Petersburg Alix knew no one. Even her sister Elizabeth, whose husband was Governor-General of Moscow, was seldom in the imperial capital. Nicholas himself was overwhelmed with work and saw little of his wife in the daytime. In the family circle Alix could speak her native English. But outside it, in Petersburg society, Russian or French was necessary. The young Empress had only just begun to learn the former. She was never very happy speaking the latter, which tended to desert her in moments of stress. In the first months of her marriage such moments were plentiful, for as Empress she was forced to be on perpetual show.

Problems quickly arose with her mother-in-law. Because Nicholas's marriage had been arranged so hurriedly, no apartments were available in the Winter Palace or at Tsarskoe Selo until well into 1895. In the interim the young married couple had to live in four rooms in the Empress Marie's palace. Just like Queen Alexandra after Edward VII's death, the Empress Marie stressed her precedence over her son's wife in court ceremonies and hung on to many of the crown jewels, most of which should have gone to her daughter-in-law. Though the two empresses always remained on relatively polite terms they could scarcely have been more different. Alix was much more serious and intelligent but she sadly lacked her mother-in-law's vivacity or her social skills. Living under her mother-in-law's roof, she quickly became aware of the many unfavourable comparisons being drawn between her and Marie in Petersburg society.[18]

The Petersburg aristocracy never liked the young Empress and by 1914 had come to hate her with quite extraordinary venom. Neither Darmstadt nor Queen Victoria were much of a preparation for Petersburg, whose extravagant luxury and low morals shocked Alix. This was a world in which the following conversation could be overheard between two ultra-aristocratic youths: 'Baryatinsky said to Dolgorukov that he is the son of Peter Shuvalov, to which Dolgorukov very calmly answered that by his calculations he is the son of Werder [the former Prussian Minister].' If Alix had been exposed to the world of her uncle the Prince of Wales's Marlborough House set rather than that of his widowed mother, Queen Victoria, all of this might have come as less of a shock. Not even the Prince of Wales's circle, however, could have prepared Alix for the torrent of jealous, malicious gossip that was the hallmark of Petersburg high society.[19]

It was difficult for an outsider to understand or come to terms with the Russian high aristocracy. Like their peers elsewhere, many of Petersburg's grandees were extremely proud. At its best such pride meant a shrinking from the servile flattery common in bureaucratic and, above all, court circles. At its worst it entailed unlimited arrogance and heartless self-indulgence. Some Russian aristocrats were not averse to remembering that their own families were older than the Romanovs and had participated in successful palace coups in the eighteenth-century 'golden age' of the Russian nobility. Petersburg high society was always elegant and sophisticated. It was often sharp and witty. Of all Europe's nineteenth-century aristocracies, the Russians had produced by far the most renowned literary and musical figures. Even the head of Nicholas II's Personal Chancellery, A.S. Taneev, was quite a well-known composer. Many aristocrats, as we have seen, regarded the last two generations of Romanovs as rather uncouth. Almost uniquely in Europe, Russian aristocrats had no equivalent of a House of Lords through which they could aspire to a political role and enjoy the entertainment, status and glory that such a chamber provided. The aristocracy's civil rights were also not fully secure since the Russian state opened private correspondence and sometimes mistreated even members of the upper classes because of their religious views and activities. For a European aristocracy at the turn of the twentieth century all this seemed a shameful and humiliating relic of barbarism. In addition, by the late nineteenth century agricultural depression and the growth of a powerful state bureaucracy were beginning to push the aristocracy to the margins of Russia's economy, government and society. With rapid industrialization in the 1890s this process speeded up. So too did aristocratic resentment and criticism. The Bavarian diplomat, Count Moy, recalls that the term 'bureaucrat' was the supreme insult in Petersburg high society in the 1890s. The 'easily excited ladies of Petersburg society' were made so angry by reports of police repression that 'a good number of them took the side of the revolutionary elements'. The Empress Marie had lived in Petersburg high society for decades and understood its ways. She shared its love for a constant round of luxurious and extravagant entertainments. But Petersburg's aristocracy was by no means prepared to throw itself at the feet of the shy, aloof and in some ways rather *gauche* newcomer whose husband inherited the throne in 1894.[20]

The young Empress was ill-equipped by temperament to win this society's loyalty. She danced badly, was extremely shy and loathed large gatherings of strangers, at which she became stiff, cold and silent. Prince Serge Volkonsky, who as Director of the Imperial Theatres met Alix frequently in the 1890s, commented that she

> was not affable; sociability was not in her nature. Besides, she was painfully shy. She could only squeeze a word out with difficulty, and her face became suffused with red blotches. This characteristic added to her natural indisposition towards the race of man, and her wholesale mistrust of people, deprived her of the slightest popularity. She was only a name, a walking picture. In her intercourse with others, she seemed only to be performing official duties; she never emitted a congenial spark.

Quite unlike her mother-in-law, who was an expert in smoothing over awkward moments by her warmth and tact, Alix's combination of shyness and obstinacy made her extremely rigid. Even in trivial matters she seemed unwilling or unable to adapt herself to Petersburg society and its ways. Volkonsky recalled that when Nicholas II came to the theatre or ballet alone, he would chatter away amiably. 'But I must add, this was only when he was alone – without the Empress. Alexandra Feodorovna evidently acted as a restraining influence on her husband. She was cold and composed. Her entrances and her exits were in pantomime. She never made an observation or uttered an opinion, or asked a question.'[21]

Alix was proud. She had a high sense of the majesty of her husband's position and of the need to support and maintain it. Knowing only too well Nicholas's natural modesty and shyness, she understood how these were seen as weak and un-imperial qualities by much of Petersburg society. No doubt this accentuated her determination to uphold the monarch's dignity. In addition, however, the Empress was simply an Englishwoman in a very foreign land.

In character Alix was very different to her far more resilient first cousin, Victoria Eugénie of Battenburg, who married King Alfonso XIII of Spain. Nevertheless, as English consorts in very un-English countries, the two women had something in common. In temperament, religion and

habits Victoria Eugénie was at variance with the Spanish aristocracy, to whom she always remained an outsider, an Englishwoman. The
Queen trod on many Spanish toes. Very much an English princess of
the Victorian era, Victoria Eugénie enjoyed organizing charities and
involving herself in activities which in Spain had always been the preserve
of the Church. Faced with haemophiliac sons, a notoriously unfaithful
husband and the harshly critical high society of Madrid, the Queen's very
self-discipline, most prized of Victorian royal qualities, gained her 'a
reputation of frigidity. She was suspected of being all the things most
Spaniards least admired: cold, aloof, insensitive, Anglo-Saxon.' The
equally Victorian Empress Alix 'was never able to understand the intrica-
cies of the Russian character, with its suppleness, its Slavic charm, and its
languid indifference to what the morrow might bring.' C.S. Gibbes, an
Englishman who came to know both the Empress and Russia well, concluded that her unpopularity owed much to 'her want of a "theatrical"
sense. The theatrical instinct is so deep in Russian nature that one feels the
Russians act their lives rather than live them. This was entirely foreign to
the Empress's thought, shaped mostly under the tutelage of her grandmother Queen Victoria.'[22]

A whole series of minor 'scandals' erupted between the Empress and
Petersburg society. In 1895, for instance, Alix patronized a charitable
bazaar which was allowed to take place in the Ermitage, an unprecedented
gesture of imperial goodwill. The resulting discontent was universal: other
charities were jealous; shopkeepers complained of unfair competition since
the bazaar's goods were untaxed; the director of the Ermitage and the chief
of security for the imperial family protested bitterly; and gossips in
Petersburg society had a field day. Some of the hostility no doubt reached
Alix's ears and the Empress behaved at the bazaar in an even more than
normally shy and stiff manner. Nor did Alix win friends by her efforts to
inject Victorian earnestness into Petersburg society by setting up sewing
circles to make clothes for the poor. The smart set scoffed, the proud kept
their distance from anything that might seem like seeking imperial favour,
and others complained that the ways of an English vicarage were inappro-
priate in Russia. Since some of the great ladies who avoided Alix's sewing
circles were active in encouraging and marketing peasant handicrafts from
the neighbourhood of their estates their criticisms were not always merely
selfish or without point.[23]

It is true that in the 1890s the gulf of mutual bitterness and resentment
between the Empress and Petersburg society was not nearly as great as in
the years after 1905, when it was much increased by the collapse of Alix's
health and the arrival on the scene of Rasputin. V.I. Mamantov, who
served cheek-by-jowl with the imperial family in Nicholas II's personal
suite, recalled that in the 1890s

Her Majesty was different to what age, illness and difficult moral sufferings subsequently made her . . . At that time the Empress still fully enjoyed life . . . Extremely shy with outsiders, and at that time still hampered by imperfect knowledge of Russian, which she later completely mastered, the Empress soon became accustomed to us, who were part of her everyday life, and enchanted us by her friendliness, simplicity and attention. Being very observant and quickly noticing each of our weaknesses, the Empress never lost an opportunity to tease us but she did this very delicately without the slightest wish to offend.[24]

Alix also still had her defenders in high society. Vladimir Lambsdorff, himself a recluse, responded to complaints that the Empress looked bored and ill-at-ease in society by saying that she was evidently a serious woman who had no time for nonsense. General Alexander Kireev commented in his diary that, months before Alix even arrived in Russia, Petersburg society was slandering her and 'already saying that the future Tsarevna has a difficult character'. In January 1896 he added that the young Empress was lovely and sweet but was very easily embarrassed and terribly in need of encouragement to talk. Despite what the idiots of the Petersburg *beau monde* said, she did not possess a permanently bored expression but was simply very shy. Even by 1900, however, Lambsdorff and Kireev were very much in the minority. Alix always found it much easier to get on with the very old or with children, rather than with people of her own age. At the turn of the century Kireev remarked of Alix's position: 'Poor unfortunate Tsaritsa! Naryshkin says that the young Empress commented that she and the Tsar saw few people. [Naryshkin replied] "Then you both need to see a few more people." Alix answered, "Why? So as to hear still more lies?" '[25]

How much Alix's estrangement from Petersburg society actually mattered is debatable. Partly because of this estrangement the imperial couple lived a very isolated life in their suburban palaces of Tsarskoe Selo and Peterhof. Petersburg society was the source of much of the slander that so damaged the dynasty's prestige in the last years before the revolution and much of this slander was rooted in hatred of the Empress. In addition, by distancing himself from Petersburg society Nicholas reduced his circle of acquaintances and the opportunity of drawing on men and opinions different to those he encountered through official channels. None of this would have mattered if the Emperor and Empress had replaced traditional links with the Petersburg aristocracy by forging ties with newer Russian élites. By 1900 Petersburg high society was by no means as important as it imagined. The monarchs could justifiably have asked themselves whether leading the capital's social round should absorb so much of their time and energy at a crucial moment in Russian history. The Romanovs' regime was too closely associated with the landowning aristocracy for its own good. It would have been an unequivocally positive move if Nicholas and his wife had tried to build bridges to the new industrial and financial élites of Petersburg and Moscow, some of whose members were not only powerful, but also exceptionally cultured and interesting. Nor were Russia's entire intellectual and cultural élites so radical in sympathy that they would have been immune to all advances from the crown.

Even Wilhelm II had some friends among his country's industrial tycoons. Edward VII got on famously with some of his country's new millionaires and played a role in the forging of the aristocracy and plutocracy into a new upper class. Prince Regent Luitpold of Bavaria carefully cultivated intellectual and artistic circles in Munich. By accident Nicholas's younger brother, the Grand Duke Michael, also mingled in such circles through his marriage to the divorced daughter of a Moscow lawyer, one of whose friends was the composer Rachmaninov. Not surprisingly, Nicholas and his mother were appalled at the news of Michael's marriage, which Marie described as 'another terrible blow . . . so appalling in every way that it nearly kills me'. No European monarch before 1914 would have viewed a son's *mésalliance* in any other way. Nevertheless there ought to have been less dramatic methods by which the monarch and his family could have come into contact with the new Russia that the government's own policies were helping to create.[26]

Nicholas occasionally visited a shipyard. The imperial couple toured the All-Russian Exposition of Trade and Industry in 1896. But old Russia, the world of the Guards officer, the peasant and the priest, was far more congenial to the Emperor and Empress than the milieu of industrialists, financiers or intellectuals. Court etiquette, tradition and lack of imagination also stood in the way. It was impossible to have sensible meetings with representatives of middle-class Russia unless the court's rules were relaxed and opinions could be freely exchanged. The conventions and pecking order of Victorian royalty and the aristocracy had to be disregarded. Nicholas and his wife were too conventional, too afraid to tread on their entourage's toes, to do this. Staying at Sandringham in 1894 the Tsarevich Nicholas was bewildered by the guests of his uncle, the Prince of Wales, who included the Jewish financier, Baron Hirsch. In this company he kept as silent as possible. Conscious of the Romanovs' need to embody the cause of Russian nationhood, Alix tried to get the *Almanach de Gotha* to drop the words Holstein-Gottorp from the imperial family's name. Perhaps inevitably, despite their idealization of the Russian peasantry, the world of the *Gotha* remained a part of Nicholas and Alix's way of life, as did the archaic and intricate rules and conventions which guided the Romanov house and the imperial court. The son of Evgeni Botkin, the imperial family's doctor, commented that although 'the Sovereigns themselves insisted that they valued in people nothing so much as simplicity and sincerity . . . at the same time, without being conscious of it, they actually appraised people almost solely according to the amount of attention these people gave to quite outward and often nonsensical etiquette'. A view of the world partly shaped by the court's etiquette and the pages of the *Gotha* was inevitably in many respects out of touch with contemporary Russia.[27]

Appropriately enough Nicholas and Alix spent most of their married life in a little town called Tsarskoe Selo, fifteen miles south of Petersburg. The town's name means 'Tsar's Village' and Tsarskoe was indeed a world apart from the rest of Russia. Tsarskoe contained two adjacent imperial palaces. The enormous and superb Catherine Palace was used for parades and other ceremonial occasions. In the smaller but very elegant Alexander Palace the imperial family lived. The interior decoration of the family's apartments was largely English Victorian and was executed according to the Empress's tastes. As Nicholas's cousin, Prince Gavriil Romanov, remarked, 'its style did not at all fit that of the Alexander Palace, which was consistently constructed in *style Empire*', in other words on strictly classical lines.[28]

Nicholas himself, however, loved the family's quarters. On first seeing the newly decorated apartments in September 1895 he wrote to his mother,

> our mood . . . changed to utter delight when we settled ourselves into these marvellous rooms: sometimes we simply sit in silence wherever we happen to be and admire the walls, the fireplaces, the furniture . . . the mauve room is delightful . . . the bedroom is gay and cosy; Alix's first room, the Chippendale drawing-room is also attractive, all in pale green . . . Twice we went up to the future nursery: here also the rooms are remarkably airy, light and cosy.[29]

The best-known room in the private apartments was Alix's boudoir where, particularly as she became older and iller, she spent much of her day. The Empress's loyal friend, Lili Dehn, wrote that the boudoir 'was a lovely room, in which the Empress's partiality for all shades of mauve was apparent. In spring-time and winter the air was fragrant with masses of lilac and lilies of the valley, which were sent daily from the Riviera . . . the furniture was mauve and white, Heppelwaite [*sic*] in style, and there were various "cosy corners". On a large table stood many family photographs, that of Queen Victoria occupying the place of honour.' Baroness Buxhoeveden, no less loyal but possessed of rather better taste, commented that Alix liked things more for their associations than for their beauty and that the rooms were, therefore, rather cluttered: 'her's was a sentimental rather than an aesthetic nature'.[30]

Nicholas lived in these apartments for most of the autumn, winter and spring of each year. His daily routine seldom varied.

> The Emperor's day began early. Around 8 o'clock the Emperor came out of his bedroom, which he shared with the Empress, and swam in the swimming pool. He dressed, had breakfast and went for a walk in the garden. From 9.30 until 10.30 the Emperor received Grand Dukes and court officials who had business with him, as well as the Marshal of the Court, the Palace Commandant and the commander of the Combined Regiment. From 10.30 until 1.00 were the reports of ministers, each of whom had his appointed day and hour. At 1.00 or 1.30 lunch was served in one or other drawing room, according to Their Majesty's instructions, on tables specially brought in. Lunch lasted for 45 minutes, after which the Emperor drank coffee in the Empress's boudoir. After lunch and until 5 p.m. were receptions for ambassadors, foreign guests and trips for various reviews. At 5 tea was served in the intimate family circle and daily from 6 until 8 there were ministerial reports. At 8.00 dinner began, after which the Emperor usually spent the time until 10.00 in the Empress's boudoir in the company of his children. After 10 o'clock the Emperor went into his study, where he worked alone, sometimes until late at night.[31]

From Nicholas's point of view one of the great advantages of living at Tsarskoe Selo rather than Petersburg was that he could indulge his passion for exercise and fresh air in the enormous Alexander Park. On occasion, the Emperor also went hunting, though for this the great forests of the game reserve around Gatchina, thirty miles to the west, offered better sport than the immediate neighbourhood of Tsarskoe. Business also took the Emperor away from his palace, though usually only for a few hours at a time. The most frequent cause for such trips were military reviews, above all the annual festivals of the Guards regiments. Since there were three entire divisions of Guards infantry and two of Guards cavalry these festivals were a regular occurrence. Like much of the rest of any monarch's ceremonial duties they followed an unchanging pattern. The Emperor exchanged greetings with his troops, all according to a set formula, and there followed inspections, a march-past, religious services, the parading of standards and a fine lunch in the presence of the monarch for present and former officers of the regiment. The tedium of such occasions was reduced for Nicholas by the fact that, unlike his father, he loved military display. He enjoyed his officers' company. The care lavished on the Guards regiments also, however, had political causes and was to yield rich dividends in 1905–7 when the regime's survival hung by a thread and the loyalty of the Guards was to be a major factor in the monarchy's survival.[32]

For the first nine years of his reign Nicholas followed tradition by hosting a number of great balls at the Winter Palace during the Petersburg season. On 6 January the Emperor always participated in the 'Blessing of the Waters' which took place on the River Neva and was a combination of an outdoor religious ceremony and a court spectacle in the Winter Palace. In mid-January a huge ball for 3,000 guests was given in the Nicholas Hall of the Winter Palace, all those invited being seated for dinner. A number of smaller balls then occurred, usually for 800 guests at a time, for which the Nicholas Hall was turned into a cross between a fantastic winter garden and a dining-room. The season ended with the coming of Lent. In 1903, the last year that Nicholas and his wife gave these balls, the season was crowned by a performance of *Boris Godunov* in the Ermitage, followed two days later by a costume ball. On both these occasions all the guests were dressed in the uniforms of the seventeenth-century Muscovite court. Even by the exacting standards of Petersburg, the clothes and jewellery were superb.

First the Russo-Japanese War and the 1905 revolution, then the collapse of the Empress's health, meant that no more balls or great spectacles occurred after 1903. This deprived Petersburg society of its fun, for the court balls had always been the most beautiful and extravagant high-point of the winter season and the pride of Russian high society. Equally angry were those in the Petersburg luxury trade, who lost a good deal of business due to the court's disappearance from the capital. Disgruntled dowagers linked the decline of correct behaviour in aristocratic circles to the court's absence, claiming that in former days the monarchs had set an example to high society and had disciplined those who misbehaved by dropping them from court guest lists or showing their disapproval in other ways.[33]

The end of the court's domination of Petersburg high society was in fact just one element in a far wider process, namely the increasing liberation of all elements of Russian society from the state's supervision and control. There were deep-lying economic, cultural and political reasons for this process which, even as regards the aristocracy, went far beyond the issue of whether the monarchs should participate in the Petersburg winter season. Nevertheless by withdrawing from the life of Petersburg high society the Emperor and Empress did make a direct, if unwitting, contribution to the weakening of the crown's hold on the lives and loyalties of the Russian élites.

In summer the imperial family moved from Tsarskoe Selo to Peterhof, eighteen miles to the west of Petersburg and situated on the shore of the Baltic Sea. As at Tsarskoe they did not live in the main palace at Peterhof, which was used only for great ceremonial occasions. Instead they inhabited a large villa called Alexandria, tucked away in the huge and splendid park of the palace very close to the seashore. Alexandria in fact consisted of more than one building. It included the so-called Cottage, a rambling villa which Nicholas I had built for his wife in 1831. Alexander III loved the Cottage, which continued to belong to his wife after his death.

The building in which Nicholas II and his family actually lived was a rather extraordinary affair. Its core was a large watch-tower built by Nicholas I during the Crimean War as a vantage point from which the movements of the Anglo-French fleet in the Baltic could be observed. Alexander III rebuilt the original wooden tower and adjoining pavilion in stone and Nicholas II then added a two-storey building which was linked by a covered gallery to the tower. The Emperor's office was on the second floor of the tower and was surrounded by a veranda covered in glass. From the veranda and from the study's windows there were splendid views over the Baltic Sea, with Kronstadt visible to the left and Petersburg in the far distance to the right. Particularly during the magnificent northern sunsets the office and veranda were places of enchantment. Inside 'a small writing desk made of walnut stood beside the window. Chairs in the English style, comfortable and elegant, covered in dark green leather, furnished the room. The walls were lined with walnut panelling.' Though the whole of the so-called New Palace was simple and comfortable, the Emperor and Empress loved the study and veranda best of all. It was here that Nicholas received his ministers.[34]

Tsarskoe Selo and Peterhof were Nicholas II's chief residences. In them he spent much the greater part of each year. In addition, he visited his hunting lodges in Poland in the autumn and usually spent some time at Livadia in the Crimea as well. As regards its natural setting, the latter was the most spectacular and beautiful of all the imperial residences. The Crimea was Russia's still unspoilt Riviera, with climate and vegetation to match. Alix loved the flowers in the Crimea and Nicholas enjoyed the walks. The sea air, the lovely weather and the superb views contributed to an atmosphere of blissful contentment. Livadia was a real holiday resort for the imperial family, far away from the intrigues and bustle of Petersburg. For that very reason the Emperor's sometimes long stays at Livadia caused trouble for his ministers, not to mention for foreign governments seeking negotiations with Russia. In 1903 one of his advisers pointed out to Nicholas 'how difficult it was for the government to be situated for so long away from the centre of administration', only to be interrupted by the Emperor's retort that 'where I am . . . is the centre of administration', a sentiment praised by Kireev as showing that 'the Emperor is beginning to become independent'! But this was an era in which Wilhelm II of Germany threw his ministers into despair by his constant travels in pursuit of escape and amusement, and even Britain's constitutional monarch could expect a busy Prime Minister to travel to the South of France for an audience in order not to interrupt the royal holiday. Fortunately for Russian ministers, until the completion of the new palace at Livadia in 1911, the imperial family's residence in the Crimea was rather cramped, which was a deterrent to very long stays. Moreover, the old palace was dark and even lacked running water above the first floor.[35]

Only on the imperial yacht, the *Standart*, did Nicholas II escape from the world of politics and government as successfully as in the Crimea. A beautiful ship of 4,334 tons, the *Standart* was built in Denmark and was completed in 1896. At full speed she was capable of 22 knots. Sometimes Nicholas II made state visits to other countries on the *Standart*. The yacht was, for instance, used for the visits to Britain and France in 1896. On other occasions, such as at Bjorkoe in 1905 and Reval in 1908, Nicholas had 'summit meetings' with foreign monarchs who arrived to meet the *Standart* in their own yachts. In general, however, he sailed in the *Standart* for pleasure and relaxation, varying his cruises by making excursions on the shores of Finland. The Emperor's own suite of rooms included a bedroom, study and bathroom. Those of his family were equally light and luxurious and there was plenty of room also for his very numerous entourage. The imperial dining-room could seat 80 people with ease and there was also a large reception room. No other officers were as close to the imperial family as those who served on the *Standart*. Nicholas and Alix, 'loving the ship like their child', were on intimate terms with its officers, none of whom were appointed or transferred without their permission. More than in any of their palaces, Nicholas II and Alix felt entirely *en famille* and out of the public eye when they were aboard.[36]

Day by day, week by week and year by year the Emperor's life passed according to a well-established routine. Nicholas would know without much risk of error precisely where he would be, whom he would be receiving in audience, and what he would be wearing at any moment for years ahead. Only revolution, war or death seemed capable of changing his immutable regime. A very few alterations did, it is true, occur of the Emperor's own volition. From 1900 on, for instance, the imperial family came to spend every Easter at the Kremlin in Moscow. They did so because Nicholas and Alix were deeply moved by their participation in religious services in the Orthodox capital at the high point of the Christian year. In addition, it made political sense for the monarchs to show themselves in Russia's second capital and to associate themselves with their country's spiritual heritage.

Other high points of the 1890s included state visits to foreign countries and the welcoming of foreign sovereigns to Russia. On the whole these visits tended to be of symbolic rather than practical significance. Court ceremony was at its most grand, etiquette at its most precise and, after constant repetition, tedium very quickly set in. Some state visits were, however, memorable and important. Wilhelm II from the very inception of Nicholas's reign sought to use cousinly links and the Tsar's inexperience to push German initiatives during private meetings with the Russian

Emperor. For this reason foreign ministers, both Russian and other, awaited meetings between the two monarchs with some trepidation. Nor was the purely symbolic side of state visits necessarily devoid of significance. When Nicholas II visited Paris in 1896, for instance, no new treaties were signed and little serious discussion of foreign policy occurred. But the huge, ecstatic, almost hysterical welcome given to the Tsar proclaimed to the world the existence of the Franco-Russian alliance and France's relief that it was no longer isolated in the international arena.

But for Nicholas II, by far the most important ceremony in which he participated during the 1890s was his own coronation. This was in his eyes far from being merely the symbolic act through which he signified to the world his assumption of the responsibilities of government. The coronation was a religious service of communion, binding together God, the Tsar and the Orthodox people. In the words of General A.A. Mosolov, the chief assistant to the Minister of the Court, 'the Tsar took his role of God's representative with the utmost seriousness'. At his coronation the Emperor prayed to God 'to direct, counsel and guide him in his high service as Tsar and Judge of the Russian Empire, to keep his heart in the will of God, to help him so to order all to the good of his people and the glory of God, that at the day of Judgement he may answer without shame'. Nicholas believed that through his coronation he had assumed before God a responsibility for the fate of his empire from which no human being could ever absolve him. He believed quite sincerely that the Tsar's heart was in God's hands and that through his coronation he was a vehicle for God's purposes. Within him rational political calculation was always to coexist with the conviction that the wisdom which sprang from the instincts and heart of a tsar was superior to any purely secular reasoning. Never could he compare his own God-given position and responsibility with that of politicians or statesmen, however wise. To be a tsar was to listen to all advisers, ignore all selfish interests or motives, but ultimately to decide on the basis of one's own conscience and reason. After this, the responsibility was God's, for He had put the Emperor in his present position and given him whatever faults and virtues he possessed. At the very height of the 1905 revolution, when the regime's fate hung by a thread, Baron R.R. Rosen found the Emperor's calm almost uncanny. Nicholas responded to the ambassador's incredulity by reminding him that, 'if you find me so little troubled, it is because I have the firm and absolute faith that the destiny of Russia, my own fate and that of my family are in the hands of Almighty God, who has placed me where I am. Whatever may happen, I shall bow to His will, conscious that I have never had any other thought but that of serving the country He has entrusted to me.'[37]

When Nicholas made his ceremonial entry into Moscow on 21 May

1896 in preparation for his coronation he did so, therefore, with a very serious, not to say solemn, sense of what the crowning and anointment of a tsar signified. That sense could only be strengthened by the emotional reaction to the beauty of the coronation service itself. Almost other-worldly singing, dramatic ritual, superb vestments and uniforms, the tremendous physical and mental strain of being the centre of a religious pageant which lasted for three hours: all of this must have made a deep impact on an impressionable young man who believed with all his heart in the role which God had called upon him to play. The Emperor's cousin, Prince Gavriil Romanov, witnessed the coronation. He recalled that the coronation service

> proceeded with quite exceptional solemnity. Everything was so beautiful that it cast into the shade anything that I had ever seen. The Uspensky Cathedral was a witness to many centuries of Russian history and all tsars of the House of Romanov had been crowned there; the clergy grouped together and in magnificent vestments, with the metropolitan at their head; the lovely music – all this gave the ceremony a deeply mystical character.

In the coronation service itself the Tsar placed the crown first on his own head and then on that of the Empress. He read prayers and then received the congratulations of the whole Romanov clan, who mounted the steps of the throne one after another to kiss his hand. There followed the liturgy, which included both the anointment and the taking of the Eucharist which, on this day for the only time in his life, the monarch received in the form reserved for the priesthood. Then the Emperor and Empress led a solemn procession around the cathedrals and squares of the Kremlin to show themselves to the people. After this came a ceremonial banquet, illuminations and the end of an exhausting day.[38]

Four days later disaster occurred. As part of the coronation festivities a great celebration was arranged for the public on the Khodynka field on the outskirts of Moscow. At ten in the morning food and mementoes were to be handed out. At noon the Emperor would arrive and be present for a range of afternoon entertainments. Although the Khodynka field had always been used for these coronation festivities, on this occasion the booths from which the presents were to be distributed were ill-sited. The ground near the booths was uneven, and much of it was laced with ditches, trenches and even wells. A crowd of over half a million gathered without sufficient police or planning to control its movements. The growing crush of people led to panic, which was exacerbated when mementoes began to be distributed and those at the rear of the crowd tried to push their way towards the booths. Even the official figure for the dead was 1,350, and in fact probably more than this died in the tragedy.

Hundreds were trampled underfoot, fell into trenches or were simply suffocated. That evening a particularly grand ball was given by the French ambassador. Because of the extravagant preparations for the ball, caused in part by French delight at the recently signed alliance with Russia, the failure of Nicholas and Alix to attend would have been a great slight. The Emperor's sister wrote that

> I know for a fact that neither of them wanted to go. It was done under great pressure from his advisers. The French government had gone to immense expense and trouble to arrange the ball. Tapestries and plate were brought over from Versailles and Fontainebleau and 100,000 roses from the south of France. Nicky's ministers insisted that he must go as a gesture of friendship to France. I know that both Nicky and Alicky spent the whole of that day in visiting one hospital after another.[39]

Whatever the Emperor's private feelings, the Khodynka catastrophe created a number of images and impressions which were to colour all later views of Nicholas, his government and his reign. The first such image was of a young monarch dancing at a fabulous ball on the evening of a day when hundreds of his subjects had lost their lives as a result of the incompetence of his own government. The image was unfair, for even Witte, the Tsar's enemy, commented that Nicholas 'looked sick' and was 'obviously depressed'. Not for the last time, however, the Emperor's self-control exposed him in temperamental Russian eyes to accusations of heartlessness and indifference.[40]

The causes of the tragedy on Khodynka field lay in part in a battle over jurisdiction between the Ministry of the Imperial Court, headed by Count I.I. Vorontsov-Dashkov, and the Governor-General of Moscow, the Grand Duke Serge. Well before the coronation festivities began these inter-departmental wrangles had been exacerbated by the tactlessness, explosive temperaments and simple arrogance of many of the personalities involved. Inevitably, after the catastrophe, everybody tried to blame everybody else and partisans of Vorontsov-Dashkov and Serge lined up behind their leaders in order to throw mud at their opponents. General Kireev, who thoroughly disliked Vorontsov-Dashkov, claimed that on this occasion the Ministry of the Court had managed arrangements for the coronation far less efficiently than under Count Adlerberg's direction in 1883. It was in large part responsible for the disaster at Khodynka field because of Vorontsov-Dashkov's tactless treatment of Serge and the Ministry's insistence on pushing aside the Moscow administration and seeking to monopolize control over arrangements. On the other hand, some of the younger Romanovs, headed by Nicholas's cousin and brother-in-law, the Grand Duke Alexander Mikhailovich, argued that Serge was to blame for the disaster and should resign. Serge's brothers leapt to his defence, and the Dowager Empress Marie supported Vorontsov-Dashkov, an old friend both of herself and of Alexander III. Count Constantine von der Pahlen, the former Minister of Justice, concluded his investigation of the disaster by remarking that 'whenever a Grand Duke was given a responsible post there was sure to be trouble', a remark which contained a good deal of truth. Witte commented that 'Count Pahlen's report did not endear him to the Grand Dukes' and 'from this time on Count Pahlen was never to receive a substantial appointment'. Immediately after the disaster General Kireev noted in his diary that one thing was certain: junior officials would take the blame for what had happened, their masters getting off scot free, for 'in our country the principle of escaping without punishment reigns'. And so it turned out. Colonel A.A. Vlasovsky, who was in charge of the Moscow police, was dismissed – a fate which, admittedly, he richly deserved. Neither Serge nor Vorontsov-Dashkov was touched. The impression that emerged from all of this was of an administration, even a Romanov family, at loggerheads with itself and careless of the fate of those for whom it was responsible. Over this mess there presided a monarch unable to control or discipline even his relatives, let alone his leading advisers. As is always the case, first impressions, particularly when established in a manner as dramatic as the Khodynka disaster, are never easily dispelled. Certainly Nicholas and his government never erased the image which Khodynka implanted in the public mind.[41]

CHAPTER 4

Ruling Russia,
1894–1904

In the 1880s, before he inherited the German crown, Prince Wilhelm of Prussia liked to send photographs of himself to friends and acquaintances. These bore the inscription, 'I bide my time'. It was during this period that Wilhelm built up his relationships with some of the individuals who were to play key roles in his reign. Even in 1882 Wilhelm, aged only 23, was calling regularly on General Count Alfred von Waldersee, whom he was to appoint Chief of the General Staff soon after his accession to the throne. In 1883 the young Prince first met Count Philipp zu Eulenberg, then a mere secretary in a minor diplomatic legation but later to be the Kaiser's closest friend and chief ally in his effort to assert his personal control over German government. In the mid-1880s, however, the Prince's greatest friend was Captain Adolf von Bulow, through whom Wilhelm became acquainted with Bulow's brother, Bernhard, then a junior diplomat in Petersburg but subsequently the Kaiser's Chancellor and right-hand man in the era when personal imperial rule came closest to realization. By the time he ascended the throne in 1888 the young Kaiser was surrounded by a small group of close friends and allies who had hitched their ambitions to his determination to rule his empire in fact as well as in name. Some of these people were obnoxious but their ability was beyond question.

Wilhelm created not just an heir's party but also a distinct political profile for himself. He broke entirely with his parents' liberalism, stressing instead his loyalty to Prussian conservative and militarist traditions. This brought him into the orbit of Otto von Bismarck, his grandfather's Chancellor, Prussia's Prime Minister since 1862 and the effective ruler of Germany. Within two years of his accession, however, Wilhelm had toppled Bismarck. The two men had differences over policy, both domestic and foreign. Indeed Bismarck's fall was soon to be followed by the lapsing of the German-Russian security treaty, which in turn was to lead to the signing of the Franco-Russian alliance and Europe's division into two blocs. But the basic reason for Wilhelm's removal of Bismarck had more to do with political ambition than disagreement over policy. Bismarck was Europe's leading statesman, Germany's legendary unifier and a man of very autocratic temperament. Wilhelm was determined to assert himself and to show that in Germany only the Kaiser ruled.[1]

The contrast between Wilhelm and his Russian cousin was tremendous. As Tsarevich, Nicholas was far too modest, too loyal and too much in his father's shadow to create anything like a crown prince's party. When he ascended the throne in 1894 he had no political profile or programme. No one knew what he really thought about political issues. In addition, Nicholas was a man who found it very difficult to make friends. He was always polite, often charming and talkative, but in the end elusive. His very politeness was a barrier to intimacy. He was in general very sensitive and careful as regards the feelings of those who worked with him, but one felt always a reticence, an aloofness, a fear of getting too close to anyone lest intimacy impair his dignity or threaten his independence. These characteristics, evident throughout his reign, existed already in 1894. Within days of Nicholas's accession A.A. Polovtsov recorded in his diary, 'Count S.D. Sheremetev says that the present Emperor is very much without warmth and is incapable of enthusiasm. Count Sheremetev's children played with the heir since childhood but none of them can say what his views really are.'[2]

No leading political or military figure in Nicholas's reign had been a friend of his before he ascended the throne, unless of course one counts members of the imperial family. Even among the Romanovs, however, grand dukes who exercised political influence were almost always men of the older generation. The only Romanov who did play a political role and was Nicholas's contemporary was the Grand Duke Alexander Mikhailovich. 'Sandro' was the Emperor's cousin by birth and married his sister, Xenia. Even he, however, only exercised an intermittent influence and politically he was distinctly less significant than many ministers. Of the latter, none were the Emperor's real personal friends. Admiral Fedya Dubasov, who crushed the Moscow uprising in the winter of 1905, was an old acquaintance of Nicholas, whom he had accompanied on his tour round the world in 1891. But the only true personal friend worth noting from the Emperor's youth was General A.A. Orlov, with whom Nicholas had served in the Guards Hussars. One of Nicholas's aides-de-camp described Orlov as 'the Emperor's single real friend, with whom His Majesty very often spoke in private, expressing his thoughts and ideas'. Both Nicholas and Alexandra had great faith in Orlov and were extremely upset by his death, at a relatively youthful age, in 1908. The Empress described Orlov as her husband's 'sole and single' friend and, in the manner common in Petersburg society, was subjected to a torrent of malicious and envious gossip because of her habit of periodically placing

flowers on his grave. But Orlov, though he played an important role in
the suppression of the revolution in the Baltic provinces in 1905–6, never
rose beyond the rank of major-general or the command of a Guards cavalry
regiment.[3]

The Emperor's lack of close friends or even acquaintances of his own
age or somewhat older created many problems for him during his reign.
He was never able to draw on a pool of people young enough to possess
energy and fresh ideas and with whom he had close personal links.
Instead, in the first years of his reign he was wholly dependent on
statesmen inherited from his father's era. Although he later gained a
reputation for shedding ministers easily, this was true only in the years of
confusion and crisis towards the end of his reign. In the 1890s, on the
contrary, he was loyal to his father's ministers, sometimes retaining them,
or even recalling them to office, when they were too old to do their jobs
properly.

The dominant figure in Russian politics during the 1890s was Serge
Witte, the Minister of Finance. Nicholas inherited him from his father
and kept him in office until 1903, despite his own increasing distaste for
Witte's rather overbearing and abrasive personality and despite the
enormous criticism to which Witte's policies were subjected from all
sides. The ministries of justice and communications were run by Nicholas
Muravyov and Prince Michael Khilkov respectively for the whole of the
first decade of Nicholas's reign, and the navy was dominated by the Tsar's
uncle, the Grand Duke Aleksei, to the extent that the latter's sybaritic and
self-indulgent lifestyle allowed him to direct any serious business. In 1898
General P.S. Vannovsky retired as Minister of War at the age of 76, after
seventeen years in the post, only to be brought back three years later with
the aim of instilling order in the crisis-ridden Ministry of Education.

Only in two departments did ministers change frequently in the first
decade of Nicholas's reign. These, however, were the crucial ministries of
internal and foreign affairs. Even here, nevertheless, the changes were very
seldom of the Emperor's own volition. Nicholas's first three foreign
ministers all died in office and although the first two were in their seven-
ties, the third, Michael Muravyov, collapsed suddenly at the age of 55. Of
Nicholas's first four ministers of internal affairs, Dmitri Sipyagin and
Vyacheslav Plehve were assassinated. Ivan Durnovo was the obvious
candidate for promotion to chairmanship of the Committee of Ministers
when Nicholas Bunge died in 1895. Of all Nicholas's leading advisers, the
only one to be dismissed for political reasons in the nineteenth century was
Ivan Goremykin, who lost his job as Minister of Internal Affairs in
October 1899 after an unsuccessful clash with Serge Witte which confirmed the latter's pre-eminent position in Russian politics.[4]

Continuity in personnel was matched by faithfulness also to the policies

pursued by Alexander III. Nicholas's first political statement of any significance was made in a speech in January 1895, during which the Emperor
responded to very polite and timid requests by a handful of local government (*zemstvo*) councils for greater public participation in government.
The young monarch, 'very nervous before going into the Nicholas Hall'
to make his speech, responded that 'I know that recently, in *zemstvo*
assemblies, there have been heard voices carried away by senseless dreams
about the participation of *zemstvo* representatives in governmental affairs.
Let everyone know that, devoting all my strength to the good of my
people, I will preserve the principles of autocracy as firmly and undeviat-
ingly as did my unforgettable late father.' Nicholas's commitment to
autocracy and his sense that this was threatened by the *zemstvos*' ambitions did not alter in the 1890s. Ivan Goremykin's dismissal in 1899 was
caused in large part by his efforts to spread elected *zemstvos* to Russia's
western borderlands where local government was still in the hands of
appointed state officials. Witte, Goremykin's enemy, pounced on this
initiative and used it to persuade Nicholas that his Minister of Internal
Affairs was expanding *zemstvo* power at the expense of monarchical
prerogatives. Indeed Witte wrote a small book for the occasion, in which
he argued that the principles on which autocracy and the *zemstvo* worked
were incompatible.[5]

Continuity meant not just preserving the autocratic powers which
Nicholas inherited from his father but also using them to pursue very
similar goals. In the first six years of his reign Nicholas made no basic
changes in his father's domestic policies. In foreign affairs the alliance with
France was upheld and even the increasing emphasis on Far Eastern affairs
had been foreshadowed by Alexander III's decision to build the Trans-
Siberian railway, despite the huge costs involved. Nicholas himself
commented that 'when my Father died I was simply the commander of
the Escort Squadron of the Hussars and for the first year of my reign was
just taking the measure of how the country was run'. In fact it was to be
a good deal more than a year before Nicholas put his stamp on Russian
government. Only at the turn of the century did his influence become
palpable, at least as regards domestic affairs. In part the Emperor's
expanding role reflected his growing experience and self-confidence, in
part his increasing impatience with his official advisers and the bureaucratic machine they ran. Very important too was the developing sense, fed
by criticism from all sides, that Russia was in the midst of crisis, and that
continuity in policy was therefore no longer enough. Yet the Emperor's
increasing personal intervention was to be both result and cause of this
crisis, leading not to new and coherent policies to steer the empire out
of danger but rather to the further disorganization of Nicholas's
government.[6]

As far as the 1890s were concerned, the causes of continuity in government policy are not hard to find. They lie in part in Nicholas's inexperience, in his lack of any clear political programme or of a circle of 'Young Turk' friends who might have sought to use him to push new principles and promote themselves into office. Filial piety, reinforced by a deep sense of personal loss and bewilderment, encouraged him to listen favourably to those who told him that his father had bequeathed an empire that was running well. Immediately after his father's death, Nicholas told his uncle Vladimir how difficult things were for him because he had been kept so far from government affairs in the past. The Grand Duke replied that

> he remembered the accession to the throne of both his father and his brother. On both of these occasions Russia was in a very difficult and troubled situation, quite different to now when, on the contrary, she had enjoyed a thirteen-year peace. Undoubtedly the life of the state and the people required some changes but there was no need to hurry with the latter. One should not give anyone grounds to think that the son condemns the order created by his father or the choice of people whom the latter had summoned to work with him. Initially one should suspend changes and should follow the main line of his dead father's policy.[7]

A.A. Polovtsov recorded that 'the young Emperor accepted his uncle's words with great sympathy'. For this there was good reason. Not only was Vladimir's advice comforting, but on the surface at least it appeared to be true. Nicholas II was the fifth Romanov to ascend the throne in the nineteenth century but the first whose accession had not occurred in the midst of tumult and crisis. Both Alexander I and Alexander III had succeeded fathers who had been assassinated. In the former's case the conspiracy which overthrew Paul I aimed to reverse the state's foreign policy and, in domestic politics, to return to the policies and manners of Alexander I's grandmother, Catherine II. In 1825, when Alexander I died, important issues of policy were immediately thrust under the nose of his successor, Nicholas I. He faced an attempted military *coup d'état*, whose aim was the abolition of the absolute monarchy, in the very first days of his reign. On Nicholas's own death in 1855 his son, Alexander II, ascended the throne peacefully but he did so in the midst of a defeat in the Crimean War which undermined the legitimacy of his father's system of government and put urgent and fundamental reform on the political agenda. Twenty-six years later Alexander III succeeded to the throne during an even worse political crisis, caused in part by a terrorist campaign which had culminated in his father's assassination. Days before he died, Alexander II had ratified a plan to allow representatives of the *zemstvos* and nobility to participate in discussion of legislation and government policy. Confirmed but as yet unpublished, this plan for a first timid step towards constitutional government lay on the new Tsar's desk when he ascended the throne, forcing him to make a fundamental political choice in the first days of his reign. In comparison to this, the dilemmas facing the young Nicholas II did not seem grave nor the desire to continue his father's policies unreasonable.[8]

Of the ministers whom Alexander III bequeathed to his son, the most interesting and unusual was Serge Witte. Witte's background was typical of Russian senior bureaucrats in the last decades of the old regime. His family, of West European origin, had become Russian in culture and religion over the generations, had produced a number of relatively senior civilian and military officials, and had married into the old Russian aristocracy. What did set Witte apart was his education, his career and his manner. Many Petersburg top officials had been educated at either the Alexander Lycée or the School of Law, the empire's two great civilian boarding colleges which were reserved for sons of the aristocracy and senior bureaucracy, and which were designed specifically to produce well-educated, loyal 'highfliers' for the civil service. Most other senior officials were graduates of Petersburg or Moscow university, though in the higher ranks of the Ministry of Internal Affairs one always found quite a large number of former army officers, most of whom had been educated in the more aristocratic cadet corps and had served in the Guards. With the exception of these soldiers, the great majority of élite officials shared a legal education, though in pre-1914 continental Europe this implied a broader and intellectually more demanding course of studies than that faced by an undergraduate studying law at a contemporary British university.

Serge Witte, on the other hand, was among the rather small minority of top officials who had passed through the very demanding university course in physics and mathematics. He was almost alone among his peers in having graduated from Odessa's 'New Russia' university. And he was rare, though not unique among Ministry of Finance officials, in having spent many years in private enterprise, in Witte's case the railways. Serge Witte's manner always made him stand out a little in high official and court circles. The average Petersburg high official who had spent his life in the bureaucracy's key central offices tended to be not just an efficient administrator but also something of a wary politician, even perhaps a smooth operator. He guarded his tongue carefully, knew how to flatter the powerful, and kept a careful eye on which way the wind was blowing at court and among the ministers. In general he was not only intelligent but also often rather cynical and world-weary as a result of many years' exposure to the Petersburg political world. Usually too, at least on the surface, he was refined and polite: certainly these were characteristics that the Alexander Lycée and the School of Law took pride in inculcating in their students.[9]

When Serge Witte first appeared in the Petersburg firmament, Madame Bogdanovich commented that 'in appearance he is more like a merchant than a civil servant'. Witte was a big man, full of practical energy. He could be tactless and overbearing. He had strong opinions and lacked the civil servant's long experience of having to defer to the wisdom of his superiors in a hierarchical chain of command. Few honest and informed observers of Russian government in the 1890s doubted that Witte was the Tsar's most impressive servant. As Minister of War from 1898 to 1904 General Aleksei Kuropatkin had many ferocious battles with the Minister of Finance. Nevertheless, Kuropatkin wrote in his diary that he could not help admiring 'this strong and highly talented man', despite all the trouble that Witte had caused the army. 'I have told him more than once that he is greater than all of us, his colleagues, by several heads and I recognize this to be true.' The trouble was, Kuropatkin added, that he was fearful as to where Witte's policy of rapid industrialization was leading Russia. Though no military genius, Kuropatkin himself was an intelligent man and an honourable patriot. Both his admiration of Witte and his fear of his policies were shared by many.[10]

Serge Witte's impact on Russian government in the 1890s was not just a product of his own personality. It also reflected the enormous power of the ministry he headed. Alexander Polovtsov commented in 1894 that 'without the Ministry of Finance it was virtually impossible to decide any serious question'. One element in the ministry's power was the high intellectual calibre of its élite officials. Even Vladimir Gurko, from the rival Ministry of Internal Affairs, admitted that Witte 'assembled a fine group of assistants and other officers in the Ministry of Finance'. Above all, however, the Finance Ministry's power was a product of the enormous range of its activities. As one would expect, the ministry controlled the state's income and expenditure, thereby exercising a powerful influence over all other government departments. The State Bank was a mere offshoot of the ministry, which monopolized control over monetary and fiscal policy. In addition, until the creation of the Ministry of Trade and Industry after the 1905 revolution, all commercial and industrial policy was directed by the Ministry of Finance, whose power was all the more formidable because, by Western standards, the Russian government pursued an extremely interventionist policy designed to protect, subsidize and channel the rapid development of Russian industry. To grasp the strength of Witte's ministry one would perhaps need to think of Japan in the 1950s and 1960s, and even then to imagine the situation had the Ministry of Finance and MITI been contained under one roof.[11]

Under Witte's direction, this enormously powerful department became something akin to a 'ministry of national development', whose tentacles spread into most areas of Russian life. It would be naïve to imagine that Serge Witte came to the ministry in 1892 with a complete plan for Russia's development in his head. On the contrary, it is clear that in some important areas, agriculture for instance, his ideas changed considerably during his term in office. Nevertheless, from his first moment as minister Witte did pursue the goal of Russia's rapid industrialization, used a whole range of policies to advance this programme, and was able to justify his aims in terms of a wide-ranging analysis of why Russia had no option but to become an industrial nation at all possible speed if she wished to retain her independence and her status as a great power in the highly competitive and ruthless world of the imperialist era. In his view, Russia's options were stark. Either she would become an economic colony of the world's leading industrial powers, contenting herself with providing them with food and raw materials at prices they would dictate. In the imperialist era, the final station on such a road was likely to be the empire's political subjection and dismemberment at the hands of these powers. Alternatively, the Russian government could use its revenues, its tariffs, its monetary policies and its control over the railways to protect and subsidize Russian industry, and to encourage the investment in Russia of foreign capital, entrepreneurial talent and technology. Though this path would entail hardship for the population and unpopularity for the government in the short term, it alone promised Russia a secure future as a prosperous and mighty great power.[12]

Witte's policies won him many enemies. In Imperial Russia anyone who promoted capitalism and put the interests of industry above those of agriculture was bound to be widely hated. Noble landowners, most liberal and socialist intellectuals, and all the other departments of state could unite in denouncing the all-powerful Ministry of Finance and its overweening chief. Some of their criticisms have been echoed by later historians, who have stressed in particular the high cost in terms of monetary and credit policy of Witte's adoption of a gold-backed currency in 1896, a move designed to encourage foreign investment in Russia. The Minister of Finance's ability to face down his critics depended on Nicholas II's support. Though the Emperor was capable of overruling his Finance Minister on points of detail, in the 1890s he gave solid support to the core of Witte's policy. In 1896, for instance, he used his autocratic powers to impose the gold standard over the objections of most of senior officialdom.[13]

Only after 1900 did the monarch's support begin to waver. This was partly because of Witte's opposition to aspects of the Emperor's Far Eastern policy. It was also due in part to the way that the industrial depression which set in after 1900 seemed to call into question many of Witte's achievements. The industries which he had helped to create now had to be propped up by the state budget or allowed to form cartels and thereby keep prices artificially high. Above all, however, the rising tide of discontent in Russian society, part of which was easily attributable to Witte's policies, was too threatening to ignore and seemed to demand a strong hand at the head of the Ministry of Internal Affairs, whose responsibility it was to defend domestic political stability and the regime's existence. In the 1890s, Witte's pre-eminence was owed in part to the fact that neither in intelligence, energy nor political skill could the ministers of internal affairs during this decade match him. When the kindly, brave but not very intelligent Dmitri Sipyagin was assassinated in April 1902, Nicholas replaced him with the much more formidable Vyacheslav Plehve who, unlike Sipyagin, was also anything but a personal friend of Witte. Sixteen months later Witte himself was removed from his power-base in the Ministry of Finance through 'promotion' to the largely meaningless chairmanship of the Committee of Ministers. In his place was appointed Edvard Pleske, an efficient, very hard-working and rather shy civil servant with none of Witte's force of personality or breadth of vision. The balance of power between the Ministry of Internal Affairs and that of Finance had been tilted firmly in the former's direction.[14]

After 1907 the Ministry of Agriculture, run by the canny Alexander Krivoshein, emerged as a major force in Russian domestic politics. Before then, however, the only department of state whose potential weight equalled that of the Ministry of Finance was the Ministry of Internal Affairs. More than any other department, the Ministry of Internal Affairs was responsible for supervising the villages, where the overwhelming majority of the population lived. Although the peasants elected fellow-villagers to run local affairs, these peasant officials were themselves watched and controlled by the police and the Land Commandants. They, in turn, were subordinate to the provincial Governor, who was himself an official of the Ministry of Internal Affairs. The Governor never controlled all branches of the state bureaucracy in the provinces because other departments of state fought ferociously to avoid their subordinates falling into the grip of the Interior Ministry. The Governor was, nevertheless, much the most important figure at the provincial level and could make life difficult for officials of other departments who crossed him. He chaired all the key inter-departmental committees at the provincial level and had considerable power to intervene in the affairs of the elected local government councils (*zemstvos*), which ran most matters concerning public health, education and rural development. At the centre, too, the Ministry of Internal Affairs was extremely powerful. Press censorship, the post and telegraph services and, above all, the vitally important Police Department were all under the direction of the Minister of Internal Affairs. In any matter concerning the peasantry, the landowning nobility, the *zemstvos*, the press, migration to Siberia or other borderlands, or the huge field of public order and state security, the Ministry of Internal Affairs was almost certain to play the leading role.[15]

Serious conflict between the departments of finance and internal affairs was inevitable. The Interior Ministry, like all other departments, resented Finance's control over its budgets and noted sourly that officials of the Ministry of Finance were often paid much more generously than their equivalents elsewhere in the government. The background of officials in the two ministries was also rather different. Very few officials in the Ministry of Finance were landowners and most came from what, in the West, would have been described as professional middle-class back-grounds. By contrast, the Ministry of Internal Affairs contained many aristocrats, a large number of whom were big landowners and, quite often, former Guards officers. Such men did not usually have great sympathy for industrial or financial capitalism and thought naturally in traditional terms of order, paternalism and the need for control over, so it was assumed, an unruly and almost childlike peasantry. Both tsarist tradition and the instruments at its disposal inclined the Ministry of Internal Affairs to try to run Russia through administrative and police controls. The Finance Ministry, on the other hand, was more attuned to the rules of the market and the use of economic levers to get its way. Above all, however, the two departments' main functions diverged. The Ministry of Finance existed to balance budgets and promote economic development. The Ministry of Internal Affairs' duty was the preservation of political stability.

One of the most interesting and important conflicts between the two ministries in the 1890s concerned labour policy. Rapid industrialization entailed the growth of a proletariat which, as is always the case at this stage of industrial development, tended to be both exploited and militant. The Ministry of Finance was acutely conscious of how difficult it was to foster rapid capitalist development in Russia. In fact a sizeable body of the Russian intelligentsia argued that it would be impossible to do so, since Russia lacked a prosperous domestic market for industrial goods and could not win export markets because her produce would be incapable of competing with better quality and often cheaper Western artefacts. Witte and his lieutenants also knew that in Russia neither property nor contracts enjoyed the same degree of protection by law or public opinion that existed in the West. If for these reasons their attitude to Russia's expanding capitalist industry tended to be nervously protective, many senior officials of the Ministry of Finance, including Witte himself, did in time accept that strikes, trade unions and free collective bargaining were inevitable if dangerous aspects of capitalist economic development. It was therefore safer to legalize them than to repress them by police methods.

The Ministry of Internal Affairs disagreed. The tsarist regime looked askance at any social group organizing itself autonomously of the state. Not only professional organizations but even the landowning nobility were closely controlled in this respect. The government, aware that proletariats bred socialism and that the revolutionary parties would pounce on any opportunity to control trade unions, was unlikely to relax its principles where factory workers were concerned. Nevertheless, the Ministry of Internal Affairs was acutely conscious of the fact that bad conditions, poor pay and unjust treatment by managers and foremen were creating discontent among the growing masses of workmen who were congregating in the empire's major cities, which were the state's key nerve centres of government and communications. The most influential report on strikes in the late nineteenth century was written in 1898 by General A.I. Panteleev, a former colonel of the Semyonovsky Guards regiment and a senior official of the Ministry of Internal Affairs. It concluded that 'the causes of the agitation and strikes, which are recurring more and more frequently, lie chiefly in the exploitation of the workers by the manufacturers, when the latter, making a huge profit, pay the labour force little and besides, with rare exceptions, do almost nothing for the improvement of the way of life of the workers and their families'.[16]

The Ministry of Internal Affairs' most interesting and radical response to labour unrest was the attempt, under the leadership of Serge Zubatov, to set up its own trade unions and itself lead the labour movement. Zubatov was a fascinating and intelligent man, who was both an intellectual and the head of the security police in Moscow for much of the 1890s. Zubatov saw the absolute monarchy as a force which could stand above the various classes, control their inevitable conflicts, and guide society with unselfish wisdom in the long-term interests of all. Though perhaps naïve, he was certainly sincere. After his dismissal in 1903 Zubatov could easily have turned his back on the imperial regime. Other police officers did so with less personal cause. Instead, on hearing of Nicholas II's abdication in 1917, Zubatov immediately retired to his study and committed suicide in an act of loyalty that was almost unique at that time.

Zubatov shared General Panteleev's belief that exploitation was the key to labour's discontent. He was convinced that if the state could protect the workers' dignity and their material interests, the revolutionary parties would have no hope of winning the proletariat's allegiance. Correctly, he believed that many strikes and stoppages resulted from minor infringements by management of workers' rights and dignity which the police only heard about after conflicts had erupted into the open. He was determined therefore to create an early-warning system. Unlike some high officials of the Ministry of Internal Affairs, Serge Zubatov understood that workers were not just peasants who happened to live in cities. The factory and the town were changing mentalities. To a considerable extent workers had to be allowed to organize themselves, elect their own articulate leaders and defend their interests. To make this process safe the police had closely to supervise these labour unions and leaders, intervene early in disputes, force management to obey the law and, in general, act as a fair and friendly referee. If Zubatov's immediate goal was to hold working-class loyalty for the regime and cut the ground from under the feet of the revolutionary parties, he also had broader strategic objectives. A loyal labour movement could be a major weapon in the state's hands, a force with which the financial and industrial élites could be balanced, and therefore a means by which the monarchy could continue to preserve its autonomy from all groups in society and its ability to rule in the long-term interests of the country as a whole.

Zubatov's unions, launched in 1900–1, had great initial success both in Moscow and amongst the largely Jewish proletariat of Belorussia and the Ukraine. Nevertheless, from the very start his plans aroused great fears among many senior officials of the Ministry of Internal Affairs. Plehve's deputy, General Victor von Wahl, for instance, believed that all trade unions were 'extremely harmful and corrupting', saw Zubatov as 'the first revolutionary' and found his schemes 'fantastic in conception and harmful in results'. Not all Zubatov's opponents were as unimaginative or wholly unsympathetic to his ideas as the narrow-minded and brutal Wahl. They did, however, fear that Zubatov would organize the workers and excite their hopes of justice and a better life by encouraging their deeply held dislike of capitalists and their age-old conviction that the Tsar was on the people's side and would intervene in an all-powerful manner to right their wrongs. He would, in short, by inspiring aspirations that the crown could not satisfy, play into the hands of the revolutionaries. The Odessa general strike of 1903 and the capture of government-run unions by the revolutionaries in Petersburg in January 1905 showed that these fears were not altogether groundless.[17]

Given the doubts aroused by Zubatov's activities in the Ministry of Internal Affairs and the fury they caused in the Ministry of Finance it is obvious that Zubatov had to enjoy protection at a very high level if his schemes were not to be killed off at their inception. This protection he received from the Grand Duke Serge, the Governor-General of Moscow. A governor-general was the Tsar's personal representative and viceroy, and as such stood beyond the direct control of the Minister of Internal Affairs. In the early nineteenth century governors-general had often existed in the Great Russian heartland of the empire, but by 1900 they were almost always confined to the non-Russian borderlands of Finland, Poland, the Caucasus and Central Asia. The great exception to this rule was Serge in Moscow. A governor-general who was also the Tsar's uncle and brother-in-law was beyond any control save that of the monarch himself. The Grand Duke, a reactionary paternalist of very authoritarian disposition, sympathized with Zubatov's efforts to hold working-class loyalty and protected his police chief from his enemies. A.A. Polovtsov complained that 'in his intimate conversations with his nephew' Serge had succeeded in persuading Nicholas II of the correctness of Zubatov's approach. It would certainly not be at all surprising if the Emperor found Zubatov's ideas attractive, for they fitted in with many of his own conceptions about the monarchy and its relationship to the masses. In addition, however, Nicholas was close to his uncle and regarded him as a useful and loyal family counterweight to the overweening Witte and the other senior officials who of necessity made up the majority of the monarch's advisers. Giving Serge his head permitted the Emperor a certain autonomy from bureaucratic control and a little room for manoeuvre. It also allowed a potentially useful policy, namely Zubatov's schemes, to be tested in a limited area of the empire in the teeth of ministerial chagrin. No doubt Nicholas also recognized that the price of employing strong-willed personalities like Witte and Serge was that both men had to be permitted a degree of freedom to pursue their schemes. If the result was a certain blurring of overall policy goals and the existence of conflict between institutions and individuals, so be it. The Emperor's position as the only possible mediator in such conflicts would be enhanced.[18]

By the end of 1903 the government's labour policy was in a mess. Accused of fomenting worker radicalism, Zubatov had finally been dismissed after the Odessa general strike and 'police socialism' partly discredited. In Petersburg, however, a watered-down version of the Zubatov programme was to be continued under the leadership of a priest, Father Gapon. Meanwhile the alternative policy, that of legalizing trade unions and strikes, was also being pursued under the auspices of the Ministry of Finance. Opposition to liberalizing labour laws from within the ministry, from the employers and the police was, however, so strong that the June 1903 law permitting the election of workers' representatives was so hedged around with controls and constraints as to be largely meaningless. As a result, instead of looking to trade union leaders inured to the give and take of wage negotiations, sections of the working class increasingly turned towards the revolutionary parties.

At the turn of the century, however, the government was less scared by working-class militancy than by growing evidence of peasant discontent. In June 1901, A.A. Polovtsov wrote: 'after the students' disorders there have followed strikes and factory workers' battles with the police. Next the peasant mass will rise up with a demand for land. Today's militia [the conscript army], torn away from this very land for a short period, will not use its weapons to curb these appetites, which it itself shares. This will be the end of the Russia which we know.' Nine months later, when a wave of arson and rioting swept the countryside in Poltava and Kharkov provinces, Polovtsov's prediction seemed amply justified. In the wake of these agrarian troubles the Secretary to the Committee of Ministers, Anatol Kulomzin, sought to reassure his wife. There had always, he wrote, been agrarian riots of this kind in Russia, during which peasants customarily paid back stewards and foremen for a multitude of old scores and minor injustices. Troops had refused to open fire on only one occasion, and even then out of simple dislike for the officer who gave the order. Alexander Kireev had less reason to hide his fears since his comments were confined to his private diary. 'I think we can cope with the students and co. without difficulty but millions of peasants . . . that's a completely different matter.'[19]

During the first decade of Nicholas II's reign three questions topped the agenda as regards the government's policy on agriculture and, specifically, the peasant question. Were the peasants becoming poorer? If so, who or what was to blame? What could the government do to rectify the situation? In the dock were Serge Witte and the Ministry of Finance, who were accused, at best, of ignoring the peasant and, more frequently, of ruining him by crushing tax demands and the high prices for industrial goods created artificially by protective tariffs.

Witte's response was to claim, correctly, that 'the picture of the peasants' miserable condition is greatly exaggerated', particularly by opponents of the government's economic policy who sought to hide their selfish interests or ideological preferences behind claims that the Ministry of Finance was ruining the peasantry. Throughout the 1890s Witte opposed direct subsidies or cheap credit to agriculture as a waste of scarce resources. In his view investment in industry was more useful even for the rural population because jobs in the cities would reduce land hunger in the villages and, above all, provide agriculture with markets for its produce and therefore with the incentive to modernize. Witte doubted whether big capital investments in noble estates could ever be justified given the low costs of production in the Americas and Australasia, whose agricultural produce was now flooding the world market. Though more sympathetic as regards cheap credit for peasant farms, he argued that the structure of peasant landowning made large-scale lending to the peasantry very dangerous. By law most peasant farms belonged not to individuals or even families but to the whole village community. Nor could this land be sold or mortgaged. As a result there was no way to secure loans or recover debts from the peasantry, as the latter knew only too well.[20]

By the early twentieth century, however, it was no longer possible for Witte to shrug off attacks on his indifference to peasant needs. Political pressure to 'do something about agriculture' was building up, as was fear of peasant discontent. After a tour of the provinces at the turn of the century even the rather dim Dmitri Sipyagin, the Minister of Internal Affairs, commented that 'we are standing on a volcano'. In addition, the state's finances were in increasing disarray, and the need to increase its revenues pressing.[21]

Nicholas II was kept well informed about the problems of both the peasantry and the treasury. In addition to receiving regular reports on these subjects from his ministers, he also on occasion was sent special memoranda by other high officials. In the spring of 1903, for instance, the Emperor received an analysis of his country's budgetary crisis from Peter Saburov, a senior official whose career had included service both as an ambassador and as a financial expert, a very unusual combination in Victorian Europe. Saburov warned Nicholas that the huge and always increasing costs of the arms race 'together with the sad economic position of the mass of the tax-paying population naturally arouse fears for the stability of the state's finances . . . To restore the state's fiscal power is only possible by means of raising the economic position of the peasantry . . . But it is already becoming clear that to fulfil this necessary but complicated task heavy sacrifices from the treasury will be needed.'[22]

Both Serge Witte and Vladimir Kokovtsov, who succeeded the critically ill Edvard Pleske as Minister of Finance in 1904, shared Saburov's concern about the parlous state of Russia's finances. Kokovtsov indeed commented that 'I look with alarm on our economic and financial position' and condemned what he described as the 'fantasies' that underlay much government expenditure. 'These fantasies I see all around,' he added: 'in the exorbitant and unreasonable strengthening of the fleet, in our active foreign policy waged at the expense of the peasant's hungry stomach . . . [in] the automatic attempt to get money for everything instead of stopping this saturnalia of expenditure and beginning to reduce the tax burden to a measure where it corresponds with the growth in income'. But whereas Witte and Kokovtsov, like Saburov, believed that excessive armaments were the key to Russia's financial problems, neither shared his view that international agreement on the reduction of armaments was possible, or indeed his conviction that the first step in this direction should be made through a deal between Nicholas II and the German Kaiser. Nor could the Tsar have any illusions on this score since the failure of his appeal for a reduction of armaments in 1898 had taught him the impossibility of halting the arms race. But, as Serge Witte pointed out to Nicholas in January 1902, if the escalation of defence costs could not be halted, it was hard to see how the peasants' tax burden could be greatly reduced or large sums provided for the modernization of village life and peasant agriculture. The conclusion drawn by Witte was that improvement of the peasants' lot would have to come less from the largesse of the treasury than from changes in the system of peasant landholding. The farmer, he told Nicholas, must have individual rights and freedom, including unrestricted property rights to his land. In other words, Witte was calling for the abolition of the peasant commune, the cornerstone of Russia's rural economy and society.[23]

Ever since the abolition of serfdom in 1861, indeed to some extent even before that, the commune had been the most important institution in Russian rural life. The peasant community, which was usually but not always made up of inhabitants of a single village, administered and judged its own members through officials elected by itself. It also bore collective responsibility for paying the state's taxes. Although in principle the administrative, judicial and fiscal institutions of the village were distinct from the community's collective ownership of land, in practice the power of the commune was enormously enhanced by the fact that it controlled, and in many cases periodically redistributed, the villagers' basic source of wealth.

Defenders of the commune believed it was a form of social welfare, which would ensure that no peasant would go without the means of survival. They felt that at least until the capitalist economy had developed to the point where millions of secure jobs existed in the cities, the only way to avoid pauperization was to ensure that any peasant, even if he was temporarily resident in a town, would have a plot of land on which to fall back. Because the masses would not be destitute and would have rights to the use of property, it was believed they would be more immune to radical and socialist propaganda than urban workers and landless agricultural labourers in the West. Not even the most ardent defenders of the commune would probably have argued that, from the narrow perspective of agricultural modernization, it was the best form of landownership; they did deny, and probably rightly, that it was as serious an obstacle to technical improvement as its enemies suggested. The fact that the commune was seen to be an old Russian institution which would preserve the country from the perils that had attended modernization in the West also added to its appeal. Anatol Kulomzin, for instance, was very much on the liberal and Westernizing wing of the ruling élite. He wrote, however, that even he swallowed whole the Russian nationalist view of the commune, so flattering to patriotic pride, and 'only the troubles of 1905–6 which pointed to the socialist spirit which the commune had bred in the life of the peasantry finally sobered me'.[24]

For some enemies of the commune, its greatest danger had always seemed to be the semi-socialist principles on which it was based.

Alexander Polovtsov, for instance, was convinced that economic progress in the countryside depended on the firm rooting of the principle of private property in peasant society and village mentalities. But above all he feared the egalitarian, collectivist principles underlying the commune and the way it potentially united the peasants against the landowning class and private property. 'We must stop uniting this dark, credulous and unstable mass into a single group', he told Nicholas II in June 1901, 'and on the contrary we must break it up, differentiate it, pushing forward the hard-working, thrifty and orderly, the support of progress in a direction desired by the government, in opposition to the unreliable, riotous groups of the population who are avid to cause agrarian chaos.'[25]

In the 1890s the enemies of the commune gained ground within the government. In 1894, for instance, Witte had refused to get involved in the debate on the commune, saying that 'this is not his business and that if he touched it they would begin to curse him even more than they do now for interference in other people's affairs'. Eight years later, however, the Minister of Finance was arguing that 'for the success of the market economy it is necessary to raise the whole economic standard of living and this is only possible if peasant life is rearranged on the basis of individual property and communal possession is abolished'. The most powerful opposition to abolition came from the top of the Ministry of Internal Affairs but even in this department some key younger officials, Vladimir Gurko for instance, had turned against the commune. To achieve the transformation of peasant landownership, Witte appealed directly to Nicholas II in January 1902. 'These questions can only be properly solved if you yourself take the lead in this matter, surrounding yourself with people chosen for the job. If your grandfather, the Emperor Alexander II, had not acted in this way over the emancipation of the serfs then we would have serfdom to this very day. The bureaucracy cannot solve such matters on its own.'[26]

Witte's analogy was a false one. Alexander II had been fully committed to emancipation and had possessed a clear sense of the key principles by which he wanted the matter to be arranged. His grandson was uncertain as to the commune's fate and fearful of the effects of its abolition. The Emperor's doubts can to a great extent be understood. The merits and disadvantages of communal tenure are still bitterly disputed by scholars and the issue is very complicated. Eliminating the commune was a huge and dangerous task, both technically and politically. The creation of millions of independent farmsteads would, for example, entail a vast amount of surveying and boundary making in a countryside where surveyors were few and far between and where disputes over boundaries, property rights and access to wood and water were already endemic and bitter. To shift landownership from the village community to the heads of individual households would transform the basic property rights of the overwhelming majority of the population. No government does this lightly or expects the process to occur without turbulence or opposition.

Nicholas therefore moved in cautious but typical fashion. He appointed Witte to head a special commission to investigate agricultural conditions in January 1902 and allowed him leeway to develop his proposals to transform peasant landownership. Simultaneously, however, the Ministry of Internal Affairs was encouraged to run rival committees and in 1905 Witte's old enemy, Ivan Goremykin, was designated to take the lead in preparing a reform programme for the countryside. To many observers, Witte of course among them, the Emperor's behaviour seemed the epitome of indecisiveness and bad faith. Playing ministers off against each other caused them immense frustration, wasted their time and paralysed government policy. On the other hand it did mean that Nicholas remained independent of any minister or group of advisers, receiving information and advice from more than one point of view. General Kireev's diaries are, for instance, packed with criticisms of Nicholas's slipperiness and indecisiveness, but in a way the Tsar was doing no more than following the advice that Kireev himself gave the Grand Duke Michael, at that time still the heir to the throne. Warning the Grand Duke that advisers and ministers were not always to be trusted, he told him to make sure he always received advice and information from more than one side on any issue. A monarch, he explained, must learn 'to control one lot of people with another'.[27]

At the same time that it was grappling with the discontent of workers and peasants, the government was also arousing increasing opposition among the non-Russian sections of the population. In part the causes were one and the same. Non-Russian workers experienced the same conditions but on the whole enjoyed even less government protection than their Russian equivalents. Belorussian and Ukrainian peasants, like Russian ones, believed that the land should belong to those who worked it and regarded the big estates, particularly if run on capitalist lines, with hostility. In addition, however, the government's efforts to impose administrative uniformity and even, in some regions, Russia's language and culture aroused opposition, particularly among the educated classes.

The government's policy differed from one minority to another. The Jews were worst treated; not merely were most of them confined to a specific region, the so-called Pale of Settlement, they were also deprived of a range of civil rights. Even in the Pale, for instance, no Jew could legally own rural land. As regards non-Russian Christians, the government regarded the Poles with greater suspicion and hostility than was the case with the peoples of the Baltic and Transcaucasian provinces or the Romanians. Where the Muslim peoples were concerned, the government usually confined itself to preserving order and raising taxes. Whereas many high officials believed they could Russify Christian, and particularly Slav, peasants who had no historical 'high culture', very few thought that attempts to convert and Russianize Muslim peoples had any chance of success. Over and above these generalizations, however, the policy pursued in a specific region, and still more the skill and tact with which it was implemented, depended greatly on the personality of the area's governor-general.

Finland provides a graphic example of this point. Conquered in 1809, the Grand Duchy of Finland enjoyed a high degree of autonomy throughout the nineteenth century. In Russian terms its status was anomalous, not only because it was uniquely free of Petersburg's control but also because it possessed representative institutions and a secure rule of law. In the last two decades of the nineteenth century pressure increased from Petersburg to bring parts of Finnish law and administration into line with Russian norms. It stuck in Russian gullets, for instance, that Russians resident in Finland enjoyed fewer rights than ethnic Finns, something that was not true of Finns living in Russia. With Russo-German antagonism growing and Sweden a very possible ally of Germany in any future war, the extent to which Helsinki was almost completely free from Petersburg's supervision also caused worry. So long as Finland was governed by Count N.V. Adlerberg (1866–81) and then Count F.L. Heiden (1881–98) the very sensible rule prevailed that infringements on Finnish autonomy must be kept to the strictly necessary minimum. When General N.I. Bobrikov was appointed Governor-General in 1898, however, not only did he arrive with sweeping plans to increase Petersburg's control, he also implemented this policy with a tactless, ham-fisted brutality which turned Finland into a hotbed of opposition.

Real trouble with Finland began when Petersburg imposed its own military conscription system on the Finns and sought to unify the Russian and Finnish armies. Though this scheme had been in the making for a number of years, it was pushed hard by the new Minister of War, Aleksei Kuropatkin, who was appointed in 1898. The majority of Russian senior officials opposed Kuropatkin's conscription law in the belief that it would needlessly antagonize the Finns and it was actually voted down in the State Council, the body of senior statesmen who advised the Tsar on legislation. As was his right, however, Nicholas overrode the council and Kuropatkin's conscription law went into effect. In the Emperor's defence it could be argued that had he failed to back up his new Minister of War the latter's authority would have been fatally damaged. Moreover the government's case *vis-à-vis* Finland was not entirely unjustified, its fears for the security of Petersburg, very close to the Finnish border, causing it particular alarm. In terms of political wisdom and tact, however,

Kuropatkin's law, not to mention Bobrikov's antics, were a disaster. The government, which had hoped to play off the ethnic Finnish majority against the country's Swedish élite, quickly united the whole country against itself. Among those who protested to Nicholas about Bobrikov's policy was his mother, herself a Scandinavian princess. In what was, coming from her, an extremely angry letter, she accused her son of going back on his promise to her that Bobrikov would be reined in and commented that 'all that has been and is being done in Finland is based on lies and deceit and leads straight to revolution'. Apart from asserting that the Finns would come round if the government showed itself resolute, Nicholas's reply to his mother skated around the main issue at stake. Seen from the Russian perspective this issue was, in Kireev's words, that 'thanks to Bobrikov and his system we have created a new Poland at the gates of Saint Petersburg! And it would have been so easy to avoid this.'[28]

In its approach to the Finnish question Petersburg made mistakes which were typical of the Russian government of the time. Policy towards Finland was decided on its own, not in the wider context of an overall strategy for achieving the government's aims and avoiding danger across the whole range of the empire's affairs. It made no sense to challenge Finnish nationalism at a time when the regime already had its hands full with a host of other domestic enemies. Nor did the government clearly define its essential interests in Finland in the light of its overall commitments, and then devote the necessary means to achieve these limited goals. By the time Governor-General Bobrikov was assassinated in June 1904 Finland was moving towards open insurrection. By then, however, much of urban Russia was moving in the same direction, with the threat of peasant risings lurking ominously in the background.

Opposition to the government in the cities came from both workers and members of the middle and upper classes. Among educated Russians the single most radical group were the students, and their riots in 1899 presented Nicholas II with his first domestic political crisis. In part student discontent was rooted in grievances common to the bulk of educated Russia: the lack of civil and political rights, and the country's poverty by European standards, for which the government was held responsible. But the student world also had its own distinct radical culture and grievances. Russian students in the late nineteenth and early twentieth century were in general much poorer and of far humbler origins than the bulk of their contemporaries in, for instance, German or English universities. In both background and political commitment they had more in common with Western students of the late 1960s. In addition, however, the Russian student very often arrived at university full of resentment over his years of education at a state gymnasium (high school), whose prying authorities and dry classical curriculum were in general loathed by students. Once at university students were further antagonized by rigid controls over clubs and welfare associations, all of which the police considered, often quite rightly, to be embryonic revolutionary cells.[29]

The student riots of early 1899 presented Nicholas II with a difficult dilemma. Some of his advisers, including his uncle Serge and his Minister of Internal Affairs, I.L. Goremykin, argued that the riots were politically motivated and should be met with stern repression. Others retorted that the causes of the troubles were the students' lack of rights of association at university, hatred of the classical curriculum in high schools, and other purely educational and non-political grievances. The Emperor's old tutor, Professor N.N. Beketov, was received in audience and urged the latter point of view on Nicholas. The Tsar had no strong personal opinions or independent sources of information on this issue. The regime's response to continuing student violence was therefore mixed. Some students were expelled from the universities and conscripted into the army, which was after all the normal lot of non-student males of this age. On the other hand, a number of specific grievances were rectified.

The students were far from satisfied with these measures, however, and the troubles resumed in the winter of 1900–1. In February 1901 the Minister of Education was assassinated by a former student, twice expelled from university for revolutionary activity. In his place Nicholas appointed the veteran General P.S. Vannovsky, who had earlier headed a committee of enquiry into student disturbances. Vannovsky's appointment first to the chairmanship of the committee and then as minister was a compromise choice which reflected Nicholas's own uncertainty and the divided counsels by which he was surrounded. Vannovsky was an impeccably conservative general with great respect for discipline and order, but he was also surprisingly sympathetic towards many student demands and was a strong opponent of the classical curriculum forced down pupils' throats at high school. His appointment further stirred up an impassioned debate about what the gymnasium should teach and how free students should be to organize their own affairs at university.

Nicholas did his best to influence education in the direction he desired. According to G.E. Saenger, who served as Minister of Education from 1902 to 1904, the Emperor was no great advocate of the classics and failed to understand the issues involved in the defence of the classical curriculum. Certainly the Tsar put no obstacles in the way of the latter's abolition. Apart from a natural desire to restore peace and order in the high schools and universities, Nicholas's strongest personal wish was that Russian education should cultivate a spirit of patriotism, as was done in British, German and French schools of the time, rather than allowing a radical and socialist sub-culture to dominate student life. The Emperor's chances of influencing Russian schools and universities in this direction were, however, slim. Nicholas knew little about the Russian educational system and had few acquaintances or potential allies in this world. Professor Alexander Schwartz, who served as Minister of Education from 1908 to 1910, wrote of Nicholas that 'our ministry was entirely alien to him – he was interested mostly in disorders or in individuals whom for some reason he knew and remembered. He very rarely gave me any special commissions or instructions.' By the time Schwartz arrived as minister Nicholas was indeed under few illusions about his chances of imposing his will through the ministry. In 1901–2 he had drafted his father's old crony, Prince V.P. Meshchersky, to help him in his efforts to inculcate a better spirit into Russia's schools but to no avail. Even most officials of the Ministry of Education, in the great majority of cases of middle- or lower-middle-class origin, were liberal or even radical in sympathy, and the same was still more true of the majority of teachers. Moreover, given the increasingly radical, even revolutionary, mood of Russian society in the first years of the twentieth century, this was not the most auspicious moment to convert the students to conservative, patriotic sentiments.[30]

By 1902–3 rumblings of revolution, or at least of fundamental constitutional change, were in the air. Not everyone heard them. Even in April 1904, three months before his assassination, the Minister of Internal Affairs, Vyacheslav Plehve, did not believe in 'the closeness of danger' to the regime. Plehve's optimism was partly based on the belief that 'in the event of things going to extremes, the government will find support in the peasantry and urban lower-middle class'. In addition he recalled having survived earlier times of crisis and panic. 'I have lived through more than one moment like the one we are living through now,' he commented. 'After the First of March [1881: the day Alexander II was assassinated] Count Loris-Melikov said to Plehve on the day after Alexander III rejected Alexander II's constitution that "the Tsar would be killed and you and I will be hanged on a gallows". Nothing happened though.'[31]

Other senior officials were less optimistic, often understanding better than Plehve that opposition to the government was by now much broader and deeper than had been the case a quarter of a century before. Kireev himself commented, as early as October 1900, that 'I have seen a lot of intelligent people recently and in one voice, some with joy . . . others with horror, they all say that the present system of government has outlived its era and we are heading towards a constitution.' Even the very conservative Konstantin Pobedonostsev agreed on this. A year later Kireev stated that in upper-class and senior bureaucratic circles 'in the eyes of the great majority a constitutional order is the only salvation'. He himself believed, however, that 'it is precisely this [constitutional order] which will in fact destroy us'. Like Alexander Polovtsov his eyes were turned

towards the peasant masses, with their huge numbers and their potential
for anarchy and socialism. 'For the *time being* the peasants are still firm,
still untouched. They are, as before, monarchists. But anyone can throw
them into a muddle.'[32]

Those with the greatest interest in throwing the masses 'into a muddle'
were of course the revolutionary socialist parties. Russian revolutionary
socialism in the early twentieth century was divided into two currents,
one Marxist, the other not. The former strand was represented by the
Social Democrats, who in 1903 split into two factions, Menshevik and
Bolshevik. The non-Marxist strand comprised the Socialist Revolutionary
Party, formally constituted only in 1901, but deriving its ideas, traditions
and older cadres from the nineteenth-century Russian socialist movement.
In terms of ideas, the greatest distinction between the two was that the
Marxists believed that the urban workers would spearhead the socialist
revolution, which could only occur after capitalism had fully developed.
The Socialist Revolutionary Party, on the other hand, claimed that a
coalition of peasants, workers and poorer members of the intelligentsia
and lower-middle class would achieve the socialist revolution, which could
come immediately if the revolutionary parties pursued the proper tactics
and exploited their opportunities.

Unlike the Social Democrats, the Socialist Revolutionaries carried out a
campaign of terror against leading officials as part of their strategy, killing
three ministers between 1901 and 1904 alone and in the process sowing a
good deal of alarm and confusion in the government. Partly for this reason
the security police tended to regard the Socialist Revolutionaries as a more
immediate and dangerous threat than the Social Democrats. The evalua-
tion was not the product of mere panic or short-sightedness. The Marxists'
dogmatism and their obsession with the working class seemed to make
them unlikely leaders of a successful revolution in a still overwhelmingly
peasant country in which capitalism was only beginning to take root.
Moreover, the fact that the majority of Social Democratic leaders were
non-Russians, and a great number were Jews, made it seem less likely than
ever that they would be able to compete with the Socialist Revolutionaries
for the support of the Russian masses. Events were in part to prove the
police right. When the monarchy fell in 1917 it was indeed the Socialist
Revolutionaries who enjoyed by far the most popularity among the
masses, not only in the countryside but also generally in the cities.
Russia's socialist future should have lain in their hands. The combination
of their own ineptitude, Lenin's intelligence and ruthlessness, and the
specific conditions of wartime Russia were to deprive the Socialist
Revolutionaries of the spoils of victory.[33]

In Russia socialist parties existed long before liberal ones. The Russian
intelligentsia borrowed its ideas from the more developed societies of

Central and Western Europe and had already created revolutionary socialist groups by the 1860s. The origins of Russia's liberal parties on the other hand only go back to the foundation of the so-called Liberation Movement in 1901. From the very start this movement was divided into two main currents, which were to split in 1905–6 into the more radical, Constitutional Democratic, and more conservative, Octobrist, strands of Russian liberalism. In sociological terms this split roughly coincided with the division between members of the professional and intellectual middle class on the one hand, and liberal landowners on the other. In terms of ideas, the basic divide came over whether one would insist on full-scale parliamentary government or accept some compromise combining elements of popular representation with parts of the existing regime. All sections of the Liberation Movement were, however, united in demanding civil rights and the end of the absolute monarchy. By 1904–5 the movement proved capable of mobilizing a broad coalition of supporters from middle- and upper-class Russia and of forging links with parts of the workers' movement too. Though never likely in the long run to be able to compete with the socialists for mass support, the Liberation Movement was nevertheless a great challenge to the regime. Its wealthy activists, who often dominated the *zemstvos*, provided protection and patronage for a wide range of people opposed to the regime, some of them very radical. Many figures in the Liberation Movement came from the same world as senior officialdom and were even at times close relations. Such people were not easy to silence by mere repression and their arguments often carried conviction with liberal members of the ruling élite, weakening the government's unity in the face of revolution.[34]

By early 1904 the government's position was a very difficult one. Opposition, actual or potential, existed in almost all sections of Russian society. Liberal and socialist parties stood ready to exploit, organize and channel this opposition. In tsarist Russia, particularly in the early twentieth century, the wealth and status of many members of the Liberation Movement and their positions in the *zemstvos* gave them some legal room to operate and to mobilize support. By contrast the socialist parties were kept underground and their cadres regularly culled by the police. But new recruits quickly filled the gaps that opened up. If the regime weakened or attempted to liberalize in the face of opposition, the freedom of action of the socialist parties would inevitably grow and they would seize every opportunity to turn inchoate resentment and revolt into organized socialist revolution. As if all this were not bad enough, in February 1904 Russia found itself involved in a war with Japan which not only further overstretched already inadequate resources but also undermined the government's prestige and self-confidence.

In Russia foreign and domestic affairs were very closely linked. In a

sense the whole of the state's domestic policy was determined by the need
to maintain Russia's position as a great power while surviving the strains
this would impose on imperial society. Russian foreign policy, on the
other hand, was inevitably hugely influenced by the country's internal
situation, and in particular its finances, which *inter alia* had great relevance
to the empire's ability to pursue a determined diplomatic line, with all the
risks of war that this entailed in the imperialist era. Nor was foreign policy
made with no concern for domestic public opinion. Even Alexander III,
determined to preserve his prerogatives as absolute monarch, could tell his
Foreign Minister that Russian nationalist sentiment could not be ignored,
for 'if we lose the confidence of public opinion in our foreign policy then
all is lost'. While the Emperor was deliberately exaggerating in order to
score a point against his cautious Foreign Minister, N.K. Giers, the
comment is none the less striking.[35]

But although foreign and domestic affairs were intimately connected,
the actual making of foreign policy within the government occurred in a
void, with virtually no involvement by the domestic ministries and their
chiefs. Up to a point this merely followed the normal Russian rule,
whereby each ministerial empire pursued its own policy in isolation. But
the degree of isolation of foreign-policy making from the domestic ministries went even further than the Russian norm. Indeed not merely were
Russian diplomats a race entirely apart from the rest of the civil service, in
the great majority of cases they spent their entire careers abroad, not even
serving in the Foreign Ministry in Petersburg. Their whole lives bound up
in the world of diplomacy and the great-power struggle, it was often difficult for them to grasp Russia's overall interests, domestic as well as
foreign. In 1892–4, Russia entered into a political and military alliance
with France, designed to check any German attempt to dominate Europe.
This was a momentous step; any move to confront Germany had huge
implications for Russia's finances, for the security of its western borderlands and indeed for the survival of the regime itself. But in Russian
circumstances it was unthinkable to consult the ministers of finance and
internal affairs before signing the treaty of alliance, and considered scarcely
proper even to inform them of its terms subsequently.

The alliance with France, concluded in the last months of Alexander
III's reign, was the cornerstone of Russian foreign policy for the rest of
the empire's existence. The logic underlying the alliance was that continental Europe's two second-ranking countries were ganging up together
to ensure that they were not bullied in peace or defeated in war by
Europe's most powerful country, Germany. The terms of the military
convention which was the alliance's cornerstone were that any German
mobilization would be countered immediately by the full mobilization of
both France and Russia's forces, and that in the event of a German attack

France and Russia would fight side by side as allies with all the troops at their disposal.[36]

Although in the long run the alliance with France can be seen as a fateful step towards Europe's division into two armed camps, in the 1890s it enhanced Russia's position and even in a sense improved its relations with Germany. Wilhelm II came to regret having abandoned Bismarck's treaty with Russia and thereby having thrust the latter into France's arms. For much of the 1890s Germany wooed Russia. So too did France, which was overjoyed to have escaped the international isolation which it had suffered ever since its defeat by Prussia in the war of 1870–1. Petersburg was able to use its desirability to good effect, in 1895 for instance persuading both Berlin and Paris to join Russia in forcing the Japanese to abandon the dominant position they had attained in southern Manchuria as a result of their defeat of China. The thinking behind the policy of Russia's Foreign Ministry is encapsulated in a conversation in October 1895 between Aleksei Lobanov-Rostovsky, the minister, and his chief assistant, Vladimir Lambsdorff. In their view the alliance with France was an essential step towards preserving the latter's position as an independent great power. With France removed from the scene Russia would be wholly dependent on the more powerful Germany, which would be fatal for Petersburg's own interests, independence and prestige. But alliance with France must go so far and no further. Russia must guarantee France's survival while actually restraining her anti-German ambitions and instincts.[37]

The Foreign Ministry's optimism that it could preserve this advantageous equilibrium was enhanced by its success in coming to terms with Austria on Balkan issues in 1897. Austria and Russia were traditional rivals in this region and it was their conflict over Balkan questions which had broken up alliances of the three great conservative monarchies (Romanov, Habsburg and Hohenzollern) in both the 1870s and the 1880s. The agreement with Vienna in 1897 to preserve the status quo in the Balkans was therefore not merely in itself of major advantage to international stability but was also a great aid to better relations with Berlin, Austria's ally. When in 1903 Russia and Austria responded to revolt in Macedonia by agreeing to act together to bring about reforms in that province, the prospect for good relations with the so-called 'Central Powers', in other words Germany and Austria, appeared better than ever.[38]

Appearances could, however, deceive. Beneath the veneer of diplomatic etiquette and polite dealing the reality of international relations was very much Thomas Hobbes's war of all against all. In a sense it was quite right to insist that a country's safety lay only in its own power and its reputation for using its strength, where necessary, with vigorous determination.

But one country's power was another one's insecurity. Where Russo-Austrian relations were concerned, suspicions were enhanced by a tradition of rivalry and the knowledge, shared by both governments, that it was very hard to freeze the spread of revolutionary nationalism in the Balkans or to avoid competition between Petersburg and Vienna if and when Ottoman rule in this region collapsed, as seemed inevitable in the near future. Nor could Russian diplomats be unaware that German power – economic and political – was growing steadily and, as a result, Germany's interests were expanding into areas hitherto outside its influence. In May 1906, for instance, the Russian ambassador in Berlin warned the Foreign Ministry that German ambitions in Asia and the Muslim world were growing quickly and that 'for the first time' this made Berlin 'a possible adversary' of Russia in these regions. Nicholas II himself had made this point to the German Foreign Minister, Bernhard von Bulow, in 1899. The Emperor had remarked to him that

> there is no problem that finds the interests of Germany and Russia in conflict. There is only one area in which you must recognize Russian traditions and take care to respect them, and that is the Near East. You must not create the impression that you intend to oust Russia politically and economically from the East, to which we have been linked for centuries by numerous national and religious ties. Even if I myself handle these matters with somewhat more scepticism and indifference, I still would have to support Russia's traditional interests in the East. In this regard I am unable to go against the heritage and aspirations of my people.[39]

Before 1904 Nicholas's priorities in terms of foreign policy were clear. Unlike Russians of so-called pan-Slav sympathy, he did not believe that his country's manifest destiny lay in the Balkans, nor did he feel that Petersburg must necessarily support the Balkan Slavs just because they were people of the same race and religion. The Emperor was determined that, should the Ottoman Empire collapse, no other power must steal Constantinople, thereby barring Russia's route out of the Black Sea and assuming a dominant position in Asia Minor. To avoid such a possibility in 1896–7 he was even willing to contemplate very dangerous military action. But, above all, Nicholas was intent on developing Russia's position in Siberia and the Far East. Particularly after 1900, his personal imprint on Russia's Far Eastern policy became very important.

Many of the Emperor's advisers were dismayed by the diversion of Russia's resources and attention to the Far East. The Ministry of Finance resented the cost of building up the Pacific fleet. The Foreign Ministry feared that it would no longer be strong enough in Europe to balance between France and Germany. But it was above all the Minister of War, obsessed by the dangers of a conflict with Germany and Austria on the western front, who was most alarmed by Russia's Far Eastern policy. Bemoaning the money and troops being lavished on Manchuria, Kuropatkin commented in 1900 that 'never in the whole history of Russia has our western frontier been in such danger in the event of a European war as is true today'. In January 1902 Kuropatkin repeated that 'we have to return again to the West from the East' since the situation in Europe was potentially very dangerous.

Such arguments seem to have cut little ice with the imperial couple. In August 1903, for instance, the Empress told Kuropatkin that he was wrong to worry so much about Europe. The 'yellow peril' in the East was a real threat whereas no danger at present existed in the West. Nicholas believed that Russia's future lay in Siberia and Asia. In this era most intelligent Europeans tended to see their country's future greatness as dependent on the possession and development of large colonies. In this competition Russia had great advantages. Her empire, second only in size to Britain's, was potentially immensely rich. It was also a single land mass and therefore far more defensible than a maritime empire scattered across the globe. The Russian population, already much larger than that of any other European state, was growing at tremendous speed. In marked contrast to the last decades of the Soviet regime, demographic trends seemed to be in the Russians' favour. Certainly the Romanovs' empire was multi-national but in Nicholas II's reign the Slav element was growing much more quickly than the Tsar's Asian and Muslim subjects. Economic development was very rapid. The people's initiative and creative energy had not been stifled and crippled by the economic system, again unlike in the late Soviet era. Instead they were beginning to blossom. It was in Nicholas II's reign that the British geographer Halford Mackinder began to expound his theory that domination of the Eurasian heartland was the key to future global supremacy. At the same time the famous Russian scholars Dmitri Mendeleev and V.P. Semyonov-Tyan-Shansky argued that Russia's centre of gravity must and would shift to Asia. The geographer A.I. Voeykov stressed the vital future significance of the Pacific economy and its trade routes. Such voices were very much in a minority within the psychologically insecure Eurocentrism that dominated the Russian intelligentsia. It was, however, to Nicholas's credit that he shared this Eurasian outlook and believed that time was working in its and Russia's favour. It is only against the background of Nicholas II's largely correct perception of this geopolitical trend that one can understand his long-term optimism about Russia's future. Set against this majestic vision of Russia's unique and powerful Eurasian destiny many of the complaints of Russian educated society and not a few of the country's problems appeared to be relatively small and transitory difficulties in the Emperor's eyes.[40]

It would, however, be naïve to think that the main reason why Russia's attention shifted to the Far East between 1894 and 1904 was simply Nicholas II's views on his country's priorities. The background to Russia's Far Eastern policy was the competition between the great powers to control territories, markets and raw materials across the whole globe. China was the biggest plum still hanging on the tree and, given the increasing decrepitude of the Manchu government, it seemed ripe to fall. There was therefore a strong incentive to reserve one's place in the Far Eastern sun by snatching valuable Chinese provinces before one's rivals cut one out. Securing railway concessions in desirable regions was the first step in this process. In this competition Russia had both advantages and difficulties. Because it bordered on China, once the Trans-Siberian railway was completed it was better placed geopolitically than any of its European rivals. On the other hand, the population of Siberia was less than one-fifth that of Japan. Russia's Pacific fleet was weak and her only port, Vladivostok, was ice-bound in winter and easily blockaded. Moreover, Russia's industrial products were seldom able to compete in an open market with those of Europe and the USA. To corner part of the Chinese market Russia would probably have to discriminate against foreign competition by political means, which was bound to incur the wrath of the other powers.[41]

The first step towards confrontation with Japan came in 1895. In the peace treaty that followed its victory over the Chinese, Tokyo secured, amongst other possessions, the naval base of Port Arthur and control over southern Manchuria. Russia masterminded a coalition with Germany and France to force the Japanese to give up these gains. It also helped the Chinese to pay off their war indemnity. As a reward, in the autumn of 1896 Petersburg won from the Chinese the right to link Vladivostok to the Trans-Siberian railway which it was building by a short cut across northern Manchuria.

This scheme was Witte's and it possessed clear advantages. The Manchurian route was easier and cheaper to build than a line across Russian territory. It also opened up the prospect of Russian domination of Manchuria, which was potentially a very rich province. By forestalling foreign competitors and dominating northern Chinese markets Witte hoped to recoup many of the costs of building the Trans-Siberian railway. With Nicholas II's support, he imposed his policy despite the doubts of some other Russian ministries. These doubts were well justified. It was extremely dangerous to place hundreds of miles of Russia's main line of communication to the East in a foreign and turbulent province. Witte's hopes of wringing quick profits out of Manchuria were always fanciful, whereas the financial and political costs of defending his railway soon proved to be exorbitant. Moreover, by travelling across foreign territory the railway partly sacrificed one of its main objectives, namely the encouragement of colonization in Russia's Far Eastern provinces.

The next stage in Russia's advance in the Far East was not initially of Petersburg's choosing. In November 1897 the Germans occupied the Chinese port of Kiaochow. The Russian Foreign Minister, M.N. Muravyov, believed that the British were likely to take Port Arthur in response. He therefore advocated that Russia should move into Port Arthur first. At a meeting on 26 November chaired by the Emperor, both the Minister of Finance and the Naval Minister opposed the seizure of Port Arthur, the latter on the grounds that a Korean port would be far more suitable for the navy's needs. Perhaps for this reason Nicholas concurred with the majority view not to take Port Arthur, despite his personal view that it was vital for Russia to have a warm-water port in the Far East. Two weeks later, however, after private conversations with Muravyov, Nicholas changed his mind, a pattern of behaviour which drove his ministers to despair. In March 1898, under heavy pressure, the Chinese agreed to lease Port Arthur and its hinterland to Russia. In compensation for German and Russian gains the British took the port of Weihaiwei. The Japanese therefore had the mortification of seeing Russia ensconced in a port from which Tokyo had been evicted only three years ago amidst pious claims that the European powers were acting to protect China's territorial integrity.

In 1900 a revolt against foreigners, the so-called Boxer rebellion, spread across much of northern China, including Manchuria. Russian troops poured in to protect Witte's precious railway. Once in possession of Manchuria Petersburg was disinclined to retreat, at least until absolute security could be guaranteed to its railway and the Chinese would concede Russia's economic domination of the province. This Peking was unwilling to do. Its stand was strongly backed by Britain, the USA and Japan, all of which demanded free access for foreign trade to Manchuria. The signing of the Anglo-Japanese alliance, clearly directed against Russia, in January 1902 further stiffened Chinese resolve.

The Manchurian issue was, however, complicated by the fact that a simultaneous dispute existed between Russia and Japan as regards control over Korea. Russia's main interest in Korea lay in the proximity of that country's northern border to Vladivostok, which made domination of the whole country by another great power worrying. In addition, the Russian navy lusted after a Korean port and feared that if the Japanese controlled both sides of the Straits of Tsushima they could easily cut communications between Vladivostok and Port Arthur. The Koreans themselves looked to Russia for protection from Japan, which was clearly the greatest threat to their independence, and offered Russia many inducements to occupy itself in their affairs. But the greatest single complicating factor in Russia's relations with Korea was the large timber concession which a number of aristocrats close to Nicholas had secured on the river Yalu, with the aim of building up a Russian bridgehead in northern Korea.

The leaders in the Yalu enterprise were A.M. Bezobrazov and V.M. Vonlyarlyarsky. Both came from prominent families of the Russian aristocracy and were former officers of the Chevaliers Gardes, the most exclusive regiment in the Russian army. Bezobrazov gained access to Nicholas II through the former Minister of the Imperial Court, Count I.I. Vorontsov-Dashkov. Neither Bezobrazov nor Vonlyarlyarsky were interested in the Yalu enterprise for the sake of personal gain. They saw their company as a means by which non-official patriots could out-manoeuvre bureaucratic caution and push forward Russia's cause in the East. Theirs was to be a latter-day version of Britain's East India Company but without its initially commercial priorities. The whole scheme bore the stamp of aristocratic arrogance and amateurism. Its leaders were convinced of their own innate superiority to mere bureaucrats. Without knowing the East, they nevertheless urged on Nicholas the belief that Orientals would back down in the face of a confident show of Russian power. There was more than a touch of opera to the Bezobrazov affair. Rather typical was the fact that at one point secret correspondence between Bezobrazov and Nicholas II was sent through their respective batmen so that the ministers should be kept in the dark about it. But there was nothing funny in the effect of Bezobrazov's influence, which was both to increase Nicholas's distrust of his official advisers and to encourage him to take a tougher and more intransigent line with the Japanese and Chinese governments. In October 1901, for instance, the Emperor told Prince Henry of Prussia that 'I do not want to seize Korea – but under no circumstances can I allow the Japanese to become firmly established there. That would be a *casus belli*.' Here was the voice of Bezobrazov not of Nicholas's ministerial advisers, whose position on Korea was much less bellicose.[42]

Bezobrazov, Vonlyarlyarsky and their supporters in particular urged on Nicholas two ideas to which he was very inclined to listen. They told him that Russia was a proud and mighty country which should speak in a strong voice and take no cheek from foreigners, least of all Orientals. This Guards officers' patriotism was music to his ears. His aristocratic advisers, loathing the bureaucracy and above all Witte, also told Nicholas that he was the captive of his ministers, who colluded in keeping information from him, imposing their own views and sabotaging his instructions when they conflicted with their own interests. By 1900 Nicholas felt this to be true, not merely as regards Far Eastern policy but across the whole range of government business. Frustrated by his seeming powerlessness and aware of mounting criticism of his rule, he turned more and more to

unofficial advisers in an effort to secure alternative sources of information
and greater freedom from ministerial control. Among these advisers
Bezobrazov was typical in his aristocratic origins and in his appeal to
Nicholas's patriotic and anti-bureaucratic instincts. In July 1901
Alexander Polovtsov commented that

> in no field of policy is there a principled, well considered and firmly directed
> course of action. Everything is done in bursts, haphazardly, under the
> influence of the moment, according to the demands of this or that person and
> the intercessions emerging from various corners. The young Tsar feels more
> and more contempt for the organs of his own power and begins to believe in
> the beneficial strength of his own autocracy, which he manifests sporadically,
> without preliminary discussion and without any link to the overall course of
> policy.[43]

As in his domestic policy Nicholas sought to balance between his
groups of advisers, drawing information from both and thereby seeking a
basis on which he could determine policy for himself. This had a disastrous
impact on Russia's Far Eastern policy in 1902–3 and on the way it was
perceived by foreigners, above all the Japanese. It was not merely that
Bezobrazov's advice was dangerous and mistaken. Outsiders did not
know what Petersburg's policy was. Faced by criticism that divisions
between ministers and unofficial advisers were causing government policy
in East Asia to be incoherent and uncoordinated, in August 1903 Nicholas
appointed Admiral Alekseev Viceroy of the Far East and subordinated to
him all responsibility not only for civil and military affairs but also for
diplomatic relations with Tokyo and Peking. This was to make a bad
situation worse. Alekseev was a sailor, not a diplomat or a statesman. By
definition neither he nor other officials in the East could have a balanced
overall grasp of the Empire's many interests for they were committed to
pursuing a forward policy in their own bailiwick.

The Japanese now had to deal with Alekseev in Port Arthur but they
knew, of course, that the Viceroy's decisions would have to be ratified by
the Tsar, and therefore by those high officials to whom he chose to listen,
in Petersburg. Confusion was compounded by the fact that during the
critical period between August and November 1903 Nicholas II was
seldom in his capital, spending most of his time on official and private
visits to Western Europe. Though Japanese counsels were themselves
divided, had Russia consistently stood out for a free hand for herself in
Manchuria in return for Japanese control over Korea, Tokyo would
almost certainly have agreed in the end. The demilitarization of northern
Korea could have been obtained through such a deal had Petersburg
offered some concessions in southern Manchuria. But the Russians

overestimated the strength of their position, and the incoherence and delay in their responses to Tokyo convinced the Japanese that Petersburg was simply prevaricating. Nicholas's own statements betrayed his uncertainty and miscalculations. In October 1903 he telegraphed to Alekseev: 'I do not want war between Russia and Japan and will not permit this war. Take all measures so that there is no war.' In late December, however, he commented that the situation reminded him of the 1895 crisis when Japan backed down under firm Russian pressure and surrendered Port Arthur. Referring to Japan, Nicholas remarked: 'all the same it is a barbarian country. Which is better: to risk a war or to continue with concessions?' In February 1904 the Japanese permitted Russia no more wavering and attacked Port Arthur.[44]

The disastrous and unnecessary war with Japan was more Nicholas's fault than anybody else's. First and foremost he underestimated Japan's resolution, its willingness to take great risks in challenging the seemingly much mightier Russia, and the skill with which it would wage war. For this he cannot be entirely blamed. In 1903–5 Japan surprised the whole world. Perhaps more culpable was Nicholas's faith in Russian might, his inability to distinguish between parade-ground glitter and military effectiveness. The Emperor was also to blame for failing to measure his Far Eastern policy against Russia's overall interests, problems and resources. His vision of Russia's future in Asia and the East was a grandiose one. Like everything he did it was fired by great patriotism and an uplifted sense of his country's destiny. Nor was the Emperor wrong to see Siberia and the Pacific as more suitable fields for his country's energies and ambitions than the Near East and the Balkans. But the enormous diversion of resources to the Far East even before the war began was excessive given Russia's domestic needs. And Russia possessed interests in Europe which she could not abandon and to which her Far Eastern policies did great harm. In 1902–3 a wise policy could have retained many of the advantages secured in earlier years in the Far East without the risk of war. A more balanced and realistic policy would have weighed the risks, benefits and costs of intransigence in the Far East rather differently.

Of course Nicholas was by no means solely responsible for having led Russia to disaster in the Far East. Many of his advisers must also share the blame. Even Serge Witte, for instance, though he took a relatively pacific line after 1900, was largely responsible for having lumbered Russia with the problem of defending its key strategic artery to the East across hundreds of miles of hostile foreign territory. But Witte was only able to build his railway across Manchuria because the departmental perspective of the Ministry of Finance was allowed to triumph over a more balanced assessment of not merely the financial but also the strategic, diplomatic and economic implications of this decision. In the Russian system of government, however, only the monarch or a lieutenant to whom he delegated full authority could hope to impose a balanced, co-ordinated view of the country's interests on the various departments which made government policy. This Nicholas proved unable to do, even to the extent that it was possible. And he was much too jealous of his autocratic powers and too distrustful of his advisers to let anyone else do the job for him.

CHAPTER 5

Autocratic Government

By the first years of the twentieth century the Russian government was clearly in a mess. Problems were accumulating at great speed with solutions nowhere in sight. A growing sense of crisis pervaded senior officialdom. So too did the sense that the government was confused, divided and without firm policies. Ministers blamed each other for this state of affairs. They also, with increasing unanimity, blamed the Tsar. His handling even of domestic issues aroused their impatience and anger. When the blunders that led to war with Japan also came to be recognized indignation mounted. By 1905 very many top officials believed that unless fundamental changes occurred in the way in which government policy was formulated and co-ordinated the regime was doomed.

The same criticisms of Nicholas were made by one minister after another. He was said to be very impressionable and therefore much inclined to alter his opinions to accord with the views of the last person to whom he spoke. As Vladimir Lambsdorff commented in the winter of 1896, 'our young monarch changes his mind with terrifying speed'. One result of this was that ministers were nervous about leaving Nicholas alone with their rivals for any length of time, sometimes dogging his footsteps while he was on holiday at Livadia like a posse of bloodhounds. Ministers knew that even when they had secured the Emperor's approval to a policy they could not take his continued support for granted, especially if that policy came under severe criticism. Alexander Schwartz recalled a conversation with S.N. Rukhlov, the Minister of Communications, 'who in a moment of sincerity said to me: God preserve you from relying on the Emperor even for a second on any matter; he is incapable of supporting anyone over anything'.[1]

Given the enormous pressures and criticism to which all ministers were subjected in the last decades of the old regime, the sense that one could not rely on the monarch's support could be a heavy cross to bear. Though no minister could ever be described as the monarch's personal friend,

Nicholas clearly liked some more than others. Not surprisingly, given his background and personality, he tended to prefer people of aristocratic origin with roots in the countryside to the more normal product of Petersburg high officialdom. The latter, part veteran politician and part bureaucrat, seldom inspired him with much enthusiasm.

Among his favourites in the first decade of his reign was Prince Aleksei Lobanov-Rostovsky, an amateur historian and an amusing story-teller whose life in the diplomatic service had taken him through most of the major courts of Europe. Of equally elevated origins but even more colourful was the Minister of Communications, Prince Michael Khilkov, who as a young man had abandoned service in the Guards to go off and work for a number of years as an engine-driver in South America and a shipwright in Liverpool. Aleksei Ermolov, also from an old landed family, got on well with Nicholas and was generally regarded as a considerable scholar in his specialist field, agriculture. What these three shared, apart from their aristocratic backgrounds, were abnormal careers and charming, pleasant personalities. There was a touch of amateurism about all three men, a lack of the obsessive political ambition and the craving for status that long immersion in the Petersburg official world could encourage among the capital's veteran officials. None of these three men could remotely be described as bureaucrats: though Lobanov-Rostovsky was a highly intelligent man and proved to be Nicholas's best Foreign Minister, his relaxed style of work horrified more professional administrators; both Ermolov and Khilkov were famous for combining great technical knowledge with an inability to manage their ministries effectively.

More typical ministers had less satisfactory relations with the Emperor. The latter gave most of his attention to defence, foreign policy and the Ministry of Internal Affairs. Intervention in other departments tended to be spasmodic. Most ministers felt that Nicholas was not greatly interested either in themselves or in the affairs of their department. Alexander Schwartz, for instance, recalled that Nicholas was always friendly, polite and welcoming but that a minister did not take long to realize that the warmth was only skin-deep. Politeness and the desire not to hurt the feelings of those with whom he worked could not disguise the fact that at heart Nicholas did not greatly like most of his senior counsellors and was largely indifferent to their fate. In addition, in Schwartz's words, the Emperor 'was sincere with scarcely anyone'. The Tsar seldom disagreed with ministers directly but his seeming consent to their views did not stop him from taking alternative counsel or secretly harbouring many doubts about a minister and his policies.[2]

At times experiencing this hidden distrust, ministers were bitter. They felt themselves to be by right the monarch's chief advisers in the specific sphere of policy covered by their ministry. In practice they sought to monopolize the flow of information and counsel to the Emperor in their field. Often they felt that unless they could do so the difficulties involved in running their ministries would become insuperable. Russian ministers faced many frustrations in trying to impose their will on a far-flung administration whose low-level officials were often of poor calibre. In rural Russia, right down to 1917, government officials were not held in check by public opinion, since most of the population was barely literate and the local press very weak. Officials were also to some extent beyond the control of the law, especially when provinces were placed under a state of emergency. Even in normal circumstances prosecution required the consent of an official's administrative superiors. Nor was the bureaucracy responsible to an elected legislature, though after 1906 deputies in the new parliament, the Duma, could shame wrongdoers by asking embarrassing questions in public of ministers. In these circumstances ministers found it very difficult to control their provincial officials. Faced with very similar problems in the 1920s and 1930s the Soviet regime, having destroyed all elements of legality and free public opinion that had existed in Imperial Russia, resorted to increasingly large-scale and bloody purges to ensure local officialdom's obedience to orders from the centre. Such methods were unthinkable in the Russia of Nicholas II. But ministers were very concerned by problems of discipline and control in their department and, partly for this reason, greatly resented any imperial interference which would weaken their prestige and authority.

In the upper levels of the bureaucracy personnel were in general educated and efficient but here the problems of control could be equally great. Senior Russian officials were not always noted for strict obedience to their superiors' commands. No line divided politics and administration in Russia. Ministers were in most cases merely very senior civil servants. Political battles in the government or at court sent ripples down the bureaucratic hierarchy. Senior officials often tended to be politicians, keeping a wary eye on currents at court and in ministerial circles. To some extent they had to be if they were to protect their jobs and promote their careers. In this very political upper bureaucracy promotions and appointments often depended on patronage. Particularly in some ministries the securing of patrons could be as important as administrative skill for an ambitious man. Little groups of patrons and their clients formed, sometimes taking on a political colouring. Given these realities a minister who lacked the unequivocal support of the monarch might find it very difficult to impose his will on some of his subordinates. This was particularly true if the latter had powerful patrons elsewhere in the government or, worst of all, were directly in contact with the monarch. The ultimate nightmare was to have grand dukes in one's department since they by definition had easy access to Nicholas and were therefore impossible to control. In addition, a minister whose support from the Emperor was weak would seldom prevail in the conflicts with other departments which are the everyday reality of any government.

By 1903 General Aleksei Kuropatkin, the Minister of War, felt that his prestige was being severely undermined by Nicholas's relations with unofficial advisers such as A.M. Bezobrazov. Still worse were the Emperor's direct links with some of Kuropatkin's own subordinates. The final straw was Nicholas's decision to create a viceroyalty in the Far East, hiving off some of Kuropatkin's responsibilities in the process, without even asking the Minister of War's advice in advance. Kuropatkin wrote in his diary:

> I said to the Emperor that none of his subjects had the right even to think about penetrating the Emperor's designs in respect of any of his acts. Only before God and history are sovereigns responsible for the paths they choose to take for the well-being of the people. Therefore, although I am opposed to subordinating the Amur [i.e. Far Eastern] region to Alekseev, I have absolutely no pretensions about supposing that my opinion is necessarily correct. I would therefore bow before each of the Sovereign's decisions and would apply all my strength to their fulfilment in the best possible way. But, being placed by the Sovereign at the head of an important ministry, by law I bear the responsibility for the correct execution of business in this department. With the Sovereign's trust I can cope with the heavy burdens that lie on me but if that trust is lost and if it becomes evident to all that the trust no longer exists then the Sovereign's relatives, the commanders of troops and other ministers will begin to slight me and go around me and my successful fulfilment of my duties as a minister will become impossible.[3]

As Minister of War Kuropatkin was more exposed to Nicholas's interventions than was the case with most heads of department. In addition, the army was almost the only permitted career for a grand duke and its upper reaches were therefore always inhabited by many of the Tsar's relatives. But few ministers entirely escaped the frustrations which Kuropatkin expressed so vividly in this conversation with Nicholas. Moreover all of them experienced the lack of co-ordination between ministries and the absence, therefore, of coherent balanced policies taking in all aspects of the state's interests. This was the greatest single failing of Russian government before 1905, and since co-ordination was the Tsar's responsibility he inevitably was widely blamed for its absence.

Konstantin Pobedonostsev, the chief civil administrator of the Orthodox Church, had much to say on this score in the years before 1905. Since he was an intelligent man and had known Nicholas for longer than any of the other ministers his comments are of particular interest. Pobedonostsev was furious that Nicholas was consulting outside advisers, who in his view were rogues and charlatans, and was allowing them to influence the government's policy. He noted that the Emperor was inclined to agree with one adviser's ideas and then change his mind when he spoke to someone else. Collegiate institutions which were designed to co-ordinate government policy were not being properly used. Taxed with his failure to unite his government Nicholas did for a time preside over weekly meetings of his ministers in 1901 but the experiment was not successful. Pobedonostsev described the meetings in the following terms: 'The discussions begin. Some people, Ermolov for instance, chatter away without ceasing. The Emperor begins to get bored. The time approaches for lunch. He begins to look at his watch and after about ten or fifteen minutes announces that the question under discussion will be on the agenda again the following Friday. The ministers bow and disperse. He lacks strength, energy and passion.'[4]

Pobedonostsev believed that it was because the Tsar failed to use collegiate institutions such as the Committee of Ministers properly that power was exercised individually by ministers. Policy was decided in face-to-face audiences between the monarch and individual ministers, which made co-ordinated and balanced decisions impossible. 'Since the representative of authority [i.e. the Tsar] had in fact resigned the use of his power, it had been picked up by the ministers, and there was therefore no unity and no directing thought.' In Pobedonostsev's view, however, the Emperor's failure to unify government policy was rooted not only in his inability to direct collegiate and co-ordinating institutions but also in Nicholas's personality and education.

> He has a naturally good brain, analytical skills and he grasps what he is told. But he only grasps the significance of a fact in isolation without its relationship to other facts, events, currents and phenomena. On this isolated trifling fact or view he stops . . . Wide general ideas worked out by an exchange of views, argument or discussions are lacking. This is shown by the fact that not long ago he said to one of his entourage: 'Why are you always quarrelling? I always agree with everyone about everything and then do things my own way.'[5]

It would, however, be a mistake to take ministers' criticism of Nicholas at face value and to imagine that theirs is the last and only word on the matter. If senior officials blamed the Emperor for the government's failings, he reciprocated in good measure. Indeed by 1900 his suspicion and contempt for the bureaucracy was widely noted. The imperial family's dislike of the ministers was expressed most succinctly by the Empress Marie, who in February 1904 commented that 'it's they who get in the way of everything'. Nicholas's sense of frustration, isolation and bewilderment is evident from a letter written by his wife to her sister in February 1905.

> My poor Nicky's cross is a heavy one to bear, all the more so as he has nobody on whom he can thoroughly rely and who can be a real help to him. He tries so hard, works with such perseverance, but the lack of what I call 'real' men is great. Of course they must exist somewhere, but it is difficult to get at them . . . We shall try to see more people but it is difficult . . . Poor Nicky, he has a bitter hard life to lead. Had his father seen more people, drawn them around him, we should have had lots to fill the necessary posts; now only old men or quite young ones, nobody to turn to. The uncles no good, Misha [Nicholas's brother] a darling child still . . .[6]

In part Nicholas's isolation, frustration and inability effectively to run his government were rooted in his personality. Loneliness is the inevitable lot of any monarch, especially if he ascends the throne at an early age. Nicholas's reticence and self-control, the fact that he opened his heart to almost no one, contributed, however, to his isolation. Probably the majority of mankind, if dropped by fate into the world of Russian high politics, would have thoroughly disliked most of the men and the morals they encountered. In Nicholas's case, the innocence and high ideals of his upbringing must have made exposure to this world all the more shocking. The Tsar's ethics were those of the honourable if naïve Guards officer. His conception of patriotism and duty was a high one. The intrigue, ambition, jealousy and frequent pettiness of the political world revolted him. Years of exposure to this world hardened him and made him indifferent and cool to its inhabitants. In Peter Bark's view this 'stopped him, despite his very great personal charm, from creating around himself a group of devoted friends, loyal and faithful'. Fully trusting almost nobody outside his own family, in the first decade of his reign Nicholas often turned to his relatives for advice on people and even policies. Many of the other Romanovs, however, not only drew their friends and acquaintances from a narrow circle but also lived superficial and self-indulgent lives which made them easy targets for all sorts of flatterers and fools. Very few of his relatives' protégés did Nicholas much service, the prize for awfulness going to the acquaintances of the Tsar's brother-in-law, the Grand Duke Alexander. Nor did the Emperor's own innocent and closeted upbringing prepare him well to judge people.[7]

Nicholas II's nature was delicate and sensitive. He disliked coarseness, bullying and personal confrontations. Alexander III had loved to play cards with members of his suite, who in the excitement of winning and losing, 'uninhibited by the Sovereign's presence, allowed themselves impermissible pranks and expressions. This left an indelible impression on the Emperor for his whole life and robbed him of any desire to become acquainted with card games.' In December 1896 Madame Bogdanovich recorded that during an argument between two ministers, 'Witte flared up with such anger against Khilkov that the Tsar went out of the room, leaving the two together and didn't return to them . . . It's evident that the ministers don't pay attention to the Tsar and that he can't cope with them.' Nicholas's method of dealing with ministers was not to confront them but rather to evade arguments, seek alternative advice and go his own way. This won him a reputation for cowardice and shiftiness.

Once he had gained some experience in government, the Tsar's shyness and dislike of argument did not mean that he was easily swayed by ministers. Michael Akimov, the President of the State Council from 1907 to 1914, knew Nicholas well. He commented that 'for all his seeming pliability and gentleness, His Majesty at times revealed an unexpected independence, in some circumstances producing an impression of stubbornness'. Gentle and rarely angry, indulgent towards mistakes, impressionable but sometimes stubborn, always suspicious and elusive – Nicholas's personality meant that he failed to impose his will and strength of purpose on his ministers in a consistent manner. As was the case in a number of ways, the Emperor's virtues sometimes told against him. Nicholas never allowed himself to indulge in the explosive Russian outbursts of temperament that soothed the nerves and satisfied the egos of so many figures in Russian political life at the time, though at the cost of endless unnecessary and debilitating personal battles that did nothing to enhance the effectiveness of the political system. But his calm, moderation and self-control – very un-Russian virtues – were often interpreted as indifference and weakness. His wife complained with some justice that 'it cost the Emperor a tremendous effort to subdue the attacks of rage to which the Romanoffs are subject. He has learnt the hard lesson of self-control, only to be called weak; people forget that the greatest conqueror is he who conquers himself.' Terror has always been one method by which dictators have held their subordinates in awe. In Victorian and Edwardian Russia it was unthinkable that the Emperor should in the literal sense of the word terrorize his lieutenants like a medieval despot or Josef Stalin. It did not help his cause, however, that he was incapable even of scaring his ministers.[8]

Though Nicholas's personality was of course an important factor in his dealings with his government, it would be a mistake to imagine that it was the only one. During the reign of the last Russian Emperor, some ministers were inclined to look back on Alexander III's reign as a golden age. Despite Alexander's powerful and imposing personality, however, many of the difficulties faced by his son as regards the direction and co-ordination of the machinery of government were already fully in evidence in the 1880s.

A.A. Polovtsov commented in 1889 that Alexander III was 'full of contempt for the entire higher bureaucracy' and that, together with the Grand Duke Vladimir, the Tsar bewailed his isolation and the lack of good candidates for jobs. Polovtsov responded to Vladimir's complaint by arguing that 'both the Emperor and you live in conditions which make it very difficult if not impossible to know people . . . You live your lives under lock and key, see people at official receptions and speak to two or three whom fate or intrigue have brought close to you and who find in you a means to the attainment of their goals.' Though himself a senior official, Polovtsov, like most Russians, despised the bureaucracy. His comments to Alexander III on its evils no doubt fed imperial prejudices on this score.

> Formerly the throne was surrounded by a hereditary aristocracy, which could tell the truth to the monarch, if not in the course of official service, then in everyday social intercourse and during entertainments. Now the aristocracy has been destroyed and high society itself scarcely exists any more. The Emperor is only accessible to servile bureaucrats who see in him a means to the achievement of their own egotistical goals.[9]

As revealing are the diaries of Alexander Kireev from the 1880s. Kireev complained that nobody and nothing co-ordinated the activities of the various departments, which simply pursued independent policies. 'In our country each ministry is a separate state which has nothing to do with any other one.' Alexander III, rather than preside over the State Council or Committee of Ministers, ran Russia through private audiences with individual ministers. As a result he got a one-sided view of problems. The Tsar was isolated and saw far fewer people than his father, Alexander II. With the press censored and the aristocracy in decline, the Tsar knew Russia through what his officials chose to tell him. In Kireev's view the Tsar was completely in the bureaucracy's hands, knew and resented this fact but could do nothing about it. 'The Emperor said to Zhukovsky that he despises the administration and had drunk a toast to its obliteration.' Kireev's conclusion was that 'the poor Emperor lives in a vicious circle from which there is no exit. He puts his trust in the ministers, strictly watches that each of them keeps only to his own business and doesn't allow intervention in their neighbours' affairs. This makes each minister completely outside monarchical control.'[10]

In August 1903 Aleksei Kuropatkin complained bitterly to Vyacheslav Plehve, the Minister of Internal Affairs, about the Emperor's suspicion and lack of confidence in his official advisers. Plehve responded:

streaks of distrust for ministers and the publishing of important acts without their involvement were common to all sovereigns beginning with Alexander I. This trait is connected with the basic principle of autocracy. Autocrats appear to listen to their ministers and on the surface agree with them but almost always people from the side find easy access to their hearts or instill in the monarchs distrust for their ministers who are represented as encroaching on the rights of the autocrat. Hence the bifurcation of the state's actions. Even such a strong personality as Alexander III was not averse to this sort of activity.[11]

Plehve was right to stress that conflict and suspicion between the autocrat and his ministers were built into the Russian system of government and had existed throughout the nineteenth century. Nevertheless, relations between the monarch and senior officialdom had changed fundamentally during this period. The most obvious reason for this was simply the vast growth of the bureaucracy. Even if one excludes the horde of clerks, secretaries, janitors and messengers who served in the bureaucracy's lowest ranks, the number of civil servants in Petersburg alone grew from 23,000 in 1880 to 52,000 in 1914. Moreover, the administration grew not just in size but also in the range and complexity of the tasks it was seeking to fulfil. Alongside defence, diplomacy and law and order, the traditional spheres of government activity, there emerged new fields in which the Russian government often played a much greater role than was the case elsewhere in Europe. At one extreme lay the increasingly large-scale operations of the security police, as always particularly difficult to supervise or control because of the secrecy with which they acted. At the other stood the wide-ranging activity of the ministries of finance and, particularly in the twentieth century, agriculture. A vast range of questions, many of them very technical, were decided in the upper reaches of the government. One result of this was that in many areas it was difficult for an amateur without specialist skills to understand the issues or to make intelligent decisions.

The civil service was changing not merely in its size and functions but also in its mentality. In the 1890s there were many ministers who saw themselves primarily as the Tsar's servitors and assistants. In their view their duty lay in executing the monarch's decisions, whatever they might be. By 1905 such views seemed increasingly anachronistic. The focus of most civil servants' loyalties had shifted from the dynasty to the state and nation. Senior officialdom, by now almost always possessing a higher education and a considerable *esprit de corps*, felt that its expertise gave it a right to considerable autonomy *vis-à-vis* the Tsar. This shift occurred even in the Foreign Ministry, the department over which traditionally the monarch exercised the closest supervision. When he succeeded Count

Lambsdorff as Foreign Minister in 1906, A.P. Izvolsky made it clear that a fundamental shift in mentality had occurred. He would not follow in the footsteps of his predecessor, who 'advanced the stupefying theory that in Russia the Minister of Foreign Affairs could not quit his post until dismissed by his sovereign, and that his sole function was to study the questions pertaining to the Empire's foreign relations and present his conclusions to the Emperor, who, in his quality of autocrat, would decide for or against, and his decision would thereupon be obligatory for the Minister.'[12]

By the early twentieth century, a monarch who intended to dominate the machinery of government and direct its policies along his own lines faced far more formidable obstacles than those that had confronted his ancestors in 1800 or 1850. One quite interesting way to illustrate this fact is to look at the travails of a number of great aristocrats who occupied top positions in government under Nicholas II. These landowning magnates from the old aristocracy were quite a small minority among Nicholas's ministers, most of whom were professional civil servants. Like the Tsar himself, they were amateurs in government, without years of experience of managing large administrative organizations. Their mentality, values and lifestyle, like those of the monarch, marked them out as members not merely of a leisured class, but also of a class bred to the conviction that it was its right to govern, and its duty to do so in a paternalist manner. Unlike the Emperor, however, aristocratic ministers were responsible only for the affairs of one department and were not chained to their office for life.

Two senior aristocratic officials in Nicholas II's government were the brothers-in-law Prince Alexander Obolensky and Count Aleksei Bobrinsky. Both men were not only great landowners but also great industrialists. They were very wealthy. Obolensky served first as a Senator and then as a member of the State Council, in other words in the empire's highest judicial and legislative bodies. Bobrinsky, also a member of the State Council, subsequently held ministerial office. Both men discovered on first entering senior executive positions in the bureaucracy that little in their backgrounds had prepared them for the daily grind and long hours entailed by their jobs. Alexander Obolensky wrote to his wife that 'I am simply not accustomed to doing my work sloppily and I just won't do this. But there's not the time to do it as it ought to be done.' Soon after Bobrinsky became a minister he wrote to his daughter that 'my role is exhaustingly hard labour. I work from morning until night . . . I had imagined this post differently. There is the appearance of power but in fact thousands of plots, conferences and discussions.'[13]

Bobrinsky at least was more politically ambitious than most aristocratic magnates and quite enjoyed the world of Petersburg high society and its

salons. By contrast Alexander Obolensky was much more like Nicholas II
in his detestation of Petersburg and its political intrigues, and in his preference for the life of a country gentleman. In the autumn of 1904, for
instance, as Russia lurched towards revolution, Obolensky wrote of
Petersburg that 'here there is futility, sadness, gossip and cold – to sum
things up, it is foul'. By contrast, his estate was a haven of serenity where
people got on with their daily lives and concentrated on practical tasks. In
his part of the countryside 'everyone has got a lot of bread and so they are
all satisfied. When one is here and is plunged into the local atmosphere
and interests you forget quite a bit about questions concerning the war and
domestic politics'. He added that 'Petersburg, with all the tragic, busy
and disturbed times it is going through, seems something far away. One
thinks about what is going on there but doesn't really feel it.' The
Emperor would have given almost anything to flee with Obolensky to the
backwoods serenity of his estate in Penza province. In comparison, his
almost suburban palaces at Tsarskoe Selo and Peterhof, though at least an
escape from Petersburg, were a poor substitute.[14]

Prince Boris Vasil'chikov was, like Alexander Obolensky, a great
aristocratic landowner who far preferred rural life to Petersburg politics
and accepted the job of Minister of Agriculture in 1906 with great reluc-
tance. Managing a large estate, dealing with the local peasantry and working as a provincial Governor on a person-to-person basis with local notables
were jobs that Vasil'chikov enjoyed and felt that he did well. By contrast,
he himself wrote that he was 'no good as a minister'. He commented that
to succeed at the top level in Petersburg you had to love power and be very
ambitious. Since politics at this level was a constant battle you had both to
enjoy the fight and to take pleasure in mastering and imposing your views
on other people and departments. In addition, wrote Vasil'chikov, he had
no training in the task of managing a large organization like a ministry
and very little experience of the Petersburg bureaucracy and its ways. Professional Petersburg bureaucrats shared Vasil'chikov's view that he was
unsuited for his job as minister. Serge Witte described him as 'not a busi-
nesslike man'. Vladimir Gurko called him 'a typical Russian gentleman'
and commented that he was 'an honorable and intelligent man, but
neither a good worker nor a statesman. He represented a type of minister
of the period of Nicholas I [1825–55]; he was upright, honest and could
speak openly and frankly even to the Monarch, yet he had no knowledge
of any problem; he relied simply upon his own common sense but was
utterly incapable of handling skilfully any complicated matter.' Gurko's
comments reflected the widespread and growing belief of Petersburg officialdom that government and politics were full-time occupations best left
to professionals. Impatience with, and disdain for, the efforts of aristocratic amateurs to participate in this world are frequently encountered in

officials' memoirs and correspondence. Such views were bound in time to colour senior officialdom's attitude to Nicholas II, who was by far the most important aristocrat involved in the politics and government of his country.[15]

Peter Bark commented that Nicholas had 'old-fashioned ideas' about his country and the officials through whom it was governed. 'He considered himself to be the chief of his people or a landowner on a grand scale, though no sacrifice seemed to him too great if it was for the good of his subjects. The huge Russian Empire was to him a sort of ancestral family estate, private property. Ministers acted in his name as servants attached to his person and obligated to carry out his will might have acted.'[16]

It is clear from many of the Emperor's statements that he did not make a clear distinction in his own mind between public and private, the realm of the state and that of the imperial household. His defence of his autocratic powers was in part linked to the idea that these were a family heirloom of which he was the guardian rather than the outright owner. His attitude towards government was coloured by similar conceptions. He saw himself as his people's protector, father and friend rather than simply as the head of an impersonal institution called the state. He looked back nostalgically to the days before Peter the Great created Russia's modern bureaucratic apparatus, fondly believing that in these faraway times simple patriarchal and almost family ties linked the Tsar and his people. Far from fully trusting his bureaucracy and its plethora of rules and regulations, Nicholas felt that his duty lay in part in protecting his subjects from his own officials. To find a modern version of the Tsar's vision of personal, fatherly and accessible authority one would have to look to the Arab monarchies of the Middle East. But Nicholas II was not the tribal sheikh of a tiny kingdom, he was the ruler of an empire of 150 million people.

Great efforts were made to preserve the personal, patriarchal, unbureaucratic aspect of the monarchy. Personal requests and pleas poured into the Emperor's Petitions Chancellery on a vast range of subjects. The Emperor's position as patriarch of the Russian tribe, for instance, meant that until 1913, when family and matrimonial disputes were handed over to the courts, the personal sanction of the monarch was required before a wife could live apart from her husband. Unbelievably, right down to 1917, no Russian subject could change his name without the Emperor's consent, which meant that the Chancellery was flooded with petitions from newly respectable and educated peasants whose families had a generation or so before been blessed by fellow villagers with rude nicknames. By Nicholas II's day well over a hundred administrative officials worked in the Chancellery, handling not only such trivial petitions but also serious appeals for clemency or requests for subsidies, pensions or other forms of protection. According to V.I. Mamantov, the last head of the Petitions Chancellery, service in this organization was more like work in a private household than a government department. Its officials took their jobs very seriously and regarded it as their duty to do their utmost to listen to petitioners in a kindly and personal way and to redress the wrongs of the 'injured and insulted' wherever possible. Once a week the head of the Chancellery would report personally to Nicholas on the most difficult and serious cases for up to ninety minutes and the Emperor, blessed with an excellent memory and a quick grasp of complicated issues, would issue instructions to ministers where petitions were to be granted or complaints further investigated.[17]

In a sense the Petitions Chancellery was a cross between, on the one hand, the most ancient conception of monarchy in which the king sat under a tree and dispensed justice personally to his subjects and, on the other, a modern ombudsman, deputed to handle citizens' complaints against the bureaucracy. Despite the efforts of the Chancellery's officials to be as unbureaucratic as possible, to many Russians – above all peasants – Mamantov and his subordinates were just another species of civil servant. Only a petition pressed personally into the hands of the monarch, thereby avoiding any possibility of bureaucratic interference, was deemed by such people to have any hope of success. Peasants in particular attempted to waylay the Tsar on his travels or came to his palace to present their petitions to him in person. 'Every day the aide-de-camp on duty was obliged to receive and listen to each petitioner and then, returning to the duty office, had to draw up a short summary of each petition on a special form, attach and number all the petitions, place them in an envelope and at eight p.m. hand them over to the Emperor's valet, who would place this packet on the Emperor's writing table.'[18]

Like it or not, however, Nicholas II was not only father of the Russian tribe but also chief executive officer of the imperial government. In this context, one extraordinary fact is of great importance. During the nineteenth century the machinery of government in Russia had evolved enormously. Ministries became large and formidable institutions with a will of their own. The imperial administration was capable not merely of preserving order and raising taxes across a sixth of the world's land surface but also of implementing a policy of rapid industrial development and beginning the transformation of Russian peasant society as well. But while the machinery of government was developing in spectacular fashion, the institutions which surrounded the man who was supposed to be Russia's chief executive officer changed not at all. A twentieth-century governmental machine was presided over by a man whose throne was serviced by the offices of an eighteenth-century royal household.

In fact not only did no imperial secretariat develop to match the growth of government institutions but the offices which had earlier aided the monarch had a tendency to atrophy or even disappear, their functions being taken over by the ministries. Under Nicholas I, for instance, the Emperor's Personal Chancellery had been a formidable institution. Its Third Section, for example, had run the Gendarmerie, which Nicholas I conceived of not merely as security police but also as the monarch's eyes and ears, an élite super-bureaucracy through which he could supervise all other government institutions. By the 1860s and 1870s the Third Section had ceased to fulfil this role and was becoming a mere department of state security. Even so the Third Section's abolition in 1880 and the transfer of its functions to the Police Department of the Ministry of Internal Affairs was a key landmark in the shift from autocratic to bureaucratic rule.[19]

By the 1880s the monarch's Personal Chancellery was a shadow of its former self. All that remained was the old First Section. Under Nicholas I this section's most significant function was to act as the civil service inspectorate, checking promotions and appointments in the civil bureaucracy on the monarch's behalf. In 1858, however, the inspectorate was abolished and ministries became in practice almost autonomous managers of their own personnel. In an attempt to reimpose a greater degree of monarchical supervision over the bureaucracy Alexander III re-established the inspectorate in his Personal Chancellery in 1894 but this move proved ineffective. This was partly because the reform was not properly thought through, and partly because the Emperor died shortly after it was implemented. The result, however, was that the Russian monarch in practice had less control over civil service appointments and promotions than his Prussian cousin, who for this purpose worked through an effective personnel office called the Civil Cabinet which was part of the monarch's private secretariat.[20]

In contemporary Western governments chief executive officers come in two forms, one prime ministerial, the other presidential. Prime ministers tend themselves to chair regular sessions of their cabinet of ministers, seeking thereby to enhance co-ordination of policy between departments. At the turn of the century many of Nicholas's advisers believed that he should play a similar role. In their view the existing system whereby most business between the monarch and his ministers was conducted in private one-to-one audiences was a recipe for confusion. The monarch's authority allowed individual ministers sometimes to force through policies of which their colleagues could be unaware. As a result, one department's interests or perspectives swept aside those of other ministries. Nor were any records kept of these audiences. Confusion, disunity and, even worse, inter-departmental conflict were the result. Nicholas appears to have listened to these complaints. As we have seen, in 1901 he did for a time regularly chair meetings of the Committee of Ministers. On rare occasions, particularly over questions of foreign policy, he chaired smaller *ad hoc* ministerial sub-committees. And in 1905–6 he presided effectively over a number of crucial meetings of ministers and other senior officials designed to create a new constitution and to define how the new legislative and executive institutions established in 1905 should function. Nevertheless Nicholas soon tired of chairing the Committee of Ministers in 1901 and never truly functioned for long as his own prime minister.

Russian precedents were against the monarch acting in this way. No nineteenth-century tsar had chaired ministerial meetings save on very rare occasions. Nor did the Austrian emperors or the kings of Prussia do so. In addition, much of the business of the Committee of Ministers was very technical and detailed. Nicholas read the minutes of both the Committee and the supreme legislative body, the State Council, with great conscientiousness. No doubt he felt that this was preferable to wasting his time presiding over the often very boring and lengthy sessions of these bodies. The Tsar was after all an exceptionally hard-working member of a leisured class, not a professional administrator. He was sometimes away from Petersburg and its suburbs for long periods. Political considerations also counted, however. If the monarch presided over collegiate bodies he might well find himself dominated by them and bound by the decisions they took. Nicholas was impressionable. He also could not be as well informed as his ministers on most of the issues under discussion. Individuals or groups of ministers might overawe him by their arguments, committing him in semi-public to decisions he would later regret. The monarch's dignity and autonomy might well be better served by mulling over the minutes of these meetings on his own, subsequently consulting with ministers on an individual basis.

In comparison to the best-known of contemporary presidential systems, namely that of the United States, the most obvious weakness of a Russian tsar was his lack of an effective private secretariat. No American president would be able to control or co-ordinate the executive branch of government without the White House staff and its chief, the National Security Council and other such bodies. A chief executive officer who is simultaneously head of state carries an appalling range of obligations in the modern world. His time has to be controlled and rationed carefully. Trivia must be kept off his desk. On the other hand his staff must ensure that he alone makes the truly vital decisions and that he receives information sufficient in quantity and form to make this possible. This means the presentation of short, effective briefing papers setting out policy options. It means exposing the chief executive officer to different perspectives and opinions so that he does not simply become the captive of ministers and their expert bureaucratic advisers. It also entails following up the leader's directives to ensure that they are actually implemented rather than simply lost or distorted by the bureaucratic machine. A chief executive who wishes to control his government must surround himself with energetic and able advisers whose personal loyalty to him is linked both to shared beliefs and to their awareness that his power serves their ambitions and career prospects. In the 1920s and 1930s Josef Stalin faced the task of controlling the vast Russian government machine and imposing his will on the same country that Nicholas II had struggled to rule a few years before. One key to his 'success' was the formation of an immensely powerful personal secretariat packed by ambitious, able and ruthless clients through whom he imposed his decisions on the machinery of government.[21]

Nicholas II had no personal secretariat. Indeed, amazingly, he did not even have a private secretary. The Tsar was very tidy and meticulous. He prided himself on his ability to find any document in his files even in the dark. He hated anyone else to touch his papers. Nevertheless, the fact that the autocrat supposedly responsible for the fate of 150 million people actually stamped his own envelopes and wrote little notes asking for carriages to be made ready for him is almost bizarre. Trivia poured on to the monarch's desk. If on the one hand the Petitions Chancellery was inundated by the personal supplications of his subjects, ministers on the other hand were obliged to refer absurdly unimportant questions, for instance about personnel matters, to the monarch in person. In theory this was all in the cause of the Emperor's control over his administration. The reality was that, engulfed in trivia, Nicholas's actual ability to determine government policy was reduced. In the summer of 1912 Baron Roman Rosen, a former ambassador and present member of the State Council, devoted many weeks to writing a memorandum for Nicholas II on Russia's geopolitical position, her options as regards foreign policy, and the growing danger of war with Germany. Nicholas, however, was 'too busy' to read the lengthy memorandum. No doubt this was partly an excuse: the Emperor disliked 'outsiders' pushing their noses into the making of foreign policy, which he considered his personal prerogative. Even so the incident is instructive. Firstly, while too busy to read a politically important memorandum the monarch was devoting many hours a week to trivia. Secondly, if the Emperor was genuinely to be a chief executive officer he needed to listen to the opinions of people like Rosen, well-informed outsiders with different strategies to those of his official advisers. Thirdly, an effective personal secretariat with a trusted chief would not only have encouraged the monarch to read such memoranda but would also have ensured that they were presented in a digestible form rather than, as in Rosen's case, virtually at book-length.

An effective personal secretariat might well have reduced the frustration felt by both the monarch and his ministers. Nicholas read reams of documents with great care and attention. He often annotated them copiously and intelligently, passing on advice and instructions to his subordinates by this means. More often than not the documents then disappeared into a bureaucratic void and had no effect on either the formulation or execution of policy. The Tsar felt cheated and chafed at ministerial sabotage of his wishes. Had he possessed energetic and politically mature officials in his Personal Chancellery whose job it was to pursue these documents and try to ensure that they were implemented some of the Tsar's frustration could have been reduced. In fact not only did he have no real private office but he never even discussed politics with his entourage, most of whom were honourable but politically illiterate officers drawn from the Horse Guards regiment.

The absence of a private office was also sorely missed when ministers came for their weekly private audiences with the monarch. No documents were submitted in advance and no independent source existed to brief the Emperor on the topics a minister would be raising. Since most of these topics were narrow and specialized, Nicholas would generally have been hard pressed to dispute or debate them with his minister. Subsequently, however, he might well discuss the issues in question with someone else he met, in the process changing his mind on the subject. A more systematic approach to business, backed by an effective secretariat, could have avoided this danger in part, thereby reducing the Tsar's reputation for slipperiness and changeability.

In the autumn of 1898, speaking to V.I. Mamantov, Nicholas 'expressed his regret that when he was at Petersburg and Tsarskoe reports began from early in the morning. He therefore did not always succeed in familiarizing himself with the contents of the two newspapers which he had for a long time been accustomed to read every morning.' In response, Mamantov, then an official in the Emperor's tiny so-called Campaign Chancellery, began to organize a press-cuttings service so that the Tsar could read a digest of the press before 9 a.m. every morning. After initial enthusiasm, however, Nicholas allowed the scheme to lapse, supposedly because he did not wish to ask the Ministry of Finance for the very small extra sum required for its success. In Mamantov's view the real reason for the Emperor's retreat on this issue lay in malicious gossip at court, many of whose members envied anyone who appeared to be closer than themselves to the monarch and were fully capable of playing on Nicholas's suspicion that Mamantov's selections from the press might be slanted to support causes to which he personally was committed. If so this is one example of features often noted in Nicholas, namely his fear of falling into the hands of any adviser, his suspiciousness, his lack of personal friends, and his susceptibility to malicious gossip. The chief executive officer of a government needs to know what the press is saying. He gains thereby both a certain sense of public opinion and insights into ideas and information different from those that his official advisers provide. In abandoning the service Mamantov offered, Nicholas was turning his back on what could have proved a very useful aid to someone who aspired to the role of genuine head of government.[22]

For only one brief period in his reign did Nicholas have even the rudiments of a genuine Personal Secretariat. In October 1905, after his resignation as Governor-General of Petersburg, General Dimitri Trepov was appointed Commandant of the Imperial Palaces, a position he held until his death one year later. Normally this job, though it brought one into close contact with the Emperor, was limited to watching over the monarch's physical security. In Trepov's case it was always much more than this. In February 1906 Nicholas reported to his mother that 'Trepoff is absolutely indispensable to me: he is acting in a kind of secretarial capacity. He is experienced and clever and cautious in his advice. I give him Witte's bulky memoranda to read, then he reports on them quickly and concisely. This is of course a secret to everybody but ourselves.'[23]

Trepov had all the qualifications for the job. Most crucial of all, he enjoyed Nicholas's confidence to an almost unique extent. In October 1905 the Emperor had written to Trepov that 'you are the only one of my servants on whom I can rely completely. I thank you with all my heart for your devotion to me, for zealous service to the Motherland, and for rare honesty and straightforwardness.' Trepov was an ex-officer of the Horse Guards, whose former colonel, Vladimir Frederycksz, was the Minister of the Imperial Court. He was also the brother-in-law of Frederycksz's deputy, General A.A. Mosolov, another officer of the same regiment. Trepov was honourable, upright, straightforward and totally devoted to Nicholas and his dynasty. Such qualities were not uncommon among officers of the Imperial Guard. Much rarer in this milieu was Trepov's political experience and relative sophistication. As Governor of Moscow, Trepov had been the immediate boss of Serge Zubatov, both men being clients of the Grand Duke Serge.[24]

Dimitri Trepov's unique position in Nicholas's household was not, however, merely the result of his personal qualities or the trust which the Emperor felt for him. With revolution threatening the dynasty's survival by October 1905 Nicholas had been forced to create a new Council of Ministers, whose chairman was supposed to play the directing and co-ordinating role of a prime minister. This new institutional structure threatened to deprive the monarch of much of his power. Moreover Nicholas had been forced to appoint as chairman Serge Witte, for whom by now he had developed deep dislike and mistrust, since no other candidate seemed to have the necessary stature required by the critical times. With Witte now installed as Prime Minister the Emperor had better reason than ever to try to strengthen his personal position and his ability to keep an effective watch over his government.

Trepov functioned precisely as the head of the monarch's Personal Chancellery ought to have done. According to Andrew Verner, who has studied Nicholas II's response to the 1905 revolution with great care,

> instead of promoting his own views, the new court commandant sought to present for the tsar's consideration the recommendations of others whom he regarded as more knowledgeable and experienced than himself, be they bureaucratic traditionalists or members of the Kadet party. As a result, both Trepov's advisors and his advice appear to have changed repeatedly. The only constants were his untiring loyalty to the emperor, his eagerness both to expose Nicholas to different opinions in good autocratic fashion and to protect the autocrat from being dominated by any one person or group . . . Nicholas probably trusted and confided in Trepov precisely because he was neither a member of the hated bureaucracy nor an exponent of a particular viewpoint.[25]

Serge Witte's comments on Trepov's role are interesting and important. Soon after Trepov's resignation as Governor-General of Petersburg, wrote Witte,

> it was quickly evident that, far from having lost power by giving up all his previous posts for the comparatively lowly one of palace commandant, he had become even more powerful, answerable to no one, an Asiatic eunuch in a European court. His power was enhanced chiefly because this decisive and imposing man was now in a position to exercise great influence on the weak-willed Emperor, whom he was seeing every day . . . Note, moreover, that he was privy to all the counsel that reached the Emperor. And it should be remembered that all confidential material intended for the Emperor went through his hands, a fact of particular importance given the Emperor's passion for secret documents and meetings. It was Trepov who now decided what was worthy of the Emperor's attention and what was not. After all, didn't His Majesty have more than enough to read? And if one of the documents that passed through Trepov's hands provided material for getting rid of an undesirable minister, it could be touched up in a beautiful and humble style to make the point very evident. In addition, Trepov was now able to influence the Emperor's political views.

Dimitri Trepov brought in assistants to aid him.

It was not long before Garin, the director of the Department of Police, gave up his post and joined Trepov. The Emperor informed Manukhin, the minister of justice, that he was appointing Garin to the Senate . . . Once Trepov and Garin were ensconced at Peterhof, I noted that the Emperor's comments on documents returned to me were being written in a long-winded chancery style, e.g. 'This opinion does not agree with the cassational decisions of the Senate of such and such a date concerning such and such case, which explained the true sense of article such and such, volume so and so . . .' The handwriting was the Emperor's but the words and style were not his . . . Knowing the Emperor's ignorance of legal niceties I was puzzled by the new style until I learned that virtually all reports from ministers and the like, except those dealing with foreign affairs or defence, went to General Trepov, who, with the aid of Senator Garin, drafted the Emperor's comments and notations . . . As things turned out, Trepov had more influence over the Emperor than I did and was virtually the head of the government for which I bore responsibility.[26]

For the first time in his reign Nicholas II had acquired the beginnings of a Personal Secretariat which greatly increased his ability to act effectively as head of government. Witte's angry reaction to this development illustrates most ministers' belief that they should monopolize the flow of counsel and information to the monarch. Since Witte had become Prime Minister he believed that his sphere was now universal and was clearly intent on depriving the Tsar of most of his real power. Because neither Witte nor most other senior officials were prepared to concede the principle of popular sovereignty or make the government responsible to an elected legislature they had no alternative but to accept the concept of monarchical sovereignty as the source of ministerial legitimacy. This meant that the Emperor must have the right to appoint and dismiss his ministers. But once these ministers were in place, so Witte believed, the monarch must put his full trust in them and abstain from intervention. It is not difficult to see why Nicholas revolted against being turned by this means into a mere cipher. It is also easy to understand why Witte and other ministers wished him to become one.

As sovereign and sole source of political legitimacy Nicholas possessed enormous potential power. Unless that power was placed squarely behind ministers their task even in normal circumstances was very difficult. For a chairman of the Council of Ministers in the crisis-ridden last decade of the old regime it was impossible. The merest hint that the monarch disapproved of his policies, anticipated his fall or was adopting an independent stance would make it impossible for the premier to impose his will on the legislature, his bureaucratic subordinates and, above all, his ministerial colleagues. There was simply no room in the Russian system of government for two simultaneous chief executive officers, an emperor and a premier. Perhaps one could imagine circumstances in which the personalities involved would have made possible a trusting and stable partnership between the two office-holders. Conceivably the Gaullist constitution, with its powerful president and premier, offers a model for this. If so this model never became a reality in Nicholas II's Russia. And to do the Emperor justice, it was also never realized in Imperial Germany, Imperial Japan or the Iran of the Pahlavis, all of which had political systems rather akin to that which existed in late Imperial Russia.

To gain a sense of the dilemmas faced by Nicholas and the constraints under which he acted it is useful to stand back a little from the political battles of his day and to look at his regime from a comparative perspective. Traditionally a European monarch had been expected to lead his armies into battle and to conduct foreign policy but his role in domestic affairs was a limited one. Society was seen in basically static terms, its order reflecting divine and natural law. The ruler might have to raise taxes to support his armies but apart from this his duty was to arbitrate between conflicting groups and individuals on the basis of divine law, not to pursue an interventionist policy designed to transform his realm. The historian of the Roman imperial monarchy comments that 'it is the essential passivity of the role expected of the emperor both by himself and by others which explains the very limited and simple "governmental" apparatus which he needed.' Even in the heyday of the Spanish imperial monarchy the king was still seen 'as a judicial arbitrator between society's interest groups, rather than as an active intervenor'. It was the seventeenth and, above all, the eighteenth century which were responsible for introducing the idea that the state's role was to improve society by mobilizing its human and material resources. With the growth of cities, industry and education in the nineteenth century this duty entailed the creation of a large and complicated administrative machine. In Russia, as in some other relatively backward countries, this state bureaucracy was even larger and more formidable than elsewhere because it combined many of the police institutions of the old absolute monarchy with new ministries designed to encourage economic development in a society where government had to give private enterprise a considerable shove if capitalism was truly to take off. Unless he was on campaign a Roman emperor could easily combine his domestic governmental duties with the leisurely lifestyle enjoyed by Italy's upper class. By the twentieth century the demands on a sovereign who wished to control his government's affairs were far greater.[27]

Among the European powers Hohenzollern Prussia had traditionally been closest to Russia both in sympathy and in its system of government. It is true that after the 1848 revolution Prussia acquired a constitution, a parliament and a prime minister, which Russia was only to do after its own revolution of 1905. Because the Prussian king needed ministers who could steer legislation and budgets through parliament these ministers were on occasion able to play off crown and legislature, thereby at times achieving a degree of autonomy. In 1871 the picture was further confused when Prussia became the core of the new German Empire, a state which possessed both its own parliament, the Reichstag, and a number of other federal institutions which placed some constraints on the power of the German Emperor, King of Prussia. Most important, by 1900 Germany was a much more modern society than Russia with a well-developed public opinion and a free press which could thoroughly embarrass a monarch who indulged too blatantly in autocratic policies and gestures. Nevertheless the basic fact of Prussian and German politics was that ministers were responsible solely to the monarch, whose array of powers was awesome.

Between 1862 and 1890 the real ruler of this state was Otto von Bismarck, Prussia's Prime Minister and, from 1871, Chancellor of the new German Reich. Bismarck had partly won the trust of his master, Wilhelm I, by deft handling of the legislature. Far more important, however, was the fact that within four years of taking power Bismarck had defeated the liberal opposition, ended the seemingly insoluble constitutional crisis on the crown's terms, and secured Prussian domination of Central Europe. Had any Russian statesman won victories on this spectacular scale at such speed then it is more than possible that Nicholas II would have kept him in office for a very long time. But none did and in Russian circumstances it was barely conceivable that anyone could. In addition, however, Russian tradition did not smile on tsars who devolved their autocratic powers to others. The head of the House of Romanov was the heir of Peter the Great, Catherine II and Nicholas I. The monarchy's most devoted adherents usually called upon him to rule as well as reign. During the First World War the Empress Alexandra could urge her husband to 'be Peter the Great, John the Terrible, Emperor Paul – crush them all under you'. The less excitable General Kireev, in late 1904 mulling over plans to create a prime minister, could comment that the idea was both good and bad: good because it might increase inter-ministerial co-ordination, bad because a prime minister would 'completely hide' the Tsar, whereas the answer to Russia's problems was to make the monarch the real and effective head of government. The comment is particularly striking because it came from a man who knew Nicholas II quite well and had few illusions about his personality.[28]

In 1888 there ascended the Prussian throne a young monarch who was determined to rule as well as reign. Quite soon a number of key senior officials came to the conclusion that unless Wilhelm II was brought under ministerial control and deprived of real power Germany was headed for disaster. A key figure in this group was Friedrich von Holstein, who wrote in 1895 that 'the Kaiser as his own imperial chancellor would be questionable in any circumstances but especially now under this impulsive and unfortunately very superficial ruler'. During the 1890s a running battle occurred between Wilhelm and many of his more intelligent ministers. A particular target of the latter's wrath were the chiefs of the Emperor's civil and military cabinets, whom they often saw as shadow ministers who used their access to the monarch to sabotage the policies of the official government. The only way in which ministers could hope to control the Emperor was, however, for them all to threaten simultaneous resignation. Traditional conceptions of loyalty to the crown, together with individual ambition and the fact that ministers were not united by party ties or common political opinions, made this kind of concerted action impossible to sustain. The mere hint of ministerial 'strikes' infuriated Wilhelm II. Even if temporarily successful they aroused in him a determination in time to remove 'faithless servants' and strike-leaders. In the Kaiser's own words, 'I have the right and the duty . . . to be the leader of my people. I will also continue not to be deterred from following my conviction and practising the rights bestowed on me by God by the eternal fault-findings and intrigues I encounter.' One lesson of Germany in the 1890s which was relevant to Russia was that ministers who denied the principles of popular sovereignty and parliamentary government were in the long run incapable of controlling their acknowledged sovereign lord, the Emperor. But although Wilhelm II could undermine the authority of his Chancellor by personal intervention in politics and administration he was quite incapable himself of truly directing and co-ordinating government policy. As in Russia, the result was great confusion.[29]

In 1900 Bernhard von Bulow's appointment as Chancellor seemed to promise an improvement in this respect. Bulow was an old personal friend of Wilhelm, whose unlimited personal trust he retained for a number of years. As a result, Wilhelm's intervention in politics decreased temporarily. Armed with imperial support Bulow could impose unity on the Prussian ministers and found it easier to cajole the monarch into making occasional tactical concessions to the legislature. Both Bulow and Germany, however, paid a price for the Chancellor's absolute dependence on his personal relationship with the monarch. Constitutional reform or a curbing of naval armaments were ruled out, for instance, by Wilhelm's views. Correctly, given his reliance on Wilhelm, Bulow was obsessively concerned lest any other person gain the Emperor's ear or come between the Kaiser and his Chancellor. In an effort to drive the Kaiser out of politics Maximilian Harden, one of Germany's leading newspaper editors, destroyed Wilhelm's closest friend, Prince Philipp zu Eulenberg, by successfully pinning on him accusations of homosexuality. Though Bulow and Eulenberg were old friends, and old allies in the cause of Wilhelm's personal rule, the Chancellor appears to have connived at Harden's campaign in order to remove a dangerous rival. In the end, however, Bulow lost the Emperor's confidence. The complete failure of Bulow's foreign policy in 1905–6 undermined Wilhelm's previously limitless faith in his Chancellor. Meanwhile Bulow himself tired of the task of managing the Emperor's impossible personality and covering up for his irresponsible outbursts. When an incautious imperial interview in the *Daily Telegraph* united a wide cross-section of German parliamentary and press opinion in an effort to humiliate Wilhelm and force him to act with discretion, Bulow put up a feeble defence of his master in the Reichstag, thereby forfeiting Wilhelm's confidence and dooming his chances of remaining as Chancellor.

Nicholas II's Russia had no precise equivalent to Bernhard von Bulow. Not even Peter Stolypin, the premier from 1906 to 1911, stood as close to the Tsar as Bulow did to Wilhelm. Simultaneously attempting to manage both the monarch and the legislature was an exhausting experience shared by Russian and German statesmen after 1906, however. So too were incessant worries about the public display of full imperial support for a minister and concern about who might secretly be whispering in the monarch's ear. Moreover the publicizing by press and parliament of personal and sexual scandals in the monarch's entourage occurred in both Russia (after 1905) and Germany, and in both cases it was linked in part to efforts to undermine the monarch and push him out of politics. The way in which the Rasputin affair was used in Russia had a strong whiff about it of Harden's campaign against Eulenberg. Certainly both scandals represented the unhappy exposure of royal courts to the glare of the modern press and the questions of parliamentary deputies.

In 1889 the Japanese modelled their constitution on that of Prussia. A parliament was created and a prime minister also existed to co-ordinate government policies. As in Prussia the armed forces were kept entirely separate from both the legislature and the civil government, being subordinated in theory directly and exclusively to the monarch. Civilian ministers were also responsible not to parliament but to the Emperor. Sovereignty resided in the crown, from which all office-holders and indeed the entire political system drew their legitimacy.

In some respects similarities between the Japanese and German political systems existed not only on paper but also in practice. The armed forces in both countries were in practice controlled by no one and were a law unto themselves. Integrated military, diplomatic and political policy was impossible both in Berlin and Tokyo, a fact which led directly to militarily rational but politically insane decisions such as attacking France through Belgium in 1914 and launching the assault on Pearl Harbor in 1941. In

Russia before 1905 control over the armed forces was less of a problem, though colonial generals were inclined to thumb their noses at orders from Petersburg. Until the creation of a parliament and the Council of Ministers in 1905 Russian generals were far less worried than the Prussians and Japanese about stressing the armed forces' total divorce from the civilian ministries. After 1905, however, control over the armed forces did become a major political issue and in 1914–17 the gap between the civilian and military authorities was to yawn as wide as in First World War Germany or Second World War Japan. It was partly in order to bridge this gap that Nicholas II assumed personal command of the armed forces in 1915.

The most basic difference between Japan, on the one hand, and Germany and Russia, on the other, was, however, that in the former the monarch reigned but never attempted personally to rule. Japanese tradition was totally opposed to the Emperor actually attempting to act as the chief executive officer of his government. For centuries the Emperor's role had been purely ceremonial and priestly, actual power being exercised by the Shogun. In the last decades of the Tokugawa era even the Shogun did not rule personally, his powers being used by subordinates in his name. Although in theory the Meiji restoration returned power to the monarchy's hands, it was never the intention of the restoration's key statesmen that the monarch should literally run his own government like a Russian or German emperor. On the contrary, the monarchy's role was to provide legitimacy for the Meiji era's reformist oligarchy and to act as a symbol around which the Japanese nation could rally. As in Europe, however, one key reason for the oligarchy's determination to locate sovereignty in the Emperor was their opposition to accepting the only alternative principle, namely the sovereignty of the people exercised through elected institutions.

In a way that was not true even in Prussia, let alone Russia, court and government were always sharply separated in Meiji Japan. The court was the world of priestly rites and Confucian moral virtues, never of actual political rule. Though in theory the Emperor chose prime ministers, in fact they were selected by the *genro*, in other words the tiny group of elder statesmen who constituted a sort of supreme privy council and presented the monarch with a candidate whom he never rejected. Recommendations on policy were submitted to the crown in the unanimous name of the government. The Emperor was never asked to adjudicate personally between conflicting choices or groups, still less to devise his own policies and find ministers to support them. The traditions of the imperial house meant that the monarchs did not revolt against this passive role. The Emperor Meiji, for instance, is said to have rebuffed efforts to draw him more directly into government by commenting that 'when one views

[our] long history one sees that it is a mistake for those next to the throne to conduct politics'. In any case since no modern Japanese emperor, Meiji included, had ever possessed real political power there was never any question of the need to surrender it into the oligarchy's hands. When the Emperor Hirohito contemplated intervening personally to tilt the balance against military extremists in 1937 he was warned by the sole remaining *genro*, Prince Saionji, that the monarchy must not endanger itself by active political engagement. Only in the apocalyptic circumstances of 1945 did the monarch decisively enter the political arena and even then this happened because the government was split down the middle on the issue of peace or war and requested his intervention.[30]

Most Russian and Prussian senior officials by the twentieth century would have given almost anything for a system like the Japanese one, which preserved the legitimacy provided to oligarchical rule by the monarchy while ensuring that the monarch himself was silent and politically inactive. By 1912 the veteran president of the State Council, Michael Akimov, would certainly have been defined as an elder statesman, or *genro*, in Japan. In that year Akimov commented that 'our sovereign is the personification of the most complete uncertainty. You cannot hope to know and can't even guess what he will be up to tomorrow.' A.N. Naumov, a member of the State Council, recalled that 'Akimov looked on the personality of the monarch and his immediate entourage very pessimistically . . . According to him, among Petersburg statesmen there had more than once arisen the question of how to protect the throne from chance backstairs influences, and to form around it a special Supreme Council (on the Japanese model).'[31]

Unlike the Emperor Meiji, however, Nicholas II exercised real power, believed it was his duty to continue to do so, and would not be removed from the political arena without a struggle. Least of all would the Emperor willingly surrender power to an oligarchy of senior bureaucrats such as the Japanese *genro*. One has to remember that in Russia state officialdom enjoyed far less prestige than in Japan or Germany. Indeed the one point on which most articulate Russians tended to agree was their loathing for the bureaucracy, which was blamed for most of the country's ills. This was particularly true in the aristocratic and conservative nationalist circles which enjoyed the easiest access to Nicholas and with which he often sympathized. Thus in December 1904, for instance, General Kireev, who was both an aristocrat and a nationalist, wrote to the Tsar that 'everyone knows, Your Majesty, that you don't nourish any great trust in the bureaucracy and everyone rejoiced and rejoices in this . . . Society sees in the bureaucracy the cause of all our evils and discord.' Faced with such attacks on the bureaucracy and constantly confronted with appeals to protect individuals from the injustice or inaction of his officials, it was

hard to expect the Emperor to abdicate his powers in favour of officialdom's senior representatives.[32]

Nicholas's ideal of Russian monarchy made him very disinclined to
accept the role of a mere symbol and source of legitimacy for the rule of
some coalition of élites. He believed very strongly in the union of
Tsar and people. In Peter Bark's words, 'in his opinion the peasant question was the main one'. Nicholas always felt uplifted at moments of communion with his people; at Easter services in Moscow; at the celebrations
of the anniversaries of the battles of Poltava and Borodino; during his
journey through the Russian provinces to celebrate the dynasty's tercen-
tenary. Though no doubt his self-portrayal as the peasants' Tsar was good
propaganda, since peasants after all made up the overwhelming majority
of his subjects, it also came from the heart. Nicholas would certainly have
agreed with his sister Olga's opinion that the Russian peasant was in
general both more honest and more Christian than members of the upper
classes, let alone the intelligentsia. Like her, he believed that the 'truly
dedicated affection' of peasant Russia for the Tsar 'embraced their feelings
for God and their country' and 'was the main support of the Romanov
sovereigns in their unrewarding task of wielding absolute power'. If the
peasants sometimes opposed his government's policies and had to be
treated with a firm hand, this was because they were immature and easily
misled by outside agitators as to their own interests. Alternatively, they
were being mistreated by capitalists, bureaucrats or Jews. No doubt such
rationalizations appear self-serving and naïve to most modern scholars
and perhaps they were so, but no one can doubt Nicholas's sincerity in
this matter. He saw himself as his people's father, and a parent does not
abdicate responsibility for his or her children's welfare however ungrateful
the child or unrewarding the task.[33]

Autocrats seldom renounce their power willingly to become mere
symbols of sovereignty and legitimacy. Nor is it always a pleasant or safe
existence to be the powerless totem pole of this or that oligarchy acting in
one's name. In the 1930s the Emperor Hirohito suffered the frustration of
seeing expansionist military policies of which he disapproved pursued in
his name. It made matters worse that it was those who proclaimed their
devotion to him most fervently who were most inclined to ignore his
wishes. In 1936 he faced the ultimate humiliation of a revolt by officers of
the imperial guard who murdered or attempted to murder many of his
leading servants in the name of devotion to the imperial house. One could
no doubt argue that Hirohito's ultimate fate, along with that of the
Japanese monarchy, was nevertheless preferable to that of the Romanovs,
Hohenzollerns and Pahlavis. To say this is, however, to read history
backwards. In the modern era Emperor Hirohito is the exception to the
rule that dynasties and their heads seldom survive lost wars. In Allied

circles the wartime debate over the fate of both the Emperor and the monarchy was fierce and its outcome far from certain. Having surrendered its fate into the hands of fascism the House of Savoy was ultimately pulled down by Mussolini's lost war and the same could easily have happened in Japan.[34]

The last Shah of Iran certainly came to understand in the first period of his reign just how precarious and humiliating could be the life of a monarch who exercised no real power. This experience is one explanation for Mohammed Reza's later insistence on an extreme and grandiose autocratic regime. In Iran the world witnessed, almost certainly for the last time, an attempt at enlightened royal despotism, though admittedly by the monarch of a very new dynasty. The problems encountered by the Shah are a warning to those who believe that, had the Romanovs produced a would-be Peter the Great in 1894, the dynasty's future would have been secure. As we have seen, there are some rather surprising similarities between the personalities of Mohammed Reza and Nicholas II. The former was, however, not merely superficially more imposing but also loved politics and power in a way that Nicholas did not. In addition the Shah's childhood, Iran's constant humiliations at the hands of the great powers, and the Pahlavis' own position as parvenus created a monarch driven by insecurities and resentments in a way that was certainly not true of Nicholas II.

There are, however, interesting parallels between autocratic government and the problems it encountered in Russia and Iran. One banal but important point is that a man who inherits a throne when still young is expected to bear the burdens of political leadership throughout his life. Given the pressures on even a half-conscientious political leader in the modern world, this is more than the human frame can bear. After all, it is a very rare politician indeed in a contemporary Western democracy who holds the top executive office for over ten years in a row. Moreover, politicians choose their career and prove they possess the temperament to go with the job. This is not true of monarchs. Nicholas II had an almost obsessive need for fresh air and physical exercise. Mohammed Reza was equally obsessed by young women and aeroplanes. None of this was an adequate antidote to a lifetime's work as both chief executive and head of state. Not surprisingly, by the last years of their reigns both Mohammed Reza and Nicholas II were showing signs of physical and mental exhaustion. Nor, after a lifetime of isolation behind a fog of courtiers' flattery, was either monarch proof against many illusions about his regime's stability and popularity.

As autocrats both Nicholas II and Mohammed Reza were overburdened by trivia but often regarded subordinates' attempts to reduce this workload as subtle efforts to encroach on imperial power. In 1971 the Shah's

Minister of the Imperial Court, Asadollah Alam, pointed out to his over-stretched master that 'by no means all of this work is essential. "The burden could easily be reduced", I said, "but whenever I make any suggestion you merely accuse me of empire-building. What can I do if you won't trust me?" '

Like Nicholas II, though to a somewhat lesser extent, Mohammed Reza's autocratic tendencies undermined his prime ministers' authority and made it impossible for them to control, balance and co-ordinate government policy. Yet the monarch himself proved incapable of impos-ing this unity by his own efforts, despite the fact that he had a pro-gramme, a quite impressive personality and worked hard. In Alam's view part of the reason for this lay in the weakness of the Shah's personal secre-tariat. In January 1971 Alam told the Shah that 'the modern world demands deep thought and penetrating analysis; every problem requires examination by first-rate experts before its submission to you'. Admitting that the head of the personal secretariat was 'honest and loyal', Alam nevertheless added that 'he has next to no academic qualifications. He never attended university, speaks no language other than Persian and has no grasp of the problems of the modern world'. Alam confided to his diary that evening:

> More and more I get the impression that national affairs are uncoordinated with no firm hand on the tiller, all because the captain himself is overworked. Every minister and high official receives a separate set of instructions direct from H.I.M. and the result is that individual details often fail to mesh with any overall framework. Thank God, the Shah is a strong man, but he's no computer; he cannot be expected to remember every one of the thousands of instructions he issues each week. Occasionally one set of instructions contra-dicts another.[35]

A year later Alam returned to the same subject in conversation with the Shah. 'I reminded him', wrote Alam in his diary,

> that at present each minister receives his orders direct from H.I.M. Once such orders have been issued the minister in question quite naturally tends to ignore the wider aspects of government policy. On occasion this has led to something little short of chaos and has severely disrupted the co-ordination of any overall policy. There is a pressing need for a regulatory authority, which would best be located in H.I.M.'s personal secretariat. But H.I.M. would have none of this and asked straight out, 'Did anyone ever "advise" me to achieve the many great things I have done for this country?' 'Of course not, Your Majesty,' I told him, 'but the issues which face you today are of much greater technical complexity. No one could cope with all of them single-handed' . . . He made no reply.[36]

More than sixty years after the fall of the Romanovs the government of the Pahlavis collapsed in the face of revolution on the streets of the capital. The imperial regimes of Russia and Iran differed in many ways, as did the causes of their collapse, the people whom they governed, and the eras in which they existed. But when one reads the diary of the Shah's Minister of the Imperial Court the echoes from the Russia of Nicholas II are often very strong.

CHAPTER 6

The Years of Revolution, 1904–1907

On 28 July 1904 Vyacheslav Plehve, the Minister of Internal Affairs, was travelling through Petersburg *en route* to an audience with the Tsar. Not far from the Warsaw railway station a young Socialist Revolutionary, Yegor Sazonov, hurled a bomb which shattered Plehve's carriage and killed the minister. That evening Nicholas wrote in his diary, 'in the person of the good Plehve I have lost a friend and an irreplaceable Minister of Internal Affairs'. Such a statement in the Emperor's laconic daily record was the equivalent of pages of tearful comment in another man's diary. Nicholas had known Plehve since before his accession to the throne. Still worse, the Minister of Internal Affairs had been the linchpin of the Emperor's domestic policy.[1]

Few of Plehve's contemporaries even among senior officials shared Nicholas's sorrow at the minister's death. At best their reaction was similar to that of Prince Alexander Obolensky. 'Not many people would probably feel any sincere sorrow for him but the event itself, especially since it comes shortly after the killing of Bobrikov, has an oppressive effect and inspires no very confident thoughts.' Two years earlier senior official-dom had greeted Plehve's appointment as Minister of Internal Affairs very differently. Even the relatively liberal Anatol Kulomzin had written to his wife,

> I finally calmed down today when I read about V. K. Plehve's appointment as Minister of Internal Affairs . . . This was the only sensible appointment but rumours were going around about Bobrikov. Plehve knows the Governors, knows police business and will put everything in order. This is the general calming feeling which has seized everything and everyone . . . What is needed is a clever man who won't hound the *zemstvos* and won't agree with Witte about everything.[2]

During Plehve's two years in office much had happened to cause the collapse in sympathy for the minister. For the general public, especially outside Russia, the most shocking event had been the pogrom which struck the Jewish community of Kishinev in April 1903, killing forty-seven people. This was the first major outbreak of anti-Semitic violence since the 1880s and it had occurred partly because of the inaction, and in some cases even connivance, of many local officials. Plehve's anti-Semitism was notorious and rumour quickly blamed the minister for inciting the pogrom to distract attention from Russia's domestic problems. A skilfully forged letter to this effect from Plehve to von Raaben, the Governor of Bessarabia, was widely circulated and believed. In fact Plehve was innocent of this charge, above all because, like all other top officials, he was far too terrified of anarchy to take the risk of inciting mob violence. But the pogrom badly damaged the government's prestige and even those who realized that Plehve bore no direct responsibility for events in Kishinev argued, with reason, that the minister's open dislike of the Jews encouraged some of his subordinates to feel that they faced little risk in turning a blind eye to anti-Semitic violence.[3]

In conservative and high official circles, however, the pogrom at Kishinev was not the main cause of complaint against Plehve. While many senior officials deplored the savagery and loss of life, more regretted the pogrom's impact on Russian prestige in Europe. But in these circles the Jews had few friends. Plehve was above all blamed for following a purely repressive domestic policy, in the process alienating from the regime loyal members of the educated classes. A.A. Kireev greatly admired Plehve. By the summer of 1903, however, even he was becoming exasperated by what he saw as the minister's exclusively bureaucratic approach to solving Russia's problems. In August 1903 Kireev commented that Plehve was to blame for the fact that his position was weakening. It was simply not possible to govern a modern country by police methods and without the support of any substantial element of educated society. Few provincial nobilities in Russia were less liberal than that of Kursk. The Marshal of the nobility of Belgorod district, Kursk province, was the extremely conservative Count V.F. Dorrer. Even he was driven to protest when Plehve sought to force a fellow Marshal to retire for political reasons, in the process infringing the autonomy which Catherine II had granted to the provincial noble corporations in 1785.[4]

Plehve's strategy was rooted in his belief that the masses were more loyal to the regime than the élites. Above all, in his view, the peasantry and the army were still reliable. Intelligent, purposeful reforms had to come from above, in other words from the government. Concessions to liberal members of the upper and middle classes were both useless and dangerous because these groups were weak and deferred to the radical left. To use Plehve's own metaphor, Russian society was a raging torrent which only a powerful and self-confident government could dam and channel. Liberals would open up so many holes in the dam and allow the revolutionaries such freedom and encouragement that the whole structure would be swept away. The machinery of government required a radical overhaul, one element of which needed to be decentralization and a more co-ordinated and efficient relationship between the bureaucracy and the *zemstvos*. But Plehve was adamant in trying to minimize the opportunities for educated Russians and the organizations they created to secure greater autonomy from the regime. In his view, to give potential opposition leaders more freedom and room for manoeuvre would be suicidal, since they would use this freedom to destroy the authoritarian regime on which Russian political stability rested.[5]

Plehve's sudden death faced Nicholas with the choice of a new Minister of Internal Affairs. Three candidates for the job were widely canvassed. One was Plehve's assistant minister, General Victor von Wahl. Wahl was an unimaginative, rather brutal but quite efficient policeman who could be trusted to carry out an unwavering policy of repression if ordered to do so. Another alternative was Boris Sturmer, who had won a good reputation as a provincial governor and was currently the head of one of the key departments of the Ministry of Internal Affairs. Sturmer's political views did not differ greatly from those of Wahl and Plehve but he was known for his ability to smooth over conflicts and achieve a *modus vivendi* with liberally inclined provincial noblemen. The third candidate was Prince Peter Svyatopolk-Mirsky, the Governor-General of Lithuania and part of Belorussia. Unlike Wahl, Plehve and Sturmer, Svyatopolk-Mirsky was a great landowning aristocrat and a member of Petersburg high society. In common with many of his peers, Svyatopolk-Mirsky inclined to rather Whiggish anti-bureaucratic opinions and enjoyed the sympathy of the Dowager Empress Marie. Before Plehve's death Nicholas had shown no sign of dissatisfaction with his minister's policy. It therefore seemed logical to expect that Plehve would be succeeded by Wahl or Sturmer, since they came closest to sharing their dead chief's policy and opinions.

What happened is explained – probably accurately – in a letter from the Grand Marshal of the Court (*Oberhofmarshal*) Count Paul Benckendorff to his brother, the Russian ambassador in London. 'Wahl was going to be appointed Minister of Internal Affairs. A *scène de famille*, during which one [the Empress Marie] almost threw oneself at his [Nicholas II's] knees, stopped this nomination.' Instead Svyatopolk-Mirsky was appointed, little attention being paid to the great differences between his and his predecessor's political views. Benckendorff commented that 'one cannot absolutely change one's political colour just to give one's mother pleasure'. In the Grand Marshal's opinion, the appointment was of a piece with other decisions made by the Tsar at this time. 'Everything was understood in the wrong way and one only paid attention to trivia.' Matters were not thought through properly. Svyatopolk-Mirsky's appointment would only have made sense if a fundamental decision had been made to re-orient the state's whole domestic policy. Even if this had been the case, Svyatopolk-Mirsky was the wrong man for the job. 'The poor boy has neither the health nor the personality for this position.' In fact, though the new minister had no doubt made his 'profession of faith' to Nicholas, the latter was not committed to a consistent policy of liberalization. Once Svyatopolk-Mirsky began to embark on such a policy he would run into 'passionate opposition' from conservative officials who, up to the moment of Plehve's death, had been following a strategy of repression with the Emperor's publicly expressed support. The inevitable result would be confusion.[6]

Svyatopolk-Mirsky's appointment was a classic example of the Romanov 'family firm' in operation. No doubt the Empress Marie was spurred into action more by political than personal motives. Very much *au fait* with the opinions of Petersburg high society, she shared its resentment at Plehve's methods and its conviction that his policy could only lead to revolution. Undoubtedly, her pleas partly convinced Nicholas that some concessions to society were needed. Nevertheless this was scarcely a very sensible way to make a key appointment at a crucial moment for the future of both the imperial regime and Russia.

Svyatopolk-Mirsky himself tried to dissuade Nicholas from the nomination. He told the Emperor on 7 September, 'you barely know me and perhaps think that I share the views of the two previous ministers; on the contrary I have precisely the opposite views . . . The state of affairs is such that one can consider the government in hostilities with Russia; reconciliation is necessary, otherwise we will soon reach the situation in which Russia is divided into those who are under police surveillance and those who are carrying it out. And what then?' The new minister then set out his 'programme' to the Tsar, which included religious toleration, autonomy and expansion for the *zemstvos*, civil rights, and the need to consult elected representatives of local society on central government policy and legislation. To all of this Nicholas seemingly agreed, delighted as always to find a top official who shrank from ministerial office rather than grabbing it with ambitious and power-hungry hands.[7]

Disillusionment soon set in on both sides. Svyatopolk-Mirsky spoke in eloquent but rather nebulous terms to the press about a new era of trust and reconciliation between government and society, in the process unleashing a torrent of hopes about fundamental political change. In early October the Grand Duke Constantine, an intelligent and decent cousin of the Emperor, wrote in his diary that the new minister had come to dinner. 'He makes a good impression by his broad views. It frightens me that everyone – society and the press – are very carried away by him. How can disenchantment not follow, since in the nature of things it will be impossible for him to put into effect much of what he would like to do?' Very soon Svyatopolk-Mirsky found himself under increasing pressure from a growing liberal movement which wanted to go much further than the minister desired or the Tsar would allow. Paul Benckendorff commented that Svyatopolk-Mirsky 'is very astonished by what is going on' and was bewildered by the forces he had unleashed. Public opinion was getting more and more excited but the minister, bereft of firm ideas, had no hope of steering it. Conservatives, led by the Grand Duke Serge, sought to persuade Nicholas II to stop Svyatopolk-Mirsky's reforms, warning him that otherwise the regime was doomed. The Minister of Internal Affairs, on the contrary, told the Tsar that 'if you don't carry out liberal reforms and don't satisfy the completely natural wishes of everyone then change will come but in the form of revolution'.[8]

The denouement came in December 1904 when the Emperor presided over a conference of ministers, grand dukes and other top officials to discuss Svyatopolk-Mirsky's ten-point programme of reforms. The latter included not only promises of civil rights but also a proposal that elected representatives of society participate in discussing legislation and central government policy. Under strong pressure from the Grand Duke Serge and warned by Witte that Svyatopolk-Mirsky's proposal was a long step towards a constitution, Nicholas rejected the key point of his minister's proposal. The Emperor commented that 'I will never agree to a representative form of government because I consider it harmful to the people whom God has entrusted to me.' What remained of Svyatopolk-Mirsky's programme after the conference, namely some rather vague promises of civil rights, would not satisfy society. Reading the decree which followed the conference, the very loyal and conservative Prince Alexander Obolensky wrote to his wife, 'I will admit to you that it made a sad impression on me. All this smacks of insincerity, of an act which was forced on them by the need to promise something in whose saving grace they don't really believe.'[9]

The deep suspicion that reigned between Nicholas and Svyatopolk-Mirsky by December 1904 is well illustrated in the words of the two men's wives. For Princess Svyatopolk-Mirsky the Tsar was 'the most false man in the world', who said one thing to a minister's face and another behind his back. He was 'indifferent and blind' to what was happening in Russia, incapable of understanding that the existing system of 'arbitrariness and bureaucratic wrongdoing' was turning even naturally conservative owners of property into enemies of the government. For Nicholas autocracy was, in her view, a sort of absurd 'fetishism'. The Emperor was the perfect 'embodiment of infirm degeneracy, into whose head they have beaten the idea that he must be strong. And there's nothing worse than a weak man who wants to be firm.' Under cover of the Tsar bureaucracy ruled supreme. Her husband had failed in his efforts to bring European standards to Russia because 'in his character and ideas he was opposed to all the traditions of bureaucratism and wanted to give goys access to the Holy of Holies', in other words to allow representatives of society some say in political affairs. The bureaucrats were too powerful, however, to allow such a reform to go through. Princess Svyatopolk-Mirsky's diary is an accurate reflection of the values and opinions of Petersburg aristocratic liberalism. In early September 1904, for instance, she quoted with seeming approval her husband's comment to Nicholas II that there was no cause to repress gatherings of workers for 'in England no constraints whatever are placed on the social movement but the rights of property are incomparably better protected than in our country'. Subsequently, in January 1905, when a huge crowd of workers attempting to present a petition to Nicholas II was fired upon by the Petersburg garrison, the Princess changed her mind. 'It is sufficient to start any sort of robbery or assault and then in a crowd of 150,000 it is hard to say what would have happened . . . it was impossible to allow a huge crowd to gather on Palace Square.'[10]

Not surprisingly, the Empress Alexandra's interpretation of political developments was very different to that of Princess Svyatopolk-Mirsky. At the beginning of 1905 she wrote to her eldest sister, Princess Louis of Battenberg, that

> the Minister of Internal Affairs is doing the greatest harm. He proclaims grand things without having prepared them. It's like a horse that has been held very tight in hand, and then suddenly one lets the reins go. It bolts, falls and it is more than difficult to pull it up again before it has dragged others with it into the ditch. Reforms can only be made gently with the greatest care and forethought. Now we have precipitately been launched forth and cannot retrace our steps.

In the same letter the Empress expressed a view which was as central to her political instincts as hatred of bureaucracy was to Petersburg aristocratic society: 'Petersburg is a rotten town, not an atom Russian. The Russian people are deeply and truly devoted to their Sovereign.'[11]

Underlying the mutual recriminations between Nicholas II and Svyatopolk-Mirsky there was a deeper problem. In his classic study of the origins of the French Revolution Alexis de Tocqueville commented that the most dangerous moment for a repressive regime was when it began to reform itself. Under a resolute and united authoritarian government, opposition was deterred by the knowledge that it would be repressed without hesitation or mercy. Once the government began to allow greater leeway to society, however, difficulties mounted. Brave spirits were tempted to see how far freedom could be pushed. For the government, finding the right mix of repression and concession required much more skill and judgement than simply sticking to an unwavering policy of coercion. As reforms were introduced and society began to emancipate itself from the regime's control, splits almost inevitably occurred within the government between those who argued that change was coming too rapidly and others who claimed it was not coming fast enough. Both sides tended to believe that their opponents' line threatened political stability and the regime's survival. Divisions within the government led to uncoordinated and tentative actions which themselves encouraged the regime's opponents. Prince V.P. Meshchersky, the very conservative editor of *Grazhdanin*, made most of these points in an editorial which appeared shortly after Svyatopolk-Mirsky announced the onset of an era of trust between government and society. Meshchersky added that in Russia at present ordered reform would be particularly difficult since the government's prestige was low, many of its enemies were irreconcilable, and reforms could easily be interpreted as concessions born of fear and weakness. Meshchersky was a reactionary, a homosexual, a past-master at Petersburg intrigue and a well-known unofficial adviser to both Alexander III and Nicholas II. For all these reasons he was widely hated by his contemporaries and has enjoyed a very bad press with historians. But the Prince was not stupid and on this occasion, as on many others, his political analysis was quite shrewd.[12]

By December 1904 it was clear that Svyatopolk-Mirsky had lost Nicholas II's confidence and could not survive in office much longer. Svyatopolk-Mirsky himself was convinced that he was not suited for the job. Even in October he had told the Emperor, 'no – I am not a minister'. Six weeks later he commented that 'it is not in his [that is, Svyatopolk-Mirsky's] character to battle constantly'. His wife added that her husband was a far less effective and ruthless political operator than those against whom he had to struggle in the Petersburg political jungle. Both Count Paul Benckendorff and Vladimir Gurko, a senior official in the Ministry of Internal Affairs, agreed that Svyatopolk-Mirsky lacked energy, drive or force. For Gurko, Svyatopolk-Mirsky was another example of an aristocratic amateur attempting to do a job best left to tough and experienced professionals.

> His outstanding trait was a desire to remain at peace with everyone and live in an atmosphere of friendship. It was not that he sought popularity but simply that by his very nature he could not irritate anyone . . . His marriage with Countess Bobrinsky had brought him great riches and opened the road to preferment . . . By the time the Prince was appointed Minister of the Interior he had undoubtedly acquired some political opinions, but they were those of

the man in the street. He never did realise the responsibility for the peace of the state which his new position placed upon him . . . He had entered the office of Minister of the Interior with a light heart. He left it in the same way to make the centre of his existence the fashionable Yacht Club.[13]

One result of Svyatopolk-Mirsky's period in office was that the Ministry of Internal Affairs completely lost control over the workers' movement in Petersburg. Though Plehve had been wary of Zubatov, he had allowed a watered-down version of Zubatov's unions to exist in Petersburg under a priest, Gapon. Supposedly, these unions were simply to provide workers with concerts, excursions and other harmless forms of relaxation. Zubatov, an intelligent and professional police chief, had understood that police trade unions had to be closely and carefully supervised otherwise they could result in a labour movement organized by the government being captured by its opponents and escaping from the regime's control. By 1904 the Petersburg police leadership was much less careful and professional than Zubatov had been. Even while Plehve was still alive, Gapon was being converted to socialism by the lieutenants whom he was supposedly using on the government's behalf to create a loyal workers' movement. 'By March 1904 he conspiratorially revealed a "plan" to his group, a radical plan aiming at civil liberties, a responsible ministry, the eight-hour day, unions, universal education, and sweeping land reform, a plan they [his supposed lieutenants] had put in his mind in the first place.' Throughout 1904 the police regarded Gapon as loyal and left him unsupervised, though by the autumn the threat represented by his movement should have been clear. Suddenly, in January 1905, the government was faced with Gapon's plan to lead a huge demonstration to the Winter Palace to demand a string of very radical political and economic reforms, including the convocation of a constituent assembly.[14]

It was inconceivable that Nicholas II would personally accept such demands, presented by a huge demonstration in terms little short of an ultimatum. The question was, what to do about the demonstration. Like Communist regimes in the late 1980s, the tsarist government, having always banned demonstrations, had no experience of dealing with them and no policemen trained to handle them. In any event the Russian government was much too poor to employ the number of policemen required to cope with a crowd of this size. The only option therefore was to call in the army. Bringing in the troops was, however, very dangerous. Soldiers had neither the training nor the equipment to control large crowds or act as riot police. Even given its narrow range of options, however, the government's response to Gapon's demonstration was clumsy and cruel. Cavalry and cossacks were brutal and terrifying when used to disperse crowds but at least their whips and the flat sides of their sabres seldom killed anyone. In contrast, infantry turned out against crowds were in general either ineffective or lethal. Always outnumbered and armed with nothing but their rifles, their only way to stop or disperse crowds was by using their firearms. This is what happened on Bloody Sunday, 22 January 1905, when Gapon's demonstration tried to push its way through to the Winter Palace at the heart of official Petersburg. Over a hundred demonstrators were killed and many more were wounded. It is difficult to dispute the subsequent judgement of Peter Durnovo, the very intelligent former head of the Police Department, that 'it is in many circumstances possible to avoid battles with the troops . . . The mistake had been to summon infantry units whereas it would have been more appropriate to limit oneself to cossacks and cavalry, who could disperse the crowd with whips, especially since the demonstrators were not armed.'[15]

The massacre of unarmed workers in the centre of the empire's capital was a disastrous blow to the regime's prestige both at home and abroad. Nicholas commented in his diary that evening: 'a sad day. In Petersburg serious disorders occurred as a consequence of the workers' wish to reach the Winter Palace. The troops had to open fire in various parts of the town and there were many killed and wounded. Lord, how painful and sad.' The fact that most demonstrators were quite sincere in their hope that the monarch would respond to their petition and some even carried his portrait made matters worse. At a time when new ideas were spreading among an increasingly literate peasantry an event such as Bloody Sunday was an exceptionally dangerous affront to the people's traditional faith in their ruler's benevolence.[16]

Nevertheless it would be naïve to follow Lenin in asserting that Bloody Sunday spelled the end of the people's faith in the Tsar. Loyalties as deeply rooted as Russian peasant monarchism do not disappear overnight, especially when a very large number of those who hold these beliefs are illiterate villagers living in the back of beyond. Plentiful evidence exists that much peasant faith in the Tsar survived not only Bloody Sunday but also the many other shocks this traditional set of beliefs received between 1905 and 1907. The Soviet historian A. Avrekh commented that even 'the Trudoviki – who were the conscious expression of the interests and dreams of the revolutionary [section of the] peasantry, and who put forward in their programme a wide range of democratic freedoms and reforms, up to and including the convocation of a constituent assembly and the confiscation of all landowners' estates, never advanced the slogan of a republic'. Nor were these Russian radicals unique either in refraining from a direct attack on the monarchy or in understanding that the Russian peasant made a distinction between the Emperor on the one hand and oppressive élites and political institutions on the other. During the Second World War the

Japanese Communist Nosaka Sanzo told a Chinese Communist party conference that

> the Japanese people may hold the Emperor . . . in religious awe, but they do not worship the system of despotic rule. We must abolish the Emperor system immediately and establish a democratic system . . . However, we must be very careful in defining our attitude to . . . his [the Emperor's] semi-religious influence . . . Many soldiers captured by the [Communist] Eighth Route Army said they could agree with the [Communist] ideology, but if they sought to destroy the emperor, they would be opposed. This can be seen as a general pattern of thought held by the majority of the Japanese people.[17]

Although Bloody Sunday raised the political temperature, it did not change the basic course of government policy. As before, the regime sought to restore stability through a combination of concessions and repression. As tends to happen under such circumstances, the concessions were insufficient to pacify opposition but did persuade the regime's enemies that tsarism was on the run. Meanwhile the degree of repression sufficed to anger but not to subdue the population. Some ministers, with A.S. Ermolov in the lead, urged Nicholas to convoke an assembly drawn from all classes of the population and to listen to its advice 'before it is too late'. And indeed, in early March, a manifesto announced that a consultative elected assembly would be convoked. On the other hand, to take but one example, General D.F. Trepov, the newly appointed Governor-General of Petersburg, warned that further concessions 'will completely shatter power and satisfy nobody'. The old complaint about government disunity was heard more and more loudly, and pressure mounted on Nicholas to agree to the creation of a prime minister who could co-ordinate policy. At the same time, however, Serge Witte's ambition to force his way back to office in the guise of tsarism's saviour caused fear and alarm not only to Nicholas but also to many other members of the political élite.[18]

As always the Emperor remained deeply unwilling to surrender his autocratic power. He told Svyatopolk-Mirsky in October 1904: 'You know, I don't hold to autocracy for my own pleasure. I act in this sense only because I am convinced that it is necessary for Russia. If it was simply a question of myself I would happily get rid of all this.' Some of the factors behind Nicholas's stubborn defence of autocracy are well-known and have already been discussed. They include his conviction that supreme power was an obligation he had received from God at his coronation and was therefore a responsibility he had no right to thrust on to the shoulders of others. Also important was his sense of his family's hereditary privilege and duty to exercise power over their Russian land. In 1905 these religious and dynastic instincts were strongly upheld by the Empress Alexandra, who began to play a, albeit still minor, role in Russian domestic politics for the first time and whose opposition to any retreat from autocracy was described by Paul Benckendorff in June 1905 as 'ferocious'.[19]

It would, however, be wrong simply to ascribe Nicholas's defence of autocracy to wifely pressure or the Tsar's religious or dynastic instincts. More down-to-earth and rational calculations also played their part. Ever since Alexander II had initiated his policy of 'modernization from above' in the late 1850s, the crown had periodically come under pressure to concede part of its power to a representative assembly. Alexander's response to this pressure when it first occurred in 1861 was expressed in terms with which both his son and his grandson would certainly have concurred.

Alexander II explained to Otto von Bismarck, who was then the Prussian minister in Petersburg, that

> the idea of taking counsel of subjects other than officials was not in itself objectionable and that greater participation by respectable notables in official business could only be advantageous. The difficulty, if not impossibility, of putting this principle into effect lay only in the experience of history that it had never been possible to stop a country's liberal development at the point beyond which it should not go. This would be particularly difficult in Russia, where the necessary political culture, thoughtfulness and circumspection were only to be found in relatively small circles. Russia must not be judged by Petersburg, of all the empire's towns the least Russian one . . . The revolutionary party would not find it easy to corrupt the people's convictions and make the masses conceive their interests to be divorced from those of the dynasty. The Emperor continued that 'throughout the interior of the empire the people still see the monarch as the paternal and absolute Lord set by God over the land; this belief, which has almost the force of a religious sentiment, is completely independent of any personal loyalty of which I could be the object. I like to think that it will not be lacking too in the future. To abdicate the absolute power with which my crown is invested would be to undermine the aura of that authority which has dominion over the nation. The deep respect, based on an innate sentiment, with which right up to now the Russian people surrounds the throne of its Emperor cannot be parcelled out. I would diminish without any compensation the authority of the government if I wanted to allow representatives of the nobility or the nation to participate in it. Above all, God knows what would become of relations between the peasants and the lords if the authority of the Emperor was not still sufficiently intact to exercise the dominating influence.'[20]

Nicholas II's own ideas were very close to those of his grandfather. Once, during the First World War, he spoke to his neighbour at dinner, a senior British general, 'about empires and republics'. The Emperor commented that

> his own ideas as a young man were that he had, of course, a great responsibility, and felt that the people over whom he ruled were so numerous and so varying in blood and temperament, different altogether from our Western Europeans, that an Emperor was a vital necessity to them. His first visit to the Caucasus had made a great impression on him and confirmed him in his views. The United States of America, he said, was an entirely different matter and the two cases could not be compared. In this country, many as were the problems and the difficulties, their sense of imagination, their intense religious feeling and their habits and customs generally made a crown necessary, and he believed this must be so for a very long time, that a certain amount of decentralisation of authority was of course necessary, but that the great and decisive power must rest with the Crown.

To some extent the Emperor's view of his people was an old-fashioned one. Literacy and the disciplines of a capitalist economy were changing Russian habits and mentalities. Such changes do not, however, occur overnight nor indeed could even capitalism turn Russians into Anglo-Saxons. Moreover, change was anything but painless and it exacerbated the class conflict to which Alexander II had referred a half-century before. After listening to Alexander's words Bismarck commented that if the masses lost faith in the crown's absolute power the risk of a murderous peasant war would become very great. He concluded that 'His Majesty can still rely on the common man both in the army and among the civilian masses but the "educated classes", with the exception of the older generation, are stoking the fires of a revolution which, if it comes to power, would immediately turn against themselves.' Events were to show that this prophecy was as relevant in Nicholas II's era as it had been during the reign of his grandfather.[21]

To understand the Tsar's dilemma it is worth recalling the immediate origins of the French revolution. Certainly, the fate of Louis XVI weighed very heavily on the minds of nineteenth-century old regime monarchs. In the mid-1780s the French absolute monarchy had come under great pressure from the country's élite to concede some form of constitutional government. Bowing to this pressure, the King summoned the Estates General, a long defunct body drawn from the various estates of the realm whose power was in theory purely advisory. Very similar were the calls by which Nicholas was surrounded in 1905 to summon some sort of consultative assembly drawn from 'all estates of the Russian land'. Convoking the Estates General aroused great expectations among the previously rather inert French masses. Very soon the assembly began to assert its claims to

much more than purely consultative power. Still worse, opening up political debate created conditions in which latent tensions between classes
exploded. The army, officered by nobles and manned by members of the
lower classes, began to disintegrate under the influence of these tensions,
especially after being employed for two or three years in a domestic police
and peace-keeping role. The result was full-scale revolution, the fall of the
monarchy and civil war. There were quite enough similarities between
France in 1789 and Russia in 1905 to give pause for thought. Not for
nothing did senior officials shudder when they saw the portrait of Marie
Antoinette, a rather tactless gift from the French government, hanging in
the apartments of the Empress Alexandra. Nor was Paul Benckendorff
unique in believing, in June 1905, that any Russian parliament would
quickly devise its own electoral law and turn into a constituent assembly.[22]

The war with Japan greatly worsened the domestic political crisis.
Writing to his brother, the ambassador in London, in the winter of
1903–4 about this 'absurd but likely war', Count Benckendorff commented that no one in Russia wanted war with Japan, understood why it
should be fought or took any real interest in the issues at stake. He added
that, if the war lasted for long, its effect on Russia would be terrible. But
he acknowledged that unless the Russian navy won quick victories over
the Japanese fleet the conflict was bound to be lengthy since it would take
many months to build up Russia's land forces in the Far East. Not even
Benckendorff, however, foresaw the continual blows to Russian pride and
prestige that the conflict with Japan would bring. The humiliation of
defeat by the Japanese, combined with awareness that the war had been
unnecessary, embittered the Grand Marshal of the Court. In May 1905 he
wrote, 'we have become at best a second-rank power for two generations'
and Russia might even be destroyed altogether by the conflict. Anger
against the incompetent and irresponsible conduct of public affairs boiled
over in sharp criticism of the Tsar. In March 1905 Benckendorff wrote that
Nicholas II was 'ridiculous', that he 'was beginning to annoy everyone'
and that 'there is something absurd in any and every monarchy'. Such
comments, coming as they did from a senior military courtier of impeccably loyal and aristocratic origins show just how far the monarch's prestige
had fallen even in conservative and patriotic circles as a result of humiliation in the Far East.[23]

Russia's defeat by Japan was in part the product of geography. When
the war began, only two of Russia's twenty-nine army corps were in the
Far East and it took months of effort to transfer sufficient troops to the
theatre of operations. Supplying the field army along the single-track
Trans-Siberian railway was a difficult task. The Russian navy could not
bring its full strength to bear since the Black Sea squadron, one-third of the
fleet, was not allowed by international treaty to pass the Bosporus. The

Baltic fleet needed to steam round the world before it could enter the fray; by the time it arrived off the coast of Japan, Russia's Far Eastern squadron had already been destroyed. Although on paper the latter had been a match for the Japanese fleet, its lack of bases and repair facilities was a major disadvantage. Nor did Russia's Far Eastern fleet enjoy much luck. In the surprise torpedo attack by which the Japanese began the war only two Russian ships were hit but they happened to be the squadron's most modern battleships. When Russian naval morale in the Far East was restored by the arrival of Makarov, the country's best admiral, cruel luck again intervened. Of all the ships in the Russian squadron, it had to be his flagship alone which struck a mine at the crucial moment in the war between the two countries' Pacific fleets.[24]

Above all, however, Russia lost the war because of the failings of its senior commanders, military and naval. Russia's generals and admirals on the whole turned out to be administrators, veterans of internal security operations or military intellectuals rather than fighting commanders. To some extent this tends to be the fate of any armed forces after a long period of peace. In the Russian case, however, the poverty-stricken peacetime armed forces spent so much of their time and energy on administration, supply and paying their own way that military bureaucrats were bound to come to the fore. Russian generals and admirals also displayed a quite extraordinary talent for fighting among themselves. The Russian general who told a visiting British officer in 1912 that 'there will never be unselfish cooperation amongst the higher leaders as in the German army' was speaking from bitter wartime experience. In the first phase of the war the commander of the land forces, General Kuropatkin, was at loggerheads with the Viceroy, Admiral Alekseev. After Alekseev's removal, battle raged between generals Kuropatkin and Grippenberg. To some extent this endless feuding stemmed from the bitterness of defeat. It had, however, already commenced before the war had even really begun. In February 1904 Kuropatkin recorded a conversation with Admiral Avelan, the Naval Minister, who

> expressed doubt about the ability of Admiral Stark to carry out such a great naval operation independently. He said that Stark is painstaking and knows his job but lacks initiative . . . To my question why – having such admirals as Skrydlov, Birilev, Rozhdestvensky, Makarov and Dubasov – almost our entire fleet is entrusted to the incompetent Stark, Avelan said that the fleet's personnel had been decided by Alekseev himself. He had asked for Birilev but Birilev had refused on the grounds of Alekseev's character: 'on my oath,' he had said, 'I assure you that after two months I would be forced to leave'. For the same reasons, Rozhdestvensky and Dubasov can't go.[25]

Peace came rather unexpectedly in September 1905 after the Russian army had been defeated in the spring at Mukden and the Baltic squadron annihilated at Tsushima. Nicholas stood out for a hard line, initially refusing either to pay a war indemnity or to cede any part of Sakhalin Island. In his heart the Emperor would have been happy to have broken off negotiations, postponing peace until the Russian army had won some victories. Only very reluctantly and under great pressure did he finally agree to cede southern Sakhalin. Actually, on this occasion Nicholas proved wiser than his advisers. The Japanese government, overstretched both financially and militarily, was desperate for peace and would have been prepared to accept it even without southern Sakhalin. Both the Japanese and the Russian military commanders believed that the tide was about to turn in the land war. Whereas Japanese manpower was almost exhausted, Russian reinforcements, including two of the army's best corps, were pouring into the theatre of operations. Nor was it the case, as was subsequently often argued, that the Far Eastern army was needed to crush revolution at home and was widely used for this purpose in the winter of 1905–6. The sudden peace at a time when morale was improving and the prospect of victory was in the air caused great disillusionment in the Far Eastern army. The manner in which demobilization occurred resulted in further discontent. Rather than contributing to the suppression of revolution in European Russia, much of the Far Eastern army remained cut off in the theatre of operations, while disgruntled demobilized reservists straggling back to Russia added to the chaos that prevailed along the Trans-Siberian railway.[26]

Within two months of the war's end Russia had been promised a constitution. On 30 October Nicholas II issued a manifesto offering 'unshakeable foundations of civil liberty on the principles of true inviolability of person, freedom of conscience, speech, assembly and association'. The elected assembly already promised earlier in the year was now to be 'guaranteed the opportunity of real participation in control over the legality of actions of the authorities appointed by us'. In addition, without the consent of this assembly, to be called the State Duma, 'no law can be put into effect'. Finally, the manifesto stated that the list of voters established earlier in the year for elections to the consultative assembly was now to be expanded to include 'those classes of the population that at present are altogether deprived of the franchise'.[27]

Nicholas's surrender of his autocratic powers was owed in large part to a renewed wave of strikes, demonstrations and violence which swept across Russia in the autumn of 1905, ultimately encompassing most sections of the urban population. This occurred to a considerable extent because of the government's own faulty tactics. In the summer of 1905 the promise of a consultative assembly and the prospect of peace with Japan caused divisions within the opposition and seemed to offer hope of a breathing space during which the government could regain its composure. By reopening the universities in early September, however, and allowing them wide-ranging autonomy the government opened the floodgates to revolution. University buildings, now beyond the control of the police, became centres of revolutionary organization and propaganda. Workers poured on to the campuses, the revolutionary parties had free rein for their activities, and all disgruntled elements of urban society could share their grievances and co-ordinate their protests in perfect security. By early October General D.F. Trepov was warning Nicholas that 'the moment is not far off when under the pressure of the revolutionaries who now control the universities, the disorders there will spill into the street'.[28]

Within days Trepov's prediction came true. From 2 October strikes began to spread from sector to sector of Moscow's economy. Sympathy strikes began in Petersburg. The crucial moment came, however, when the railwaymen walked out, since their action paralysed both the government and the economy and, in addition, sparked off something close to a general strike in urban Russia. 'The government was immobilized. Officials could not even travel between St Petersburg and Moscow. An October 12 conference of ministers called by the tsar to restore railroad operations all but threw up its hands in despair.'[29]

Nicholas described the situation to his mother in the following terms.

All sorts of conferences took place in Moscow, which Durnovo [P.P. Durnovo, the Governor] permitted. I do not know why. Everything was being prepared for the railway strike. The first one began in and around Moscow, and then spread all over Russia practically at once. Petersburg and Moscow were entirely cut off from the interior. For exactly a week today the Baltic railway has not been functioning. The only way to get to town is by sea. How convenient at this time of year! From the railways the strike spread to the factories and workshops, and then even to the municipal organisations and services, and lastly to the Railway Department of the Ministry of Ways and Communications. What a shame, just think of it . . . God knows what happened in the universities. Every kind of riff-raff walked in from the streets, riot was loudly proclaimed – nobody seemed to mind. The governing bodies of the universities and engineering schools were granted autonomy but they do not know how to use it. They couldn't even lock the doors in time to keep out the impudent crowd, and then of course complained they could not get any help from the police – but do you remember what they used to say in years gone by? It makes me sick to read the news! Nothing but new strikes in schools and factories, murdered policemen, cossacks and soldiers, riots, disorders, mutinies. But the ministers, instead of acting with quick decision, only assemble in council like a lot of frightened hens and cackle about providing united ministerial action.[30]

Despite the Emperor's sarcasm, pressure from within senior officialdom for the co-ordination of ministerial policy was the other key element behind the granting of the October manifesto. The confusion in both domestic and foreign policy-making before the outbreak of the Russo-Japanese War had persuaded most senior officials that radical changes were required as regards the co-ordination of ministerial activity. Once it became clear in the spring of 1905 that an elected assembly was to be created, the need for government to present a united front to the world appeared clearer than ever. From early September 1905 a special conference under the chairmanship of the empire's most distinguished elder states-man, D.M. Solsky, had been considering this issue. If the post of premier was to be created, Serge Witte was the obvious man to fill it. Witte himself craved the job. His reputation had soared as a result of his success-ful leadership of Russia's delegation to the peace conference that followed the war with Japan. Paul Benckendorff wrote in early October, 'my last hope is Witte, as it has always been'. The Empress Marie advised her son that 'I am sure that the only man who can help you now and be useful is Witte . . . he certainly is a man of genius, energetic and clear-sighted.' Witte's terms were, however, very steep. He had become convinced that only by granting a constitution and full civil rights could society be paci-fied and the government's authority be restored. In addition, if he was to head the government, Witte insisted on his right to choose all the other ministers and to determine and co-ordinate the policies pursued by the various departments. Not surprisingly, Nicholas wavered for a few days before accepting such conditions, in the meantime pondering the option of military repression. But on 30 October the Emperor gave in and Russia acquired simultaneously its first constitution and its first prime minister.[31]

Two days later Nicholas explained his decision in a letter to his mother:

One had the same feeling as before a thunderstorm in summer! Everybody was on edge and extremely nervous, and, of course, that sort of strain could not go on for long. Through all these horrible days, I constantly met Witte. We very often met in the early morning to part only in the evening, when night fell. There were only two ways open: to find an energetic soldier and crush the rebellion by sheer force. There would be time to breathe then but, as likely as not, one would have to use force again in a few months; and that would mean rivers of blood, and in the end we should be where we had started. I mean to say, government authority would be vindicated, but there would be no posi-tive result and no possibility of progress achieved. The other way out would be to give to the people their civil rights, freedom of speech and press, also to have all laws confirmed by a State Duma – that, of course, would be a constitution. Witte defends this very energetically. He says that, while it is not without risk, it's the only way out at the present moment. Almost everybody I had an opportunity of consulting is of the same opinion. Witte put it quite clearly to

1. The Emperor Alexander III (1845–94)

2. The Empress Marie (1847–1928) and her sister, Queen Alexandra of England

3. The Anichkov Palace in Petersburg where Nicholas spent much of his youth

4. Nicholas and Alexandra
in 1894

5. The Empress Alexandra
shortly after her marriage in
1894

6. The Winter Palace in Petersburg, scene of great ceremonial occasions. Nicholas and Alexandra seldom stayed here

7. The young Emperor relaxing at a country retreat shortly after ascending the throne

8. Nicholas's study in his small 'palace' at Peterhof where he spent the summer months

9. The Alexander Palace at Tsarskoe Selo, the imperial couple's main residence

10. The imperial yacht, the *Standart*

11. The new palace at Livadia, completed in 1911

12. Serge Witte (1849–1915): Minister of Finance, 1893–1903, Chairman of the Committee of Ministers, 1903–5, and Prime Minister, 1905–6

13. Nicholas leaves the Russian Orthodox Church in Paris during his state visit to France in 1896

14. Pilgrims and police await the Tsar's arrival at Sarov for the ceremonies surrounding the canonization of St Seraphim

15. General Aleksei Kuropatkin (1848–1925): Minister of War, 1898–1904, and GOC Far Eastern Army, 1904–5

16. The Tauride Palace, home of the Duma

17. Peter Stolypin (1862–1911) with his family. Stolypin was Minister of Internal Affairs, 1906–11, and Prime Minister from 1907 to 1911 when he was assassinated. Two of his children were seriously injured in an earlier assassination attempt in 1906

18. Nicholas with George V of England, *c.* 1909

19. Vladimir Kokovstov (1853–1943): Minister of Finance, 1904–5 and 1906–14, and Prime Minister, 1911–14

20. Peter Durnovo (1844–1915): Minister of Internal Affairs, 1905–6, and leader of the conservative group in the State Council, 1906–15

21. Michael Akimov (1847–
1914): Minister of Justice,
1905–6, and President of the
State Council, 1907–14

22. Ivan Goremykin (1839–
1917): Minister of Internal
Affairs, 1895–9, and Prime
Minister, 1906 and 1914–16

23. Nicholas visits his cousin, the Grand Duke Nicholas (Nikolasha) at Headquarters during the early months of the First World War. At this time the Grand Duke was commander-in-chief of the front-line army

24. Nicholas and the Tsarevich Aleksei in the uniform of the Cossack escort shortly before the First World War

25. Nicholas and his children with officers of the Cossack escort during the First World War: (*left to right*) Anastasia, Olga, Nicholas, Aleksei, Tatiana and Marie

26. Nicholas and Aleksei visit the armies of General Brusilov, *c*. 1916

27. The imperial family shortly before the revolution: (*left to right*) Tatiana, Anastasia, Marie, Olga, Nicholas, Alexandra and Aleksei

28. The imperial family in captivity at Tobolsk: *(left to right)* Olga, Anastasia, Nicholas, Aleksei, Tatiana and Marie

me that he would accept the Presidency of the Council of Ministers only on the condition that his programme was agreed to, and his actions not interfered with. He and Alexei Obolensky drew up the manifesto. We discussed it for two days, and in the end, invoking God's help, I signed. My dear Mama, you can't imagine what I went through before that moment; in my telegram I could not explain all the circumstances which brought me to this terrible decision, which nevertheless I took quite consciously. From all over Russia they cried for it, they begged for it, and around me many – very many – held the same views. I had no one to rely on except honest Trepov. There was no other way out than to cross oneself and give what everyone was asking for. My only consolation is that such is the will of God, and this grave decision will lead my dear Russia out of the intolerable chaos she has been in for nearly a year.[32]

This last sentence provides a key to Nicholas's subsequent attitude to both Witte and the new constitution. His concession had been designed to secure peace and to win back the support of the liberal movement. At least in the short run neither of these goals was achieved. In the winter of 1905–6 the regime came closer to collapse than at any other time. Great bloodshed was required after all for the government's preservation. The Tsar felt cheated. No doubt Witte's expectation of easy pacification had always been naïve. As Paul Benckendorff wrote to his brother, 'the constitution has been dragged from the government by disturbances. That is a bad position. The capitulation is complete. How will one be able to restore to this government a semblance of respect after the war and now this event?' Of course the revolutionary parties saw the October manifesto as a sign of weakness and redoubled their efforts to hasten tsarism to its grave. For six weeks 'dual power' existed in Petersburg: a Soviet of Workers' Deputies, whose outstanding personality was Leon Trotsky, existed alongside the imperial government and attempted to lead and co-ordinate the revolutionary movement. The Bolsheviks organized an armed uprising of Moscow workers in December. The main strand in the liberal opposition proclaimed that revolution must continue until parliamentary government and universal suffrage were achieved. Poland, the Caucasus and the Baltic provinces witnessed massive violence. Worse still, the Russian and Ukrainian peasantry, sensing the collapse of authority, poured on to the estates of landowners, burning manor houses and destroying crops and animals. The army, deployed in increasingly dispersed units to preserve order across the length and breadth of the empire, began to show serious signs of disintegration. In 1906 even the élite First Battalion of the Preobrazhensky Guards, the senior regiment of the Russian army, was to mutiny, prompting a horrified Kireev to write in his diary, 'This is it.' In the winter of 1905–6 the regime's life hung by a thread.[33]

If the government survived this was partly because, in the face of renewed strikes, assassinations and riots, it lost its self-doubt or equivocation. Previously repression and concessions had been combined, often in an unskilful and self-defeating manner. Now authority was to be restored at any price. The new Minister of Internal Affairs, Peter Durnovo, was the man of the hour. Resolute, self-confident and very intelligent, Durnovo was one of the most impressive statesmen to serve the old regime in the last half-century of its existence. When Durnovo arrived to take up his position in the ministry chaos reigned. The post and telegraph strike had cut off links to the provinces. The officials of the vital Police Department were locked in internecine conflict. Police informers were beginning to slip away, convinced that the regime was doomed. In the ministry's Petersburg offices officials wandered about, unsure what to do and repeating rumours. Still more bewildered were the provincial governors, unprepared for the October manifesto and deprived of firm guidance from the capital. Dmitri Lyubimov recalled that 'in a word one felt complete collapse in the ministry. In addition to this, the mood among the officials was extremely nervous.' In a revolutionary crisis, as on a battlefield, the leader requires calmness under pressure, unflinching resolution, and an acute sense of tactics and timing. These Durnovo displayed.

Vladimir Gurko, himself a senior official in the Ministry of Internal Affairs, recollected that 'Durnovo had a way of impressing on people his own firmness and the inflexibility of his own decisions . . . he and he alone . . . really understood the situation and systematically, even ruthlessly, had taken steps to prevent the break-up of the state apparatus.' From provincial governor down to private soldier, no individual in the apparatus of repression could have had any doubt that the government had the will to survive and would punish without mercy anyone who wavered in the suppression of disorder. The revolution was first smashed in the key centres of administration and communications. The Soviet was arrested, and the lack of resistance encouraged Durnovo to press on with his counter-offensive. The Moscow rising was suppressed and control reasserted over the railways and telegraph. Subsequently, punitive expeditions fanned out across the empire. The revolutionary parties found it impossible to co-ordinate the protests of workers, peasants and mutinous members of the armed forces in the face of concerted and resolute repression. Nor, unlike before October 1905, did strikes and demonstrations enjoy the support of much of the propertied classes, or even, after a time, the unequivocal sympathy of the professional and cultural intelligentsia.[34]

This was, in part, because the concession of a constitution had won support for the government among moderate elements of the upper and middle classes. Whereas the bulk of the liberal movement formed itself into the Constitutional Democratic (Kadet) party, the conservative minority split off, most of them ending up in the Octobrist party. As the latter's name suggests, its basic platform was support for the promises made in the October manifesto and a belief that these had removed any justification for further opposition, especially of a violent nature. More important than these political manoeuverings, however, were the increasing horror and resentment of the social élites as the revolution of the masses grew more radical and violent, turning its attention to the property of upper- and middle-class Russia. As workers demanded higher pay, shorter hours and better treatment, industrialists responded with lockouts and sackings. As manor houses went up in flames, the landowning classes swung far to the right, taking the *zemstvos* with them. Radical civil servants working for the *zemstvos* were sacked, and cossacks and other guards were hired to protect estates from destruction. An important sign of the shifting mood of upper- and middle-class Russia were the unpaid volunteers who offered their services to break the post and telegraph strike.

Reflecting the new mood, Paul Benckendorff wrote to his brother at the end of 1905 that people who had previously howled with indignation at the mistreatment of a single student were now screaming that no prisoners must be taken and all radicals must be shot. On 1 December Nicholas was able to write to his mother that 'more and more voices are heard protesting that the time has come for the Government to take matters firmly in hand – which is a very good sign indeed'. A week later he added that

> God is my strength and gives me peace of mind, and that is the most important thing. So many Russians nowadays have lost that spirit. That is why they are so often unable to resist the threats and intimidations of the anarchists. Civic courage, as you know, is at the best of times noticeable here only among the few. Now it hardly seems to exist at all. But, as I wrote to you last time, the state of mind of the people has lately changed altogether. The old headless Liberals, always so critical of firm measures on the part of the authorities, are now clamouring loudly for decisive action.[35]

While revolution waxed and waned in the winter of 1905–6 Nicholas and his government were hard at work drafting Russia's new constitution and electoral law. The constitution, as published finally in April 1906, did not contradict the promises made in the October manifesto. It spelt out a wide range of civil rights guaranteed to Russian subjects. It gave the Duma a veto over all legislation and considerable control over the budget. Inevitably, however, the regime was not prepared to accept anything approaching full democracy. Sovereignty was explicitly stated to remain with the Emperor, whose rights derived from God and history. As in every major European country at that time, an undemocratic upper house, in the form of the reformed State Council, was created to act as a check on the elected Duma. Half the members of the State Council were to be senior officials nominated by the crown, the other half being chosen by the key conservative institutions and interests, which meant above all the landowning nobility. Fearful of continuing instability and revolution, the government insisted in Article 15 that the Emperor retained the unrestricted right to declare provinces to be under a state of emergency, thereby allowing itself the means to set aside the civil rights it had just promised the population. Ominously for the new constitutional order, Nicholas made clear his conviction that in the last resort he should continue to bear unlimited responsibility for Russia's destiny. On 22 April he told a conference of ministers and top officials, 'all this time I have been tormented by the worry as to whether I have the right before my ancestors to change the limits of that power which I received from them . . . I say to you sincerely that if I was convinced that Russia wished me to renounce my autocratic rights then I would do this with joy for its good.' No doubt, if he hung on to his title of unlimited autocrat he would face many reproaches about going back on the promises made in the October manifesto. 'But one must recognize whence these reproaches will come. They will come of course from the side of the whole so-called educated element, from the workers and the Third Estate. But I am convinced that 80 per cent of the Russian people will be with me.' Only with great difficulty could his advisers persuade the Tsar that the opinions of educated Russia had to be reckoned with and that flagrant undermining of the promises contained in the October manifesto was not permissible.[36]

The Emperor's conviction that 80 per cent of the population was on his side reflected his faith that Russian peasants were monarchists at heart and were uninterested in political democracy or constitutions. The question of the peasants' political reliability and monarchist sympathies was indeed the cause of angry disagreements within the ruling élite when the question of the suffrage for elections to the Duma came on to the agenda. In the end the rural masses were given predominant weight by the new electoral law, the government hoping that the peasants' traditional monarchist, religious and agrarian outlook would lead them to oppose the blandishments of middle-class liberal and radical politicians, as had happened earlier in much of Central and Western Europe.

In the circumstances of 1905–6, however, when most peasants were obsessed by the opportunity to seize the big estates, a political strategy aimed at winning the loyalty of the rural masses could only succeed if it was accompanied by the promise of land reforms. Not all members of senior officialdom or even of the landowning nobility were set against making such promises. Amidst the panic caused by peasant arson and rioting in the winter of 1905 Dmitri Trepov told Witte that 'he would be ready to give up half his land if he could keep the rest'. Citing similar support for partial expropriation from Admiral Dubasov, who had commanded the detachment which had 'pacified' Chernigov and Kursk provinces, Witte claimed that in November and December 1905 'what he said was typical of the mood then prevalent in conservative circles'. On 23 January 1906 Witte reported to Nicholas II that although the urban revolution could now be considered defeated, the peasant rebellion was still in full swing. He informed the Emperor that a draft law for partial expropriation of private land presented to the Council of Ministers by N.N. Kutler, the Minister of Agriculture, had 'aroused in the preliminary general exchange of opinions complete and fundamental disagreement within the Council'. For a monarch committed to the view that the crown's most loyal ally was the peasantry here perhaps was the moment to make a dramatic gesture to bring Tsar and peasant together at the expense of a sometimes disloyal section of the educated class. Instead Nicholas II killed Kutler's project and all further discussion of the expropriation of noble land. In the margin of Witte's report, opposite Kutler's proposal, the Emperor wrote, 'I do not approve.' Further on in the report, he made another marginal comment: 'Private property must remain inviolable.'[37]

To understand the Emperor's position it is important to note that opposition to expropriation within the landowning class was already beginning to harden by January 1906. Arbitrary confiscation of a huge amount of private property was an enormously radical policy for any European government to contemplate before 1914, particularly if the land in question belonged to the country's traditional ruling class. Acting in this way, Nicholas would have faced the outrage of families who were his dynasty's oldest supporters, and whose members had been his closest companions since his youth both in his father's household and during his service in the Guards. Since expropriation without compensation was absolutely inconceivable in Edwardian Europe, the already almost bankrupt treasury faced huge potential problems in managing the transfer of property. Nor would the transfer of land from noble to peasant bring any economic advantages, if anything quite the opposite. Although in theory it might have made sense to leave to the nobles land directly farmed by them and merely expropriate fields already leased to peasants, such a policy would certainly not have satisfied the peasantry. For the latter it was precisely the big estates which were farmed directly by their owners in an efficient, modern and capitalist fashion which were the most objectionable. The fundamental argument against expropriation was indeed that unless it was total the process was likely to whet appetites and to inflame rather than assuage peasant anger. The first congress of the United Nobility stated that 'compulsory expropriation of private lands will not calm the population but will only ignite passions'. It is clear from his marginal comments on this and similar memoranda that Nicholas shared this view and saw partial expropriation as counter-productive. It was, however, not difficult to prophesy that without some such measure the government's chances of agreement with a Duma elected largely by peasants were not likely to be very high.[38]

One casualty of the cruel and strife-ridden winter of 1905–6 was the Emperor's relationship with his Prime Minister. Nicholas had never greatly trusted Witte, in part because he had somehow got it into his head that the latter was a freemason. Disappointment that the October manifesto had not brought peace and order soon surfaced. 'It is strange that such a clever man should be wrong in his forecast of an easy pacification,' wrote Nicholas in early November. Two weeks later the Emperor told his mother that 'I hold a meeting of the Council of Ministers every week . . . they talk a lot, but do little. Everybody is afraid of taking courageous action: I keep on trying to force them – even Witte himself – to behave more energetically. With us nobody is accustomed to shouldering responsibility: all expect to be given orders, which, however, they disobey as often as not . . . I must confess I am disappointed in him [Witte] in a way.' By the end of January 1906 Nicholas has lost all faith in Witte as Prime Minister or overlord of Russian internal affairs.

> As for Witte, since the happenings in Moscow [the armed uprising] he has radically changed his views; now he wants to hang and shoot everybody. I have never seen such a chameleon of a man. That, naturally, is the reason why no one believes in him any more. He is absolutely discredited with everybody, except perhaps the Jews abroad. I like Akimov, the new Minister of Justice, very much . . . He is no longer young of course, but vigorous and very energetic, with honest ideas – he has already cleaned up his poisonous ministry. Durnovo, the Minister of the Interior, is doing splendid work. I am very pleased with him too. The rest of the ministers are people without importance.[39]

The Emperor's opinion of Witte was actually quite justified and was widely shared. Under the strain of these turbulent and terrifying weeks the Prime Minister appeared at times to lose his nerve. His opinions veered from side to side in an alarming and contradictory way. Even by 10 December Paul Benckendorff was writing that people, including himself, who had previously believed that Witte must be supported had now turned against him. The reason was, in his opinion, that the Prime Minister had failed to stick to a consistent line and, partly through fear, was trying to parley with the revolutionaries. By now, added Benckendorff, it was an illusion to imagine that the government had any alternative but the full-scale use of force. If, despite the growing disillusionment with Witte,

Nicholas retained his Prime Minister until April 1906 this was above all because of the latter's reputation as a financial genius and the strong links he had with foreign bankers. In the winter of 1905–6 Russia faced financial disaster. Witte himself wrote to the Foreign Minister, Count Lambsdorff, 'we are within a hairbreadth of financial (and consequently general) crisis. We are getting through from week to week but there is a limit to every-thing.' Russia was within an inch of being forced off the gold standard, with disastrous consequences for its creditworthiness. Salvation lay in a large foreign loan, and Witte's skills and contacts were seen as essential for its achievement. In April 1906 the loan was finally secured and Nicholas's letter of gratitude to Witte showed both his belief that the Prime Minis-ter's role had been decisive and his sense that the deal was 'a big moral triumph for the government and a pledge of future calm and of Russia's peaceful development'.[40]

To understand the circumstances of the loan, and why it proved so very difficult to raise, it is necessary to retrace our steps a little in order to grasp the broader European context within which Russia's domestic crisis was occurring. The years 1903–6 witnessed momentous changes in inter-national relations in Europe. In the 1890s continental Europe had been divided into two power blocs. On the one hand there was the Franco-Russian alliance, on the other the union between Germany and Austria-Hungary, of which Italy was a thoroughly unreliable partner. Britain stood aloof from both power blocs, though its relations with Berlin and Vienna were in general better than those with France or Russia. Anglo-Russian rivalry in Asia went deep and had on occasion brought the two empires close to war. As late as 1898 Anglo-French confrontation in Africa had also made armed conflict between those two countries appear possible. Within the Franco-Russian alliance the chances of united military action against Britain were envisaged and planned for.

By 1900 Britain's rulers were becoming aware that although their coun-try was still the mightiest state in Europe its power was declining relative to that of its competitors, and especially Germany. Resources no longer fully matched commitments. It had long since been recognized that the security of Britain's possessions in the western hemisphere could not be maintained by force and depended on good relations with the USA. In 1902 Britain's position in the Far East was bolstered by the Anglo-Japanese alliance. In 1903 agreement was reached with France on a range of colonial questions, and relations between London and Paris quickly began to improve. This raised a big question-mark over the Franco-Russian alliance. In the first years of the twentieth century, Russia's relations with Berlin and Vienna were good. Petersburg's attention was largely concentrated on Asia, and London was seen as Russia's greatest rival. The Anglo-Japanese alliance was directed primarily against Russia and many Russians believed that without it Tokyo would never have dared go to war in 1904. In the Russo-Japanese War, Paris was Petersburg's ally and London was linked to Tokyo. When the Russian Baltic squadron *en route* to the Pacific opened fire on the Hull fishing fleet war between Russia and Britain appeared possible, to the horror of the French government. Meanwhile Germany tilted towards Russia during the war, helping to coal Admiral Rozhdestvensky's ships as they made their long passage from the Baltic to the Far East. In Paris it was clear that unless Anglo-Russian reconciliation could be achieved, France's foreign policy was heading towards the disastrous necessity of having to make a choice between Petersburg and London. In Berlin it was perceived with equal clarity that Anglo-Russian antagonism, together with the collapse of Russian military power as a result of defeat in the Far East, provided a great opportunity to split the Franco-Russian alliance and assert German pre-eminence in Europe. One strand in this policy was the effort to forge an alliance with Petersburg. The other was Berlin's attempt in 1905 to challenge the right of France and Britain to dispose of Morocco's future without consulting Germany.

In the autumn of 1904 Berlin sought to play on Nicholas II's resentment of Britain's support for Japan and his desire to stand up to London through an alliance of the continental powers. Vladimir Lambsdorff, Russia's Foreign Minister, warned the Tsar to be very careful since 'I cannot fail to perceive in the German government's proposals a continual striving to shatter the friendly relations between Russia and France'. Nevertheless, when he met the German Emperor at Bjorkoe in July 1905, Nicholas agreed to sign a secret alliance with Germany. The Treaty of Bjorkoe stipulated that if either empire was attacked by another country its ally would come to its aid with all available forces. The agreement would come into operation automatically at the end of the Russo-Japanese War, at which point the Russian Emperor would initiate the French into the treaty's terms and invite them to join the alliance. For Nicholas one attraction of the treaty may have been the additional security it offered to Russia's now very vulnerable frontiers, in Europe as well as Asia. Above all, however, the Emperor no longer perceived the German-Austrian-Italian Triple Alliance as a threat. On the contrary, Britain, whose alliance with Japan was renewed and strengthened in 1905, was seen by him to be the real danger. As he told Lambsdorff, 'nowadays the Triple Alliance is, in essence, only a historical memory and Germany, which then [when the Franco-Russian alliance was signed] seemed very aggressive, is now persistently proposing to ally itself with us in order to form, with an exclusively *peaceful* goal, a common alliance of the continental powers, able to resist English aspirations which have just been sharply confirmed in the new Anglo-Japanese treaty'. Wilhelm II's reaction to Bjorkoe shows that his Russian cousin's trust was a little naïve. The German Emperor wrote to his Chancellor, Bernhard von Bulow, 'thus has the morning of 25 July 1905 off Bjorko been a turning point in European history, thanks to the grace of God. The situation of my dear Fatherland has been greatly relieved as it will now be freed from the terrible grip of the Franco-Russian vice.'[41]

The Treaty of Bjorkoe was the last gasp of old-style monarchical diplomacy. The two imperial cousins disposed of the fate of their empires in the absence of both Bulow and Lambsdorff, the officials responsible for foreign policy. Bulow was furious both at the treaty's fine print and at the fact that Wilhelm had acted without his knowledge. He immediately threatened to resign, in the process almost causing the Kaiser a nervous breakdown. As was his wont, Vladimir Lambsdorff, a much gentler man than Bulow, merely wrung his hands in despair. The Foreign Minister knew full well that there was no chance of persuading France to join a continental alliance against Britain. For Paris, the whole purpose of the Franco-Russian alliance was to act as a guarantee against German aggression. With the Moroccan crisis escalating, French fear and resentment of Germany was at its height. In 1905 a weakened Russia was in no position to twist France's arm or force it to accept Petersburg's anti-British perspectives. The question of the loan impinged here since the French financial market was bound to be the key to success in this deal and Paris would certainly veto the loan if any threat was raised against the Franco-Russian alliance. But Lambsdorff's basic thinking rested on much deeper and longer-term assumptions than this. As he wrote to A.I. Nelidov, the Russian ambassador in Paris, in October 1905: 'from many years of experience I have drawn the conclusion that to be on genuinely good terms with Germany an alliance with France is necessary. Otherwise we will lose our independence and I know nothing more painful than the German yoke.' The point was that Russia was weaker than Germany, and never more so than in 1905. Therefore, in Lambsdorff's view, it could only ensure respectful treatment from Berlin if Paris stood by its side. Otherwise it would become a German dependency. As he warned Nicholas in September 1905, 'if the conditions of this treaty become known in Paris then, in all probability, the long-term goal of German policy will be achieved – the Franco-Russian alliance will be broken once and for all, and our relations with England will be sharpened to such an extent that we will be entirely isolated and linked exclusively to Germany'.[42]

After some crafty manoeuvring and a little humiliation Petersburg succeeded in escaping from the Treaty of Bjorkoe, though at the inevitable cost of annoying Wilhelm II. In the winter of 1905–6 the great aim of Russian diplomacy was to avoid antagonizing either Paris or Berlin, and to settle the Moroccan dispute as quickly as possible so that Russia could float its loan on the Paris market. In the end the dispute was settled and the Russian loan was successfully launched, but not before Petersburg had been forced further to sour its relations with Berlin by coming down firmly on the French side over the Moroccan question. Simultaneously, and much to the disgust of General F.F. Palitsyn, the Chief of the Russian General Staff, the anti-British aspect of Petersburg's military agreement with Paris was dropped at French insistence. In 1905–6 a significant, though by no means final, step was taken towards what would be the line-up of Europe's great powers in 1914.

For much of 1905 and 1906, however, the great question asked by foreign observers was whether Russia would ever be a great power again. Russia's internal crisis was at its most severe in the period between the October 1905 general strike and the government's successful dissolution of the first Duma in July 1906. During these months the collapse of the imperial regime was a real possibility. Should this occur, German military intervention was likely, if only to protect the very vulnerable German community in Russia's Baltic provinces. In the event of Russian politics swinging as far towards anarchy and socialism as occurred in 1917, more widespread European intervention was certain in order to protect the huge foreign investments in the empire. The thought that Russia might go the same way as China or Persia horrified patriots, not to mention Russia's diplomatic representatives abroad. The prospect also inspired great disquiet in Paris and London. With Russia eliminated from the club of great powers German supremacy in Europe would be inevitable. If a Russian regime had to be propped up by German bayonets the picture would be clearer than ever. In July 1906 the Russian ambassador in London, Count Alexander Benckendorff, confessed to the new Foreign Minister, A.P. Izvolsky, that 'I have two nightmares in my head: bankruptcy and immediate [foreign] financial interference and then, and worse, intervention. It seems mad to think this but nevertheless I can't stop myself, not as regards today but to the future. This idea of German military intervention haunts people here [in London].'[43]

In the event, Benckendorff's fears proved unfounded. The imperial regime survived. In April 1906 the first Duma was opened in an impressive ceremony at the Winter Palace, full of pomp and circumstance. The scene was described in the diary of the Grand Duke Constantine.

In the [Nicholas] Hall were many members of the Duma, some in evening dress, others in suits or in Russian costume . . . The family had to gather at 1.30 . . . We were all there . . . their Majesties arrived shortly before 2 o'clock. The Emperor was in the uniform of the Preobrazhensky regiment, the Empress Marie Feodorovna in a white satin dress edged with Russian sable, and the Empress Alexandra . . . in white and gold, with a diadem made out of the huge pearls of Catherine II. The procession moved into the Hall of

St George . . . at its head they bore the imperial regalia – the seal, the sword, the standard, the sceptre and the orb . . . After their Majesties had kissed the cross Metropolitan Anthony began the religious service before the icon of the Saviour . . . To the left stood members of the State Council, to the right members of the Duma . . . The service finished . . . When everyone had taken their places, the Emperor slowly and majestically approached the throne . . . Upon a sign from the Emperor the Minister of the Court mounted the steps and with a low bow presented a paper; the Emperor took it . . . and stood up . . . loudly, distinctly and slowly he began to read the speech. The more he read, the more strongly I was overcome by emotion. Tears flowed from my eyes. The words of the speech were so good, so truthful and sounded so sincere that it would have been impossible to add anything or to take anything away . . . the Tsar ended his speech with the words: 'May God come to my aid and yours!'[44]

Not all the Duma's deputies were as impressed as the Grand Duke by this display of imperial dignity and magnificence. Some critics argued that such ceremonies were out of date and no longer impressed ordinary people. Some deputies muttered about the contrast between imperial opulence and peasant poverty. The ceremony had been planned by the Empress Alexandra who, as always, came in for more than her fair share of criticism. Nine years later when the Empress threw off her grandeur and worked as a nurse during the Great War she also incurred criticism, though this time from precisely the opposite point of view. Even Lili Dehn, Alexandra's close friend, commented that

perhaps the Empress erred in her conception of the mentality of the Russian peasant. As an impartial critic, I fear this was the case. When she wore the Red Cross, the sign of a universal Brotherhood of Pity, the average soldier only saw in the Red Cross an emblem of her lost dignity as Empress of Russia. He was shocked and embarrassed when she attended to his wounds and performed almost menial duties. His idea of an Empress was never as a woman, but only as an imposing and resplendent Sovereign.

In early twentieth-century Russia it was difficult to know how best to stage the symbolism of monarchy. In Britain or Germany the bourgeois citizen gloried in the fantasy of royal pomp and circumstance and at the same time was comforted by the sense that the philistine patriotic values and respectable family life of George V and Wilhelm II reflected those existing around the middle-class fireside. But in Russia the average citizen, and the monarchy's key constituency, was not the cosy bourgeois but the peasant. It was not so easy for educated outsiders to understand and respond to his values and psychological needs. In fact, in an era when peasant values and mentalities were changing rapidly these needs were likely to be contradictory and often unfathomable even to the peasant himself.[45]

The government's relations with the Duma took a predictable course. The assembly was dominated by members of the liberal Constitutional Democratic party (the Kadets). They were committed to parliamentary government, an amnesty for political prisoners, and partial expropriation of the big estates. None of these principles were acceptable to the government. Moreover it was clear that Kadet domination of the Duma had only occurred because the socialist parties had refused to participate in the elections. The initially unaffiliated radicals and peasants who joined the Trudovik faction stood to the Kadets' left and demanded, amongst other things, total confiscation of all private land. The only questions were when, not if, the government would decide to dissolve the Duma and whether it would face effective mass resistance upon doing so. In July 1906 dissolution occurred and the population remained deaf to the Kadets' appeal for a tax strike. Mutinies at the Baltic fleet bases of Kronstadt and Sveaborg were quickly and brutally suppressed. When a second Duma was elected and proved even more recalcitrant than the first it too was dissolved without difficulty. This time, in the so-called *coup* of 16 June 1907, the government combined dissolution with changing the electoral law to ensure that future parliaments would be dominated by Russia's property-owning élite. The revolution had finally been defeated. The monarchy had survived, albeit in somewhat altered form, and at the price of great bloodshed, hatred and bitterness.

CHAPTER 7

Constitutional Monarch?
1907–1914

The years between the outbreak of the Russo-Japanese War in January 1904 and the dissolution of the second Duma in June 1907 were a difficult time for Nicholas. For an innocent and always optimistic patriot like the Tsar, defeat and revolution were heavy and unexpected blows. During this period Nicholas and Alexandra experienced one great joy. On 12 August 1904 an heir to the Russian throne was born. The Emperor wrote in his diary: 'an unforgettable great day for us in which God's grace visited us so manifestly . . . Words do not suffice with which one could thank God sufficiently for this comfort sent by Him in this year of hard trials.' The little boy was called Aleksei, in memory of Peter the Great's father, who was Nicholas's favourite ancestor. The child's name had symbolic resonance. Like many Russian conservatives the Emperor looked back nostalgically to the era before Peter introduced Western ideas, in the process creating the divide between Westernized élites and the Russian masses which remained so crucial right down to the empire's demise. In the reign of a new Aleksei, so his father no doubt hoped, Russia would regain the harmony and patriotism of the times when 'ancient and medieval peoples were strong in spirit, they were not confused by theories or by the various considerations of the Social Democrats, Trudoviki, and such people, but marched firmly down the road of the creation of a realm and the consolidation of their power'.[1]

Between 1895 and 1901 the Empress had given birth to four daughters: Olga, Tatiana, Marie and Anastasia. The four little girls were beautiful, healthy and lively children who were greatly loved by their parents. Nicholas was a fine father and the family circle was full of love, warmth and trust. If the Emperor had a favourite it was probably Tatiana, whose personality came closest to that of her mother. Olga, his eldest daughter, was the most thoughtful, sensitive and intelligent of the four. Marie, the third, with huge grey eyes and a warm-hearted, simple, friendly manner, was always the easiest to get on with on first acquaintance. Anastasia, born in 1901, was notorious as the family's comedian. Under Russian law, however, no woman could inherit the crown. Had Nicholas died before 1904, the throne would have gone to his kind-hearted but weak-willed younger brother, the Grand Duke Michael. Since Michael was a bachelor in 1904 and subsequently contracted an illegal and morganatic marriage, the Romanov inheritance would then have passed to a younger brother of Alexander III, the Grand Duke Vladimir, and his descendants. Tension and mutual dislike between the 'Vladimir branch' and the imperial couple were never far below the surface in the twentieth century. Much therefore hung on the life of the little boy born in August 1904. All the more horrifying was the discovery that the child had haemophilia.

In the Edwardian era there was no treatment for haemophilia and little way of alleviating the terrible pain it periodically caused. The chances were against a haemophiliac living into middle age, let alone being able to pursue a normal life. For any parents who loved their children as intensely as the imperial couple did, the physical and emotional strain of a haemophiliac son was bound to be great. In the case of Nicholas and Alexandra, however, matters were made worse by the fact that it was considered unthinkable to admit that the future autocrat of all the Russias was incurably ill and quite possibly doomed to an early death. The natural sympathy and understanding which might have flowed to the parents had therefore to be foregone. Moreover, however harrowing one of Aleksei's periodic illnesses might be, a monarch – let alone a Russian autocrat – had always to keep up appearances. It says something for Nicholas's extra-ordinary self-control that, adoring Aleksei as he did, he nevertheless never let the mask slip. As Alexandra herself once wrote to him, 'you will always wear a cheery face and carry all hidden inside'.[2]

Inevitably, however, it was the mother who bore the greater burden during her son's illnesses, not to mention the incessant worry even when he was relatively healthy. Nor could she escape the guilt born of the knowledge that she was the cause of her son's suffering and of the extra burden of worry about his dynasty's future which had been placed on her husband's shoulders. Physically frail and always very highly strung, the Empress poured her last drop of energy into watching over her son and nursing him during his attacks. As a mother Alexandra clearly out-shone her cousin, Queen Ena of Spain, who more or less banished her haemophiliac eldest child from Madrid and failed to see him on occasion for months on end. But the effort cost the Empress dear. She was often too ill and exhausted to play the role of a monarch's consort, incurring great odium as a result. Moreover, the strain of Aleksei's illness pushed his mother close to nervous collapse. As the Grand Duchess Olga rightly commented, 'the birth of a son, which should have been the happiest event in the lives of Nicky and Alicky, became their heaviest cross'.[3]

For the Empress religion was the great consolation. She never doubted that God intervened in the world, testing human beings, punishing them for their sins, but ultimately forgiving and rescuing them if they prayed and believed with sufficient purity and commitment. During the Russo-Japanese War, for instance, Alexandra ascribed Russia's defeats to God's punishment for the country's sins. Paul Benckendorff wrote to his brother in June 1904 that 'a very visible religious exaltation at present plays the major role'. Alexandra's religion was that of the heart, not the intellect. She once wrote to Nicholas that 'our church . . . needs soul and not brain'. Reason and dogma were insignificant beside direct religious experience, and purity of heart and conscience. The Empress's attitude was that of the Pietists, who had a major influence on the mentality of the eighteenth- and nineteenth-century Prussian aristocracy. It was similar, too, to that of the evangelical movement, led by Lord Radstock, which had swept Petersburg high society in the 1870s. But to this essentially Protestant conception of faith Alexandra added a strong element of Orthodox mysticism and superstition. For the Empress, as for her husband, probably the most uplifting religious experience of the whole reign was the ceremony surrounding the re-burial in the depths of the Russian countryside of the newly canonized Saint Seraphim of Sarov in the summer of 1903. By the time the church service was over evening had fallen. At least 300,000 people had gathered outside the church, in which the Emperor, both empresses and many grand dukes had participated in the service.

> Leaving the church we truly found ourselves in another temple. People standing in reverent silence filled the grounds of the monastery; every hand held a candle. Many had faced the cathedral and knelt to pray. As we passed through the wall of the monastery, we came upon the same spectacle, but now even more majestic and awesome. Stretched before us was an enormous multitude. Everyone had a candle, and some even held several . . . Here, literally, was a pilgrims' encampment . . . Chanting voices arose from various places, but the singers could not be seen, and the voices seemed to come from heaven itself . . . though the night passed, the singing continued.[4]

A.A. Kireev's views on Orthodoxy, Russian nationhood and the union between Tsar and people endeared him to Alexandra. In addition, the old general knew how to put her at her ease, liked her, thought her intelligent and sympathized with her plight. His diaries are therefore a good record of the Empress's state of mind. In March 1904 one of Alexandra's ladies-in-waiting agreed with Kireev that Alexandra was a practical Englishwoman on the surface and a mystical Russian underneath. She believed deeply in the religious significance of autocracy, in other words in the bonds of responsibility and affection that tied an Orthodox Tsar both to God and to the Russian people. 'She looks at Russia through the prism of the Sarov festivities and the people's acclamations in Moscow during Lent.' The revolution of 1905 and her son's health caused her huge anxiety. In February and March 1908, for instance, Kireev recorded that although Alexandra's health was slowly improving, she was still in a very nervous state. She kept having terrible dreams about the murder of her husband and son. She knew too that she was widely disliked and that Petersburg society was awash with calumnies about her. Two years later, in almost the last entry in his diary, Kireev wrote that Alexandra's religiosity was growing all the time but it was a strange and mystical faith, an altogether odd sort of Christianity. The Empress felt that her prayers would protect her husband. Kireev, without knowing about the heir's haemophilia, realized that Alexandra's mental state had much to do with her son. He feared 'psychic disorders' would destroy the Empress and commented that her state of mind was becoming 'terrifyingly dangerous'. Nine months earlier he had mentioned Rasputin's name in his diary for the first time. 'They probably look on "Grisha" as a sort of mascot and think that he brings good luck?! But such an influence can take very undesirable forms.'[5]

The imperial couple first met Rasputin in the autumn of 1905, a fortnight after Nicholas's October manifesto had promised Russia a constitution. Like most of the other rogues who gained access to the Emperor, Rasputin was introduced to him by Romanov relations, in this case the Grand Duke Nicholas (Nikolaevich), his wife and sister-in-law. Rasputin was a Siberian peasant who had become a full-time pilgrim and holy man. His was the voice of Russian popular religion, whose connection to the hierarchy and dogma of the Orthodox Church was often rather debatable. The Orthodox priest and the rituals he performed stood at the centre of village life but pagan spirits, sorcerers and hobgoblins lurked around its boundaries. Like others of his type Rasputin found protection both in Petersburg high society and, more important, in the Church hierarchy as a sincere, repentant, though no doubt sinful, holy man. He was also seen as the authentic voice of Russian popular Christianity. Subsequently, as the damage Rasputin was doing to the prestige of the monarchy and the Church became apparent, many of his former patrons turned against him, sometimes denouncing him to the imperial couple. Nicholas and Alexandra were, however, to a great extent armoured against the attacks of such turncoats. S.S. Fabritsky recalled that 'I personally had to hear on many occasions the same comment expressed with weariness both by the Emperor and the Empress: "We well know that we only have to get close to anyone whom we like for whatever reason, then people immediately begin to say vile things about him." ' In the deeply jealous and backbiting world of Petersburg there was much truth in this comment, even where Rasputin was concerned.[6]

Rasputin's hold over Nicholas and Alexandra was rooted in his unique ability to stop the bleeding when Tsarevich Aleksei had one of his attacks. No one has ever been able to provide a fully satisfactory medical explanation for how Rasputin achieved this. In 1913 the Tsarevich suffered his worst-ever attack while staying in his father's hunting lodge at Spala. The child lay literally at death's door, only to recover miraculously after Rasputin's intervention. The Grand Duchess Olga recalls that 'later that year I met Professor Fedorov, who told me that the recovery was wholly inexplicable from a medical point of view'.[7]

The Grand Duchess herself witnessed an earlier such 'miracle' when Aleksei had an accident in the park at Tsarskoe Selo.

> I wonder what Alicky [the Empress] must have thought – and that proved the first crisis out of many. The poor child lay in such pain, dark patches under his eyes and his little body all distorted, and the leg terribly swollen. The doctors were just useless. They looked more frightened than any of us and they kept whispering among themselves. There seemed just nothing they could do, and hours went by until they had given up all hope. It was getting late and I was persuaded to go to my rooms. Alicky then sent a message to Rasputin in St Petersburg. He reached the palace about midnight or even later. By that time I had reached my apartments and early in the morning Alicky called me to go to Aleksei's room. I just could not believe my eyes. The little boy was not just alive – but well. He was sitting up in bed, the fever gone, the eyes clear and bright, not a sign of any swelling on his leg. The horror of the evening before became an incredibly distant nightmare. Later I learned from Alicky that Rasputin had not even touched the child but had merely stood at the foot of the bed and prayed, and of course, some people would at once have it that Rasputin's prayers were simply coincidental with my nephew's recovery. In the first place, any doctor would tell you that an attack of such severity cannot be cured within a few hours. Secondly, the coincidence might have answered if it happened, say, once or twice, but I could not even count how many times it happened![8]

For the Empress, Rasputin's miraculous interventions to save her son's life showed that he was 'a man of God's sent to help' the imperial couple through the many trials and tribulations of their lives. But it mattered greatly to her as well that Rasputin was a man of the Russian people. By now the reader will be weary at the numerous references in this book to Nicholas and Alexandra's deeply held populism. This attitude was actually quite widespread in Russian educated society both on the right and on the left of the political spectrum. Viewed from one perspective, the

courage, patience and humility of the Russian peasant were a great deal
more attractive than the habits and morals of either the aristocracy or the
intelligentsia. But psychological factors also influenced many educated
Russians towards a passionate faith in 'the people'.[9]

The term 'populism' dated back to the 1870s in Russia. It was applied
to young radicals who in the 1860s and 1870s turned against the world of
their parents, the state and Victorian bourgeois society. These young men
and women created a separate little world of their own, an isolated revolutionary counter-culture based on worship of 'the people' and commitment
to their well-being. There were many reasons for the emergence of this
counter-culture, not to mention the fanatical and irrational forms it sometimes took: one such reason was the isolation and loss of emotional balance
of people cut adrift from their families and their natural social milieu and
often frantically in search of some alternative star by which their lives
might be guided and given purpose. In a curious way there were parallels
with the Empress Alexandra, lonely and isolated from upper-class Russia,
and driven by her emotions to seek a communion less with the real Russian
people than with her vision of what they ought to be. Still more obvious
was the manner in which the Empress fitted into the tradition of Russian
conservative populism. The most influential strand in nineteenth-century
conservative Russian thought was Slavophilism, whose last major publicist
was none other than General A.A. Kireev. Slavophiles preached that
Russia's religious, cultural and political values had been preserved and
guarded by the Orthodox peasantry, not by the Westernized élites.
Fyodor Dostoevsky stood partly in this tradition, strongly believing that
educated Russians must go to the simple people to learn from them the
meaning of Christian faith.[10]

Nicholas II and his family shared many of these beliefs. After her
marriage, his sister Olga was at last able to come into close contact with
the peasantry by visiting the villages of her husband's estate. 'I went from
village to village, nobody interfering with me. I went into their huts, I
talked to them and felt at my ease among them. There were hardships and
I saw penury too, of a kind I had never imagined to exist. But there was
also kindness, magnanimity, and an unbreakable faith in God. As I saw it,
those peasants were rich for all their poverty, and I had the sense of being a
genuine human being when I was among them.'[11]

The Emperor's position made it impossible for him to act in his sister's
manner. Nevertheless, on a number of occasions between 1907 and 1914
great celebrations and anniversaries allowed him to meet huge numbers
of peasants, with whom he did his utmost to come into personal contact
and from whom he in general drew thunderous applause. This helped to
reassure the Emperor that the monarchy still retained the loyalty of the
peasant masses, whose riots in 1905–6 could comfortably be ascribed to

the efforts of outside agitators from the intelligentsia, and particularly to Jews and other 'un-Russian' and unpatriotic elements. Shortly after the great celebrations in 1909 near Poltava to mark the two hundredth anniversary of the famous victory over the Swedes, Nicholas received the French military attaché at an audience. When Colonel Matton commented on the massive crowds' warm reception of the Emperor, Nicholas responded in a manner which perhaps reflected not just belief but also defensiveness and the need for reassurance.

> Yes, he said to me, making allusion to the cheers directed towards him, we were no longer at Petersburg and one could not say that the Russian people do not love their Emperor . . . He is certain that the rural population, the owners of land, the nobility and the army remain loyal to the Tsar; the revolutionary elements are composed above all of Jews, students, of landless peasants and of some workers. These elements were not represented at Poltava.

In part, too, Rasputin's role was to act as the authentic and reassuring voice of the loyal Russian people, a voice which might blot out the memory of the radicals and agitators whom the peasants had been cozened into electing to the first and second Dumas.[12]

To some extent not only Alexandra but also Nicholas fell victim to their own need to believe in the people's devotion. The great myth of the union between Tsar and people was the cornerstone of the whole tsarist political edifice. Revolutionaries and historians have expended much energy in explaining how the Russian peasant was hoodwinked by this myth and bemoaning the fact. Ironically, Nicholas and Alexandra were as effectively hoodwinked as any peasant. Nevertheless, it would be wrong to imagine that Nicholas's conception of his relationship with the Russian people was the product simply of naïvety and self-delusion. Nor was his frustration at the obstacles that divided him from the peasantry difficult to understand.

The Emperor was right to believe that the monarchy was the only political institution in Russia with some hold on the emotions and loyalty of both the élites and the masses. Nicholas's simple, patriotic and rather philistine values, not to mention the imperial couple's cosy domestic lifestyle, were mocked by much of Petersburg high society and the intelligentsia. But they were potentially more attractive to the common man and woman. The Emperor genuinely admired, even idealized, the sterling qualities of the Russian peasant and soldier. And he was not wrong in thinking that elements of traditional Russian political thinking were still deeply embedded in the Russian people's mentality. In 1910 Peter Durnovo, referring to this tradition, commented that 'according to the ideas of our people the Tsar has to be terrible but gracious, terrible first and foremost and gracious afterwards'. Aspects of Soviet political history were to bear out this comment. Tsarist religious imagery and paternalism had their echo in the Lenin cult and in the opinion, still often found among ordinary Soviet citizens even in the 1970s, that 'at least Lenin loved us'. Stalin's dictatorship was from one angle tsarism at its most medieval and ruthless, and the dictator himself consciously adopted the mantle of Ivan the Terrible.

Nor even was Rasputin's voice always merely absurd and self-seeking. Sometimes he did express genuine peasant fears and aspirations. In the autumn of 1913, scared by rumours of impending war and worried by the newspapers' incitement of pro-Slav, nationalist frenzy, Rasputin gave two interviews in which he said that peace should be preserved at all costs. Not merely should Christians not slaughter each other on principle but, in comparison to the supposedly Christian peoples of the Balkans, 'the Turks are more fair and peaceful on religious things. You can see how it is – but it comes out different in the newspapers.' A contrast to this piece of folk wisdom was the advice given to Nicholas II in Holy Week 1913 by the President of the Duma, M.V. Rodzyanko. Referring to Russian pro-Slav feeling, the elected representative of Russia's élites commented, 'one must profit from the general enthusiasm. The Straits [Constantinople] must belong to us. War will be accepted with joy and will serve only to increase the prestige of the imperial power.' There is no question as to whose words were wiser or better reflected the feelings of the mass of ordinary Russians whose blood would no doubt need to be spilt generously for the Straits and the government's prestige in the event of a European war.[13]

This is, of course, not to deny that Rasputin's closeness to the imperial couple was a disaster for the monarchy. The danger was not the influence that the *starets* ('holy man') actually wielded, which was always wildly exaggerated by Petersburg society gossip. Before 1914, despite endless stories, there is no evidence that he had any political role or influence. He did, however, help to cause turmoil and division within the Orthodox Church, the milieu from which he sprang. Rasputin was widely, and probably correctly, credited with the promotion of the monk Varnava to the bishopric of Kargopol. The ferocious battle between Rasputin and the anti-Semitic demagogues Bishop Hermogen of Tsaritsyn and his ally, the monk Iliodor, brought both the Church and the monarchy into disrepute. As was his habit, Rasputin boasted to Iliodor about his influence on Nicholas and Alexandra, giving the monk some letters from the Empress to prove his bona fides. Iliodor broadcast the boasts and the letters across the length and breadth of the empire: the boasts were taken at face value and the harmless if flowery letters augmented by pornographic counterfeit ones. When in 1912 Nicholas banished Hermogen and Iliodor from Petersburg in order to put a lid on the scandal, this was grist to the mill of those who believed Rasputin's voice in the Church was all-powerful.

At this time a ferocious argument raged in society over the need to free the Orthodox Church from the state's control. Rasputin's role was a God-given weapon to those who argued, quite correctly, that state domination was not in Orthodoxy's interest. The Rasputin issue was taken up in the Duma and, by invoking parliamentary privilege, then given wide publicity in the press. The key figure behind this move was the Octobrist party leader, Alexander Guchkov. The latter stood for the independence of the Church and for the removal of Nicholas II, the other Romanovs and their 'cliques' from an active role in politics and government. The party leader's desire to achieve this goal to some extent reflected his ambition to fill the resulting political vacuum himself but he also believed that the Romanovs' removal would contribute to a more intelligent and efficient system of government. Guchkov may well have been right but it is a moot point whether élites as vulnerable as Russia's could afford to wash their dirty linen in public and damage the monarchy's prestige in the way he did. A parliamentary system, in which rival political leaders openly competed for influence, denouncing each other and the government in the process, had its dangers from the selfish point of view of the élites. For these élites were now operating in an increasingly literate society in which preliminary censorship had been abolished and a number of mass-circulation newspapers had come into existence.

Guchkov's goals and tactics were, as already mentioned, similar to those pursued by Maximilian Harden in Germany in an effort to drive Wilhelm II and his irresponsible entourage out of active politics. Even Harden's accusations of spiritualism and homosexuality in Wilhelm's entourage had their echoes in the Rasputin affair. Both Harden and Guchkov were middle-class representatives of the new urban society created by the industrial revolution. Guchkov, the elected party politician from a family of industrialists, and Harden, the newspaper editor, were trying to rid their respective political systems of any but symbolic 'relics of feudalism'. But Harden, unlike Guchkov, was operating in a rich and relatively stable society with a huge middle class, a rather conservative peasantry and a working class, much of which had in practice given up the goal of socialist revolution. That made his campaign both safer and more likely to succeed than was the case in Russia. Nicholas II still controlled the army, the police and most of the bureaucracy. His hold on peasant loyalty was much greater than that of any political leader elected by Russia's élites and middle class. Unlike in Germany peasants still made up 80 per cent of the population. In these circumstances, unless a

Tsar voluntarily accepted relegation to a purely symbolic role, only
revolution could push him aside. But for members of Russia's élites,
as they well knew, revolution was a very dangerous fire with which to
play.[14]

For Peter Stolypin and Vladimir Kokovstov, Russia's prime ministers
from 1906 to 1914, the Rasputin affair was an extra cross to bear. Their
position was made more difficult by the fact that they never knew the full
story of the heir's illness or Rasputin's role in preserving his life. This
increased their frustration at the Emperor's unwillingness to remove the
starets from Petersburg once and for all. Nevertheless, Rasputin's significance in pre-war Russian politics should not be exaggerated. The *starets*
was an embarrassment to the government and the affair's impact on the
dynasty's prestige was a matter for concern. But among the problems
faced by Russian prime ministers between 1907 and 1914 the Rasputin
affair ranked nowhere near the top of the list.

One great difficulty was the new, hybrid and untested constitutional
set-up. Russia still had an emperor who was described in his official title as
'autocrat' and who aspired to be the final arbiter of his government's
policy. But the monarch now had a potential rival in his Chairman of the
Council of Ministers, who looked on himself as a true prime minister, at
least in embryo. Unless the Emperor gave his full backing to his Prime
Minister the latter would find it impossible to impose his will on other
ministers and senior officials, in which case the co-ordination of policy
between departments, which was the whole point behind the creation of
the Chairman's position in 1905, would become impossible. But if the
monarch did resign his governmental role in favour of his premier then his
sovereign authority could in time become somewhat akin to that of the
theoretical sovereign in a contemporary West European democracy,
namely 'the people'. All politicians and officials would act in his name and
proclaim his virtue, while often privately decrying the occasional political
activism of their naïve and ignorant sovereign. Periodically he would have
the job of appointing and dismissing his Prime Minister. In the interim,
however, his influence on how his country was governed would usually
be limited. Quite enough has already been said about Nicholas II's conception of monarchy to make it clear that he would not easily accept this
reduced role.

Nor was potential rivalry between the monarch and his Prime Minister
the only problem. Russia now had a parliament without whose consent
neither laws nor much of the budget could be brought into force. It is
in the nature of separate executive and legislative branches to fight,
particularly when both sides are anxious to assert precedents in a new
constitutional order and when, as was the case in Russia, the executive
bureaucracy is widely distrusted in society. The party leaders in the Duma

were certain to push for more power and Nicholas was equally certain to resist them. Standing between Tsar and Duma, and often feeling they had the full support of neither, the ministers' lot was an unhappy one. Moreover, the situation was further complicated by the fact that the Russian legislature had two chambers, a lower house (the Duma) and an upper one (the State Council). Even after property-owners came to dominate the Duma's electorate when the franchise was changed by the decree of 16 June 1907, the lower house was still considerably less conservative than the upper one. The State Council was packed with former ministers and senior officials, most of them both elderly and conservative. Many of these men had doubts about the viability of the whole constitutional system, not to mention the specific reforms proposed by the Duma. Some of these mandarins were also big landowners, as were the majority of their elected colleagues who comprised the other half of the upper house. Like the Tsar, the State Council possessed an absolute veto over legislation. Here, in other words, was a recipe for stalemate and frustration. The most frustrated person of all in this system was likely to be the Prime Minister who, to govern effectively, had somehow to satisfy the very different wishes of the monarch, his fellow ministers and the two legislative chambers.[15]

In the first years of Peter Stolypin's premiership matters appeared to be more or less under control. Stolypin's prestige and his vibrant, commanding personality enabled him to dominate the political system. Minister of Internal Affairs from the spring of 1906, from 23 July 1906 Stolypin combined this post with the premiership. Impressive in stature and blessed with a fine, strong face, Stolypin radiated vigour, forcefulness and self-confidence. Like a number of other ministers in the wake of the 1905 revolution, Stolypin was much younger than had been the ministerial norm in the 1890s. On appointment as Prime Minister he was only 44. Promoted straight from a provincial governorship to the post of Minister of Internal Affairs, Stolypin lacked knowledge of the workings of central government but brought a gust of fresh air into the corridors of the Petersburg bureaucracy. He had a talent for acting, oratory and public relations rare among senior officials. His powerful speeches in the Duma, together with the crushing responses he gave to revolutionary and opposition spokesmen, rallied Russian conservatives and raised their confidence. No one could doubt his courage and patriotism. Stolypin was initially helped by the fact that he was neither a Petersburg bureaucrat nor a member of the capital's high society. Like many members of the third and fourth Dumas, he came from an old and wealthy family of the provincial landowning nobility. This endeared him to both members of the new parliament and Nicholas II.

Stolypin's prestige was also enhanced by the savage bombing of his home in August 1906 which killed dozens of innocent people and crippled one of his children. Vladimir Kokovtsov, then serving as Minister of Finance, recalls that 'this awful blow directed at his own family did not disturb the outward composure and great self-control with which he continued to fight the extreme elements of the revolution . . . After August 12 . . . he acquired great moral prestige. His nobility, courage, and devotion to the state were indisputable. He gained in stature and was unanimously acclaimed master of the situation.' Four days after Stolypin's house was destroyed the Empress Marie wrote to her son, 'when will all these horrible crimes and revolting murders stop? There can be no peace or safety in Russia before these monsters are exterminated! What a blessing that Stolypin's girls are recovering, and that by a miracle he was not hurt. How awful it is for the poor parents to see the sufferings of their own innocent children!' Three months later Nicholas informed her that 'there is still a possibility of more disgusting attempts on the lives of various people. I don't feel happy about good Stolypin. He and his family are living in the Winter Palace; and he comes to Peterhof for reports by steamer. I cannot tell you how much I have come to like and respect this man!'[16]

As is the case with democratic electorates in contemporary Western politics, new Russian ministers tended to enjoy a honeymoon period with their sovereign. Stolypin's honeymoon lasted longer than most. This was in part because during his first two years in office he gave priority to repressing the revolution and reforming the system of peasant landowner-ship by weakening the village commune and encouraging the creation of separate family farms. Both these policies enjoyed widespread support within the ruling élites. In addition, memories of the revolution were still fresh and Stolypin was seen as the saviour and indispensable guarantor of the social order. Even A.A. Kireev, for instance, could not withhold his admiration for the Prime Minister despite strong misgivings about his concessions to parliamentarism. In the spring of 1907 he wrote that 'although one can't agree with the whole government programme, and despite the recognition of Russia as a constitutional country and the Octobrism which grates on my ears, one can't but welcome Stolypin's civil courage, his conviction and his skill as an orator . . . One feels that now at last we have a government again.' Even in December 1908 Kireev believed that 'it is beyond question that Stolypin is a strong character and at the present moment is irreplaceable; he is a gentleman and is not of the Milyukov [radical-liberal] stamp'.[17]

By 1909–10 Stolypin's stock among the élite was falling. Argu-ments were growing between the Duma, the government and the State Council as to whether it was yet safe to rescind the 'states of emergency' by which much of Russia was governed. This would allow the civil rights promised in the constitution to come into effect and would thereby reduce the anger of much of Russian educated society against bureaucratic arbitrariness. Some of Stolypin's proposed reforms were threatening the position of powerful groups and interests. The Orthodox hierarchy denounced efforts to widen and guarantee the rights of other religions and of non-believers. Industrialists complained about new welfare legislation for workers. Above all, the landowning aristocracy attacked Stolypin's plans to democratize in part local government while at the same time increasing the control over it of the central administration. The landowning class disliked bureaucracy only a little less than democracy. Both were seen as threats to the aristocracy's power, whose shakiness had just been rudely illustrated in the 1905 revolution. Landowners struggling to make big estates profitable were terrified at the prospect of the increased tax burdens a more democratic local government might impose. The aristocracy's intransigence was a measure of its weakness. Unlike in nineteenth-century England, the upper class felt itself too poor and too weak to be able to make concessions, buy off opposition and survive. Under the new constitutional system, the aristocracy was far better able to defend its interests than had ever previously been the case. For the first time, the landowners were allowed to organize on a national scale and their pressure group, the United Nobility, became the single most powerful lobby in Russia. Moreover, landowning nobles were now the biggest group in the Duma and were also well entrenched in the State Council. They could and did block legislation that offended their interests. The Russian situation was very similar to that of Prussia in the decades after the 1848 revolution. When absolute monarchy gave way to a conservative and very restricted constitutionalism the aristocracy gained greatly in political power in both countries. As the class most trusted by the monarchy, the landowners acquired the predominant weight in parliament in both Petersburg and Berlin. The agrarian lobby was a thorn in the flesh of Wilhelm II's government. The Russian agrarians helped to wreck Stolypin.[18]

Rather like in pre-1914 Germany, Stolypin turned to nationalism as a means to unite the various sections of the élite. This worked up to a point. After initial arguments, for instance, the government, the Duma and the State Council did to some extent co-operate in rebuilding the army and navy from the ruins of the Russo-Japanese War. Unlike in Germany, however, the Russian government was too weak militarily and too scared of revolution to run the risk of appealing to nationalist sentiment by an adventurous foreign policy. Humiliation at the hands of Austria and Germany during the Bosnian crisis of 1908–9 further damaged the government's nationalist credentials. After Petersburg had been forced to back down and recognize Austria's annexation of Bosnia in the face of an ultimatum from Berlin, Kireev wrote in his diary: 'If Russia were to have any successes at all, then one could rebuild one's fortune on them but there is nothing of the kind . . . On the conclusion of peace [with Japan] the Tsar said to me "Russia has been shamed" and from that day to this nothing has happened to redeem its honour.' Bereft of triumphs in the field of foreign policy, Stolypin was to some extent forced back on mobilizing Russian nationalist sentiment against 'disloyal' minorities within the empire, particularly the Poles and the Finns. But although anti-Finnish and anti-Polish legislation could get through the Duma and the State Council, it inevitably worsened relations between the empire's nationalities and at the same time was a very ineffective way of appealing to latent nationalist sentiment among the Russian masses.[19]

As frustration and opposition to Stolypin began to grow amongst both the élites and Russian society as a whole, the Emperor's restiveness also increased. Even with Stolypin as Prime Minister, Nicholas still enjoyed a great deal of power. When he badly wanted something, he could usually get his way. The Emperor, for instance, vetoed Stolypin's plan to remove most restrictions on Jewish civil rights, following the traditional conservative argument that the Russian peasantry was too backward and economically vulnerable to be exposed to exploitation by crafty Jewish capitalists. Nicholas forced on an unwilling government the re-creation of an ocean-going battle-fleet and destroyed the Council of State Defence when the generals tried to use it as a means to block the navy's demands for extra money. In his view a mighty navy was needed not just to reassert Russia's position as a great power after the catastrophe of Tsushima but also to make Europe's two greatest naval rivals, Britain and Germany, fearful of antagonizing Russia and driving her fleet into the 'opposition' camp. Potentially, in other words, the fleet gave Russian foreign policy the possibility of manoeuvring between Europe's two leading powers, Britain and Germany.

Equally determined was Nicholas's campaign to instill patriotic values into Russian youth by encouraging the creation of a militarized form of boy scouts – the so-called *poteshnie* – in the empire's schools. The Emperor pursued this policy in defiance of the views of his Minister of Education, Professor A.N. Schwartz, whose guiding principle it was to keep anything touching on politics out of Russian schools. Anger at imperial interference was one factor behind Schwartz's decision to quit his ministerial job, which itself is a small commentary on the limited range of possibilities for a monarch who had to balance the desire to have his own way against the need to retain effective ministers.[20]

It was with Stolypin himself, however, that this issue became most pressing. Even in the field of foreign policy, which the constitution had declared to be the monarch's sole responsibility, Stolypin began to play a major role. Very significantly, in the autumn of 1908 a threat of resignation by Stolypin resulted in the abandonment of the policy of doing a deal with Austria over Vienna's annexation of Bosnia and Hercegovina. This policy had been agreed between Nicholas and his Foreign Minister, A.P. Izvolsky, who in strict constitutional principle ought to have been the only two people with a major say in the matter. But Stolypin's position was too powerful and his personality too commanding for his opposition to be ignored. Perhaps it is not entirely surprising that Nicholas once commented to his sister, 'sometimes Stolypin is so high-handed that I get annoyed, but it does not last, and he is the best Prime Minister I have had'. When on 9 May 1909 Nicholas gathered up his courage to override Stolypin's objections and veto the Naval General Staff Bill, he felt constrained to write to his Prime Minister in the following terms: 'Remember that we live in Russia and not abroad or in Finland . . . and therefore I will not allow any thought of retirement . . . I warn you that I categorically reject a request for dismissal from you or anyone else.'[21]

The crisis over the Naval General Staff Bill seemed at first sight to have blown up out of a trivial matter. The Duma had sought to assert its legitimate role in military affairs by confirming the list of personnel of the newly established Naval General Staff, which had been created in the wake of the war with Japan. Looked at more broadly, however, the issue concerned whether the monarch or parliament was to control the armed forces and was therefore of fundamental significance. This was the question over which Charles I and the House of Commons had split in 1641–2. It was also the issue around which the confrontation between the Prussian monarch and parliament had revolved in 1862–3, thereby bringing Otto von Bismarck to power. The establishment of a parliament in Russia made it very likely that a struggle would occur over the armed forces and that both executive and legislature would be very anxious to establish firm precedents in this matter from the start. The Duma and, above all, the Octobrist leader, Guchkov, conducted a powerful and concerted campaign to build up allies in the armed forces, weaken the links to the court of both the army and the navy, and establish their patriotic credentials as responsible and legitimate actors in the military field. It was partly in order to keep the Duma at arm's length and maintain imperial control over the armed forces that General V.A. Sukhomlinov was appointed Minister of War in 1909. As Nicholas's watchdog in the army, Sukhomlinov was loathed by influential figures in the Duma, the press and society. Political battles became entangled with rivalries within the army. In time the Grand Duke Nicholas, Sukhomlinov's main military enemy, was elevated by part of public opinion to the rank of statesman and military genius, despite the fact that the Grand Duke was in fact emotionally unstable, a very poor general and no sort of liberal. By contrast, Sukhomlinov ended up in gaol. All this was to occur during the First World War, when the panic and fury bred of military defeat exacerbated political and personal hatreds existing in pre-war Russia. Moreover, in March 1917 the links established between party leaders and the High Command were to be a significant factor in Nicholas's abdication and the fall of the monarchy.

In March 1909 Peter Durnovo, now leader of the conservative opposition in the State Council, denounced the Naval General Staff Bill, and Duma intervention in military affairs, in the following terms:

> Such intervention, however insignificant, creates dangerous precedents for the direction of the state's defence and gradually entangles the military and naval ministries, all their establishments and ultimately the army and the fleet in civilian attitudes which are alien to them. It introduces discord into military relations and as a result, slowly and quietly but none the less inexorably, undermines the foundations on which the military power of the Russian state rests. Such results will occur because by these impatient interventions the military administration will be transferred into the hands of the State Council and the State Duma, which is contrary to the Fundamental Laws, to our basic beliefs, and to our conception of the high significance of that power which created Russia and personifies her strength and might.

It was with voices like this in his ears that Nicholas, for the only time in his reign, vetoed a bill which had been passed by the Duma and the State Council, in the process arousing Kireev to astonished praise of what he saw as a rare act of imperial independence and resolution.[22]

The Naval General Staff crisis is important because it was a significant stage in Nicholas's worsening relationship with Stolypin. Though the Emperor's attitude can in part be ascribed to irritation, and on his wife's part even to jealousy, at being eclipsed by his powerful and charismatic Prime Minister, the Naval General Staff crisis shows that there was room too for genuine concern about where the constitutional regime might be leading the monarchy and Russia. Conservative figures such as Kireev and Durnovo were experienced, intelligent and loyal servants of the regime. It is not surprising that Nicholas listened to their words and worried at the warnings they conveyed.

For Kireev the bottom line was always that 'a constitutional Russia won't last long'. 'A constitution here!' he once exclaimed, 'We have no restraining elements, neither English aristocracy nor German culture.' Kireev would certainly have agreed with the Bavarian diplomat, Count Moy, that the Russians were impulsive, irresponsible and liable to lurch from one extreme to another at a moment's notice. Kireev himself put down this fascination with extremes to childishness and lack of culture, since only the latter enabled people to see two sides of an issue and respect alternative points of view. Both the Russian personality and the nature of Russian society convinced Kireev that it was impossible to govern the country from the liberal centre. In June 1906, for instance, he wrote, 'the fact is that in themselves the Kadets don't represent any force. They are only strong because of the revolution.' Still weaker was the Octobrist party, on which Stolypin attempted to build his alliance with society despite the fact that Octobrism in reality had very few supporters in Russia. Kireev commented that 'it seems to me that Stolypin's mistake was that he wished to lean on something that doesn't exist, namely the centre'.[23]

Peter Durnovo's views were rather similar to those of Alexander Kireev though they were based less on the psychology of the Russian character and more on the contemporary level of development of Russian society. In Durnovo's view only an authoritarian regime operating under cover of the monarchy's prestige and legitimacy had any hope of holding the Russian Empire together or governing it effectively. Without such a regime, the problem of the non-Russian nationalities would be hard to control. More important, the great majority of the Russian people – peasants and workers – had no respect for the property, culture or values of the country's European élites. The instincts of the Russian masses were egalitarian, collectivist and even socialist. They were anti-bourgeois and un-European. Revolutionary parties existed to mobilize and channel these instincts if allowed the freedom to do so. The liberal centrist parties, in other words the Kadets and Octobrists, enjoyed no support from peasants and workers. Their pressure for civil rights, the rule of law, parliamentary government and other European liberal principles might destroy the police state but could never create an alternative system of government which could protect the interests of the propertied, preserve order, defeat the revolutionaries, or hold the loyalty of the masses. The establishment of constitutional government in Russia could therefore only be the first brief stage in what would very soon become 'social revolution in its most extreme form'. Durnovo was more of a materialist than Kireev. In his view a country's level of economic development more or less determined what type of political institutions it could sustain. Carrying out political reforms or importing Western liberal principles before Russian society had reached the stage of development where prosperity and property-ownership were widespread would be suicidal. The police state provided the essential buttresses and scaffolding which were needed to support the dwelling of propertied, 'cultured' and European Russia until the house's foundations were securely rooted in a developed capitalist economy and society.[24]

In their hearts Kireev and Durnovo rather despised Nicholas II. He was not the iron-willed, imposing and clear-sighted autocrat whom, in their view, Russia needed. Kireev complained that 'the Tsar is the central figure in our life but he is the very epitome of lack of will'. He added in December 1908, 'it is very difficult to work in the political sphere. The Emperor, who still (in the last resort) actually decides matters, wavers to such an extent that it is impossible to rely on him.' In early 1914 Peter Durnovo is said to have responded to an offer of the premiership in the following terms: 'Your Majesty, my system as head of the government and Minister of Internal Affairs cannot provide quick results, it can only tell after a few years and these years will be a time of complete rumpus: dissolution of the Duma, assassinations, executions, perhaps armed uprisings. You, Your Majesty, will not endure these years and will dismiss me; under such conditions my stay in power cannot do any good and will bring only harm.' On another, well-authenticated, occasion Durnovo called Nicholas 'the kind of man who, if you asked him for his last shirt, would take it off and give it to you'.[25]

The criticisms of Kireev and Durnovo were echoed by so many people who worked with Nicholas II that they must contain considerable truth. Nevertheless, it is possible to defend the Tsar up to a point. Peter Durnovo was a clever man but he could also be cynical and ruthless. His attitude to the ordinary Russian of his day – peasant or worker – was not only tough but also contemptuous. His was the voice of the Russian ruling élite at its least sentimental and populist. In the State Council he stressed the 'cultural weakness of the Russian people', feared that revolutionary agitators in the countryside could easily appeal to 'the half-savage instincts of the crude mob' and argued that the Russian masses had no political aspirations beyond a destructive, radical egalitarianism. Nicholas II was less intelligent and much more naïve than Durnovo but, in addition, his instinct was always to see the best in people. That is one reason why he found the ruthless world of Russian high politics so difficult. Long since dissipated by bitter experience where high society or the political world were concerned, the Tsar's instinctive trustfulness and goodwill still prevailed as regards the mass of the Russian people. Not only Nicholas's personality but also his conception of his role as Tsar and father of his people made it impossible for him to see the monarchy as simply a useful device through which Russia's cultured and Westernized élites could protect their interests and in time impose their values on the masses. The Tsar might at times regard his subjects as annoyingly wayward children but never under any circumstances as semi-savages without human values and aspirations.[26]

In addition, the line urged by Kireev and Durnovo had one obvious weakness. Both men dismissed the liberal parties in the Duma, and indeed liberal currents in Russian educated society, as unimportant. But although urban, educated, Westernized Russians still made up a relatively small part of the empire's population, in absolute terms they were a large and rapidly increasing group. Most educated and urban Russians were liberal or radical in their political sympathies, and this sector of Russian society was equal in size to the town population of one of the bigger Western European states. Already by 1914 some Russian newspapers had circulations of over 100,000. This was the world of Stravinsky, Diaghilev and Chagall. It was also the world of rapid industrial growth and of a tremendous expansion of administrative and professional middle-class jobs. Such a large, well-educated and sophisticated society demanded civil rights and a political voice. It looked with disdain and even shame on a political regime which still rested in part on eighteenth-century principles of absolute monarchy and even older, medieval aspects of tsarist ideology. The shadowy presence of a figure such as Rasputin only increased this shame. The Tsar's own officials sprang from educated society and lived within it. They were bound to be influenced by its values. As their ever more frequent marriages to commoners and divorcees showed, even members of the Romanov family were rejecting the dynasty's corporate code and putting the pursuit of individual happiness and fulfilment above group loyalty and traditional values.

Durnovo and Kireev may or may not have been right to believe that in Russia, for the present, this European, 'cultured' and property-owning élite world could only survive if protected by an authoritarian state. That was certainly not the view of most educated Russians between 1906 and 1914. After witnessing the revolution of workers, peasants and Bolsheviks in 1917, even the Kadet party, the main political voice of middle-class radicalism and liberalism, came to support a White counter-revolutionary movement whose victory would undoubtedly have resulted in a military dictatorship. The position of the always more conservative Octobrists was the same. A decade earlier, fairly enough, attitudes were different.

Nicholas II was under pressure from one group of advisers who told him that concessions to liberalism would undermine the authoritarian state and doom property and the Russian Empire to destruction. Another group, with equal insistence, told him that, without such concessions, support for the government in educated society would disintegrate and the regime would collapse. Both sets of advisers had a point. The Tsar sympathized more with the first, conservative, group of advisers. But the pressure on his regime from educated society was very great and hard to oppose. In these circumstances there was some excuse for uncertainty and wavering.[27]

In March 1911 Stolypin suffered a major political defeat over his plan to

introduce elected *zemstvos* into six provinces in Russia's western borderlands (that is, present-day Belorussia and the Ukraine). Hitherto, *zemstvos*
had been confined to the core Russian provinces because of fears that the
Polish landowners, who predominated in the Ukraine and Belorussia,
would control elected councils and use them against Russian interests.
Stolypin's new law was cleverly constructed to offer something to
different sections of the political élite. Since experience showed
that provinces with *zemstvos* provided better agricultural, medical and
educational services to the population, the new law could be defended on
purely administrative grounds. Because many members of the Duma were
liberal or liberal-conservative landowners involved in *zemstvo* affairs, the
extension of local self-government should also be politically attractive. To
ensure that the new *zemstvo* would not be controlled by the Polish nobility
Stolypin extended the franchise and set up separate electoral curias. This
could be expected to appeal to the Russian nationalist lobby. As regards
the Duma, Stolypin's calculations proved correct. The bill sneaked
through by 165 votes to 139, though not without some damaging
amendments.

The next problem was the State Council, through which the bill had to
pass before it could be put on the statute book. As was to be the case many
times between 1907 and 1914, it proved impossible to produce a law on
which both upper and lower house could agree. Some members of the
State Council objected to dividing the electorate into ethnic blocs. Others
protested that lowering the franchise to stop Polish aristocratic control of
the *zemstvos* established dangerous precedents for the democratization of
local government. Undoubtedly, personal and political antagonism
towards Stolypin also played a role. If the Emperor had exerted all his
influence on members of the State Council in support of the bill then it
would probably have been passed. Instead, when leaders of the upper
house's right wing stressed to Nicholas II their objections to the bill, both
orally and on paper, he told them to vote as their consciences dictated. As
a result, the bill was defeated by 92 votes to 68.

Stolypin was enraged. The Western *Zemstvo* Bill had been a key part of
his political strategy. More important, Stolypin saw the bill's defeat as
part of a broader campaign by 'reactionary forces', meaning the monarch
and the State Council, to block any chance of a *rapprochement* with the
Duma and the classes, interests and opinions which it represented. The
Prime Minister interpreted Nicholas's comment that members of the
upper house should be guided by their consciences as deliberate sabotage of
government policy. Stolypin was a proud and masterful man: he felt
personally humiliated by his defeat. In addition, he was ill and exhausted
by his struggle to hold monarch, government and legislature together
behind a coherent policy. Running the machinery of government, over-

seeing reforms and beating off attacks from the Duma and public opinion were difficult enough. Deprived of the monarch's unequivocal and public support the burden of office became unbearable. Stolypin resigned. He insisted that he would only return to office if Nicholas would allow him to assert his supremacy in a spectacular fashion over all other players in the political game. Peter Durnovo and Vladimir Trepov, the conservative leaders in the State Council, must be removed from Petersburg 'on leave' for the rest of the year. Both houses of the legislature must be prorogued for a few days and emergency powers used to put the Western *Zemstvo* Bill on the statute book.

Stolypin's demand presented Nicholas with a dilemma. He did not want his premier to resign. On 22 May he wrote to Stolypin that 'your devotion to me and to Russia, your five years' experience in the post you hold, and, most of all, your courageous upholding of Russian political principles on the borders of the Empire, move me to retain you at all costs'. Probably even more important in the Emperor's eyes was worry about 'what will become of the government, which is responsible to me, if the ministers resign because they have a battle today with the State Council and tomorrow with the Duma?' Very reluctantly, therefore, Nicholas complied with Stolypin's demands. No doubt the Emperor deeply disliked having to submit to such an ultimatum and must have realized that to use emergency powers in this way was illegal. Both the Duma and the State Council felt humiliated at the Prime Minister's high-handed and unconstitutional action. Well before his assassination on 14 September 1911 Stolypin's days in office were numbered, for he had succeeded in infuriating most of the key actors on the political scene. Undoubtedly, Nicholas himself drew certain lessons from the Western *Zemstvo* crisis. It helped to undermine his faith both in the wisdom of his Prime Minister and in the viability of a constitutional set-up which appeared to doom his government to paralysis and confusion. In particular, centring government strategy around a programme of reform designed to satisfy the Duma's majority seemed to be a recipe for dissension between the chambers and for legislation which caused more problems than it solved.[28]

One month after Stolypin's death, his successor, Vladimir Kokovtsov, had a long conversation with the Empress Alexandra. The new premier bemoaned the fact that it would be increasingly difficult to get legislation through the Duma since he enjoyed less support there than Stolypin, and the major parties were in any case breaking up into increasingly chaotic factions. The Empress responded with the comment that

we hope that you will never take the road of those dreadful political parties, who only dream about seizing power or subordinating the government to their will . . . Listening to you I see that you are making comparisons between yourself and Stolypin. It seems to me that you respect his memory highly and assign too much significance to his personality and activity. Believe me that there is no need to regret those who no longer live . . . I am convinced that each man fulfils his role and calling and if someone is no longer with us that is because he has fulfilled his role and had to retire into the background since he had nothing more to accomplish. Life always takes new forms and you ought not to try blindly to continue what your predecessor did. Remain yourself and don't seek support in political parties. In our country they are so insignificant. Rest on the Emperor's confidence. God will help you. I am convinced that Stolypin died in order to make way for you and that this is for Russia's good.[29]

During Kokovtsov's twenty-nine months as Prime Minister the government abandoned any attempt to present a coherent package of reforms to the Duma. This was partly because after Stolypin's death the power of the premier declined sharply. As a result, battles between ministers and conflicting departmental policies began to return to the pre-1905 pattern. Stolypin's dominance had depended above all on his personal relationship with Nicholas, his charisma and his reputation as the man who had saved Russia from revolution in 1906–7. As premier, Stolypin had succeeded in choosing most, though not all, of his fellow ministers. They were for the most part his 'team'. Vladimir Kokovtsov had none of these advantages. He inherited his fellow ministers from Stolypin and was seldom able to promote his own candidates when vacancies occurred. In the Council of Ministers Kokovtsov was one veteran Petersburg official among others. The new premier was a clever and exceptionally hard-working man with decades of experience in financial and economic matters but he had none of Stolypin's charisma or talent for publicity. A small, neat and slightly pedantic man who liked the sound of his own voice, even in physical terms Kokovtsov lacked Stolypin's stature. Moreover his relationship with Nicholas was always merely correct and official.

With the departure of the masterful Stolypin, voices were raised that the dominant role in domestic affairs should belong not to the Chairman of the Council of Ministers but rather to the monarch and his Minister of Internal Affairs. Prince V.P. Meshchersky, an old acquaintance of both Nicholas and his father, wrote in 1911 that 'the direction taken by government policy is decided not by the Council of Ministers and not by its Chairman but by the Minister of Internal Affairs, in whose hands at present lies control over all rights and freedoms, over everything relating to the realization of the act of 17 October 1905'. Constantly sniping at Kokovtsov, Meshchersky urged Nicholas to take the lead in determining his government's policy. 'Russia's salvation is in the power of its Tsar,' wrote Meshchersky in 1913. 'On the day that the Tsar is not strong, Russia will die.' Advice such as this emboldened Nicholas to insist on his own candidate as Minister of Internal Affairs in 1913. The Emperor met the young Governor of Chernigov province, Nicholas Maklakov, in 1911 and liked him. No doubt he was partly attracted to Maklakov because the latter, like Stolypin, was in his forties, was full of energy and was an official with plenty of experience of provincial life rather than a Petersburg bureaucrat. Subsequently, Maklakov commented that, 'speaking with complete sincerity', everything to do with his appointment 'was completely unexpected . . . for me, it was like a clap of thunder from a clear sky'. For Kokovtsov, the appointment of Maklakov came closer to being the clap of doom. The previous Minister of Internal Affairs, A.A. Makarov, had been Kokovtsov's ally and client. With Maklakov's appointment it was clear that control over domestic policy was slipping from the premier's hands.[30]

Within the Council of Ministers Kokovtsov had some formidable enemies. Among the most dangerous were Vladimir Sukhomlinov, Minister of War, and Alexander Krivoshein, Minister of Agriculture. Kokovtsov combined the posts of Prime Minister and Minister of Finance. In his latter capacity, determined to control spending, he incurred the wrath of the main spending departments. In Sukhomlinov's case, the battle between the treasury and the army over money was worsened by deep personal enmity between himself and Kokovtsov. In addition, the Prime Minister was desperate to avoid anything that increased the risk of war and believed some of Sukhomlinov's statements and actions to be needlessly provocative. Nicholas regarded the armed forces as beyond the premier's legitimate remit. He trusted Sukhomlinov, whom he had known for years. He also saw him as an indispensable barrier to the Duma's efforts to forge close links with the officer corps. There was no possibility of the Emperor dropping Sukhomlinov in order to please Kokovtsov.

Still more interesting was the case of Alexander Krivoshein. The Ministry of Agriculture, which he headed, had grown enormously in importance since 1905. This ministry was now responsible for implementing the so-called Stolypin land reforms, in other words for encouraging the weakening of the commune and the emergence of hereditary, consolidated, privately owned farms in place of the old system of collective ownership and the division of the village's fields into strips. By 1917 considerable progress had been made. Between one-quarter and one-third of all formerly communal land was owned outright by peasants, though the consolidation of a family's land into one enclosed farm was often a difficult task and was proceeding much more slowly. The commune was very far from dead but its influence had been weakened in some areas. Nor in any case were undermining the commune or implementing the land reforms the only strands in the government's policy towards agriculture and the peasantry. Between 1905 and 1914 about one-fifth of all noble land was sold to peasants, the government providing cheap credit to help the purchasers. Peasant consumer and trading co-operatives mushroomed. Krivoshein's ministry co-operated successfully with the *zemstvos*, whose trust it enjoyed. Central government funds poured into the *zemstvos* to improve the rural economy and rural life in general. Primary education got particular priority. By 1914 roughly three-fifths of Russian children attended school and it was reasonable to predict universal primary education by the 1920s.[31]

All these changes were not merely important in themselves but also had tremendous political implications for the imperial regime. Inevitably, the Ministry of Agriculture and Alexander Krivoshein became key actors in Russian government and politics. In the words of one senior official, Krivoshein was 'a masterful chief in his own ministry [and] . . . a subtle diplomat outside it'. Krivoshein's skilful handling of the huge and complicated tasks faced by his ministry enhanced his reputation. Astonishingly, by 1914 he enjoyed the sympathy of the *zemstvos*, much of the Duma, the State Council and even the Empress Alexandra. Nicholas discussed with his trusted minister issues which went well beyond the narrow sphere of agriculture. By the summer of 1913 Krivoshein was clearly a dangerous rival to Kokovtsov, whose stress on budgetary stringency he greatly resented. Cheap credit for peasant farmers was a particular source of conflict. Krivoshein's plan was to replace Kokovstov as Minister of Finance with his own friend and client, Peter Bark, which would ensure more money and a more favourable hearing for the agricultural department's pet schemes. For a number of reasons Krivoshein craftily preferred not to take the premiership himself but instead to replace Kokovtsov with the aged Ivan Goremykin, whom he felt he could control. From the winter of 1912, 'in the plans for Krivoshein's oral reports to Nicholas, alongside information about the course of the party struggle in the Duma (which did not at all come within the competence of the head of agriculture) there appears the point: "Goremykin". Judging by what happened subsequently, Krivoshein had begun to persuade the Tsar to appoint Goremykin as premier, in order to operate behind his back'. And indeed on 11 February 1914 Krivoshein's intrigue succeeded. Kokovtsov was replaced by Goremykin as premier and by Bark in the Ministry of Finance. Paul Benckendorff reported to his brother that Nicholas neither wanted nor expected Goremykin to do anything. The idea behind his appointment was to destroy the power of the Chairman of the Council of Ministers as it had existed under Stolypin. Meshchersky and the Empress

Alexandra were behind this move. Even under Kokovtsov, in Bencken-dorff's words, the ministers had fought among themselves 'like cats and dogs'. Further to weaken the chairman's role was 'terribly dangerous'. Benckendorff was right but it is a mark of Krivoshein's subtlety that his considerable part in Kokovtsov's overthrow was invisible even to the Grand Marshal of the Court. From February 1914 until the summer of 1915 the Minister of Agriculture was the most powerful figure in the imperial government.[32]

Meanwhile, armed with the Emperor's support, Nicholas Maklakov continued to pursue his own course as Minister of Internal Affairs both before and after Kokovtsov's dismissal. Maklakov was an impulsive man. Not unlike Stolypin, this former governor came to Petersburg with little experience of Russian high politics or of the city's character. He did not fully grasp how very much more powerful public opinion was in the capital than in the provinces. Nevertheless, Maklakov was by no means the buffoon generally depicted in Western history books. He came to office with a clear mandate from Nicholas to launch a counter-attack against the civil and political rights gained by society since 1905. He used the states of emergency which existed in many provinces to banish enemies of the regime against whom there was insufficient evidence to secure judicial convictions for subversion. He was determined to curb the press, if possible by enacting a new censorship law but if necessary by declaring a state of emergency in Petersburg itself. He resolved to stop the situation in which revolutionary parties used the Duma as a privileged tribune from which to spread their denunciations of the government throughout Russia. From the regime's point of view the logic of some of Maklakov's schemes was clear. The Bolshevik party, for instance, used its deputies in the Duma with the single avowed aim of encouraging armed revolution. By 1914 the Bolshevik newspaper, *Pravda*, published between 20,000 and 40,000 copies daily in the same cause, sending 12,000 of them through the post to regular subscribers. At least as damaging to the regime, however, were the speeches and articles of the liberal politicians and press revealing scandals such as an internal government report casti-gating the police for the massacre of workers in 1912 on the Lena gold-fields or the Rasputin affair. In the spring of 1914 Maklakov went on to the offensive against the revolutionaries. In an attempt to undermine their freedom of speech in the Duma, he indicted the socialist leader N.S. Chkheidze for subversion because of his advocacy of republicanism. The editorial office of *Pravda* was finally shut down in July 1914. But despite Nicholas's support, the other ministers blocked Maklakov's plans for a more broadly based assault on freedom of the press.

Still more horrified was the reaction of most ministers to Maklakov's plans to reduce the Duma's powers. On the right the former revolutionary and now ultra-conservative Lev Tikhomirov spoke for many when he argued that the new constitutional system created a dangerous paralysis in government since 'everyone can get in everyone else's way but there is no one who could force the institutions of state to collaborate'. Nicholas II himself wrote in October 1913 that he had long favoured a change in the statutes of the legislative bodies in order to end stalemate between them and to return to him the final say as to whether laws should be passed. 'Presenting for the sovereign's choice and confirmation the opinions of the majority and the minority [in the Duma and State Council] will be a good return to the previous calm course of legislative activity and will in addition be in the Russian spirit.' Whatever the theoretical advantages of such a course of action, most ministers shrank from the head-on collision with public opinion that a new constitutional coup would entail. Even Michael Akimov, the extremely conservative President of the State Council, told the Emperor rather gruffly that he had created the constitutional system and would now have to live with it.[33]

By 1914 talk of revolution was again in the air, fuelled by mounting labour unrest, the frustrated hopes of the middle classes and squabbling within the government. In fact the chances of revolution in 1914 were very slim. After years of good harvests the countryside was quiet. There were very few signs of discontent in the army, whose loyalty was in the immediate sense the government's main guarantee against revolution. Troops brought back into Petersburg to deal with the city's 'general strike' in July 1914 appeared completely loyal. Nor were they in the event needed since the strike collapsed and the police proved able to cope on their own. In 1914 the authorities reckoned that two-thirds of all political strikes in Russia occurred in the imperial capital. Even in Petersburg, however, the solidarity of labour never approached the levels of 1905 or 1917. Labour unrest reached its peak in July 1914 but even then most manual workers in Petersburg did not strike. Not only the great mass of commercial and domestic labourers but even the railway workers remained aloof. In the run-up to 1905 liberals and socialists had often marched side by side. Even many from the landowning gentry had sympathized with the Liberation Movement. Industrialists had also often supported the opposition, in some cases in resentment at the government's promotion of police trade unionism. Nothing similar occurred in 1914. In the previous seven years most educated Russians had turned their backs on revolutionary socialism. A few left-wing Kadets and a sprinkling of young, radical and noisy Moscow industrialists advocated an alliance with the workers and socialists but most of the party leaders in the Duma remembered the anarchy of 1905–7 and shunned this idea. The Ministry of Internal Affairs and the Petersburg industrialists opposed the strike relentlessly, efficiently and in unison. Despite the sound and fury of July 1914 in Petersburg, the government was never in any danger.[34]

In the larger perspective, however, the regime had much more reason to worry. The bulk of the Russian population had been virtually excluded from constitutional politics after the franchise was changed in June 1907. Peasants and workers remained a formidable threat both to the imperial regime and to the world of Russia's wealth and property. Though much of what had happened in the countryside since 1907 was promising from the government's point of view, most peasants remained determined to seize the big estates if the weakness of authority gave them the chance. Moreover, by encouraging peasants to split off from the communes and demand separate private farms the Stolypin land reforms had caused a good deal of conflict within the peasantry. Still worse was the situation among urban workers. The idea of police trade unionism was dead, killed by memories of Bloody Sunday and by the anger it stirred up among employers. But the alternative strategy of legalizing trade unions and strikes was never followed consistently by the regime. This was partly because most industrialists, above all in Petersburg and the Ukraine, strongly opposed unions. It was also because, with good reason, the police were terrified that legal trade unions would simply become untouchable headquarters for the various branches of the revolutionary socialist parties. Denied legal outlets even for economic grievances, the growing radicalism of workers was inevitable.

The bulk of the middle class, whose political voice was the Kadet party, were also in an angry and frustrated mood. The constitutional era had brought them neither fully secure civil rights, nor greater power and status in Russian society. The Kadet leadership felt, in the words of F.I. Rodichev, that the government's intransigence meant 'that we are being made fools of in front of all those who say that you will never achieve anything with this government save by violence'. The main representative organs of Russia's propertied élites, namely the United Nobility and the Congress of Representatives of Trade and Industry, were much more conservative than the Kadets but even in these circles the government's infringement of civil rights was often resented. In addition, industrialists grumbled at the agrarians' influence in the government and some Duma politicians drawn from the élites itched for ministerial office. Meanwhile discord between ministers and the lack of a commanding presence like that of Stolypin weakened the government's confidence and prestige. Memories of the war with Japan, rumours about Rasputin, and the general belief that the monarch was weak and wavering meant that very few members of Russia's élites had much confidence in Nicholas II's ability to lead their country.[35]

Russia's situation in 1914 did not augur well for a peaceful transition to liberalism and democracy. This was partly because the Emperor, who still retained the last word in such matters, could only be pressured into constitutional concessions by the dire and immediate threat of revolution. One can envisage circumstances in which the monarch could have been pushed aside by a coalition of élites, as to some extent happened in March 1917. Had Nicholas died, it is quite possible to imagine his invalid son or weak-willed brother becoming a mere constitutional symbol of authority, as was the case, for instance, when the 9-year-old Prince Amanda Mahidol ascended the Siamese throne in 1935. Even had the Russian élites come to power on an impeccably liberal platform, however, their weakness and vulnerability would soon have forced them back in the direction of a police state if they wished to preserve their property and status. Determination to maintain the integrity of the Russian Empire in the face of nationalist threats would have led in the same direction. Nor do comparisons with other countries on Europe's periphery in the twentieth century inspire one to optimism about the chances of constitutional liberalism in Russia. There are dangers in making such comparisons across societies and eras. A country's history to a great extent depends on its specific circumstances and on the bewildering intermingling of events and personalities which form a pattern that is never repeated. Take out the Bolshevik revolution and all the cards in twentieth-century European history have to be reshuffled. Nevertheless, it must be of some relevance to Russia that all the monarchies in inter-war Eastern Europe either became royal dictatorships or provided a respectable covering for military or even, in the Romanian case, semi-Fascist rule. In Italy, where constitutionalism was far more deeply rooted than in Russia, the House of Savoy made its compromise with Fascism in 1922 and stuck to it for twenty-one years. In Russia before 1914 the radical right was weak and divided, in large part because the continuing power of the old semi-absolutist regime gave Fascism little room or incentive to develop. But if liberals or moderate socialists had come to power on tsarism's ruins then circumstances might have changed rapidly, particularly if Fascist victory elsewhere in Europe had established a trend.[36]

The most fruitful comparison with twentieth-century Russia is, however, probably Spain. Like Russia, Spain was on Europe's periphery. Its people were poor and its middle class small by Western European, but not Russian standards. Class conflict was bitter and, in both countries, the political spectrum covered the entire range from defenders of medieval principles of absolute monarchy to numerous supporters of anarchism and Communism. Castilian and Russian centralizing nationalism fought autonomist and potentially separatist movements on the countries' periphery. The entry into politics of the socialist and anarchist masses caused intense concern to the propertied élites in both Spain and Russia in the twentieth century. In Russia in 1917 and in Spain in 1931 the political élite abandoned a hopelessly compromised monarchy and sought to preserve as much as possible of their position under a liberal republic. Very soon the upper and middle classes came to the conclusion that they could not live with the growing power of workers and peasants, let alone the danger of socialist dictatorship. In part unwittingly, Franco achieved what Durnovo and even Stolypin had advocated. Under the watchful eye of his policemen and soldiers the Spanish economy was transformed, in the process making Spain safe for property and therefore, not coincidentally, also for democracy. The nature of his regime ensured that most of the costs of modernization were met by the masses, not the élites. Spanish industrialists and landowners had far less reason to fear for their property, status and lives in the 1970s than had been the case forty years before, for under Franco Spain had acquired a huge middle class and a relatively prosperous and non-revolutionary working class as well. Even the bitter conflict between landowners and labourers on the great estates of Andalusia had been defused, thanks to the departure of most of the workers to the factories of Catalonia and Castile, and the mechanization of the latifundias.

The victory of conservatism in Spain and its defeat in Russia had roots deep in the history of each country. Quite unlike Russia, in Spain autonomous municipal, regional and corporate institutions had existed for centuries. The royal state in nineteenth-century Spain had been far weaker than in Russia. Indeed, in the Napoleonic era it collapsed altogether. The major conservative interests had therefore to a much greater extent been forced to act autonomously in defence of their interests. They had thereby acquired political strength and maturity. This was true above all of the Church and the army, the two great institutional pillars of Franco's victory in the civil war. From its earliest origins the Catholic Church had always been more independent of the secular authorities than was generally the case with Orthodoxy. But in nineteenth-century Spain, the collapse of the absolute monarchy, secularization of Church property, and open conflict between right and left forced the Church to take up an active and independent political position. Under the imperial regime the Orthodox Church had neither the means nor the need to do this. Nowhere, especially in rural Russia, were priests hated by peasants or even workers with a ferocity equal to that in southern Spain in the 1930s. Nowhere in the Russian civil war did the clergy play as active and popular a political role on the side of counter-revolution as in central and, still more, northern Spain in 1936–9.

Eighteenth-century Russia witnessed many military coups. Spain at that time witnessed none. In the nineteenth century precisely the reverse occurred. The Russian army concentrated exclusively on combating foreign enemies. Apart from losing a small-scale war with the Americans, the Spanish army's role was entirely domestic and encompassed two civil wars and a number of coups. Geopolitics reinforced tradition. Spain, protected by the Pyrenees and no longer a great power, could avoid involvement in European wars. Russia, a great power with open frontiers, could not do so. Spain's colonial campaigns in Africa created a core of ruthless professional regiments, ideal for counter-revolution. To fight the Germans Russia needed a huge conscript force, inherently less reliable as a weapon of domestic coercion. In 1914 the professional officer cadre of Russia's army, which had saved the imperial regime in 1905–6, went to war with Germany and was destroyed. Thus even a comparison between Russia and Spain brings us back inexorably to the outbreak of war in 1914, which played such a huge role in bringing on the end of the Russian monarchy and the triumph of Bolshevism.[37]

In the wake of the defeat by Japan and revolution the prospect of a European war was a nightmare for the Russian government. In the years that followed 1905 Russia's military and political weakness was only too obvious both to its own rulers and to foreigners. Weakness was a terrible burden for any government to have to carry in pre-1914 international relations. The feeble were pushed around by other powers. Humiliation further damaged a regime's domestic prestige. In its anxiety to stop this process, a government was apt to make exaggerated statements about its willingness and ability to stand up for its interests, if necessary in battle. A gap opened up between rhetoric and intentions, as foreigners soon perceived. As a result firm statements were heard at a discount. Russian diplomacy suffered from this between 1907 and 1914. To understand why Russia went to war in 1914 it is also necessary to grasp the values and mentality of the Russian ruling élites, including Nicholas II. In old regime Europe the nobleman was brought up to defend his public reputation and honour at all costs, if necessary with sword in hand. The ethic of the duel still prevailed in aristocratic and, in particular, military circles. No crime was worse than cowardice. Kings, aristocrats and generals were not used to being pushed about or humiliated. In contemporary parlance, they had a short fuse. In pre-1914 Europe, war was still widely regarded not only as honourable and even romantic, but also as a sometimes necessary and legitimate means by which great powers could defend their interests and achieve national goals unobtainable by peaceful measures. Victory was a meaningful concept even as regards wars between great powers in a way that makes little sense in the nuclear age. The catastrophe of 1914 is incomprehensible unless these underlying realities are taken into account.[38]

The main aim of Russian foreign policy in the immediate aftermath of 1905 was to remain on good terms with everyone. For a weak country in a Europe that was increasingly splitting into two power blocs this was a very difficult and, in the end, impossible task. Nevertheless, the new Foreign Minister, Alexander Izvolsky, did his best. In 1907 agreements with Tokyo and London very much reduced the risk of conflict over Asian issues. Since Britain was Japan's ally and was drawing close to France, the *entente* with London also improved Petersburg's links with Paris while further guaranteeing Russia against any aggressive moves by Tokyo in the Far East. As Izvolsky fully understood, however, agreement with Britain would be counter-productive if it led to bad relations with Berlin. The Russian Foreign Minister tried very hard to ensure that this would not happen. He signed a secret treaty with Berlin in 1907, for instance, on Baltic affairs and in his negotiations with Britain over Persia made very sure that he kept to his promise 'that no German interests either as related to the Baghdad railway or to the equality of commercial opportunity would be in the slightest degree affected'.[39]

Nevertheless, Russia's agreement with Britain made it clear to the Germans that their attempt to play on Petersburg's hostility to London and thereby split the Franco-Russian alliance had failed. In addition, domestic developments in Russia were bound to worry Berlin. As the British embassy in Petersburg reported, 'the partial emancipation of the Russian people has been accompanied by a most pronounced and almost universal outburst of feeling against Germans and Germany'. Officials with German names, though usually by now fully Russianized, played a major and often conservative role in the Tsar's government, which inspired both anger and envy among many Russians. The German Empire was seen as the most powerful bulwark of authoritarian conservatism in Europe, in contrast to Britain and France, the continent's leading democratic powers. Moreover, Germans and Austrians were the main rivals of Slavdom and Russia in Eastern Europe and the Balkans, where many Russians believed their country's historical destiny lay.[40]

Between 1907 and 1914 the outlines of a coalition between sections of Russia's economic, political and intellectual élites based on a combination of liberal and nationalist ideas began to emerge. It encompassed a number of leading Moscow industrialists, some of Russia's greatest liberal intellectuals and many Duma leaders. By 1914 this shadowy coalition had important friends in both the army and the bureaucracy. Prince Grigori Trubetskoy, who ran the Foreign Ministry's department of Near Eastern and Balkan affairs, was closely linked to the Moscow industrialists and to Peter Struve, the leading intellectual spokesman for the coalition of the liberal-conservative and nationalist élites. Even Alexander Krivoshein, the Minister of Agriculture, was a potential ally of this coalition. His ministry, and indeed he himself, maintained cordial relations with the Duma and the *zemstvos*. On the whole, they enjoyed a good press. And Krivoshein was not merely inclined towards pro-Slav nationalist sympathies, he had also married a daughter of one of Moscow's leading industrialist families. It needs to be stressed that this coalition was still in embryo in 1907-9 and that Germany's own aggressive policies played a role in bringing it to life in later years. Nevertheless the Germans were not wrong to watch Russian domestic developments with great concern in the pre-war era. The idea that the liberal-nationalist, anti-German and pro-Slav coalition represented the wave of the future was not unreasonable and was widely believed both in Russia and abroad.[41]

Nicholas II was aware of the dangers created by Russian public opinion's anti-German outbursts. In June 1908, during the meeting at Reval between the Tsar and King Edward VII, a senior British diplomat, Sir Charles Hardinge, had a long conversation with the Russian monarch.

> The Emperor admitted that from the point of view of the relations of Russia to Germany, the liberty of the press had caused him and his government considerable embarrassment since every incident that occurred in any distant province of the empire, such as an earthquake or thunderstorms, was at once put down to Germany's account, and serious complaints had recently been made to him and the government of the unfriendly tone of the Russian press. He was, however, quite unable to remedy this state of affairs except by an occasional official communiqué to the press and this had generally but slight effect. He wished very much that the press would turn their attention to internal rather than foreign affairs, but this was too much to expect.[42]

German irritation with Russia was to play an important role in Petersburg's humiliation in the so-called Bosnian crisis of 1908-9. The origin of this crisis lay in Vienna's determination formally to annex the provinces of Bosnia and Hercegovina which it had in fact occupied since 1878. This decision reflected in part a broader Austrian wish to assert itself in the Balkans. Russia was too weak to oppose the annexation so Izvolsky decided to do a deal with his Austrian counterpart, Baron Aehrenthal, whom he visited at his estate at Buchlau in September 1908. The two foreign ministers agreed that Russia would accept the annexation and Austria would subsequently support Petersburg's wish to open the Straits (that is, the sea passage from the Black Sea to the Mediterranean) to Russian warships. Izvolsky secured the consent of Nicholas II in advance to a deal. The Foreign Minister believed that opening the Straits would redound to his and Russia's prestige. Annexation on the other hand was not merely a *fait accompli* but also an act which would damage Austria's standing among the Balkan Slavs, which could only benefit Russia.

Izvolsky's self-satisfaction soon evaporated. He quickly discovered that the English and French were not enthusiastic about raising the issue of the

Straits. The Austrian circular announcing the annexation stated that it had Russia's full consent, which, although true, was not supposed to be public knowledge. Meanwhile Stolypin, many members of the Duma, and the press exploded at Russia's further humiliation, and her betrayal of Slav interests. When the Prime Minister threatened to resign, Russian foreign policy had to go into reverse. No deals were to be made with Vienna. Instead Petersburg began to call for an international conference to put a legal stamp on the annexation and, more important, to save Russia's prestige. Since Russia was too weak to force the issue, the Germans and Austrians were flatly opposed to a conference, and the British and French were lukewarm, this policy could only end in defeat and humiliation for Petersburg. This duly occurred in March 1909. Vienna demanded that Petersburg and Belgrade formally recognize the annexation of Bosnia-Hercegovina. It prepared to invade Serbia to enforce this demand. Meanwhile Germany sent Russia a fierce note calling on it to defuse the crisis by agreeing immediately and unconditionally to recognize the annexation. Given its military and political weakness, Russia had no alternative but to do so.

The Bosnian crisis was a vital turning-point in Russia's road to 1914. All trust in Vienna was gone. Already deeply humiliated by the Japanese, this further defeat infuriated both the government and public opinion. Hysteria and lack of realism reigned in much of the press. Nicholas II was furious at Russia's humiliation and shared the general indignation against Austria. In the autumn of 1908 he wrote that 'the main culprit is Aehrenthal. He is simply a scoundrel. He made Isvolsky his dupe when they met and now puts things quite differently from the way he did then.'[43]

The Emperor's attitude to the ending of the crisis in March 1909 is extremely interesting and tells one much about his basic views on Russian foreign policy in the following years. He wrote to his mother on 18 March that

last week . . . I held a Council of Ministers in connection with that wretched Austro-Serbian question. This affair, which had been going on for six months, has suddenly been complicated by Germany's telling us we could help to solve the difficulty by agreeing to the famous annexation while, if we refused, the consequences might be very serious and hard to foretell. Once the matter had been put as definitely and unequivocally as that, there was nothing for it but to swallow one's pride, give in and agree. The Ministers were unanimous about it. If this concession on our part can save Serbia from being crushed by Austria, it is, I firmly believe, well worth it. Our decision was the more inevitable as we were informed from all sides that Germany was absolutely ready to mobilise . . . But our public does not realise this and it is hard to make them understand how ominous things looked a few days ago; now they will go on abusing and reviling poor Isvolsky even more than before.

The next day Nicholas added a postscript to his letter.

Nobody except the bad people want war now, and I think we have been very close to it this time. As soon as the danger is over people immediately begin shouting about humiliation, insults etc. For the word 'annexation' our patriots were prepared to sacrifice Serbia, whom we could not help at all in the case of an Austrian attack. It is quite true that the form and method of Germany's action – I mean towards us – has simply been brutal and we won't forget it. I think they were again trying to separate us from France and England – but once again they have undoubtedly failed. Such methods tend to bring about the opposite result.[44]

In response to defeat in the Bosnian crisis Russia changed its Foreign Minister. Izvolsky was replaced by Serge Sazonov. The new leadership made three basic decisions, with Nicholas II's approval. Firstly, it remained fully committed to its agreements with France and Britain. Secondly, swallowing their pride, the Russians attempted to patch up relations with Berlin. In an effort to get the Germans to veto any Austrian aggression in the Balkans, Petersburg made concessions to Berlin on a range of Middle Eastern economic issues. By 1911, though nothing fundamental had changed in Russo-German relations, they were on the surface quite friendly again.

The third element in Russia's strategy was to build up an alliance of Balkan states which would oppose any further Austrian advances in south-eastern Europe. By the autumn of 1912 this goal had been achieved but the Balkan allies quickly escaped from Russian control and turned their efforts to carving up what was left of the Turkish Empire in Europe, which above all meant Macedonia and Albania. The Russian government was alarmed by this enormous threat to international stability but proved unable to hold back its Balkan 'clients'. With the Ottoman Empire tottering visibly as a result of defeat by Italy in the 1911 war, nothing could stop the Balkan states from settling scores with their old Turkish enemy and seizing its territory. Having achieved this, the allies then started another and much bloodier war among themselves over the division of the spoils. This horrified Russian public opinion, which cultivated naïve illusions about its Slav 'little brothers' and, as always, blamed the Foreign Ministry for its failure to achieve Russian nationalists' unrealistic goals. Though one would never have guessed it from the childish hysteria which gripped the Russian press, the real loser from Balkan developments in 1912–13 was not Russia but Austria. The two Balkan states which had gained most territory and prestige from the wars were Serbia and Romania. Many Serbs and Romanians lived within the borders of Austria-Hungary and were bound to be the next target for nationalists in Belgrade and Bucharest. Serbia was Russia's main client in the Balkans. In the spring of 1914 Romania was showing strong signs of moving away from her alliance with Germany and Austria, and towards Russia's orbit. In the nine months before July 1914 the Russian Foreign Ministry understood the risk that Vienna might seek to restore its weakened position in the Balkans by some demonstrative use of force against its Serbian neighbour.[45]

In his normal optimistic way Nicholas did not expect the Austrians to start a war in 1914 and was always inclined to discount gloomy forebodings by his advisers. In February 1912 he had commented that 'so long as the Emperor Franz Josef lived there was no likelihood of any step being taken by Austria-Hungary that would endanger the maintenance of peace; but when the aged Emperor had passed away it was impossible to say what might happen'. Concern for the future was partly linked to fears about the plans of the Austrian heir apparent, whose violent and aggressive language Nicholas recalled, to transform the empire's domestic constitution and the balance of power between its nations. The Tsar had never been close to the Habsburgs and felt little sense of monarchical solidarity with them. He had not met the Austrian heir, the Archduke Franz Ferdinand, since 1903. In 1913 he foresaw the collapse of the Habsburg monarchy without alarm.

> His Majesty spoke of the disintegration of the Austrian Empire as a mere matter of time. The day, he said, would come when we would see a Kingdom of Hungary, a Kingdom of Bohemia, and the incorporation of the German provinces of Austria into the German Empire, while the southern slavs would be absorbed by Serbia and the Rumanians of Transylvania by Rumania. Austria, His Majesty held, was at present a source of weakness to Germany and a danger to the cause of peace, and it would make for peace were Germany to have no Austria to drag her into war about the Balkans.[46]

Traditionally, the Romanovs had been far closer to the Hohenzollerns than to the Habsburgs, whose Catholicism had barred marriages with the Russian royal house. By the winter of 1913–14 Nicholas's patience with and trust in Wilhelm II were, however, wearing thin, though they had not entirely disappeared. At issue was a growing German interest in Russia's traditional spheres of influence in Asia Minor and Persia and, above all, Berlin's ambitions in the Straits. The latter was a very sensitive point for the Russians, above all because so much of their foreign trade passed through the Bosporus and the Dardanelles. A great naval power, once established in Constantinople, could strangle Russia's all-important grain trade and dominate the Black Sea, exposing the empire's whole southern coast to attack.

Nicholas had always been much more interested in Constantinople and the Straits than in the Balkan Slavs. On the eve of the Balkan wars, for instance, he had written: 'I insist on complete non-intervention by Russia in the forthcoming military activities. But of course we must take all measures to protect our interests on the Black Sea.' Both he and his Foreign Minister, Serge Sazonov, therefore reacted angrily upon hearing in the autumn of 1913 that a German general, Liman von Sanders, had been appointed to command the Turkish corps which garrisoned Constantinople and the Straits. From the German point of view von Sanders' appointment was a technical detail. Direct command of Turkish units was necessary if genuine reforms were to be imposed on the army, whose performance against the Balkan allies had been unimpressive despite years of effort by German inspectors and instructors. For the Russians, however, the prospect of direct German command over the garrison of the capital city and the Straits at a time when the Ottoman Empire appeared to be on the verge of disintegration was unacceptable, particularly in the light of Wilhelm's scarcely veiled intention to dominate whatever Turkish rump state emerged from the empire's collapse. In the end the Liman von Sanders crisis ended peacefully but not without much bad blood between Petersburg and Berlin, which subsequently was reflected in violent mutual denunciations in the two countries' newspapers. In the light of the Liman von Sanders affair Nicholas believed military intelligence delivered through spies in the Austrian High Command, who reported that the Germans were seeking control over the shore batteries on the Bosporus.[47]

Alarmed by the growing danger of war with Germany, Peter Durnovo presented a memorandum to Nicholas II in February 1914 about Russia's future foreign and domestic policy. Durnovo argued that a great European war was now likely. Contrary to general belief, it would not be a short war and would test the overall strength of a country rather than just the prowess of its armies. Economic strength, financial resources and political unity would be key factors determining defeat or victory in this conflict. In all these respects Russia was ill-equipped to fight. Any defeat on the battlefield would result in a surge of opposition to the government, which would be blamed for all Russia's failings and backwardness. Complete social revolution would be the probable outcome. Durnovo insisted that there was no reason to take such risks since Russia and Germany's interests were not in serious conflict. In his view Berlin's main argument was with London and concerned naval, colonial and economic supremacy. Russia must not be drawn into such a conflict, and least of all on the side of liberal England against conservative Germany. In one sense, Durnovo's suggestion that Russia should remain on the sidelines while Germany and Britain fought each other to a standstill had something in common with Stalin's stance in 1939.

A sense of Nicholas's reaction to such ideas is conveyed by a discussion he had with the British ambassador, Sir George Buchanan, in the spring of 1914.

> It was, His Majesty then proceeded to say, commonly supposed that there was nothing to keep Germany and Russia apart. This was, however, not the case. There was the question of the Dardanelles. Twice in the last two years the Straits had been closed for a short period, with the result that the Russian grain industry had suffered very serious loss. From information which had reached him from a secret source through Vienna he had reason to believe that Germany was aiming at acquiring such a position at Constantinople as would enable her to shut in Russia altogether in the Black Sea. Should she attempt to carry out this policy he would have to resist it with all his power, even should war be the only alternative . . . though the Emperor said that . . . he . . . wished to live on good terms with Germany.

At this point Nicholas did not believe, as Witte for instance still did, that it would be possible to split Germany from Austria.

Of course Nicholas said nothing to a foreign ambassador about Russia's domestic political situation so it is impossible to know precisely what he thought of this aspect of Durnovo's memorandum. It is a safe guess, however, that he considered the Russian people to be much more loyal to the throne and much more patriotic in any future war than his more hard-headed and more realistic adviser predicted. Nicholas worried that the Irish question might stop London acting vigorously in foreign affairs. This would be very dangerous because the old 'Concert' of great powers which had peacefully managed past crises was threatened with paralysis. As regards Balkan questions, 'it was the old story. Europe was divided into two camps, and it was impossible to get the Concert to work together.' But at present the vital necessity was for Russia, France and Britain to unite more closely in order to make it absolutely clear to Berlin that all three *entente* powers would fight side by side against German aggression. The British ambassador concluded that Nicholas wanted 'a closer bond of union established between England and Russia, such as an alliance of a purely defensive character'.[48]

On 18 February 1914 Paul Benckendorff wrote to his brother that in Petersburg 'absolutely no one wants war or adventure but over the last few months the feeling that war is inevitable has grown and grown in all classes'. It was widely believed that Berlin and Vienna would take the

opportunity to declare war when Russia was least expecting it. The Grand
Marshal of the Court confessed that he himself was beginning to think in
the same way. The arms race had got completely out of hand. The great
geopolitical issues now on the agenda could scarcely be resolved peacefully. Similar warnings came from Alexander Izvolsky, now ambassador
in Paris. In October 1912, on the outbreak of the first Balkan war,
Isvolsky had warned that the victory of the Slav nationalist states over the
Ottoman Empire would result in the latter's collapse and would endanger
the Habsburg monarchy too. 'It would bring forward, in its full historical
development, the question of the struggle of Slavdom not only with Islam
but also with Germanism. In this event one can scarcely set one's hopes on
any palliative measures and must prepare for a great and decisive general
European war.' Such fears and prophecies had their own self-fulfilling
logic. If war was probable then the key question became how to win it
rather than how to avoid it. Diplomacy strove less to restrain Balkan
clients than to ensure that their armies would stand on one's side in the
event of war. The influence of the generals rose and the military priorities
of smooth and speedy mobilization and co-ordinated offensives with one's
allies gained a greater weight.[49]

The imperial family spent April and May 1914 in the Crimea. The
Council of Ministers no longer had an effective chairman but the monarch
was hundreds of miles from his capital with communications passing by
post and courier. The explanation for this strange behaviour was the
Empress Alexandra, whom General Spiridovich remembered as being in a
state of 'extraordinary nervousness' at this time, much given to prayer and
tears. Paul Benckendorff commented to his brother that Alexandra was
making life very difficult for her husband. If the Empress could relax
anywhere it was in her new Italian-style villa at Livadia, with its court-
yards, fountains and superb gardens, all at their best in the Crimean
spring. In early June the Romanovs visited the King of Romania, an occasion which was full of political significance given the current state of
Balkan affairs. The strain of a busy one-day state visit was enough to make
Alexandra collapse entirely.[50]

Returning to Russia, Nicholas toured Odessa and unveiled a monu-
ment in Kishinev. By 18 June he was back at Tsarskoe Selo, ready to
receive an official visit from the King of Saxony. On 28 June came the
news of the assassination of the Austrian heir and his wife. The first
reaction from the Russian ambassador in Vienna, N.N. Shebeko, was
calm and entirely misunderstood the thinking in Austrian government
circles. 'There is already reason to suppose that at least in the immediate
future the course of Austro-Hungarian policy will be more restrained and
calm. That is what they believe here and beyond question that is what the
Emperor Franz Josef will strive for.' Over the next few days Shebeko

became a little less optimistic and alarming rumours, all of them stoutly denied in Vienna, began to circulate about possible Austrian action against Serbia. A British naval squadron visited Petersburg amidst great festivities. Between its departure and the arrival of President Poincaré of France, the imperial family slipped away for a few days on the *Standart*, at Alexandra's insistence. The cruise did her no good for her son fell while boarding the yacht from a small boat and suffered another bad bout of bleeding. On 23 July the French President and Prime Minister left Russia after four exhausting days of speeches, ceremonies and meetings whose most spectacular moment was a review of the Imperial Guard on the parade-ground of Krasnoe Selo. That evening the Austrians presented their ultimatum to Serbia, giving Belgrade only forty-eight hours to respond.[51]

At 10 a.m. on 24 July the text of the Austrian ultimatum reached Serge Sazonov, the Russian Foreign Minister. Sazonov exclaimed, 'This means war in Europe!' For the first time in his life the Foreign Minister made a report to the Emperor over the telephone. Sazonov stated that the Austrian note was worded with deliberate brutality and must have been concocted in agreement with Berlin. The Central Powers (Austria and Germany) must have realized that 'the ultimatum could not be complied with by Serbia' and therefore must be intending to take military action. Russia and subsequently all Europe would be dragged into the conflict. In Sazonov's opinion, the Germans 'were certainly in the most advantageous position owing to the supreme efficiency of their armies'. They were deliberately starting a war now because they believed that they would win it. The Emperor heard his minister out and ordered him to convene the Council of Ministers as quickly as possible.

Shortly afterwards, Peter Bark, the new Minister of Finance, arrived for his regular weekly audience with Nicholas. His recollections of the Emperor's attitude ring very true: as always, Nicholas was optimistic and inclined to think that his ministers were panicking. Equally familiar was his belief in the honesty and goodwill of people he had known for a long time, in this case his cousin Willy. It was hard to believe that the man who had sat in the neighbouring room twenty years before when Nicholas and Alexandra became engaged could now deliberately be starting a war which would engulf all Europe. Peter Bark wrote that

the Emperor . . . remained quite calm and told me that he thought Sazonoff was exaggerating the gravity of the situation and had lost his nerve. In latter years conflicts had frequently arisen in the Balkans, but the powers had always come to an agreement. None of them would wish to let war loose in Europe to protect the interests of a Balkan state. War would be disastrous for the world and once it had broken out it would be difficult to stop. The Emperor did not think it likely that the Note had been sent after consultation with Berlin. The German Emperor had frequently assured him of his sincere desire to safeguard the peace of Europe and it had always been possible to come to an agreement with him, even in serious cases. His Majesty spoke of the German Emperor's loyal attitude during the Russo-Japanese War and during the internal troubles that Russia had experienced afterwards. It would have been easy for Germany to level a decisive blow at Russia in these circumstances – which were particularly favourable for such an attempt – since our attention was engaged in the Far East and we were left with insufficient protection against an attack from the West.[52]

Peter Bark tended to share Nicholas's optimism. Given the immense success of the German economy in recent years, the Minister of Finance could not believe that Berlin would risk everything by starting an unnecessary war. Both the Emperor and his minister were wrong. The Austrian ultimatum to Serbia was designed to make war inevitable. Vienna believed that its position in the Balkans could only be restored by forcing Belgrade back into dependence on Austria. Other Balkan states would learn from this that opposition to Vienna did not pay and that in the last resort Russia would not protect its clients at the risk of war. The Austrians tended to believe that fear of revolution would make Russia back down. If not, Vienna and Berlin agreed that it was better to start a war now than to delay matters, since Russia's resources, together with the rapid growth of her economic and military strength, would make victory for the Central Powers unobtainable in a few years' time. In retrospect it appears certain that the only thing which might have deterred the Germans was a conviction that Britain would enter the war on the side of Russia and France. The British Liberal government was unwilling to make such a commitment at the beginning of the crisis and would have faced revolt from both Parliament and public opinion had it tried. By the time the likelihood of British intervention had begun to sink in, Austro-German policy had gone too far to make peaceful compromise possible without great damage to Austrian and German prestige. The first rather hesitant calls to Vienna for restraint from the German Chancellor were in any case being undermined by contrary advice from Moltke, the Chief of the German General Staff. Moreover, even by 29 July the Central Powers' position remained that Russia must cease military preparations while the Austrian offensive in Serbia must be allowed to proceed. No one in Petersburg could have accepted such terms. Nicholas II was much less enthusiastic about the Balkan Slavs than some of his ministers, let alone public opinion. But in January 1914 he had promised, 'we will not let ourselves be trampled upon'. Now, in July, he commented that 'punitive expeditions are only undertaken in one's own country or colonies'.[53]

At the crucial meeting of the Council of Ministers which took place on the afternoon of 24 July the dominant voices belonged to Sazonov and Krivoshein. The Foreign Minister told the Council that 'the information at his disposal and his knowledge of events in Central Europe during the past years had convinced him that Austria-Hungary and Germany were resolved to deal a decisive blow at Russian authority in the Balkans by annihilating Serbia'. Both Sazonov and Krivoshein argued that Russia could not allow this to happen. Domestic political considerations counted for something: 'public and parliamentary opinion would fail to understand why, at this critical moment involving Russia's vital interests, the Imperial Government was reluctant to act boldly'. More important were considerations of national honour and prestige. Given Russia's centuries-old role in the Balkans, if she allowed herself to be driven out of the region in so total and humiliating a fashion, no one would take her seriously again: 'she would be considered a decadent state and would henceforth have to take second place among the Powers'. Russia's obvious weakness and her many concessions since 1905 had not brought her security. Instead, they had merely encouraged her opponents to push her around. If Russia caved in again despite so blatant a challenge to her interests, no one – ally or enemy – would believe that she would ever stand up for herself. Having forfeited her Balkan allies, she could then very possibly be forced to fight in the near future in the face of further German challenges. Sazonov admitted that 'war with Germany would be fraught with great risks', particularly since 'it was not known what attitude Great Britain would take in the matter'. Nevertheless he, and with him the whole Council of Ministers, decided that if Austria refused all negotiations and insisted on the invasion of Serbia, Russia could not stand aside. In the event of invasion, Russia would mobilize four military districts in the hope that this would be a warning to Austria but not a provocation to Germany.[54]

The Emperor's diary for the nine days before the outbreak of war is a strange and revealing document. Nicholas II was in one sense Russia's chief executive. In another sense he was curiously detached from the everyday business of government. Even in these days of crisis he was to some extent a gentleman of leisure. Admittedly on one day he records that work kept him up until after 3 a.m. and still he had to start his next day at 9 a.m. Nevertheless, Nicholas found time to play tennis, to walk and canoe with his daughters, and to visit relatives for tea. Days were also crammed with the ceremonial activities of a head of state: reviews, dinners, visits to a hospital and the handing out of prizes. As Germany and Russia prepared to go to war and the collapse of European civilization began, an extraordinary piece of old regime archaism intervened in Nicholas's schedule. On 26 July Nicholas received the Master of the Horse of the Court of Mecklenburg-Strelitz, a small dukedom absorbed into the German Empire in 1871, who in time-honoured fashion had come to bring official notice of the Duke's death. What the Emperor and the courtier found to discuss in the lunch that followed is a mystery. Reading the diary one gets the impression of a man indifferent to events. The most revealing comment about the Emperor's feelings is his entry for 31 July, in which he noted that the weather was grey, as was his mood. Reality was very different. Pierre Gilliard, the tutor to the Tsarevich, commented that 'one only needed to see the Emperor during that terrible week to understand what worry and what spiritual suffering he was undergoing'.[55]

Nicholas did his best to stave off the stampede to war. He dispatched telegrams and a personal envoy to Wilhelm II begging him to restrain the Austrians. He rescinded the order for a general mobilization on the evening of 29 July on receiving what seemed a conciliatory telegram from Wilhelm II. Pressured by his military and civil advisers, who urged that war was inevitable and rapid and general mobilization vital, he held out until the afternoon of 30 July. The Emperor faced a united front of his main political, diplomatic and military advisers who argued that general mobilization must not be delayed. Krivoshein, Sazonov and the Chief of the General Staff, Yanushkevich, all agreed on this. On the afternoon of 30 July, 'for almost an entire hour the minister [Sazonov] tried to show that war had become inevitable since it was evident to everyone that Germany had decided to bring on a collision, otherwise she would not have turned down all the conciliatory proposals that had been made and could easily have brought her ally to reason'. The Emperor displayed 'extreme loathing' for war, in the words of the Foreign Minister's diary. His exceptional nervousness and revulsion at the idea were revealed by a burst of irritation which, coming from Nicholas, was almost unheard of. In the end, however, the Emperor had to agree that war was probably inevitable and that nothing remained but to wage it with the greatest possible chance of success.[56]

On the evening of 1 August, at the moment when the German ambassador presented Berlin's declaration of war to Sazonov,

> the Emperor, the Empress and their daughters were attending Vespers in the small church at Alexandria. Having met the Emperor a few hours earlier, I was struck by his very exhausted appearance: the features of his face had changed, and the small bags which appeared under his eyes when he was tired seemed far bigger.
>
> In church he prayed very hard that God would spare his people this war, which seemed so close and unavoidable. His whole being seemed absorbed by religious feeling – simple and convinced. Next to him was the Empress,

whose sad face had the expression of great suffering which I noticed so often when she was by the bedside of the sick Aleksei Nikolaevich. On this evening she also prayed with passionate strength, begging that a terrible war be avoided.

At the end of the service Their Majesties and the grand duchesses returned to the villa of Alexandria.

It was eight o'clock. The Emperor, before going to dinner, went into his office in order to look at the dispatches which had arrived during his absence, and here he learned from a report by Sazonov about Germany's declaration of war. He had a short conversation on the telephone with his minister and asked him to come to Alexandria when he had the opportunity.

Meanwhile the Empress and the grand duchesses were waiting in the dining-room. Her Majesty, worried by the long absence of the Emperor, asked Tatiana Nikolaevna to look for her father, but at that moment he finally appeared, very pale, and, in a voice which, despite his wish, showed his emotion, announced that war was declared. Hearing the news, the Empress started to cry, and the grand duchesses, seeing their mother's despair, also burst into tears.[57]

CHAPTER 8

The War,
1914–1917

On 2 August, the day after war was declared, the imperial family attended a religious service in Petersburg, after which the Emperor came out on to the balcony of the Winter Palace to bow to the huge crowd which had gathered in the square below. On his appearance, tens of thousands of his people knelt and sang the imperial hymn. Even more vast were the crowds which greeted the imperial family when they visited Moscow later in the month. On 5 August came the news that Britain had declared war on Germany and that Italy, despite its alliance with Berlin and Vienna, had decided to remain neutral. On 8 August the overwhelming majority of Duma deputies committed themselves to unconditional support for the government's war effort, in Alexander Obolensky's words displaying a unity 'which is something really surprising'. Instead of 'the usual Duma chatter and abuse . . . One felt here a very great enthusiasm and a sort of calm confidence in final victory.' Nicholas II, buoyed up by popular support, recovered from the intense worry and gloom of the preceding days. 'The State Duma', he commented, 'has shown itself worthy of its position and has truly expressed the will of the nation, because the whole Russian people feels the insult that Germany has caused it. I now look on the future with complete confidence . . . I am sure that we will now see in Russia something like what happened during the war of 1812.'[1]

The Emperor's optimism was justified up to a point. The potential resources of Russia and her allies were much greater than those of the Central Powers. Victory should therefore be attainable. Within Russia almost all sections of the upper and middle classes could unite to fight a war forced on the country by the Germans and waged in defence of the Balkan Slavs and of Russia's position as an independent great power. As leader and symbol of the nation, the Tsar's popularity was bound to soar. Ominously, the Russian Social Democrats, unlike their French and German brothers, did not vote war credits for their government. On the other hand, in the first months of the war strikes in the cities almost ceased. As regards peasant attitudes, opinions differed. Paul Benckendorff wrote to his brother that the national sentiment was excellent and that mobilization had gone far more smoothly than during the war with Japan. Other observers were less sanguine, noting peasant resignation rather than comprehension of the war's aims.[2]

So long as the war was relatively short and ultimately victorious national unity would prevail. If, as Peter Durnovo had argued in February 1914, the conflict proved lengthy and Russia suffered defeats then many of the problems he predicted with such foresight were almost sure to emerge: 'The insufficiency of our war supplies'; 'far too great dependence, generally speaking, upon foreign industry'; 'the network of strategic railways is inadequate'; 'the railways possess a rolling stock sufficient perhaps for normal traffic, but not commensurate with the colossal demands which will be made upon them in the event of a European war'; 'the quantity of our heavy artillery, the importance of which was demonstrated in the Japanese War, is far too inadequate and there are few machine guns'; 'the closing of the Baltic as well as the Black Sea will prevent the importation from abroad of the defence materials which we lack'; 'the war will necessitate expenditures which are beyond Russia's limited financial means'; 'both military disasters – partial ones, let us hope – and all kinds of shortcomings in our supply are inevitable. In the excessive nervousness and spirit of opposition of our society, these events will be given an exaggerated importance, and all the blame will be laid on the government'; 'in the legislative institutions a bitter campaign against the government will begin'; the country would resound with 'socialist slogans, capable of arousing and rallying the masses, beginning with the division of the land and succeeded by a division of all valuables and property'; the army, 'having lost its most dependable men, and carried away by a primitive peasant desire for land, will find itself too demoralised to serve as a bulwark of law and order'; and 'the legislative institutions and the intellectual opposition parties, lacking real authority in the eyes of the people, will be powerless to stem the popular tide, aroused by themselves, and Russia will be flung into hopeless anarchy'.[3]

In 1914 the overwhelming majority of informed Europeans expected the war to be brief. In fact, there were good reasons why it would be long. Germany was Europe's most formidable military power. The Austrian and Ottoman empires were huge lands with large populations. The Central Powers had the advantage of interior lines, and could shift their troops from front to front with greater ease than the Allies. Among the latter, the British Empire was potentially the most powerful. But the armies of Britain and her colonies were tiny. It would be two years before British potential could fully be realized on the battlefield. Until then Russia and France would have to carry most of the military burden. Beneath a show of bravado, most Russian generals believed their army to be inferior to that of Germany. Indeed they exaggerated its inferiority. Memories of 1709 and 1812, when military inferiority had been compensated for by strategic retreat and a war of attrition, loomed large in their minds. None of this promised a quick end to the war. In any case, in this era military technology greatly favoured the defender, entrenched and armed with the machine gun and the rifle. The old offensive weapon, the cavalry, was redundant and the tank and the dive-bomber were yet to be born. Defeated armies retreated to their railways and supply bases. Attackers plodded forward on foot, their supplies dragged forward by horse and cart. In 1941-2 the Soviet army suffered much worse defeats then the imperial one in 1914-15. But the Second World War moved more quickly than the First. By the winter of 1943, their third of the war, the Russians had Stalingrad and Kursk behind them. The tide had clearly turned in their favour. In 1916 the Russian army had won great victories but the war's final outcome was less clear that third winter than in December 1943. Morale was less easy to sustain.

The British or German soldier of 1914 was the product of many years of schooling. He was not only literate but had also gone through a course of patriotic indoctrination. The same was true of the Soviet soldier of 1941. The Russian man of 1914 might or might not be literate. In the latter case his education was probably rudimentary, his teacher a miserably paid member of the intelligentsia who despised the tsarist regime and was not trusted by it to inculcate its version of patriotism into his, or as often her, pupils. The horizons of a peasant soldier were always likely to be narrow. In 1915 the Chief of Staff, General Yanushkevich, claimed that 'it is beautiful to fight for Russia but the masses do not understand it . . . a Tambovets is ready to stand to the death for Tambov province, but the war in Poland seems strange and unnecessary to him'. In part, this was but one of Yanushkevich's many excuses for defeat brought on by bad generalship. On the other hand, it was certainly easier to arouse Russian patriotism in 1941-3, when Hitler's armies were fighting barbarously on Great Russian soil. It was harder to explain to Russian peasants in 1914-16 why they should die in Poland for the rights of Serbia and Russia's position as a great power. For all her naïve faith in peasant monarchism, in the summer of 1915 the Empress Alexandra was forced to appeal to her husband not to try to mobilize peasants from the reserve militia (*opolchenie*, second class) 'for internal peace's sake'. In 1915, as in 1941-2, Russian soldiers surrendered in droves to the Germans, sometimes in bewilderment and anger at cruel and incompetent commanders. Unlike Hitler, the Kaiser's Germany did not do its Russian enemy a good turn by murdering these prisoners in vast numbers and thus deterring further surrender. In March 1917 the imperial regime was brought down by a revolt of the Petrograd population caused, above all, by the collapse of living standards during the war (the capital's name was changed from the German-sounding Petersburg in August 1914). In 1941 the Soviet regime had greater support amongst the working class than the Tsar had enjoyed in 1914. In Leningrad, however, living conditions were incomparably worse than in 1916–17. But there was much less open inequality in suffering and more confidence in competent leadership. Above all, with German armies on the city's outskirts and Hitler threatening to raze Leningrad to the ground, revolt was scarcely an option.[4]

Not only were the defeats suffered by Russia's armies in 1941–2 much more complete than anything experienced in 1914–16, they were also to a far greater degree the result of mistakes made personally by the head of state, Josef Stalin. But there was no free press to criticize the dictator and no opposition political parties to challenge his rule. Unlike the Tsar, Stalin's regime directly controlled the economy. The Soviet dictator did not need to bargain with independent industrialists, landowners or even peasants. The state of siege and the dictatorship, for which some Russians called in 1914–17, already existed in 1941 before war began. Even in wartime it was very difficult for a twentieth-century Russian tsar, and impossible for Nicholas II, to be an Ivan the Terrible or a Peter the Great. From the start, beneath the Union Sacrée of 1914, suspicions lurked between government and educated society. Both sides knew that the war would have an immense impact on Russia's future political development. In March 1916 the Empress Alexandra wrote to her husband that 'it must be your war and your peace and your and our country's honour and . . . by no means the Duma's'. Much of the opposition leadership thought no differently. When the Tsar's armies were defeated in the spring of 1915 the press, the opposition parties and the various public organizations launched ferocious attacks on the government's incompetence. 'How unpatriotic,' wrote Anatol Kulomzin, 'not to say foul, to seize a share of political power on the grounds of the country's misfortune when in fact they are completely forgetting their country.' But there was more to the attacks than a simple struggle for power. The deepest political instinct of educated Russians, whether members of the intelligentsia or of the land-owning aristocracy, was that the tsarist bureaucracy was incompetent to run the country's affairs and that 'society' could do the job much better. Military setbacks and supply crises merely confirmed this instinct. From the very start, the war's outcome was likely to depend on a race between military victory and the disintegration of the home front. On balance, the latter was always likely to come first.[5]

In the first nine months of the war matters went reasonably well. Defeat in eastern Prussia in August 1914 was more than outweighed by a series of victories over the Austrians. By the spring of 1915 the Habsburg Empire seemed on the verge of final defeat. In the winter of 1914–15 Russian troops also often gave a very good account of themselves against the Germans in Poland. Paul Benckendorff wrote to his brother in October 1914 that the internal political situation was excellent and that he was convinced unity would survive until the end of the war. The Empress Alexandra threw herself into organizing care for the wounded and for soldiers' families. For a time she enjoyed genuine popularity. The Empress trained as a nurse and worked with the wounded in her hospital at Tsarskoe Selo. When dying men asked for her presence, she tried never to let them down. This was a great physical and still greater mental strain. 'There were several . . . unknown, solitary men, from obscure line regiments, who died in her hospital whose last hours were comforted by the Empress. She lost her shyness in her nurse's dress.' Like her husband, the Empress was full of sincerity and goodwill. But to modern eyes her time was organized with great inefficiency and lack of concern for the impact which the Empress's activities could have had on public opinion. Like her husband, Alexandra hated self-advertisement, which is an essential feature of modern politics. 'The Empress wanted every man of the immense army to have something made with her own hands and strung innumerable images all through the war. Very few knew this: and the work only tired her, without being appreciated by those for whom she worked.' By January 1915 Alexandra was exhausted, her heart in a perilous state, and her nerves in tatters. But she remained buoyed up by the mood in Russian society which she had expressed in early October. 'With God's help . . . all will go well and end gloriously, and it [the war] has lifted up spirits, cleared the many stagnant minds, brought unity in feelings and is a "healthy" war in the moral sense.' Nicholas's spirits also remained high. In December 1914, travelling in Russia's Caucasian frontier lands, he wrote to his wife that 'this country of Cossacks is magnificent and rich . . . They are beginning to be wealthy, and above all they have an inconceivably high number of small infants. All future subjects. This fills me with joy and faith in God's mercy; I must look forward in peace and confidence to what lies in store for Russia. What the country is achieving and will go on achieving till the end of the war is wonderful and immense.'[6]

In the spring of 1915 moods changed drastically. By March it was clear that Russia faced a severe munitions crisis. The artillery lacked shells and the infantry were short of rifles. In May there began a series of massive German offensives which continued until September and resulted in the loss of Poland, Lithuania and a small part of the Ukraine. All the belligerents faced munitions crises at this time though that of Russia was more severe than most because of the country's relatively low level of industrial development and her geographical isolation. In Russia, however, politics and personal jealousies confused the issue. Headquarters, meaning the

Grand Duke Nicholas and his Chief of Staff, General Yanushkevich, used the shell shortage as an excuse for their own incompetence and as a stick with which to beat their old enemy, the War Minister. The Duma and the press, with which Headquarters had built up a good relationship, joined gleefully in the attack on Sukhomlinov. The latter was accused of treason, since Headquarters turned to spy mania as another explanation for defeat. Sukhomlinov's associate, Colonel S.N. Myasoedov, was arrested by Headquarters and hanged on trumped-up charges of espionage. The whole Jewish population of the western borderlands also came under suspicion. Local Jewish leaders, in particular rabbis, were seized and used as hostages. Jews were driven from their homes and forced to flee into the Russian interior with a brutality which, in the words of the Council of Ministers, drove even some notorious Russian anti-Semites to shame and rage. The Minister of Internal Affairs commented that it was General Yanushkevich's 'plan to maintain the army's prejudice against all the Jews, and to represent them as responsible for the defeats at the front . . . for Yanushkevich, the Jews are probably one of those alibis about which A.V. Krivoshein spoke'.[7]

With panic growing both at Headquarters and in Petrograd some ministers, led by Alexander Krivoshein, decided that those of their colleagues most obnoxious to the Duma and 'society' must be removed since the government needed public support in a time of crisis. Krivoshein no doubt also rejoiced in the possibility of getting rid of Nicholas Maklakov, Minister of Internal Affairs and the only minister whose standing with the Tsar was equal to his own. On 18 June Maklakov was dismissed since, of all the ministers, he was the one most hated by public opinion. Along with him went the ministers of justice and war, together with the civilian head of the Orthodox Church, all of whom were also conservative figures odious in the eyes of liberal society. Nicholas was signalling his desire to maintain the Union Sacrée and to compromise with the Duma. Paul Benckendorff wrote that the Empress was furious at these changes: 'There are going on around me here fantastic domestic dramas.'[8]

But Nicholas had not given way entirely to pressure for concessions. The ancient, shrewd and loyal Ivan Goremykin remained as his watchdog in the Council of Ministers. The Emperor's view on Krivoshein's coup tells one much about his attitude to politics and to his ministers. Peter Bark, one of Krivoshein's allies, recalled that

at the end of my report, the Emperor . . . made it clear that he was very unpleasantly struck by our *démarche*. He said to me that he could not understand how we had decided to ask for the dismissal from our group of four ministers, who were loyal servants of their monarch. This was an act of disloyalty to colleagues and he could not but express his displeasure to all of us.

The Emperor added that he was educated in military discipline, and was accustomed to a military atmosphere. He considered unthinkable in a regiment a situation where one section of the officers asked the regimental commander to dismiss some of their colleagues who had committed no offence. The Emperor considered that solidarity and discipline were required in any body and that any business would be ruined if these necessary conditions were not observed . . . I never expected that the Emperor would make an analogy between the Council of Ministers and a regiment and equate the solidarity necessary among members of a cabinet with the corporate spirit in military formations.[9]

Despite Nicholas's concessions pressure built up on the government. On 7 September 1915 the 'Progressive Bloc' was formed, to which two-thirds of the Duma's members and a sizeable proportion of the State Council adhered. The Bloc's programme contained a mass of legislative proposals, most of which had little relevance to the war and scant chance of immediate realization in wartime conditions. Some parts of the programme, for instance its sections on Jewish rights and local government reform, were kept deliberately vague since the Bloc's left and right wings totally disagreed on these issues. But the Bloc's essence did not really lie in its programme. In the eyes of its enemies the Bloc was a conspiracy designed to remove control over the government from the Emperor's hands and to place it in the grasp of the party politicians and the legislature. The Bloc's friends argued that, on the contrary, it was designed to unite as much of the country as possible behind the war effort and to force the appointment of efficient ministers who would work with the public to achieve victory. Within the Bloc the Progressist party, whose most active core consisted of wealthy Moscow industrialists, pressed for a government formally responsible to the legislature. In this they were backed by much of the press and by most activists in two important organizations, the Town Union and the *Zemstvo* Union, which had been created in August 1914 to help the war effort and which did important work in support of the army and the horde of refugees who had fled into the interior after the retreat of 1915. To the extent that one can judge, middle-class opinion in both Moscow and the provinces backed this demand.

Most of the Duma leaders were, however, more cautious. They called for a government enjoying 'public confidence'. Decoded, this slogan meant that the Emperor must appoint a prime minister acceptable to the Progressive Bloc who must then be allowed to choose and control his fellow ministers. The party leaders shied away from demanding formal responsibility to the legislature for fear of antagonizing Nicholas II. In addition, most of them felt that in present circumstances an experienced senior official would run the government better than a parliamentarian unused to administration. The Kadet leader Milyukov, head of Russia's main middle-class party, stated that 'we don't seek power now . . . the time will come when it will simply fall into our hands, it's only necessary at present to have a clever bureaucrat as head of the government'. The Octobrist politician, A.I. Guchkov, whose ambitions were deeply suspect to Nicholas II, later claimed that he 'had always looked sceptically on the possibility of creating a "society" or parliamentary cabinet in the Russia of that time' since among the party leaders and other figures respected by society 'one did not find that civic courage which the authorities needed to show at so responsible a moment. Rather, it was possible to find this among representatives of the bureaucracy.'[10]

In the summer of 1915 most ministers sympathized with the Progressive Bloc and wished to come to an agreement with it. Indeed it may well be that some ministers played a hidden role in the Bloc's formation. The minutes of the Council of Ministers display a mood of great nervousness, at times bordering on panic. This was caused in part by the Council's sense of its own powerlessness to avert disaster. By Russian law a huge swathe of territory behind the front line came under military jurisdiction. As the army retreated, the Council of Ministers even lost control over its own capital city and found itself begging unresponsive military censors to do something to tame the furiously anti-government line taken by the press. Under increasing attack in society, the ministers also felt that their policies did not enjoy the full sympathy or confidence of the monarch. They argued that the government needed the support of public opinion and that only unity between ministers, parliament, key economic interests and the armed forces could bring victory. General Polivanov, the new Minister of War, argued that 'the very possibility of victory rests in the union of all forces in the country . . . But how can one achieve this union, this passion, when the overwhelming majority is not in sympathy with . . . the course of internal policy, nor with the government called upon to conduct this policy? How can men work when they have neither faith nor confidence in their leaders?' Polivanov warned those who advocated a policy of hard-line repression that 'one should not forget that the army is now quite different from the one which marched forth at the beginning of the war. The regular troops are badly thinned out and have been absorbed into the mass of the armed people, as it is now fashionable to call them, badly trained and not imbued with the spirit of military discipline . . . the officer corps, being filled up with speeded-up promotions and ensigns from the reserve, is not aloof from politics.'[11]

A.V. Krivoshein summed up the position of the Council's majority by stating, 'the demands of the Duma and of the whole country are reducible to the issue not of a programme but of which people are to be entrusted with power . . . Let the Monarch decide how he wishes to direct further internal policy -- along the path of ignoring such desires or along the path of reconciliation . . . We, old servants of the Tsar . . . firmly state to His Imperial Majesty that the general internal situation of the country requires a change of Cabinet and of the political course.' Most ministers made it clear that, unless a compromise was sought with society, they could not stay in office for long. Nor could they work with the Council's Chairman, I.L. Goremykin, whose views were flatly opposed to their own. Serge Sazonov expressed the mood of many ministers when he stated, 'we are not puppets . . . we do live in an age when one cannot . . . refuse to respect people, particularly when these people are ministers and speak of the impossibility of continuing to serve'.[12]

The political crisis of the summer of 1915 was sharpened by Nicholas II's decision to dismiss the Grand Duke Nicholas Nikolaevich, known as Nikolasha within the family, and himself to assume the supreme command of the army and the fleet. One element in this move was the Empress's jealousy of the tall and imposing Grand Duke, whom she saw as trying to replace her husband as a symbol of patriotism, military glory and national leadership. Stories of the Grand Duke's prestige in the eyes of the people or comments about the prayers read on his behalf in churches fuelled such feelings. The Grand Duke Nicholas Mikhailovich, another cousin, wrote to the Emperor:

> as regards Nikolasha's popularity I will say the following: this popularity was craftily manufactured from Kiev by Militsa [Nikolasha's wife], little by little and by all possible means – by spreading among the people brochures, little booklets, popular prints, portraits, calendars etc. Thanks to this well-calculated preparation his popularity did not fall after the loss of Galicia and Poland . . . I dare to say to you that it is my deep conviction that this popularity alarms me in a dynastic sense, especially in view of the excited state of our public opinion, which is becoming more and more evident in the provinces. This popularity does not at all help the throne or the prestige of the imperial family but only inflates the prestige of the husband of the Grand Duchess, who is a Slav woman and not a German . . . Given the possibility of every kind of disturbance at the end of the war, you need to be on the lookout and to watch carefully all the ways used to support this popularity.[13]

The Grand Duke Nicholas Mikhailovich was a clever man. He was also a great intriguer. His letter oozes with the envy and malice so prevalent in Russian politics and Petersburg high society. The hint at the German origins of the Empress was a particularly masterly touch. The Grand Duke was unfair to Nikolasha, who was never likely to try to supplant his nephew. Nevertheless the opinions expressed in the letter were not entirely unreasonable. As Commander-in-Chief the Grand Duke Nicholas cultivated excellent relations with the Duma leaders, the *zemstvo* and town unions, and the press. The government, and particularly the Minister of War, he tended to ignore and despise. Headquarters became potentially a major political centre of power. Well before 1914 many conservative and nationalist Russians longed for a convincing symbol of military glory and Russian power. Neither Alexander III nor Nicholas II satisfied this thirst, above all because, as Tsars, they had to bear the burden of Russia's real weakness and backwardness, which was not the stuff of which nationalist dreams were made. At the end of the First World War, a victorious and charismatic military commander could undoubtedly have played a major political role.[14]

Apart from personal and political considerations, there were also strong practical reasons for the removal of the Grand Duke. Headquarters' refusal to co-operate with the civilian government, and the cruel and unwise policies it pursued in the huge region under its control, were causing chaos. The Council of Ministers protested furiously at the antics of the Grand Duke, and even more at the behaviour of his Chief of Staff and protégé, General Yanushkevich. Still worse, both the Supreme Commander and Yanushkevich were poor generals, whose incompetence played a significant role in the disastrous performance of the army in the summer of 1915. Moreover, with his armies in full retreat, the very excitable Nikolasha was in a state of panic that came close to a nervous breakdown. It would be difficult for the dynasty's prestige to replace a defeated grand duke as supreme commander with a simple mortal. In proposing himself as supreme war leader, the Emperor never expected personally to decide strategy or military operations. These were to be the responsibility of his Chief of Staff, General M.V. Alekseev, who proved far more competent than either Nikolasha or Yanushkevich. But the Emperor was a much more calming influence at Headquarters than his nervous uncle. In addition, since peasant soldiers were not easily swayed by a modern sense of nationalism but were still often influenced by veneration for their Tsar, there was some hope that the monarch's presence at the front would improve morale. On top of this, Nicholas's assumption of the supreme command did lead to better co-ordination of military and civilian authority. It also seemed to avert the danger of the army high command falling out of the monarch's hands and forming an alliance with the political opposition.[15]

Despite these powerful reasons for Nicholas's assumption of the supreme command, the Council of Ministers reacted to the news of the Tsar's intentions with horror. In part this simply sprang from the panic prevalent in Petrograd at the time. In part, too, it was due to dismay that the monarch was taking such a momentous decision without even consulting his ministers. Most important, however, was the ministers' belief, based on information from Headquarters, that the military situation was disastrous, the surrender of Kiev certain and even the abandonment of Petrograd a possibility. The thought that the monarch himself might have to take the responsibility for impending disaster appalled the ministers. As Peter Bark wrote subsequently, the Emperor's decision to assume the command in these circumstances was 'a sublime act, full of self-sacrifice, of patriotism, of love for his country and of a profound sense of his duty'. At the time Ivan Goremykin warned his fellow ministers that the Tsar's decision to assume command went beyond mere political calculation and would never be altered by their arguments.

> I must say to the Council of Ministers that all attempts to dissuade the Emperor will be, in any event, useless. His conviction was formed a long time ago. He has told me, more than once, that he will never forgive himself for not leading the army at the front during the Japanese war. According to his own words, the duty of the Tsar, his function, dictates that the monarch be with his troops in moments of danger, sharing both their joy and their sorrow . . . Now, when there is virtually a catastrophe at the front His Majesty considers it the sacred duty of the Russian Tsar to be among the troops, to fight against the conqueror or perish. Considering such purely mystical feelings, you will not be able to dissuade the Emperor by any reasons from the step he has contemplated. I repeat, intrigues or personal influence played no role in this decision. It was prompted by the Tsar's consciousness of his duty to the motherland and to the exhausted army. I, too, exerted all efforts as did the Minister of War, to restrain His Majesty from making his decision final, begged him to postpone it until circumstances are more favourable. I, too, find that the assumption of command by the Emperor is a very risky step which can have grave consequences, but he, understanding this risk perfectly, nevertheless does not want to give up his perception of the Tsar's duty. There remains for us only to bow before the will of our Tsar and help him.[16]

The ministers would have been wise to heed Goremykin's words. The Emperor's decision to assume the supreme command was not only courageous and irrevocable but also correct. The best solution to the political crisis was for the monarch to take over the supreme command, leaving behind in Petrograd an energetic prime minister capable of uniting the government and collaborating with the Duma and the various organizations created by society to help the war effort. The ideal candidate for the premiership would have been Alexander Krivoshein. Had the ministers been less panic-stricken and supported the Emperor's decision to assume the supreme command it is just possible that such an outcome would have been achieved. But persistent and united ministerial resistance to the assumption of the supreme command merely aroused Nicholas's stubbornness. The catastrophic consequences predicted by the ministers if the Grand Duke Nicholas was removed and the Duma's session prorogued seemed unconvincing to the Emperor, who in this case too proved a better and calmer judge than his advisers. The ministers' refusal to work with Goremykin also annoyed him. At the end of September he wrote to his wife that 'the ministers do not wish to work with old Goremykin, in spite of the stern words which I addressed to them; therefore, on my return, some changes must take place'.[17]

On 22 September Nicholas wrote a letter to his wife which makes clear not just his attitude to the 'ministerial strike' but also some of the assumptions and illusions that were to guide his policy for the rest of his reign.

> The behaviour of some of the ministers continues to amaze me! After all that I told them . . . I thought that they understood both me and the fact that I was seriously explaining what I thought. What matter? – so much the worse for them! They were afraid to close the Duma – it was done! I came away here and replaced N, in spite of their advice; the people accepted this move as a natural thing and understood it, as we did. The proof – numbers of telegrams which I receive from all sides, with the most touching expressions. All this shows me clearly one thing: that the ministers, always living in town, know terribly little of what is happening in the country as a whole. Here I can judge correctly the real mood among the various classes of the people: everything must be done to bring the war to a victorious ending, and no doubts are expressed on that score. I was told this officially by all the deputations which I received some days ago, and so it is all over Russia. Petrograd and Moscow constitute the only exceptions – two minute points on the map of the fatherland.[18]

The military and political crisis of the summer of 1915 put Nicholas under immense strain. Even in June, well before the crisis peaked, the Emperor wrote to his wife: 'I am beginning to feel my old heart. The first time it was in August of last year, after the Samsonov catastrophe [at Tannenberg], and again now – it feels so heavy in the left side when I breathe. But what can one do!' On 23 June Alexandra wrote,

> everything is so serious and just now particularly painful and I long to be with you, to share your worries and anxieties. You bear all so bravely and by yourself – let me help you, my Treasure . . . I do so yearn to make it easier for you, and the ministers all squabbling amongst each other at a time when all ought to work together and forget their personal offences – have as aims the welfare of their Sovereign and country – it makes me rage. In other words it's treachery, because people know it, they feel the government in discord and then the left profit by it. If you could only be severe, my Love, it is so necessary. They must hear your voice and see displeasure in your eyes; they are too much accustomed to your gentle, forgiving kindness.[19]

Determination to stiffen her husband's resolve was a constant theme in Alexandra's correspondence. After he had overborne his ministers and assumed the supreme command the Empress asked him to forgive her for badgering him so much but wrote that she knew his gentleness and how difficult it was for him to fight with people.

> You have fought this great fight for your country and throne – alone and with bravery and decision. Never have they seen such firmness in you before and it cannot remain without good fruit . . . What the struggle here really is and means – your showing your mastery, proving yourself the Autocrat without which Russia cannot exist. Had you given in now on these different questions, they would have dragged out yet more of you . . . You had . . . to win your fight against all. It will be a glorious page in your reign and Russian history, the story of these weeks and days – and God, who is just and near you, will save your country and throne through your firmness . . . God anointed you at your coronation, He placed you where you stand and you have done your duty, be sure, quite sure of this . . . and He forsaketh not his anointed.[20]

Nicholas never put down on paper the precise reasons which persuaded him to reject the deal with the Progressive Bloc which most of his ministers urged on him in the summer of 1915. Immediately after his abdication, however, he was asked by his trusted Palace Commandant, General Voeykov, why he had resisted society's demands.

> The Emperor replied that, firstly, any break in the existing system of government at a time of such intense struggle with the enemy would lead only to internal catastrophe and that, secondly, the concessions which he had made during his reign on the insistence of the so-called public circles had only brought harm to the country, each time removing part of the defences against the work of evil elements, consciously leading Russia to ruin. Personally he had always been directed by the wish to preserve the crown in the form which he had inherited it from his late father in order to hand it on in the same form after his death to his son.[21]

In the summer of 1915, as in the autumn of 1905, huge pressure built up on Nicholas II to make concessions to society. In retrospect he believed that the constitution he had granted in October 1905 had made Russia less stable and less governable. Now further weakening of the monarch's power was demanded. A 'government enjoying public confidence' meant that Nicholas must devolve most of his power in domestic affairs to a prime minister, whose stay in office was dependent in part on the support of the Progressive Bloc. The concessions he had made in June by dismissing conservative ministers had been followed by a demand for more concessions in August. Particularly if the military situation remained bad, would not further demands be made, with any 'bureaucrats' remaining in ministerial chairs being held responsible for failures in the country's war effort whose real causes were well beyond their control? The Progressive Bloc was riven with jealousies and differing opinions. It might hold together in denouncing the government and issuing ringing declarations. Would it do so when it actually had to produce legislation satisfactory to its constituents or take some responsibility for governing Russia in the appallingly difficult conditions of war? Even on the most important and pressing domestic issue, namely how best to provide adequate supplies of food to the cities, the Progressive Bloc was split fundamentally and right down the middle. Alexander Khvostov, Goremykin's only firm ally in the Council of Ministers, argued that 'demands are being presented for changes in the State structure, not because these changes are necessary for the organization of victory but because the military misfortunes have weakened the position of the authorities and one can now act against them with a knife at the throat. Today one will satisfy some demands; tomorrow new ones, which go still further, will be announced.' Goremykin himself stated that 'while I'm alive, I will fight for the inviolability of the Tsar's power. The whole strength of Russia lies only in the monarchy. Otherwise there will be such a mess that everything will be lost. First of all, one must conclude the war, instead of occupying oneself with reforms.' No doubt Nicholas shared the opinions of both Goremykin and Khvostov.[22]

In the nine months that followed the crisis Nicholas's firmness seemed to bear fruit. Shortly after his assumption of the supreme command the military situation improved rapidly. Kiev was saved. The front was stabilized. Small but successful counter-attacks occurred. As important, the autumn witnessed a dramatic improvement in military supplies thanks to effective collaboration between the Ministry of War and Russian industry, above all the great barons of the Petersburg and Ukrainian metallurgical factories. When the 1916 campaigning season began, the Russian army was larger and better equipped than at any previous time in the war. The improved military situation and the collaboration between government and industry took much of the sting out of domestic politics. The liberal parties became much more meek, toning down their demands and criticisms. Contrary to fears expressed in the summer of 1915, Nicholas's refusal of a 'ministry of public confidence' did not result in activists in the *zemstvo* or town unions boycotting the war effort. In January 1916 M.V. Chelnokov, the Mayor of Moscow and one of the leading figures in the opposition movement, attended a supply conference at Headquarters, where, to their mutual astonishment, he and Nicholas bumped into one another. The Emperor received the Mayor in private audience. 'He breathed heavily and jumped every second from his chair when he was speaking. I asked him whether he was feeling well, to which he replied in the affirmative, but added that he was accustomed to present himself before Nikolasha, and had not expected to see me here. This reply, and his general bearing, pleased me.' Five months later the President of the Duma, M.V. Rodzyanko, had an interview with the Emperor at Headquarters. Nicholas commented that 'in comparison with last year his tone has changed and has become less self-confident'.[23]

The 1916 campaign on the Eastern Front began with failure in the so-called Lake Naroch battle. Nicholas commented: 'many generals are making serious blunders. The worst of it is, that we have so few good generals. It seems to me that during the long winter rest they have forgotten all the experience which they acquired last year! I am beginning to complain but that is unnecessary! I feel firm, and believe absolutely in our final success.' In the summer of 1916 the Emperor's faith was to be vindicated. A major offensive commanded by General Aleksei Brusilov smashed through the Austrian front. Huge numbers of Austrian and German prisoners were taken. The well-commanded Russian forces proved a match for the German army. New and young military talent, capable of adapting to the needs of modern war, was coming to the fore. With British forces at last committed in huge numbers, and Germany facing terrible attrition on the Somme and at Verdun, it looked briefly as if the last hour of the Central Powers might be nigh. In fact the Germans succeeded in stabilizing the situation. Even so there was some reason for optimism that, with Allied numbers and resources now much outweighing those of the Central Powers, the 1917 campaign could bring victory. But for this to happen, the Russian home front would have to survive its third winter of war.[24]

The basic problem here was economic rather than political. In part it had to do with the railway system, which was strained beyond endurance by the war. The Russian railway network was thinner than in Central or Western Europe. It was also geared to moving grain exports to the Black Sea ports. Now it found itself forced to supply food, forage and fuel to Petrograd and the front on the empire's western and north-western borders. The war's impact on Russian agriculture altered the pattern of regional agricultural surpluses and caused further trouble. So too did a shortage of skilled labour and the impact of inflation on workers' morale. Anyone working for the government, such as a railwayman or policeman, was badly hit by prices racing far ahead of wages. Workers in private companies in Petrograd and Moscow also suffered from this, albeit not quite so badly. The cause of inflation was that the government could only cover much of war expenditure by resorting to the printing press. Easy money helped the boom in investment in war industries but only at the expense of a major drop in urban living standards, made all the more unbearable by the fat profits of some industrialists. The head of the

Petrograd political police warned in October 1916 that great danger existed of a popular explosion brought on by collapsing living standards and exhaustion with the war. 'The economic position of the masses, despite the vast increases in pay, is more than terrible.' 'The ordinary inhabitant, condemned to a half-starved existence,' was, 'to a considerable extent ready for the most wild excesses on the first suitable or unsuitable occasion.' The head of the empire's police forces, A.T. Vasilev, agreed that the situation was 'very alarming' and added that the authorities, including the Emperor himself, were widely blamed for failure to cope with the crisis on the home front.[25]

Even worse than inflation and problems on the railways, though closely linked to both of them, was the drying-up of food supplies to the cities. By the winter of 1916–17 this problem had become acute. With Russian industry geared to the war effort and industrial consumer goods' prices soaring ahead of agricultural prices peasants had increasingly less incentive to market their grain. Massive army purchases, backed by fixed prices and administrative controls, further confused the market. A gap began to yawn between the interests of the country's northern provinces, where there was a shortage of grain, and the southern provinces, where there was a surplus. To a great extent this also meant a battle between town and countryside. Not just the government but also the Progressive Bloc and public opinion were sharply divided on solutions to this crisis. To what extent, if any, should the supply of food be left in the hands of private grain traders? At what level should grain prices be fixed? Should the government or the *zemstvo* and town unions or other public organizations assume responsibility for the food supply? If the government, then which ministry? Technical, political and institutional disagreements combined to make this a supremely intractable problem. Though the liberal opposition fiercely criticized the government's food supply policy in the autumn of 1916, when forced to take responsibility for this problem themselves after the monarchy's fall they failed entirely. In the end the Bolsheviks 'solved' the problem by ferocious requisitioning of grain from the peasantry. But by then the urban population had halved as a result of hunger and unemployment, and the end of the Great War meant there was no longer any need to feed a massive army in the western borderlands.[26]

The Emperor was aware of the crisis on the home front but bewildered as to how to resolve it. In June 1916 he reported that the Minister of Communications, A.F. Trepov, declared that the railways 'are working better than last year, and brings forward evidence to that effect, but complaints are being made, nevertheless, that they do not bring up all that they could! These affairs are a regular curse; from constant anxiety about them I cannot make out where the truth lies. But it is imperative to act energetically and to take firm measures, in order to settle these questions once and for all.' Three months later Nicholas added that,

> together with military matters, the eternal question of supplies troubles me most of all. Alexseev gave me today a letter which he received from the charming Prince Obolensky, the President of the Committee of Supplies. He confesses frankly that they cannot alleviate the situation in any way, that they are working in vain, that the Ministry of Agriculture pays no attention to their regulations, that the prices are soaring and the people beginning to starve. It is obvious where this situation may lead the country. Old Sturmer [the Prime Minister] cannot overcome these difficulties. I do not see any other way out, except by transferring the matter to the military authorities, but that also has its disadvantages. It is the most damnable problem that I have ever come across! I never was a business man, and simply do not understand anything in these questions of supplying and provisioning.[27]

The strain of wartime leadership told severely on the Emperor's health. Even in early 1915, S.S. Fabritsky recalled that, 'not having seen their Majesties and the family for about 10 months I was shaken by the change which could not but strike one. The Emperor and the Empress, who had given herself up to the care of the wounded, had a very tired and worried appearance, and in addition the Emperor had aged noticeably.' Meeting Nicholas again at Headquarters in September 1916 Fabritsky was even more alarmed. 'He had greatly aged and his cheeks were sunken. Sitting almost opposite His Majesty and not taking my eyes from him, I could not but pay attention to his terrible nervousness, which had never existed before. It was evident that the Emperor's spirit was troubled and that it was difficult for him to hide his agitation successfully from his entourage.' Paul Benckendorff told Dr Botkin, the Emperor's physician, that

> he can't continue this way much longer. His Majesty is a changed man. It is very wrong of him to attempt the impossible. He is no longer seriously interested in anything. Of late, he has become quite apathetic. He goes through his daily routine like an automaton, paying more attention to the hour set for his meals or his walk in the garden, than to affairs of state. One can't rule an empire and command an army in the field in this manner. If he doesn't realise it in time, something catastrophic is bound to happen.[28]

Nicholas complained that the ministers 'persist in coming here nearly every day, and take up all my time; I usually go to bed after 1.30 a.m., spending all my time in a continual rush, with writing, reading and receptions!!! It is simply desperate.' Especially when reporting on technical economic questions ministers often felt that the monarch was far away. As Minister of Agriculture, Alexander Naumov bore chief responsibility for supplying food to the army and the cities. In June 1916 he made a report to the Emperor at Headquarters.

> I tried to tell His Majesty in detail about the situation of the food supply, about the harvests and what was the prospective yield, and about the organization of agricultural work in the agricultural regions of the south. The Emperor kept on interrupting me with questions that related not to the business side of my official journey but rather to everyday trivia that interested him . . . how the weather was, whether there were children and flowers . . . I must admit that this kind of attitude from the Emperor towards matters of fundamental national importance at the time discouraged me greatly . . . I became clearly aware of a certain characteristic of the monarch which I attribute to general nervous exhaustion brought about by all the adversities attending his reign and the extraordinary complications he had encountered in governing the country since the outbreak of war in 1914. Like the neurotic who preserves his equanimity only until some vulnerable point is touched, the Emperor, clearly exhausted under the pressure of very complicated national concerns and tremendous responsibility, instinctively looked for peace and preferred to think and talk about lighter and happier things when we reported to him, rather than to hear and discuss urgent, difficult and worrying issues.[29]

Peter Bark served as Minister of Finance until the monarchy's fall in March 1917. He wrote in his memoirs that

> when I had to go to Headquarters to present a report to the Emperor, His Majesty more than once told me how good he felt among his army and how unpleasant to him was the whole atmosphere of the capital when he returned for short periods to Tsarskoe Selo. At the front people defended their country and sacrificed themselves but in the rear they were taken up with gossip, intrigue and personal interests. Unfortunately the apathetic attitude of the Emperor to the rear inspired him to a certain indifference as regards the tasks of government. Having taken the path of his own personal policy, having assumed the supreme command and determined the course of internal affairs despite the opinions of the majority of the Council of Ministers, the Emperor had taken upon himself the whole burden of responsibility for the administrative machine. The Council of Ministers, as a united government, had ceased to exist and the ministers had been turned simply into bosses of the departments, whom the Emperor summoned separately to hear their reports on current affairs.[30]

Bark was a little unfair on Nicholas, whose attitude to the rear and its problems was as much one of bewilderment as of apathy. But the Minister of Finance was absolutely correct in describing the civilian government as in many ways leaderless. Throughout the war the pattern established in

January 1914 prevailed. A weak Chairman of the Council sat alongside powerful heads of department, of whom the Minister of Internal Affairs was the most important as regards domestic policy. Ivan Goremykin, who served as Chairman until January 1916, was an intelligent and experienced man but he had been born in 1839. In his wartime letters Paul Benckendorff stressed on many occasions the need for a powerful and inspiring prime minister who could co-ordinate and energize government policy. In the summer of 1915 he commented that if Goremykin could obey the logic of his political views and act as a dictator, all well and good. In fact, however, he was far too old and was exhausted after one hour of conversation. In January 1916 Goremykin was succeeded as premier by Boris Sturmer, nine years his junior in age and considerably his inferior in personality. Sturmer had been a competent provincial governor many years before but as a war leader or dictator he was out of his depth. Benckendorff complained that no one could even hear his speeches in the Duma or State Council. Still older, though nicer and more intelligent, was the last premier, Prince N.D. Golitsyn. For a country in the midst of deep crisis even the symbolic presence of such elderly and tired figures at the helm of government was both depressing and psychologically disastrous. But Nicholas and Alexandra knew, liked and trusted these old men. They would not seek to push the Emperor aside or gang up with the Duma behind his back. Above all, they had the values of the older generation of senior officialdom. They would stay in office and execute the Emperor's policy even if they disagreed with it. By contrast, younger ministers were much more likely to insist on resigning if their opinions and those of the monarch diverged.[31]

With Ivan Goremykin's appointment as Chairman of the Council in February 1914 Nicholas II had established a pattern whereby a powerful Minister of Internal Affairs had the biggest say as regards domestic policy and worked directly to the Emperor. In June 1915, in an effort to appease the Duma and public opinion, the Tsar dismissed Nicholas Maklakov and replaced him as Minister of Internal Affairs with Prince N.B. Shcherbatov. Maklakov was a reactionary in the correct sense of the term, meaning that he wanted, as far as possible, to return to the pre-1905 system of government. The Soviet historian, V.S. Dyakin, comments that 'Maklakov was no fool, raised by chance to a ministerial post. He was one of the most consistent, decisive and open defenders of the autocracy.' His successor, Shcherbatov, was much more popular but also less competent. He was a conservative aristocrat, a man drawn from 'society', not a bureaucrat. One of his ministerial colleagues recalled that Shcherbatov 'won great sympathy by his straight character and his gentle treatment of people, however . . . not having any experience in the work of the huge and complicated bureaucratic apparatus he became completely lost'. For the rest of the war

Nicholas tried hard not to alienate public opinion totally, partly because he needed the support of liberal members of public organizations, for instance in the *zemstvo* and town unions, to manage the food supply, cope with the refugee problem and provide a number of services to the front-line army. This more or less ruled out the appointment of one of the small and shrinking band of tough conservative bureaucrats to run the Ministry of Internal Affairs. On the other hand, in the summer of 1915 the Emperor rejected a 'ministry of public confidence', thereby making it impossible to leave the Ministry of Internal Affairs in the hands of a liberal-conservative official of Krivoshein's type. The monarch's options in appointing men to this vital position therefore became very narrow. Many of the available candidates were mediocre and gerontocratic. A perfect reflection of this was the fact that for four months in 1916 Boris Sturmer doubled as Prime Minister and Minister of Internal Affairs. Less offensive to the Duma than Goremykin, for the last fifteen years Sturmer had enjoyed a reputation for loyalty, even subservience, to the crown, but combined with a manner and attitudes which smoothed over relations with *zemstvos* and liberal activists to the extent that that was possible.[32]

In the winter of 1915–16 the Ministry of Internal Affairs was headed by Aleksei Khvostov, whose uncle Alexander was also a member of the cabinet at that time. The younger Khvostov, who was both a former provincial governor and a right-wing member of the Duma, seemed to have the right qualifications for the job: administrative experience, loyalty to the crown, the ability to cope with the Duma. In addition, Khvostov was young and energetic. Alexandra described him as 'a man, no petticoats', who was 'energetic' and 'with cleverness and decision' would sort out the domestic political and food supply crises. The new minister's programme was to undercut the liberal opposition by reducing inflation and the cost of living, demonstratively combating speculation and loudly denouncing the role of non-Russians, and especially people of German origin, in the economy. Khvostov was not just a demagogue but also a rather shady character. Though he had cultivated Rasputin when seeking office, he quickly realized that the man was a liability to the regime and decided in desperation to have him killed. The security police was not, however, in pre-revolutionary days an organization that arranged contract murders. Its director, S.P. Beletsky, denounced Khvostov and a frightful scandal ensued, which further damaged the crown's prestige. When Khvostov was appointed, Paul Benckendorff described him, a little snootily, as a 'mediocre *arriviste*' of doubtful morals, one of a number of vulgar, unscrupulous types who were forming a clique around the Empress. Reporting to his brother on 9 March 1916 about the bungled effort to kill Rasputin, he commented: 'that is all that was lacking'.[33]

Alexander Protopopov, the last Minister of Internal Affairs in Imperial Russia, was appointed on 29 September 1916. On paper Protopopov seemed a perfect candidate. He was the Vice-President of the Duma and came not from its right wing but from its Octobrist centre. Like many Octobrists, Protopopov's political principles were distinctly flexible and, appointed to ministerial office, he proved a loyal servant of the crown. Nevertheless, since the Duma's President, M.V. Rodzyanko, had actually recommended Protopopov to Nicholas it seemed reasonable to expect that his appointment would smooth relations with the parliament. Protopopov was both a landowner and an industrialist. He enjoyed excellent relations with the Petersburg financial oligarchy, whose support for both the regime and the war effort was very important. In March 1916 Protopopov had been elected chairman of the Council of Metallurgical Industrialists, a group which played a key role in supplying the army and one whose attitude to the government was much less hostile than that of the Moscow industrialists who were linked to Alexander Guchkov and to the Progressist party. As chairman of the Duma delegation which had visited Britain, France and Italy in 1916 Protopopov had won golden opinions in Western Europe. Dyakin commented:

> a good orator and conversationalist, and anything but a stupid man, Protopopov knew how to make a good impression. The Russian ambassadors in London, Paris and Rome told Nicholas about this in their reports, the King of England expressed his joy that Russia possessed such outstanding people, some ministers made favourable comments about him . . . From his side, Rodzyanko put forward Protopopov as a candidate for the Ministry of Trade and Industry in a conversation with Nicholas in June 1916.

In early August 1916 the Emperor talked to Protopopov for the first time. He reported to Alexandra, who became a firm supporter of Protopopov, 'yesterday I saw a man whom I liked very much – Protopopov, Vice-President of the State Duma. He travelled abroad with other members of the Duma and told me much of interest. He was formerly an officer of the Grenadier Guards Cavalry Regiment, and Maximovich [assistant to the commander of Imperial Headquarters] knows him well.' In the winter of 1916–17 the story current in parliamentary circles was that Protopopov was becoming insane as a result of having contracted syphilis. Perhaps the tale was true. But Nicholas can be excused for saying wearily, when told about this, that Protopopov's insanity must have come upon him suddenly after his appointment by the crown to responsible office.[34]

For all his qualifications, Protopopov turned out to be a disastrous minister. Peter Bark recalled that in the Council of Ministers Protopopov created a very negative impression by his statements. His explanations and judgements were unusually superficial, he enjoyed no authority and seemed a pitiful figure because of his lack of competence or knowledge. Alongside this were the very best intentions to show firm authority not only in his own ministry but even to widen the activity of his department by transferring to it the food-supply question from the Ministry of Agriculture. He succeeded in doing neither, despite the fact that via the Empress he put up the latter question for the Emperor's well-disposed decision. One must do him justice as regards one talent – he was extremely eloquent and could talk without end . . . In his reception room crowds of people gathered waiting the time for their meetings with him, which never took place, and urgent current business fell into a chaotic state. But it was impossible to be angry with him. He was in the highest degree a well-educated person, attentive, courteous, winning sympathy by his kind treatment of people. He was the prototype of those of his colleagues who after the revolution formed the first revolutionary Provisional Government – dreamers, filled with good intentions, lacking any experience of statesmanship, possessing a talent for oratory and giving great significance to words, without knowing how to turn words into actions.

Peter Bark spoke with the bias of a bureaucrat and a banker but there was much truth even so in what he said. Had Nicholas and the Progressive Bloc come to an agreement in the summer of 1915 it is possible that able and experienced officials could have directed the war effort with parliamentary and even some public support. Instead, in the winter of 1916–17, the crown was lumbered with sole responsibility for the efforts of a parliamentarian promoted into a key office which he lacked the talent to manage and subjected to a barrage of frenzied and inflammatory criticism from the press and his increasingly panic-stricken former colleagues in the Duma.[35]

Assaulted on all sides by pleas to remove his Minister of Internal Affairs Nicholas gave in. On 23 November 1916 he wrote to his wife: 'I am sorry for Protopopov – he is a good, honest man, but he jumps from one idea to another and cannot make up his mind on anything. I noticed that from the beginning . . . it is risky to leave the Ministry of Internal Affairs in the hands of such a man in these times.' The Empress responded:

Darling, remember that it does not lie in the man Protopopov or x, y, z, but it's the question of monarchy and yr. prestige now, which must not be shattered in the time of the Duma. Don't think they will stop at him, but they will make all others leave who are devoted to you one by one – and then ourselves. Remember, last year Yr. leaving to the army, when also you were alone with us two against everybody, who promised revolution if you went. You stood up against all and God blessed your decision. I repeat again – it does not lie in the name of Protopopov but in your remaining firm and not giving in – the Tsar rules and not the Duma.

Descending on Headquarters, Alexandra persuaded Nicholas to change his mind about Protopopov's dismissal, no doubt appealing to his own belief that the frequent changing of key ministers under parliamentary pressure was a sign of weakness and a road to disaster. Because Nicholas kept Protopopov he was forced to accept the resignation of A.F. Trepov, Sturmer's replacement as Prime Minister, who made his own stay dependent on the Minister of Internal Affairs' removal. In Trepov's place there came the septuagenarian Prince N.D. Golitsyn, the last Chairman of the Council of Ministers in Imperial Russia.[36]

Alexandra's intervention to save Protopopov was the most spectacular example of the influence she wielded over her husband during the war. When he stood up to his ministers in the summer of 1915 and moved to Headquarters, Nicholas invited his wife to take a more active political role. 'Will you not come to the assistance of your hubby now that he is absent?' he wrote on 7 September 1915. 'I know of no more pleasant feeling than to be proud of you, as I have been all these past months, when you urged me on with untiring importunity, exhorting me to be firm and to stick to my own opinions.' 'The feminine influence is at its peak,' wrote Paul Benckendorff to his brother in November 1915 and this was a theme that the Grand Marshal of the Court was to repeat in many later letters, commenting that the only partial counterweight to Alexandra was General Alekseev at Headquarters.[37]

In one sense Alexandra's influence was nothing new in principle. The Romanov regime had always been a family firm in which the monarch was influenced by his relatives. No single Romanov in the earlier years of Nicholas's reign had been as dominant as Alexandra was during the war, partly because by that time the Emperor was increasingly isolated even from his own family. Nevertheless, the Empress Marie's influence on key appointments in the first decade of her son's reign had been considerable. There was, however, a fundamental difference between the political views of the two empresses. Marie moved easily in the capital's high society and shared its views and moods. She told Alexander Krivoshein during the war that 'it is impossible to govern a large nation without the support of enlightened people and against public opinion'. Alexandra on the other hand loathed high society, distrusted its Whig sympathies and believed in firm autocratic power resting on the supposed union of Tsar and peasant.[38]

Political sympathies aside, Alexandra was dangerous to her husband because of her German blood, which made her an easy target for the rumours and accusations of treason which flew around in the increasingly hysterical wartime atmosphere of Petrograd and Moscow. Secret police reports stressed the public belief that the Empress headed a pro-German court party anxious for peace with Germany. There was no truth whatever in these stories. Alexandra bitterly regretted the war and was made miserable by the thought that her brother, the Grand Duke of Hesse, was on the other side of the lines. But not only did she associate entirely with Russia, the land of her husband and son, she also understood that peace with Germany would be inconceivable for domestic political reasons. In June 1915, for instance, she wrote to Nicholas that she had assured his uncle, the Grand Duke Paul, that 'you were not dreaming of peace and knew it would mean revolution here'. Nevertheless, the combination of panic and rumour in Petrograd, of deliberate attempts by the press to blacken the dynasty, and of the shady dealings of some members of Alexandra's circle all encouraged the story that 'dark forces' grouped around the 'young empress' were trying to end the war on German terms.[39]

Alexandra was the victim of her own isolation, nervousness and credulity, which made it impossible for her to see through some of those who tried to win her sympathy. Paul Benckendorff described the Empress as having 'a will of iron linked to not much brain and no knowledge'. On another occasion he commented that once Alexandra had made up her mind on a subject, no amount of rational argument or fresh evidence would make her alter her views. He wrote to his brother on 10 April 1916 that he did not wish even to raise the anodyne issue of appointing George V Colonel-in-Chief of a Russian regiment since one never knew nowadays how Alexandra would react to such an innocent suggestion. As this letter makes clear, the Empress was by 1915–17 in a state of great nervous agitation and instability. The extra strains of wartime, and of the domestic political crisis, had proved too much for her. Increasingly, Rasputin came to be her tranquillizer, her amulet which would ward off the dangers which threatened her husband and family. As she wrote in November 1916, 'had we not got Him [Rasputin] – all would long have been finished, of that I am utterly convinced'. Inside the shell of seeming confidence and toughness, Alexandra was deeply uncertain of herself and her husband. Rasputin, she wrote, 'will be less mistaken in people than we are – experience in life blessed by God'.[40]

In August 1915 Paul Benckendorff mentioned Rasputin's name to his brother for the first time, his letter showing clearly his belief that the ambassador would not previously have known anything about the *starets*. During the next sixteen months much of Petrograd came to believe in Rasputin's power and thence the rumours about his role spread to the army and through the interior of the empire. Alexandra's letters certainly show that a major consideration for her as regards appointments, above all in the Church and the Ministry of Internal Affairs, was whether the man in question would defend Rasputin from verbal and physical attack.

Where key political appointments were concerned, however, it is very doubtful whether the absence of Rasputin would have made any significant difference. Given the course which Nicholas was steering, suitable candidates for key government offices were few and far between and it is easy to point to influences other than Rasputin's advice which resulted in the appointment of individuals to top positions. Even in 1915–16 what really mattered about Rasputin was not his actual political influence but the fatal impact he had on the monarchy's prestige. The *starets* frequently visited Anna Vyrubov, Alexandra's bosom friend, who was the daughter of A.S. Taneev, the head of the Emperor's Own Personal Chancellery. He also called on some top officials, including the various prime ministers. The Empress was known to respect his opinions and to rely emotionally on his support. No one could doubt Alexandra's closeness to her husband or the fact that he listened to her advice. Rumour and Rasputin's own boasts about his power did the rest. Taken up by some of the silliest elements in fashionable female Petrograd and fawned upon by unscrupulous seekers after office and government contracts, Rasputin's head was completely turned. His drunkenness and sexual antics were a further gift to the press and the monarchy's enemies. Some of the dynasty's friends and even members came to see Rasputin as the linchpin of Nicholas's political strategy, which to them appeared suicidal. On 30 December 1916 the *starets* was murdered by a group that included Prince Felix Yusupov, husband of the Emperor's niece, as well as the Grand Duke Dimitri, who was Nicholas's first cousin. Another conspirator was V.M. Purishkevich, a Duma deputy of the far right.

The murder of Rasputin by figures from ultra-conservative and high society circles reflected the great fear in such quarters of impending revolution. Increasing discontent in Petrograd, caused above all by soaring prices and growing shortages, was the background to their action. At the other end of the political spectrum in 'respectable society', a mood of panic was also setting in. When the Kadet leader, Paul Milyukov, stood up in the Duma on 14 November and accused the government of treason in a speech which reverberated across Russia he hoped to satisfy his increasingly enraged middle-class electors, to distance himself from the regime and to ward off criticisms of liberal spinelessness. But though his dangerous and irresponsible speech made an enormous impact on public opinion, the last thing that Milyukov actually wanted was revolution on the streets of Petrograd.

In the winter of 1916–17, for the second time during the war, enormous pressure built up on Nicholas II to concede a government which would rely on the support of the Duma. Even now some voices urged him to resist this pressure. Peter Durnovo had died in 1915 but his mantle had to some extent been taken up by Nicholas Maklakov. In November 1916 he wrote to the Emperor that the opinion was widespread in society, and even now in some government circles, that if the Emperor conceded a parliamentary regime in Russia 'a golden age will begin' and the government would emerge successfully from its present crisis. The reality was that the Duma majority parties were 'so weak and uncoordinated that their victory will be very unstable and brief'. The Kadets, though they were Russia's major liberal party and called themselves democrats, had no support among the mass of the population. Their constituency was almost exclusively the professional middle class. The Octobrists had far less backing even than this. They were for the most part landowners, whose pretensions to liberalism would disappear the moment a single noble estate was looted by peasant rioters. The great threat came from the left, where the socialist parties represented 'a serious danger and a real strength'. The masses might be changeable in mood, swinging from chauvinism to anarchy very easily, but they were 'strongly united by a feeling of hatred for the wealthier classes and by a fervent desire to seize other people's property and for class war'. No parliamentary government could hold the socialist revolution in check. The day after parliamentarianism triumphed would come 'social revolution . . . communes . . . the end of the monarchy and of the property-owning class and the triumph of the peasant, who will become a bandit'.[41]

In 1914 those who thought like Maklakov were a small minority. By the winter of 1916–17 even previous pillars of conservatism such as the United Nobility warned Nicholas of impending revolution and begged him to concede a ministry resting unequivocally on the support of the Duma's majority. Members of the imperial family joined the chorus. The Emperor's brother-in-law, the Grand Duke Alexander Mikhailovich, wrote to Nicholas in February 1917 that the Duma's majority did not want revolution and would be satisfied by limited concessions. What was needed was a united government led by a powerful prime minister who enjoyed the Duma's confidence. A full parliamentary regime was neither necessary nor desirable but 'the present situation in which all responsibility lies on you and you alone is unthinkable'. The legislature must share the burden of responsibility and government must be responsive to public opinion. Still more alarming in a way was a letter from Alexander's brother, the normally quiet and apolitical Grand Duke George, who in November 1916 was visiting the front commanded by General Brusilov. The Grand Duke wrote to Nicholas that

> literally everyone is visibly worried about the rear, in other words about Russia's internal condition. They say straight out that if matters go on as now within Russia then we will never succeed in winning the war and if we don't do that then it's the end of everything . . . Then I tried to make clear what

measures could heal this condition. To that I can reply that the universal cry is for the removal of Sturmer and the establishment of a responsible ministry . . . This measure is considered to be the only one which could avoid a general catastrophe. If I had heard this from leftists and various liberals then I would not have paid any attention to it. But this was said to me by people here who are deeply devoted to you and with their whole souls want only your good and Russia's, which are indivisible.

Perhaps the Grand Duke did not feel the need to underline the point that the army's commanders were the monarchy's most vital supporters and that if they came to see the imperial government as an obstacle to victory over Germany then the dynasty's cause was truly hopeless.[42]

To most observers it seemed that Nicholas II was stumbling blindfold towards revolution, whose danger he completely ignored. It is true that both the Emperor and the Empress continued to feed on illusions about popular support for the monarchy. As always during Nicholas II's reign, the cheers which greeted him on his travels helped to persuade the monarch that he enjoyed far more public sympathy than his advisers pretended. On the very eve of the revolution Nicholas said to Frederycksz's deputy, 'how can even you, Mosolov, talk to me about a danger to the dynasty, which right now everyone is trying to din into me? Can you too, who have been with me during my inspections of the troops and have seen how both the soldiers and the people receive me, also get frightened?'[43]

Nevertheless, the picture of complete blindness and stupidity is a little exaggerated. The danger of rioting in Petrograd was understood and plans were drawn up to contain it. The authorities would confront disturbances with a three-stage strategy and only if all other measures failed would soldiers be required to use firearms. Only the companies created to train non-commissioned officers would be used, since these were regarded as more reliable than ordinary troops. Battalions of the supposedly loyal Naval Guards were brought back from the front to reinforce the garrison. The police well understood popular despair at living conditions but believed that their arrests of revolutionary activists in Petrograd in January and February 1917 would deprive rioters of effective leadership. Apart from the Ministry of Internal Affairs, which Protopopov was throwing into confusion, the key domestic departments in the winter of 1916–17 were communications and agriculture. The former was headed by E.B. Krieger-Voynovsky, the latter by A.A. Rittikh, both of whom were intelligent and efficient professionals where railway and food-supply questions were concerned. Tsuyoshi Hasegawa, among Western historians the leading expert on the February revolution, considers that 'the tsarist government's over-all performance in handling this enormous task of food supply was not as bad as is often argued . . . the army did not suffer from lack of provisions and no one in the cities starved. The collapse of the mechanism for supplying food actually came after the February Revolution.' Speaking to A.I. Piltz, the former Governor of Mogilev, in early February 1917, Nicholas II betrayed an awareness of danger which he revealed only to the very few people whom he fully trusted. 'I know that the situation is very alarming, and I have been advised to dissolve the State Duma . . . But I can't do this . . . In the military respect we are stronger than ever before. Soon, in the spring, will come the offensive and I believe that God will give us victory, and then moods will change.'[44]

On 7 March Nicholas left Tsarskoe Selo for Headquarters. The next day disturbances began in Petrograd. By Sunday, 11 March, it was clear that the crowds, emboldened by the authorities' unwillingness to use firearms, were becoming uncontrollable. Almost all Petrograd's factories were on strike, food shops were being looted and enough members of the revolutionary parties were still at liberty to provide political leadership and colouring to the demonstrations. The military and government authorities in Petrograd played down the seriousness of the situation in their messages to Headquarters in Mogilev. On 11 March the moment of crisis came when troops were ordered to open fire in order to clear the central areas of the city from occupation by demonstrators. Initially force proved effective and the crowds dispersed. Ominously, a small mutiny occurred in one company of the Pavlovsky Guards regiment on the afternoon of 11 March but it was contained. The next day, however, in response to the shootings on 11 March, mutiny spread at great speed through most of the Petrograd garrison. On 12 March Nicholas learned that his government had lost control of the capital. He decided to return to Tsarskoe Selo and ordered General N.I. Ivanov to command a special force drawn from front-line units with which he was to restore governmental authority in the capital. Nicholas's own train was blocked from reaching Tsarskoe Selo and the Emperor chose to divert to Pskov, the headquarters of the northern front, where he arrived in the early evening of 14 March. The reason for choosing Pskov was its proximity to Nicholas's train and the possibility of rapid communication between the northern front headquarters and Petrograd by a primitive form of teleprinter. Meanwhile on 12 March a so-called Provisional Committee of the Duma had come into existence and began to assert control over the capital. Though some of the Duma politicians were happy to take power into their own hands, others did so very cautiously and out of fear that the alternative would be anarchy and the seizure of control by the socialist-dominated Workers and Soldiers Council (that is, the Soviet), which also began to form on 12 March.

The fate of the monarchy now depended on the Duma politicians and, above all, on the military commanders. Only if the latter were willing to sanction a rapid move on Petrograd by large numbers of troops could

Nicholas's throne be saved. On arrival at Pskov at 7.05 p.m. on 14 March
the first signs were not encouraging. General Ruzsky, the commander of
the northern front, greeted Voeykov, the Palace Commandant, with the
words: 'Look what you have done . . . all your Rasputin clique . . . what
have you got Russia into now?' Later that evening Ruzsky, who was in
touch with Rodzyanko, the President of the Duma, pressed on Nicholas
the latter's view that only the immediate concession of parliamentary rule
could save the dynasty.[45]

The Emperor's response to Ruzsky's demand tells one much about his
political and personal philosophy.

> 'I am responsible before God and Russia for everything that has happened and
> is happening,' said the Emperor, 'regardless of whether ministers are respon-
> sible to the Duma or the State Council. Seeing that what the ministers are
> doing is not for Russia's good, I will never be able to agree with them,
> comforting myself with the thought that matters are not in my hands and that
> the responsibility is not mine.' Ruzsky tried to show the Emperor that his idea
> was mistaken and that one must accept the formula: 'The monarch reigns but
> the government rules.' The Emperor said that this formula was incomprehen-
> sible to him and that he would need to have been differently educated, to be
> born again, and once more he stressed that he was not personally hanging on to
> power but only that he could not take decisions which were against his
> conscience and, having shed responsibility for the course of events before
> people, he still could not consider that he was not responsible before God. The
> Emperor, with unusual clarity, ran through the views of all the people who
> could govern Russia in the near future as ministers responsible to the legisla-
> ture and expressed his conviction that these non-bureaucratic public figures,
> who would undoubtedly make up the first cabinet, were all people without
> any administrative experience who, having taken on the burden of office,
> would not be able to cope with their task.[46]

After a tremendous struggle, during which the General browbeat the
Emperor and controlled the flow of information to him, Ruzsky finally
persuaded Nicholas to agree to a government responsible to the Duma. By
the next day, however, it became clear that the discussion had been
academic. Rodzyanko, in the name of the Duma's Provisional Committee, now asserted that only the Emperor's abdication offered any hope of
avoiding further bloodshed in Petrograd. The other front commanders,
though not as brusque or hostile as Ruzsky, all advised the Emperor that
he should abdicate for Russia's good. The senior generals were not certain
of their troops' loyalty in the event of clashes with revolutionary soldiers of
the Petrograd garrison. Most of them had lost confidence in Nicholas II's
ability to rule Russia. Above all, none of the generals wanted internal
complications which might stand in the way of fighting the Germans, a

priority which the Emperor himself fully shared. Had the military commanders been faced with anarchy in Petrograd or the coming to power of
the socialist-led Soviet then the army's intervention would have been
certain. There is also a real chance it would have been successful. But once
the Duma leaders assured the generals that they were in control of events
and that military intervention would lead to civil war the front-line commanders were prepared to compromise. Abandoned by his generals,
Nicholas II had no alternative but to abdicate. On 15 March he renounced
the throne. General Alekseev, the Chief of Staff, only agreed to the Tsar's
abdication in the conviction, inspired by Rodzyanko, that the monarchy
would be preserved in the person either of the Emperor's son or of his
brother, the Grand Duke Michael. By 16 March, however, the majority of
the Provisional Committee of the Duma had decided that, in view of the
mood of the Petrograd workers and soldiers, the continuation of the
monarchy in any form was impossible. They persuaded the Grand Duke
not to assume the crown. Alekseev was faced with a *fait accompli*. Three
hundred years of Romanov rule had come to an end. Meanwhile the
imperial train made its sad way back from Pskov to General Headquarters
at Mogilev. General Voeykov entered Nicholas's coupé, where the
Emperor was sitting in the darkness, the only light coming from the lamp
shining by the icon in the corner. 'After all the experiences of this sad day
the Emperor, always distinguished by his enormous self-control, no longer
had the strength to restrain himself. He embraced me and wept.'[47]

CHAPTER 9

After the Revolution,
1917–1918

After returning to Headquarters at Mogilev, Nicholas bade farewell to General Alekseev and the rest of his military staff. On 21 March the former Emperor issued his last address to the army. In this time of great personal agony, his overriding concern remained the fate of his country, and the need for national unity in order to achieve victory. His agreement to abdication had indeed been greatly influenced by his generals' argument that this would avoid civil war and thereby allow the struggle with Germany to be pursued successfully. 'For the last time', wrote the Emperor,

> I appeal to you, the troops whom I so fervently love. Since my abdication . . . power has passed to the Provisional Government . . . May God help it to lead Russia along the road to glory and prosperity. May God help you, my valiant troops, to defend our homeland against the cruel foe. For two and one half years you have hourly borne the heavy burden of war. Much is the blood that has been shed; many are the efforts that have been made; and the hour is already near when Russia, bound to her gallant allies by a single common striving for victory, will crush the last efforts of the adversary. This unprecedented war must be brought to full victory. Whoever now dreams of peace, whoever wishes it – that one is a traitor to his fatherland, its betrayer. I know that every honest soldier thinks so. Carry out your duty then; protect our gallant homeland; subordinate yourselves to the Provisional Government, obey your commanders.

Though the whole purpose of the appeal was to strengthen the position of those in authority, the Provisional Government did not allow the address to be published. On 21 March Nicholas was placed under arrest. The next day he was taken back to Tsarskoe Selo.[1]

For Alexandra the fortnight of her husband's absence had been a time of immense strain and agony. News of the abdication was a terrible blow. Revolutionary troops in Tsarskoe Selo came within 500 yards of storming the palace. All her children were dangerously ill with measles, not a disease to trifle with in those days. Aleksei had a temperature of 104°. In addition to measles, his sister Marie had contracted double pneumonia, coming close to death. Somehow pride and royal training allowed the Empress to preserve her outward dignity in these terrible days.

Lili Dehn, Alexandra's close friend, was in the imperial family's apartments on 22 March when Nicholas returned from Headquarters.

As we went into the red salon, and the light fell on the Emperor's face, I started . . . I now realised how greatly he had altered. The Emperor was deathly pale, his face was covered with innumerable wrinkles, his hair was quite grey at the temples, and blue shadows encircled his eyes. He looked like an old man; the Emperor smiled sadly when he saw my horrified expression, and he was about to speak, when the Empress joined us; he then tried to appear the light-hearted husband and father of the happy years; he sat with us and chatted on trivial matters, but I could see that he was inwardly ill at ease, and at last the effort was too much for him. 'I think I'll go for a walk – walking always does me good', he said . . .

The Empress and I . . . stood by one of the windows which looked out over the Park . . . the Emperor . . . by this time was outside the palace. He walked briskly towards the Grande Allée, but suddenly a sentinel appeared from nowhere, so to speak, and intimated to the Emperor that he was not allowed to go in that direction. The Emperor made a nervous movement with his hand, but he obeyed, and retraced his steps; but the same thing occurred – another sentinel barred his passage, and an officer told the Emperor that, as he was now to all intents and purposes a prisoner, his exercise must be of the prison-yard description! . . . We watched the beloved figure turn the corner . . . his steps flagged, his head was bent, his whole aspect was significant of utter dejection; his spirit seemed completely broken. I do not think that until this moment we had realised the crushing grip of the Revolution, nor what it signified . . .

The Empress said nothing, but I felt her hand grasp mine; it was, for her, an agonizing experience . . . that day the Emperor and the Empress dined and spent the evening together. The Empress told me afterwards that the Emperor lost his self-control when he was alone with her in the mauve boudoir; he wept bitterly. It was excessively difficult for her to console him, and to assure him that the husband and father was of more value in her eyes than the Emperor whose throne she had shared.[2]

The five months that the imperial family were to spend in captivity at Tsarskoe Selo brought many further humiliations. Some were trivial though hurtful, such as the soldiers' insistence on taking away Aleksei's toy gun. Others were more serious. For the whole of April, for instance, Nicholas and Alexandra were kept apart and not allowed to have any conversation in private. The mood of the soldiers was fickle and unpredictable. In many units the officers were terrified of their men, over whom they had no control. Clashes between the soldiers and the palace servants occurred on a daily basis. The disloyalty of supposedly devoted friends and servants was a great blow, just as the faithfulness of some of the court officials, such as Paul Benckendorff and Sofia Buxhoeveden, was a tremendous consolation. The fate of the heir's two sailor 'minders' was typical of the times. One, Derevenko, turned on Aleksei, abused him and abandoned the palace. The other, Nagornyy, remained loyal and later, in Siberia, paid for his faithfulness with his life. A tremendous extra worry for Nicholas was all that he heard from the front about the disintegration of the army and the faltering of the war effort. In the words of the children's tutor, Pierre Gilliard, this caused the Emperor 'great grief'. As always, however, Nicholas's optimism struggled against bad news. 'I get a little hope from the fact that in our country people love to exaggerate. I can't believe that the army at the front has become as bad as they say. It couldn't have disintegrated in just two months to such a degree.'[3]

Nevertheless, life at Tsarskoe Selo had its compensations for the Emperor. Bearing sole responsibility for Russia's government in wartime had been an appalling strain. Holding out for months on end against overwhelming pressures for political change had demanded a toughness and self-confident resolution which did not come easily to Nicholas and cost him dear in terms of emotional stress. At Tsarskoe he could spend all his time with his family, whom disaster had united more closely than ever. In office the Emperor's gentleness and his lack of self-assertiveness had been weaknesses. Now they were strengths. His personal humility and his self-discipline stood him in good stead. Not only at Tsarskoe but also later in Siberia no one ever heard the Empress or her husband complain about their fate. On the contrary, it was for their children, their friends and their servants that they worried. As Alexandra wrote to Lili Dehn in March 1918, 'for us, in general, it is better and easier than for others'. During the war the Empress's stubbornness, her irrationality and her political activities had driven Paul Benckendorff to frenzy. Now it was her courage and dignity that impressed him. 'She is great, great . . . but I had always said that she was one of those people who rise to sublime heights in the midst of misfortune.'[4]

On the throne the religious convictions of the imperial couple had been a hindrance. They had encouraged a certain fatalism in Nicholas and persuaded him that his duty to God demanded of him an active role as autocrat which did not fit his personality. Alexandra had searched for

God's hand in politics. Now that the imperial couple were helpless victims of fate their submission to God's will, faith in His mercy, and natural otherworldliness became pillars of strength. Alexandra wrote to Lili Dehn in the spring of 1918 that

> I feel the Father's presence near me and a wonderful sense of peaceful joy thrills and fills my soul . . . one cannot understand the reason for it, as everything is so unutterably sad, but this comes from Above and is beside ourselves, and one knows that He will not forsake His own, will strengthen and protect . . . Do not worry about us, darling, dearly beloved one. For you all it is hard and especially for our country!!! This hurts more than anything else – and the heart is racked with pain – what has been done in one year! God has allowed it to happen – and therefore it must be necessary so that they might understand, that eyes might be opened to lies and deceits . . . everything generally hurts now – all one's feelings have been trampled underfoot – but so it has to be, the soul must grow and rise above all else; that which is most dear and tender in us has been wounded – is it not true? So we too have to understand through it all that God is greater than everything and that He wants to draw us, through our sufferings, closer to Him. Love him more and better than one and all. But my country – my God – how I love it, with all the power of my being, and her sufferings give me actual physical pain.[5]

Immediately after the revolution, it seemed possible that the imperial family would go into exile in Britain. To his honour, the Kadet leader, Paul Milyukov, now Foreign Minister in the Provisional Government, requested that the British government offer Nicholas and his family asylum in England. Initially the British felt constrained to agree. Very quickly came second thoughts and it was the King, an old personal friend of his Russian first cousin, who took the lead in closing off the possibility of asylum. His secretary, Lord Stamfordham, queried, on King George's behalf, how the imperial family would support themselves financially in exile. Political worries were, however, the decisive factor. Fearful of reaction from British socialists and the labour movement, King George did not want his dynasty to be associated in the public eye with the hated, and now fallen, Russian Tsar, let alone with his half-English wife. Lord Stamfordham wrote to the Foreign Secretary that 'from the first the King has thought the presence of the Imperial family (especially of the Empress) in this country would raise all sorts of difficulties, and I feel sure that you appreciate how awkward it will be for our Royal Family who are closely connected both with the Emperor and the Empress.' Requests for visas from two grand dukes were also turned down. As regards Nicholas and Alexandra, it may well be that the

British decision made no difference. It would have been politically very difficult for the Provisional Government to have allowed the Emperor and the Empress to leave the country, even in the first weeks after the revolution. Moreover, both Nicholas and Alexandra were resolutely opposed to abandoning Russia, come what may, for neither of them gave much priority to their personal fates. Products, as they were, of Victorian Europe, it was inconceivable to either of them that anyone should seek to harm their children, a boy of 13 and four girls. In King George's defence, it can be said that 1917 was not a good time either for compassion or for risk-taking by ruling dynasties. On learning of the Emperor's death, King George overruled Stamfordham and attended the memorial service for his cousin, commenting in his diary: 'I was devoted to Nicky, who was the kindest of men and a thorough gentleman: loved his country and people.' Nevertheless, the British response to the Romanovs' need for asylum leaves a somewhat sour taste in the mouth.[6]

Early in August the imperial family learned that they were to be sent to Tobolsk, a provincial backwater on the border between the Urals and western Siberia, far from the turbulent politics of Petrograd. The day before their departure, 12 July, was Aleksei's birthday and a religious service was held to invoke God's protection for the family on their journey. The icon from the Church of Our Lady of Znamenie was brought to the palace across Alexander Park in a solemn procession. Paul Benckendorff recalls that 'the ceremony was as poignant as could be: all were in tears. The soldiers themselves seemed touched, and approached the holy Ikon to kiss it. They followed the procession as far as the balcony, and saw it disappear through the Park. It was as if the past were taking leave, never to come back. The memory of this ceremony will always remain in my mind, and I cannot think of it without profound emotion.'[7]

The Romanovs were escorted to Tobolsk by P.M. Makarov, the Provisional Government's emissary, and by the commander of the guard, Colonel Evgeni Kobylinsky. Both were decent men who did their best for the prisoners. Kobylinsky, twice wounded in the war, was a regular officer. 'Makarov was a professional architect: a socialist revolutionary, he had, under the old regime, been in prison for a time. He was an honest man and we owed him nothing but thanks.' Among Makarov's services to the family were his strenuous efforts to clean up and make habitable the house of Tobolsk's former Governor, which was to be their residence until April 1918. The house was relatively comfortable and, especially in their first months in town, the Romanovs did not go short of food. Their main problems were lack of news and physical exercise. Dr Botkin's son, who lived with his father opposite the Governor's house, 'could see the Grand Duchesses walking in a dirty courtyard – a cut off portion of the street, really, converted into a yard and surrounded by a wooden fence, some eight or ten feet high . . . They could walk only in that abominable yard and a small garden on the other side of the house.'[8]

Tobolsk was neither an industrial centre nor on a railway line and in 1917 was therefore not greatly infected by the revolutionary mood. 'Far from showing any hate towards the Emperor, the good citizens of Tobolsk took off their caps and crossed themselves every time they passed the house in which the Imperial family were held captive. And hardly a day passed without a cake or some candies, or an icon or some other present being sent to the Imperial family.' Nor were the soldiers of the guard by any means all hostile to the Romanovs. The escort was made up of men from the First, Second and Fourth Guards Rifle Regiments. The Second Regiment was unfriendly and became more and more unpleasant as Bolshevik propaganda spread. But the men of the First and Fourth Regiments were much more kindly disposed, especially to the children. 'Part of the guard from the Fourth Regiment, which consisted almost entirely of older men, showed special affection to the imperial family and it was a joy for the whole family to see these honest people on duty. On those days the Emperor and the children used to go secretly to the guard house to talk and play cards with the soldiers.'[9]

Events in the rest of Russia were, however, to seal the Romanovs' fate. In November 1917 the Bolsheviks overthrew the Provisional Government. Given the ruthlessness of Russia's new rulers, it was never likely that the imperial family would escape with their lives once Lenin had come to power. In January 1918 the Bolsheviks closed the democratically elected Constituent Assembly, in which they had only one quarter of the seats, though the winter of 1917–18 represented the peak of Bolshevik popularity. In March peace was signed with the Germans at Brest-Litovsk, which bought the new regime time at the price of surrendering all the territorial gains made by Russia since the mid-seventeenth century and risking German domination of Europe. These actions, antagonizing wide sections of political opinion and allowing no peaceful means to oppose Bolshevism, made civil war inevitable. Civil war breeds ruthlessness and Nicholas II and his family were always likely to be among its first victims. Bolshevik rule was shallowly rooted in the Urals and western Siberia in 1918. The overwhelming majority of the population in both regions had voted for other parties in the elections to the Constituent Assembly. In the spring of 1918 armed resistance to Bolshevik rule exploded, spearheaded by the Czech Legion.[10]

The centre of Bolshevik power in the Ural region was the city of Ekaterinburg. Here were to be found the Bolshevik-run Ural Soviet, in other words the headquarters of the regional government, as well as the directorate of the local Cheka, the secret police. The Chairman of the Soviet was A.G. Beloborodov. The top Chekist was F.N. Lukoyanov. The former was an electrician with a rudimentary education who had had a spell in gaol for aiding Bolshevik 'fighting detachments' during the 1905–7 revolution. The latter was an official's son, a former student of Moscow university, who prided himself on his skill as a journalist. Both were ruthless men in their mid-twenties, who already had blood on their hands before they helped to organize the murder of Nicholas II's family and that of other Romanovs imprisoned in their region. After a successful career in the 1920s as head of the Russian People's Commissariat of Internal Affairs (that is, *inter alia*, police chief) Beloborodov, like most of the former Ural leadership, was to fall foul of Stalin because of his links with Trotsky. He was killed in 1938. Exceptionally, Lukoyanov survived both the 1930s and the Second World War, dying in his bed in 1947. His life may well have been saved by the nervous breakdown he suffered in 1919, from which he never fully recovered, as a result dropping out of the murderous race for high office in the Soviet Union. Illness did not, however, stop him from denouncing a good many party enemies in Stalin's heyday.[11]

The most powerful Bolshevik in the Urals was 'Filipp' Goloshchekin, the region's Military Commissar. Forty-two years old, and a party member since 1903, Goloshchekin had spent six years in exile in Siberia, where he had met Jakob Sverdlov, who in 1918 was Lenin's right-hand man and the supremo for internal affairs throughout Russia. 'Sverdlov and Goloshchekin were linked not only by common views but also by personal friendship,' wrote Sverdlov's wife in her memoirs. The veteran revolutionary socialist and historian Vladimir Burtsev, 'who knew Goloshchekin personally, characterised him thus: "an executioner, a cruel man, with some features of degeneracy".' Subsequently Goloshchekin was to make a brilliant career as party secretary in the Urals and Siberia, as a member of the Cheka's ruling collegium, and from 1924 as head of the Central Asian republic of Kazakhstan. In the latter role Goloshchekin was to purge all honest and even remotely independent native cadres from the party leadership. Despite the new regime's anti-imperialist claims, Goloshchekin upheld the colonial land settlement inherited from the monarchy. Even in the supposedly 'tolerant' 1920s he carried civil war into the Kazakh villages in order to break the power of local native leaders, fully aware of the economic chaos this would cause. From 1929 to 1932 he was to preside enthusiastically over what was probably the greatest crime committed by white colonial rulers in twentieth-century Asia, namely the forced collectivization and deliberate mass starvation of the Kazakh people. 'Archival data show that the number of Kazakh households declined from 1,233,000 in 1929 to 565,000 households in 1936' as a result of the drastic collectivization imposed in the first three years of this period, during which four-fifths of the cattle belonging to the still largely nomadic Kazakhs were destroyed. The party leadership ruthlessly purged all officials who protested or attempted to slow down this policy. In the West the Ukrainian collectivization and famine are quite well known, and the purges of the Communist élite and of intellectuals in the late 1930s are the subject of a large literature. It is seldom remembered that in the 1930s 'loss of human life was proportionately greater in Kazakhstan than anywhere else in the Soviet Union'. Goloshchekin outlived many of his former comrades in the Ural leadership, but Stalin finally had him killed in 1941. Needless to say, the death sentence had nothing to do with the crimes previously committed by this evil man.[12]

In the spring of 1918 the Ekaterinburg Communists wished to get their hands on Nicholas II and his family. They concocted schemes to abduct the Romanovs from Tobolsk. The central party leadership, however, had decided to bring the Tsar to Moscow and with that aim in mind sent V.V. Yakovlev to Tobolsk with an armed detachment. Because Aleksei was ill Yakovlev left him and three of his sisters behind in Tobolsk and set off with Nicholas, Alexandra and the Grand Duchess Marie. *En route* he was intercepted by the Ekaterinburg Bolsheviks and a furious argument occurred as to the Romanovs' destination. Yakovlev was believed to be trying to spirit the imperial family away, possibly in the direction of Japan and safety. In the end the locals won the argument, in Richard Pipes's view 'possibly after the intervention of Moscow, which did not wish to antagonize the Ekaterinburg Bolsheviks and was not quite certain what to do with the Romanovs in any event'.[13]

On 30 April 1918, Nicholas, Alexandra and Marie arrived in Ekaterinburg where they were imprisoned in the house of Nicholas Ipatev, an engineer, which had been commandeered for this purpose. On 23 May the rest of the family arrived. The Ipatev House's inhabitants now included seven Romanovs, Dr Botkin, the Empress's maid and three other servants. The regime in the Ipatev House was strict and humiliating. Guards, all of whom were male, accompanied the grand duchesses to the lavatory and scrawled obscenities over the walls. Almost all communication with the outside world was ended. Initially the guards were workers from the Zlokazov factory, lured by high pay and an easy billet, infinitely preferable to being sent to fight the counter-revolutionary threat on the Siberian front. Their commander was Alexander Avdeev, who had worked for the Bolsheviks as a propagandist in the Zlokazov works. The guards, who stole everything on which they could lay their hands, were reinforced in May by workers from the town of Syserti.

Once again high pay and easy conditions were used as bait, though in this very Bolshevik town the authorities also reminded workers that failure to back the Communist cause might lead to the victory of the counter-revolution, and with it revenge for the murderous treatment of the local peasantry by worker detachments.

Goloshchekin spent the first days of July in Moscow, where he stayed in the flat of his friend Sverdlov. It was at this point that the decision was taken to kill all the Romanovs in the near future. Although the Soviet regime right down to its last days claimed that the Romanovs' murder was purely the responsibility of the Ural Bolsheviks, recent evidence coming out of Russia shows conclusively that this was not the case, and that the command came from Lenin personally and from the top party leadership. This had in fact been known in the West for many years as a result of the publication of Trotsky's diary. In it he recorded a conversation with Sverdlov, which took place after the fall of Ekaterinburg and after Trotsky's own return to Moscow from a short expedition to the provinces. Informing him that all the family had been killed, the Commissar for Internal Affairs commented that 'we decided it here [Moscow]. Ilich [Lenin] considered that we could not leave them [the counter-revolution] a live banner, especially in the present difficult circumstances.' Sverdlov's justification for the murders was rubbish. The Bolsheviks had ample time and means to remove the Romanovs from Ekaterinburg and the war zone had they wished to do so. The White leaders were not intending to restore the monarchy and would certainly have preferred a Romanov other than the discredited Nicholas II or his invalid son had they ever decided to change their minds. For the counter-revolution a martyred Tsar was more useful than a live Nicholas. As the liberal historian Yuri Gote put things with cruel accuracy on hearing of the Tsar's death: 'his disappearance constitutes the untying of one of the innumerable secondary knots of our Time of Troubles, and the monarchical principle can only gain from it'.[14]

On 4 July Avdeev was replaced as commandant of the Ipatev House by Yakov Yurovsky, the deputy head of the Ekaterinburg Cheka. With him Yurovsky brought his assistant, Grigori Nikulin, a rather handsome and presentable young man who was already an experienced killer, despite having only worked for the Cheka since his factory closed in March. Nikulin had taken up factory work in order to avoid conscription during the First World War. Unlike many of the worker guards in the Ipatev House he was cold-blooded, fully literate, ruthless and sober. When Nicholas arrived in Ekaterinburg from Tobolsk he brought with him his former aide-de-camp, Prince V. Dolgorukov, who was Paul Benckendorff's stepson. Dolgorukov was arrested immediately on arrival and shot by Nikulin, who subsequently complained about having to carry his dead victim's suitcases. Yurovsky, 40 years old in 1918, described Nikulin as his 'son' and remained close to him for the rest of his life. He made Nikulin the executor of his will. Without much formal education, Yurovsky was an intelligent and cruel man. He appears to have been a true believer in Communism and he was not a thief, unlike many of those who guarded the Romanovs. A Bolshevik since the 1905 revolution, Yurovsky was considered by Lenin to be 'the most reliable of Communists'. His brother Leyba on the other hand commented that 'he enjoys oppressing people', to which his sister-in-law added that he was 'a despot and an exploiter'. Like his peers in the Ural Bolshevik leadership Yurovsky became part of the Soviet élite and lived quite comfortably in the 1920s and 1930s. Cancer saved him from his probable fate at Stalin's hands though his daughter Rimma, who in Ekaterinburg had played a prominent role in the campaign against the Orthodox Church, was to spend twenty years in Soviet camps.[15]

Immediately after Yurovsky took over at the Ipatev House, preparations for the killings began. The murder itself was left to Yurovsky but disposal of the bodies was the responsibility of P.Z. Ermakov, the Military Commissar of Verkh-Isetsk, a Bolshevik stronghold. Ermakov was an old acquaintance of Goloshchekin, who was his direct boss. Before the revolution he had robbed banks and other commercial establishments to raise money for the Bolsheviks. Like many others involved in this activity, he was part political activist, part bandit. In 1917 he had set up his own marauding band to 'squeeze' the local rich. In his memoirs he boasted about having personally killed leaders of local peasant protests against Bolshevik rule. His most famous exploit was the decapitation of a former police agent. The day after the murder of Nicholas and his family, fellow Bolsheviks of Ermakov's type were to hurl Alexandra's sister, the Grand Duchess Elizabeth, and a number of other Romanovs down a mine-shaft at Alapaevsk, not far from Ekaterinburg. The victims were left to die slowly of their wounds and hunger.

Confirmation that Nicholas and his family were to be killed immediately came from Moscow on 16 July. The murders were scheduled for that night. Matters were delayed for ninety minutes by the late arrival of Ermakov with the lorry that was to remove the bodies. Ermakov ordered his driver to start the lorry's engine at his command in order to muffle the sound of firing. The Romanovs and their servants were woken before 2 a.m. and, after being given some minutes to dress, were led down into one of the rooms in what was a semi-basement. To avoid panic or resistance they were told that there was disorder in the town and it was safer to come down from the exposed upper floor. The ploy worked and it seems that none of the victims showed particular fright or alarm. When they were brought into the room Alexandra, by now barely capable of standing for long, asked for chairs for herself and her son, who was recovering from another attack of bleeding. Chairs were brought and immediately afterwards Yurovsky and his squad entered the room.

Yurovsky himself reported to Moscow that the squad consisted of twelve men, of whom seven were non-Russians. Though usually described as Latvians, these seven men were, it seems, Hungarian ex-prisoners of war from the Habsburg army. At the last moment two Hungarians refused to shoot the young women. Among the other members of the gang were Yurovksy himself and Nikulin, together with P.S. Medvedev, who commanded the detachment of worker guards from Syserti. Subsequently captured by the Whites, Medvedev's testimony was to be the centre-piece of the very thorough investigation of the murders by Nicholas Sokolov, virtually all of whose findings have been confirmed by new evidence coming out of the Soviet Union since 1988. Ermakov and one of his assistants also participated in the killings. Edvard Radzinsky claims that the murder gang had another member, Aleksei Kabanov, and cites his memoirs.

Immediately after the squad entered the room Yurovsky said that in view of the attacks on Soviet Russia by Nicholas's relatives, the Ural Executive Committee had decided to shoot the Romanovs. The Tsar had no time to do more than exclaim before the firing began. To get a sense of the hideous butchery that followed it is necessary to remember that the room was small: in all at least twenty-three people were packed into a room of only twenty-four square metres. Murderers and victims were almost standing on each other's feet. Some members of the murder squad got burned by their neighbours' guns. The Emperor, the Empress, Dr Botkin and three of the servants died quickly. Most of the children did not. Nor did the maid, Anna Demidov. The grand duchesses had to go through a terrible and lengthy agony partly because the bullets ricocheted off the jewels that they had sewn into their corsets. But Aleksei, now just 14, was protected by no jewellery, and he also took a long time to die. Yurovsky reported his 'strange vitality'. Even after the shooting and screaming was finished and the victims lay on the floor in pools of blood, all was not over. Some of the girls were still alive. Ermakov stood on the arms of the Grand Duchess Anastasia and stabbed her repeatedly with a bayonet. It says something about the men who committed this atrocity that they always took great pride in their act but fell out amongst themselves, since at least three of them claimed to have killed the Tsar with the night's first shot. In the 1930s Ermakov was frequently turned out to describe the murders, which he did in graphic detail, to summer camps of Pioneers, the Soviet equivalent of scouts and guides.

Presented with flowers, he was held up as a heroic model for Russian youth.

The night's horrors did not end with the murders. The bodies, dumped in the lorry, were driven to an area of mine-shafts in Ermakov's fiefdom of Verkh-Isetsk. Ermakov had arranged a guard of roughly twenty-five men around the mine-shafts and others were on patrol to keep away unwanted visitors. The guards, some of whom at least had the excuse of being drunk, were indignant that the Romanovs were not brought to them alive. Some amused themselves after the bodies were stripped of their clothes. But gloating over the grand duchesses' bodies gave way to other feelings when the jewellery in their corsets was revealed. Immediately after the murders in the Ipatev House the guards had begun to steal their victims' watches, jewels and other possessions. Now the same story began again. Yurovsky had to dismiss most of Ermakov's 'trusties' and put a stop to their Bacchanalia. He was furious to discover that the place to hide the bodies had been ill chosen and no spades or other equipment prepared. The bodies were tipped down a shaft and grenades thrown in after them. Whether Yurovsky always intended this to be a temporary hiding place is a moot point. It may be that on his return to Ekaterinburg he discovered that Ermakov's heroes had talked and that the Romanovs' grave was no secret. The Bolsheviks were determined that when the Whites took Ekaterinburg, which was now a matter of days, they should not find the bodies. So on the night of 17 July Yurovsky returned to the mine-shaft, recovered the bodies and set off towards deeper shafts in an area more suitable as a permanent hiding spot. On the way there the lorry got stuck in the mud and it was decided to bury the bodies on the spot. Just in case the Whites should discover the corpses, the bodies of Aleksei and one of the women were burned and buried separately. In this way the corpses in the grave, whose faces were deliberately smashed and disfigured, would not be associated with the victims from the Ipatev House. This ploy proved unnecessary. Not until the 1970s was the Romanovs' burial place suspected. Only after the fall of the Communist regime could it be excavated and the bodies identified.[16]

For many years the Soviet government pretended that Nicholas alone had been killed. Only among themselves could the Communist veterans take pride in the massacre of the Tsar's children and servants. For that reason Trotsky's attempt to explain the extermination of the family by the need to terrify friend and foe alike makes little sense. In July 1918 the order went out from Moscow to kill all the inhabitants of the Ipatev House because individual lives meant nothing to Lenin and the Bolshevik leadership. Murder was the quickest and least troublesome way to be rid of a hated and inconvenient group of class enemies. But perhaps Richard Pipes is right in suggesting a deeper rationale.

Like the protagonists in Dostoevsky's *Possessed*, the Bolsheviks had to spill blood to bind their wavering adherents with a band of collective guilt. The more innocent victims the Bolshevik Party had on its conscience, the more the Bolshevik rank and file had to realize there was no retreating, no faltering, no compromising, that they were inextricably bound to their leaders, and could only march with them to 'total victory' regardless of the cost, or go down with them in 'total doom'.[17]

CHAPTER 10

Then and Now

After 1917 Imperial Russia and its history lived in the shadow of the Soviet present. Soviet Communism was an attempt to organize a modern society, economy and system of government in an entirely novel way. It aroused great enthusiasm among some outside onlookers, and fear and hatred among others. Particularly after 1945, when the Soviet Union became one of the world's two superpowers, the one attitude which never existed was indifference: no one could deny the importance of Communism or of the Soviet superpower which embodied the Communist ideal. By contrast Imperial Russia seemed an irrelevant medieval relic rightly consigned to history's dustbin. This attitude was the official Soviet line but it also had very many adherents in the West. Tsarist Russia and its system of government were completely alien to Western, and above all Anglo-American, traditions. Most British or American historians of Russia were liberals or socialists. Their sympathy and interest were largely directed towards individuals or groups which shared these loyalties in pre-revolutionary Russia. Much good history was written but tsarism got a bad press. More important, explicitly or otherwise, a great deal of the history of Imperial Russia was defined by the attempt to explain why it was that Bolshevism triumphed in 1917.

The collapse of the Soviet regime in 1991 has altered perspectives. The huge body of knowledge built up on Soviet politics and economics is suddenly threatened with redundancy and 'irrelevance'. The Soviet dinosaur can no longer be studied on the hoof. It must now be pursued to the museum. Particularly for students of political science and international relations, for some of whom Russia and the world only began in 1917 or even 1945, the simultaneous disappearance of the Soviet Union and of bi-polarity in world affairs is a cause of some bewilderment. The laws of nature have been abolished. The earth no longer orbits the sun.

By contrast, a weak but friendly light warms the historians of Imperial Russia. Suddenly they are no more 'irrelevant' than anyone else. Psychologically, they are attuned to the idea of dramatic change in Russian affairs. Their perspectives on Russia are long. The world of the 1990s is very different to the one that existed before 1914 but important similarities do exist and useful comparisons can be made. The same is true where the collapse of the imperial and Soviet regimes is concerned. Within Russia there is enormous interest in the pre-Soviet era. Much that was hidden or never discussed can now be revealed. Honest answers can be sought in Russia's past for the tragedies of her twentieth-century history. For the last seventy years Marxism-Leninism has defined Russian statehood. Russia was subsumed in a Soviet and Marxist identity. Now the collapse of Communism and of the Soviet Union means that a new Russian political identity must be found. It can only be discovered in Russian history and culture, and in the country's geopolitical position. This has ensured a great debate about Russia's past. Old battles have resumed between 'Slavophiles', 'Westernizers' and 'Eurasians'. Even so serious a newspaper as *Literaturnaya gazeta* can discuss the possibility of the monarchy's restoration. Of more importance, the age-old question of Russia's boundaries and borderlands is now on the agenda. This adds further heat to the argument over Russia's historical values and identity, as well as over where her interests should lie in the future.[1]

In the last four years tremendous interest has been shown in Russia about the murder of the country's last monarch and his family. In part this is simply the desire to know about a famous tragedy which was never allowed to be discussed in the Soviet era. More significantly, it reflects concern about the origins of the Stalinist system and of the moral nihilism which came to pervade so much of Soviet society. Many Russians now feel that the murder of the Romanovs was an important moment in this process. The event's bestiality and lawlessness, the trumped-up accusations that the family was 'attempting to escape', above all the ruthless contempt even for the lives of children – all these were to be familiar hallmarks of the Soviet regime and represented a clear break with the world of Victorian Europe. When one looks at the later lives of some of those who took a prominent part in the Romanovs' murder it is hard to dispute the link between Leninist and Stalinist terror. Against this it is sometimes argued that civil war breeds horror and that the Reds behaved no worse than the Whites. There is something in this argument but not much. The civil war did not occur by accident. In 1917 the other socialist parties, in other words the Mensheviks and Socialist Revolutionaries, were partly guided by their fear of and revulsion for civil war. In the winter of 1917–18 the overwhelming majority of Russians supported one or other of the socialist parties. An all-socialist coalition would have made counter-revolution inconceivable, particularly since it would have rested on the only legitimate authority in Russia, namely the Constituent Assembly. Some

Bolsheviks would have accepted a socialist coalition but Lenin was not one of them. The Bolshevik leader rejected this course and pursued policies which, as he well knew, made civil war inevitable. Political leaders who wish civil war on their own people bear a heavy responsibility for its horrors, especially when most of the premises and calculations behind their actions turn out to be mistaken. He cannot therefore be absolved from responsibility for its horrors. It is certainly true that the Whites often acted with chaotic brutality. Their treatment of the Jews in particular was an abomination. But to the best of my knowledge no one has ever shown that the top White leaders, General Denikin or Admiral Kolchak for instance, ordered the extermination not just of enemy politicians but of their whole families, children included. Even Yurovsky's mother survived untouched during the White occupation of Ekaterinburg. The cold-blooded rationalization of class terror carried the world into a new dimension of political crime.[2]

Before the revolution the Tsar was the embodiment of Russian statehood and, to some extent, the symbol of Russian national identity. He was both a secular and a religious leader. Not surprisingly the contemporary debate over his murder therefore involves questions of statehood, national identity and religion. The call to canonize the Tsar, along with other victims of Bolshevism, arouses passions on both sides. An important point here is that Yurovsky, Goloshchekin and Sverdlov were all Jews. The Jews were traditional targets of Russian nationalist hatred. Anti-Semitism is still strong in Russia. The accusation that it was Jews who destroyed the bearer and symbol of Russian nationality and statehood is a powerful weapon in the anti-Semitic arsenal. Those who wish to use it seldom have the honesty to admit that Yurovsky's murder squad contained more Russians than Jews; that Ermakov's gang at the mine-shaft was over-whelmingly Russian; and that the final decision to commit murder came from Lenin at least as much as from Sverdlov.[3]

Contemporary interest in the last decades of Imperial Russia goes beyond the debate on statehood, national identity or political morals. In this era Russia was becoming integrated into the world capitalist economy. This was the classic time of bankers, stock exchanges and Russian entrepreneurship. In 1917 revolution reversed this process. The Bolshevik seizure and consolidation of power, the workers' revolt and the peasant rebellion were three distinct though linked phenomena. But all of them were directed against capitalism and private property as they existed in Edwardian Europe. In the 1990s Russia is once again attempting to join Europe and the world market. Popular attitudes to entrepreneurship, inequality and property will in part determine the extent to which this attempt proves successful. This adds interest to the study of Russian economic and political history in the late imperial era. At the very least one can expect more realistic and sympathetic studies of the achievements and problems of Russian capitalism in this era to be written by Russian historians in the next few years.[4]

But it is not only Victorian and Edwardian Russia which are in some ways very familiar to the contemporary observer. The same is true of the pre-1914 world as a whole. In that era Russia was part of Europe. The Edwardian world economy was unequivocally capitalist. Its monetary principles, based on the gold standard, were severe. The European banks, backed if necessary by gunboats, were its IMF. The stability of the international financial and commercial systems was linked to British pre-eminence and threatened by Britain's decline. Commercial rivalry caused bitterness between 'mercantilist' Germany and free-trade Britain, whose economies were structured and managed in rather different ways. Among the key debates of the time were questions about the levels of state intervention and social welfare which were compatible with efficient capitalism. Another major issue concerned which country would prove itself to be the most powerful and competitive bearer of capitalist progress in the twentieth century. All of these issues are still very much with us in the 1990s, though the USA now stands in Britain's place and its major commercial rival is Japan rather than Germany.

In politics the strong trend in the late Victorian and Edwardian world was towards constitutionalism and, beyond it, liberal democracy. Most educated Russians were convinced that their country too must be subject to this universal law of historical development. The majority of Marxist socialists merely argued that the last stage on the road would be not 'bourgeois democracy' but socialism. Even most conservative tsarist statesmen, rather than opposing liberal constitutionalism in principle, held that their country was not yet ready for it. Belief in liberalism reflected an optimistic faith that as human beings became richer and better educated they would become happier and more reasonable. Conflicts could therefore be resolved peacefully within a constitutional framework. Some people believed that this might be possible not merely within societies but also between them.

From the 1880s the world's domination by liberal capitalism came under threat from both the right and the left of the political spectrum. By 1914 Europe possessed political parties which carried the seeds of Fascism and Leninism. The threat to the Victorian order from the extreme left was in principle less anti-rational and more anti-capitalist than was the case with Fascism. But in time both far left and far right evolved messianic ideologies which were anti-liberal to the core. These ideologies were a serious threat in themselves. They became immensely dangerous when they captured Germany and Russia, the continent of Europe's only two potential superpowers. In the last hundred years only Germany and Russia have possessed the demographic, military and economic resources potentially to dominate all Europe. Two great wars in this century above all revolved around their competition to control people and resources in Eastern and Central Europe, thereby acquiring a power which would inevitably make them masters of the whole continent. The first stage in this conflict destroyed Nicholas II, his family and his empire. In 1940, after France's collapse, the alliance between Hitler's Germany and Stalin's Russia meant that Victorian civilization and its heirs had been subjugated throughout the whole European mainland. Thanks to the British and, above all, the Americans, Fascist Germany was destroyed in 1945 and Soviet Communism was undermined and worn down in the Cold War. Miraculously, fifty-three years after the Nazi-Soviet pact, liberal and capitalist values appeared to triumph from Dublin to Vladivostok. Whether this perspective of 1992 will continue to prevail is a moot point. But at present much of European history between 1917 and 1991 appears to be merely an abberation, a detour.

The same is true if we think of contemporary developments in Europe and Northern Eurasia under the heading of decolonization. This has been a major theme in the history of Eastern and Central Europe and the Middle East for the last 170 years. In 1800 all of this vast area was controlled by four great empires: Ottoman, Habsburg, Romanov and Hohenzollern. The Ottoman Empire was the first to crumble and the Balkans, the first region from which it retreated, became a zone of instability and a major cause of the First World War. A war originating in the Balkans resulted in the break-up of the Austrian and German empires and the Balkanization of all Eastern and Central Europe, creating a string of small and unstable states in the region locked in conflict with their neighbours over borders and ethnic minorities, and too weak to defend themselves against Germany or Russia, the area's great powers. The vacuum created by decolonization in this region was a major cause of the Second World War. Victory in 1945 brought a *pax Sovietica* to Eastern and Central Europe and Northern Eurasia. Between 1945 and 1991 the basic geopolitical fact about this huge region appeared to be that whereas all other empires had collapsed, the Russian one had survived and had even been strengthened under Soviet rule. This fact had not been inevitable. In 1917–18 the Russian Empire had disintegrated and German domination of Europe seemed likely, but Berlin's defeat on the Western Front in 1918 saved Lenin and allowed the Russian Empire to be reconstituted in Bolshevik form.

The survival of a Russian empire, which seemed an immutable fact in the post-war era, now, however, appears to have been a mere delay in the long-term historical process of decolonization. As a result, European statesmen are once again gazing in bewildered horror at the Albanian, Bosnian and Macedonian problems, all of them long-established nightmares of pre-1914 diplomacy. Moreover, in the late 1980s the basic law of European geopolitics reasserted itself. As Russia rises, Germany falls and vice versa. The collapse of the Soviet Union was accompanied, by no means accidentally, by German reunification. In time that seems likely to entail German pre-eminence in most of the area of the former Habsburg Empire and many of the western republics of the former USSR.

Of course the world of the 1990s is a very different place to Nicholas II's Europe. The existence of nuclear weapons, a single non-European superpower and the feminist movement – to take but three examples almost at random – makes this clear. Modern German society has values and ambitions very different to those that drove the Kaiser's Reich. Nevertheless, in significant ways Europe is closer to what it was in 1900 than to the continent of the 1930s or 1970s. This adds tremendous interest to the study of Europe and Russia before 1914. It also presents a rather different perspective on the events of those pre-war decades. However much historians may wish to divorce themselves from the present and study the past in and for itself, in reality the end of the Cold War and the collapse of the Soviet regime are likely to lead to considerable changes in the way the history of Imperial Russia is conceived and written, above all in Russia itself, but also to some extent in the West.

The most obvious and traditional comparison between Imperial and Soviet Russia is that between Peter the Great and Stalin. This comparison is in many ways unfair. The Tsar was not only more selfless than Stalin, but also has a far better claim to have brought enlightenment to Russia. But both men were cruel autocrats who imposed immense suffering on their peoples in order to strengthen their empire and ensure its status as a great power. After Peter's victory over the Swedes Russia became a European great power, a position which it has retained to this day. Only in the 1920s was this position really in question but Stalin's forced industrialization, followed by victory in the Second World War, not only reasserted Russia's great-power status but also turned the Soviet Union into one of the world's two superpowers. Neither Peter nor Stalin transformed the system of government which they inherited. Rather, they emphasized and developed all the most oppressive and authoritarian aspects of that system. In Peter's case this meant compulsory state service, heavy taxation and serfdom; in Stalin's it entailed a reversion to the Leninist terror and forced requisitioning of 1918–20, combined with taking authoritarian tendencies within the party to their logical limit. After the death of Peter and Stalin the élites received some relief from the political system's harshest aspects. In eighteenth-century Russia this meant the end of compulsory service and security for property. After 1953 the Soviet élites achieved freedom from terror and, under Brezhnev, job security as well. In both cases, however, the core principles of the political system remained.

The greatest contrast between Imperial and Soviet Russia is that whereas Peter's legacy survived until the 1860s, and arguably even 1917, radical reform of the Stalinist system began within four decades of the dictator's death. Thirty-eight years after Stalin's departure his regime had fallen.

Ever since the days of Peter the Great, Russian governments have judged their country's success or failure in relative terms. The standard against which they have measured Russia has always been the power, wealth and prestige of the leading Western states. For the imperial government the decisive measure was always military power and security. In the nineteenth century, however, Russian educated society increasingly based its comparisons on relative prosperity and freedom, as a result coming to conclusions which were unflattering both to Russia and its government. In the Soviet era the regime was able for many decades to isolate its people from the outside world, thereby making comparisons much more difficult. In addition the new élites and new middle class created by Stalin in the 1930s constituted a public opinion which was less cosmopolitan and sophisticated than its tsarist equivalent at the turn of the century. For the Soviet regime military power *vis-à-vis* the West remained very important but the ideological factor also entered the picture. In competition with Western capitalism, Marxism-Leninism was supposed to show superior efficiency and justice, thereby proving that progress and history were on its side. Particularly after Khrushchev's commitment to peaceful coexistence, the decisive sphere for competition between the two systems became the economy. To legitimize itself in the eyes of the Soviet peoples, and indeed of the ruling élites themselves, Marxism-Leninism had to prove itself more capable than capitalism of producing goods and distributing them widely and fairly.

Precisely because competition with the West has been a key factor in Russian history since Peter, it is possible to see the last three centuries in Russia in terms of three great cycles of modernization, each of them initiated from above, by the state, and each of them designed to achieve parity or better in the competition with the leading Western great powers.

The first of these cycles could be described as 'catching up with Louis XIV'. Its aim was to make Russia the equal of the other great European absolute monarchies which dominated the continent in the eighteenth century. The best-known figure associated with this cycle is Peter the Great though in fact the attempt to catch up with Russia's European neighbours preceded his reign and only achieved full success later in the eighteenth century. Not until the 1760s and 1770s was Russia regarded abroad as the equal of Habsburg Austria or Bourbon France. By the end of the century, however, Russia's position as one of the continent's three or four greatest military powers was universally recognized and completely secure. Alexander I's defeat of Napoleon further increased his country's prestige and in the first half of the nineteenth century Russia was generally perceived to be the continent's leading military power. A key point to remember about this first great cycle of modernization, which lasted from the 1690s to the 1850s, was that the factors which determined a country's power changed slowly during this period. All the leading continental states were agrarian societies with rather small industrial bases and urban populations. Power was to a considerable extent the product of rulers' intelligence and of the effectiveness with which they taxed and recruited their subjects. As a result of the revolution of 1789 the French state became more streamlined and effective. Popular enthusiasm could, up to a point, be mobilized in a way that was difficult in the states of the European old regime. Even the revolution and Bonaparte, however, allowed a more effi- cient use of the existing factors of power rather than their fundamental transformation. This helps to explain why in 1812–15 the European old regime monarchies could succeed in overthrowing Napoleonic France.

In the mid-nineteenth century the factors of power changed fundamen- tally because of the industrial revolution. The Crimean War brought home this lesson to the Russian government in a shocking and humiliating fashion. As a result the government initiated the second great cycle of modernization, which one could describe as Russia's attempt to remain a great power in the smokestack era. This cycle lasted from the 1850s to the 1970s. Just as Alexander I's entry into Paris in 1814 symbolized Russia's success in the first great cycle of modernization, so the capture of Berlin in 1945 marked the Soviet Union's achievement of great-power status in the industrial era. A process begun by the imperial regime and interrupted by the First World War and the revolution had been completed, albeit by socialist means, under Stalinist rule. By the 1970s the Soviet Union had achieved seemingly assured superpower status through military parity with the USA. Not since the days of Nicholas I (1825–55) had Russian power been rated so high at home or abroad. Realities were, however, as deceptive in the Brezhnev era as they had been in the reign of Nicholas I. Beneath the menace and glitter of military might, the factors of power in the world were changing quickly. In Nicholas's day it had been the spread of the industrial revolution in Western Europe which had jeopardized Russia's status as a great power. Under Brezhnev it was the revolution of the micro-chip and the computer. Gorbachev initiated the third great cycle of modernization from above in order to catch up with Russia's Western competitors in this new era of the scientific and technical revolution. He did so because he understood that unless fundamental changes occurred in the Soviet economy, society and system of government, there was no chance of his country remaining one of the world's superpowers into the twenty-first century. The pride and patriotism of the Soviet ruling élites were at stake. So too, in the longer run, were the regime's legitimacy and even its survival.

Striking parallels exist between the eras of Nicholas I and Brezhnev. The Tsar had participated in Russia's military triumph in 1812–14 and Brezhnev was a product of the years of victory between 1942 and 1945. Not surprisingly, neither leader was inclined to question the basic principles of a society and system of government which had proved so successful in the supreme test of war. Radical domestic reform is always difficult and can be dangerous for rulers, who are bound to come into conflict with powerful vested interests. In rigid but brittle authoritarian systems of government such reform is not only notoriously hard to manage but also can actually prove fatal to the regime itself. With military security and great-power status seemingly certain, neither Nicholas nor Brezhnev had the incentive to risk radical domestic change, though the Tsar believed serfdom to be both immoral and economically inefficient. In their first years both men pursued a policy of conservative, cautious but often intelligent incremental reform. In time, however, gerontocracy, immobility and fear paralysed efforts at change. In foreign affairs a combination of Russia's seeming power and its government's bullying and bluster succeeded in uniting against it a wide coalition of enemies. In the Crimean War an isolated Russia was opposed by the British, French, Turks and Piedmontese. Justified fear of Austrian and Swedish intervention was a further incentive for Petersburg to agree to a humiliating peace in 1856. By Brezhnev's death the Soviet Union was faced by a coalition of all the capitalist powers, having cemented the American-European alliance by its hamfisted policy on introducing SS-20s. Soviet behaviour had also succeeded in adding China to its list of potential enemies. In both eras a very high financial price was paid for policies which won for Russia such an extraordinarily large number of possible foes.[5]

Among the younger generation of the governing élite the last years of the Nicholas and Brezhnev eras brought increasing frustration at the incompetence of gerontocratic bosses and growing awareness of Russia's dangerous backwardness. Gorbachev and his peers had almost exact equivalents among the Milyutin brothers and other 'enlightened bureaucrats' of the 1840s and early 1850s. Many of the directors of departments in Nicholas's administration were much better educated and more energetic than their bosses. They understood which way the world was moving. Thanks to the American historian Bruce Lincoln, we know a great deal about the lives, ideas and values of these officials, who in the 1850s and 1860s were to spearhead Alexander II's reforms. It is possible to see how reformist ideas and Western influences spread from educated society to reach these key decision-makers in the government. We can trace the schools, clubs, salons and personal friendships which played a role in this process. One day a historian of Gorbachev's reforms will need to do similar work. No doubt he or she will pay much attention to the research institutes from which so many of Gorbachev's advisers came. Perhaps, too, attention will be paid to the younger relations of the Soviet Union's rulers, whose changing perceptions and openness to Western influences may have been another channel through which the ruling élite and the broader educated class was linked. In pursuing this line it will be necessary to remember that, by the standards of the rich in the West, the relatives of the Soviet élite did not actually live as well as is sometimes imagined even in material terms, let alone as regards security, freedom and self-esteem. At this level knowledge, confidence and dissatisfaction could unite.[6]

The reform programmes of Alexander II and Gorbachev had much in common.[7] Their aim was to mobilize Russia's human and natural resources more effectively, in the process creating a more prosperous and powerful country able to withstand international competition and satisfy its rulers' pride. Economic initiative and energy had to be raised through the abolition of serfdom and the dismantling of at least part of the Soviet command economy. If society was to show initiative and generate wealth it needed security for an autonomous existence beyond the reach of arbitrary bureaucratic action. Legality (*zakonnost'*) was a catchword of both eras. So too was publicity (*glasnost'*). New ideas had to be allowed to circulate. Censorship had to be scaled down. Locked in battle with powerful vested interests, a reformist leader needed to release critical voices which would undermine the intellectual case for conservatism.

But in both eras reform had strict limits. Its end result was never expected to be democracy. Public opinion was to be listened to but it was only to play an auxiliary role in government. Real power was to be retained by the centralized authoritarian bureaucratic machine. Both Alexander II and Gorbachev knew that their own position depended on this machine's survival. They believed that their empire could only be preserved, and ordered reform from above implemented, so long as this machine retained the dominant say in Russian life and government. This belief may have been self-serving but it was not unjustifiable and in personal terms was probably sincere.

As always, controlled liberalization proved an extremely difficult policy for an authoritarian regime to manage. It was easier to sanction critical voices than to silence them when they went too far. Under Nicholas I and Brezhnev some dissidents had espoused beliefs so radical that the existing regime, even in its most liberal mood, could never satisfy them. Both Alexander and Gorbachev soon found that, despite their reforms, they had enemies on the left as well as the right. Both the imperial and the Soviet reformers were terrified of exposing the bulk of the population to the full blast of a market economy. The existence of the commune under the last three tsars, for instance, meant that peasant land could neither be sold nor mortgaged. Gorbachev put strict fences around the private enterprise and private property which his reforms were supposed to encourage. Free prices were anathema. In the non-Russian borderlands the imperial and Soviet regimes were usually less legitimate than in the Russian heartland. Even more than in Russia proper, political stability rested on force and inertia. Liberalization under Alexander II led in 1863 to revolution in Poland. Under Gorbachev the explosion of nationalism in many of the republics was a decisive factor in the collapse of the Soviet regime.

Given the similar goals and intended limits of the two reformist leaderships one has to ask why the end result of their policies was so different. Imperial Russia survived for sixty years after Alexander II's accession and even then its destruction required a world war. Six years after Gorbachev came to power the Soviet regime and the Soviet Union itself disintegrated in the midst of peace. One reason for the difference was that, from the start, Alexander II was very clear in his own mind about the limit beyond which he would not go. Though pressed to concede a constitution and set up a parliament in the early 1860s he refused to so so. When he decided to crack down on opposition no institution could challenge his action. Gorbachev, on the other hand, permitted semi-democratic parliaments to come into being at the central and republican level. No doubt in part this was a tactical ploy designed to increase the General Secretary's freedom from the control of the party élite. Perhaps, too, it was a bow to the norms of an age much more democratic than the 1860s, as well as a reflection of the fact that in theory legislative institutions had always existed in the Soviet Union and simply required reinvigoration. Whatever the causes, however, from the point of view of the Soviet regime the result was disastrous. Alternative centres of power and legitimate authority emerged. Most fatal was the opposition's capture of the Russian presidency and parliament. Parliament and press formed a front and their influence on public opinion was great. By the time Gorbachev decided that enough was enough, power had to some extent slipped from the regime's hands. Its recapture would have required an extremely risky and bloody military crackdown which would have ruined Gorbachev's historical reputation and put him at the mercy of hardliners who loathed him and blamed him for the regime's collapse. By refusing to lend his legitimate authority to a crackdown Gorbachev doomed conservative efforts to save both the Communist party and the Soviet Union.

In comparison to the rulers of late Imperial Russia Gorbachev was very fortunate as regards the international and military situation. The existence of nuclear weapons and the whole climate of Western public opinion by the 1980s made any outside attempt to challenge the Soviet Union's territorial integrity inconceivable. The equation of economic backwardness with military danger was nowhere near as stark as under the tsars or in the 1930s. The economy, however, was much more of a problem than in the last decades of the monarchy, which had witnessed very impressive economic growth. By 1986–7 it seemed clear that the socialist command economy, even when purged of Brezhnevite sloth by Andropov's reforms, could not hope to compete with capitalism in the era of the micro-chip and the computer. But, as the 1990s have shown, even in countries where the transition from socialism to the market is inherently easier than in the Soviet Union the process is bound to be lengthy, risky and very painful. Moreover, the nationalities problem was also much more serious than in the monarchy's last years. The bulk of the non-Russian population were no longer peasants and nomads, largely immune to nationalist appeals. Large middle classes existed in all the republics. Under Soviet law these republics were states in embryo, possessing even the constitutional right to secede. A Soviet regime which stressed its allegiance to the rule of law and began to breathe democratic life into representative institutions which previously had been merely a façade faced enormous risks.

Difficult 'objective circumstances' were therefore one reason why, unlike under Alexander II, Gorbachev's attempt to introduce controlled modernization from above went swiftly off the rails and led to the collapse both of Communism and of the Soviet Union. Nevertheless, the 'human factor' cannot be ignored. The disintegration of the economy was, to a very great extent, due to a string of disastrous blunders made by the Gorbachev leadership itself, whose grasp of the principles underlying economic reform was very weak. By 1989 the economy was being integrated and disciplined neither by the old methods of command nor by a market. Complete financial irresponsibility reigned. Moreover, until it was far too late the leadership vastly underestimated the threat of minority nationalism and had no policy with which it might realistically be combated. Even in March 1990 a decision to accept the Balts as a special case and to offer generous levels of autonomy to other republics might well have held the core of the Soviet Union together but blindness continued to prevail. Economic collapse, which devastated Moscow's prestige and appeal, coupled with republican nationalism killed the Soviet Union but the process was far from inevitable.[8]

The story of the Soviet Union's collapse makes the last years of the imperial government look relatively good. The Romanovs' regime only fell under the immense strains of the First World War. As regards economic policy there is no comparison between the intelligent professionalism of the imperial Ministry of Finance and the awful bungling which wrecked the Soviet economy in the 1980s. Even the illusions cultivated by Nicholas II about the monarchist faith of the Russian peasantry seem to me a little less naïve and extraordinary than the blindness of the Gorbachev leadership to the nationalist threat. Yet in both the imperial and Soviet cases the rulers' blindness was not the result of stupidity. Its cause was the extraordinary degree to which the state's supreme leaders were isolated from the people whom they governed.

Seen against the panorama of the whole of modern Russian history, how should we judge the life and reign of the last Romanov Emperor? From everything said in this book it should be clear that the tasks facing any ruler of Victorian and Edwardian Russia were formidable. It was almost impossible to reconcile the demands of external security and domestic stability. The economy and society had to be modernized at great speed if Russia's survival as an independent power was to be ensured. In postwar India, for instance, multi-national and poor though it is, economic development has occurred alongside a surprising degree of democracy and political stability. One key to this lies in the policies designed to buy off peasants, the lower middle class, scheduled castes and trade unionists at the expense of seriously impeding capitalism and economic growth. Even if, miraculously, the Edwardian élite of a European country had been prepared to swallow Indian-style policies, for instance the expropriation of the big estates, the demands of great-power competition would still have made it impossible for Russia to accept any drag on economic development. Rapid capitalist industrialization occurred, to some extent, at the expense of the working class, and capitalist values were very different to those of either the peasantry or the intelligentsia. The Russian entrepreneurial and landowning classes were weak by European standards. In cultural even more than in economic terms a great gulf yawned between the Westernized élites and the Russian masses, and history added distrust and sometimes even hatred to mutual incomprehension. In time the development of a capitalist economy would have changed much of this picture but, above all for geopolitical reasons, time was something that Russia's rulers did not possess. A key problem for the imperial government was that the country's élites wanted to keep their property, status, values and income intact while enjoying the civil and political rights of their European peers. I do not myself believe that it was possible to satisfy both these wishes in anything but the short run, given the vulnerability of the élites' position.

Nicholas II was the victim not the cause of these problems. The last of Russia's monarchs can be faulted for his isolation, above all from the élites and currents which were beginning the transformation of his country. The Tsar's heart lay in old Russia. Since most of Russia was still rural, peasant and 'old' there was some justification for Nicholas's attitude but it went too far. Father George Shavelsky, the last Chaplain-General of the armed forces, wrote that Nicholas and Alexandra promoted the building of churches which copied sixteenth- and seventeenth-century styles, 'extolling the ancient and belittling the contemporary', in the process ignoring 'modern great masters of religious art – Vasnetsov, Nesterov and others'. This reflected instincts and attitudes on matters well beyond the narrow confines of church architecture and decoration. Unlike the last German Emperor, Nicholas was consistently old-fashioned, not a curious and tension-ridden combination of ancient and modern. As we have seen, the Tsar often had no time to read the newspapers and gave up the habit altogether during the First World War. By contrast, a surprised senior German official noted that Wilhelm II 'reads thirty to forty newspaper clippings one after the other and makes marginal comments on them'. Wilhelm's biographer remarks that this reflected less the Kaiser's vanity than 'his sense that public opinion played a crucial role in determining the political behaviour of nations'.[9]

As chief executive officer of the Russian government Nicholas was responsible for a number of blunders. Of these, the most disastrous and culpable were the errors that led to the war with Japan in 1904. The greatest difficulty was, however, that the Emperor could not co-ordinate and manage his government effectively but was in a position to stop anyone else from attempting to do the job for him. By the early twentieth century no human being could have acted as chairman of the Russian government throughout his adult life. The strain of the job was simply too great. The Russian administration was a large and quite sophisticated organization carrying out varied and complicated tasks. Contemporary chief executives who serve for over a decade tend to exhibit signs of exhaustion, a declining grasp of reality, and a desire to concentrate on favourite issues and, above all, on foreign affairs. These presidents and prime ministers are not selected by hereditary chance, brought up in the isolated world of a court, or dumped in the top executive office at the age of 26. They are served by effective personal offices, which are part of the fabric of government. It is not at all surprising that Nicholas liked to retreat to his palace at Livadia in the Crimea or that, during the First World War, he showed signs of physical and emotional collapse. But it was precisely during that time that Russia suffered most glaringly from the lack of an effective and formidable chief executive capable of co-ordinating and energizing the machinery of government and symbolizing resolution and strength in the pursuit of victory.

Nicholas's failure was partly personal but was more a product of the system of government which he inherited. The élites, not just in Russia but in many other countries too, were unwilling to vest sovereignty in 'the people' and thereby accept a democratic system of government. In the pre-1914 world the only alternative source of sovereignty was the monarch. This to some extent worked in Japan where history and dynastic tradition ensured that the Emperor's role was largely symbolic. The various groups within the élite were left to work out compromises and policies among themselves. Even in Japan, however, the result of this species of political system was that nobody could co-ordinate military and civilian policy, or keep the armed forces under control, with disastrous results in the 1930s.

The Russian dynastic tradition expected a monarch to rule as well as reign. If the country's affairs appeared to be going well, the sovereign might feel justified in distancing himself somewhat from affairs of government. This was much less easy when, as in Nicholas II's Russia, signs of crisis existed wherever one looked. No doubt, if he could find a Bismarck a monarch might take a back seat but Iron Chancellors are not easily found and in any case both international and domestic realities for the moment ruled out Bismarckian solutions to the Russian government's problems. Bismarck's Prussia was likely to defeat its great-power rivals in war: Russia was not. Nicholas II was served by some very able ministers, of whom the best known were Serge Witte and Peter Stolypin. Both men's policies aroused tremendous opposition within Russian society, however, above all in sections of the élite which were the monarchy's oldest supporters. The monarch could not shut his ears to their complaints, particularly since the policies pursued by both Witte and Stolypin did indeed entail serious disadvantages and dangers.

Nicholas II was not stupid. On the contrary, his problem tended to be that he could understand many points of view and wavered between them. The dangers Russia faced were very great. Responses, let alone solutions, to the country's difficulties were often mutually exclusive. The Russian Empire was neither a nation nor a bourgeois society. A Russian monarch could not save himself or his dynasty simply by putting on a top hat and becoming a citizen king. Nicholas interpreted fate as the will of God. The latter had imposed on him the duty of acting as guardian of his country's destiny. The sentry does not abandon his post just because conditions are hard and danger threatens. This is doubly true when he believes that no one else could do the job adequately if he deserted. Under the Russian system of government the Emperor bore ultimate responsibility for everything. The burden was crushing, not least because a corollary of autocracy was that Russian people tended to accept responsibility for nothing, blaming their own sins and their country's failings exclusively on the empire's rulers. Nicholas II loved his country and served it loyally and to the best of his ability. He had not sought power and he was not by temperament or personality very well equipped to wield it. He was a very kind, sensitive, generous and initially naïve man. Russian high politics in

these traumatic years required something very different and would probably have destroyed any man who sat on the throne. There is a bitter irony
in the fact that a ruler who idealized the ordinary Russian and wished only
for his or her well-being should go down in the collective memory of
twentieth-century Russians as Nicholas the Bloody. With the collapse of
the Soviet regime comes the moment not for whitewashing or mytho-
logizing old Russia and its last ruler but instead for presenting a fairer,
more human and more balanced judgement than that imposed on the
Russian people for the last seventy-five years.[10]

Notes

Chapter 1: The Inheritance

1. The first two volumes in Longman's *History of Russia* are good up-to-date guides to the subject: J. Fennell, *The Crisis of Medieval Russia, 1200–1304* (Harlow, 1983); and R.O. Crummey, *The Formation of Muscovy, 1304–1613* (Harlow, 1987). For an interesting essay on the Tatars' influence on Russia see C.J. Halperin, *Russia and the Golden Horde: The Mongol Impact on Russian History* (London, 1987).

2. On Imperial Russia as a great power there is a very good recent book by William Fuller, *Strategy and Power in Russia, 1600–1914* (New York, 1992). On the growth of the Russian Empire see also M. Rywkin (ed.), *Russian Colonial Expansion to 1917* (London, 1988).

3. There are a number of surveys of Imperial Russian history and society. In my view the most interesting is R. Pipes, *Russia under the Old Regime* (London, 1974).

4. On eighteenth- and early nineteenth-century Russsian government see: J. Le Donne, *Absolutism and Ruling Class* (New York, 1991); and I. de Madariaga, *Russia in the Age of Catherine the Great* (London, 1981). On Uvarov, see C.H. Whittaker, *The Origins of Modern Russian Education: An Intellectual Biography of Count Serge Uvarov* (DeKalb, 1984).

5. D. Field, *The End of Serfdom* (Cambridge, Mass., 1976), p. 55.

6. A good introduction to this theme is S.P. Huntingdon, *Political Order in Changing Societies* (New Haven, 1968), especially Ch. 3.

7. Benckendorff expressed this fear *inter alia* in an interesting letter to the new Foreign Minister, Alexander Izvolsky, dated 12/25 July 1906. See A.P. Izvolsky, *Au Service de la Russie, Alexandre Iswolsky, Correspondance Diplomatique* (2 vols., Paris, 1937 and 1939), Vol. 1, pp. 335–8.

8. On international relations in this era, A.J.P. Taylor, *The Struggle for Mastery in Europe, 1848–1918* (Oxford, 1971), remains a classic. I have tried to look at these issues from a Russian angle in D.C.B. Lieven, *Russia and the Origins of the First World War* (London, 1983).

9. N. Stone, *Europe Transformed, 1878–1919* (Glasgow, 1983), is a quirky and fascinating study of European society in this era.

10. Many recent works tackle these themes when looking at the history of various groups in late Imperial Russia: see, for instance, D.R. Brower, *The Russian City between Tradition and Modernity* (Berkeley, 1990); G.L. Freeze, *The Parish Clergy in*

Nineteenth-Century Russia (Princeton, 1983); S.J. Seregny, 'Zemstvo Rabbits, Antichrists, and Revolutionaries: Rural Teachers in Saratov Province, 1890–1907', in R.A. Wade and S.J. Seregny (eds.), *Politics and Society in Provincial Russia* (Columbus, 1989), pp. 113–38; and W. Fuller, *Civil-Military Conflict in Imperial Russia, 1881–1914* (Princeton, 1985), especially Ch. 2.

11. K.B. Pyle, 'Meiji Conservatism', in M.B. Jansen (ed.), *The Cambridge History of Japan. Volume 5: The Nineteenth Century* (Cambridge, 1989), Ch. 11, p. 696.

12. In January 1887, for instance, Alexander III told his Foreign Minister: 'if we lose the confidence of public opinion in our foreign policy then all is lost'. A.F. Rotstein (ed.), *Dnevnik V.N. Lamzdorfa, 1886–1890* (Moscow, 1926), p. 36.

13. The first chapters of R. Pipes, *The Formation of the Soviet Union* (Cambridge, Mass., 1970), remain the best overall survey of the nationalities problem in the last decades of Imperial Russia.

14. There is a huge literature on Russian labour before the revolution. T. McDaniel, *Autocracy, Capitalism and Revolution in Russia* (Berkeley, 1988), is a useful introduction to this issue. His bibliography is a good guide to the literature. See also, for example, R.E. Johnson, *Peasant and Proletarian: The Working Class of Moscow in the Late Nineteenth Century* (Rutgers, 1979). The capitalists' perspective has received far less attention. The best English-language source on this is O. Crisp, 'Labour and Industrialization in Russia', in P. Mathias and M.M. Postan (eds.), *The Cambridge Economic History of Europe* (Cambridge, 1978), Vol. 7, Part 2, pp. 308–415.

15. Pyle, 'Meiji Conservatism', p. 710. Apart from McDaniel, *Autocracy*, see also M.K. Palat, 'Police Socialism in Tsarist Russia, 1900–1905', *Studies in History*, Vol. 2, No. 1, 1986, New Delhi; and J. Schneiderman, *Sergei Zubatov and Revolutionary Marxism* (Ithaca, 1970).

16. I have discussed the Russian aristocracy's position within a comparative European framework in D. Lieven, *The Aristocracy in Europe, 1815–1914* (London, 1992). Two contrasting works on the upper class in late Imperial Russia are S. Becker, *Nobility and Privilege in Late Imperial Russia* (DeKalb, 1985), and R. Manning, *The Crisis of the Old Regime in Russia* (Princeton, 1982).

17. H-D. Löwe, *Die Lage der Bauern in Russland, 1880–1905* (St Katherinen, 1987).

18. Apart from Löwe three collections of essays on the Russian peasantry have recently been published in English: B. Eklof and S.P. Frank (eds.), *The World of the Russian Peasant* (London, 1990); R. Bartlett (ed.), *Land Commune and Peasant Community in Russia* (London, 1990); and E. Kingston-Mann and T. Mixter (eds.), *Peasant Economy, Culture and Politics of European Russia, 1800–1921* (Princeton, 1991).

19. On middle-class Russia there is a very good recent collection of essays edited by E.W. Clowes, S.D. Kassow and J.L. West, *Between Tsar and People: Educated Society and the Quest for Public Identity in Late Imperial Russia* (Princeton, 1991).

20. The literature on the radical and revolutionary movement is colossal. No single work synthesizes all this literature and provides a simultaneous guide to the radical intelligentsia's counter-culture and the revolutionary movement's various strands throughout the last half-century of the old regime. As regards political ideas, the best guide is A. Walicki, *A History of Russian Thought from the Enlightenment to Marxism* (Oxford, 1980). On the spirit of the intelligentsia, F. Venturi, *Roots of Revolution* (London, 1960), remains a classic work.

21. On Tkachev see D. Hardy, *Petr Tkachev: The Critic as Jacobin* (Seattle, 1977).

Chapter 2: Childhood and Youth

1. Marie, Grand Duchess of Russia, *Education of a Princess* (New York, 1931), p. 14.
2. For photographs and a description of the statue see B. Ometev and J. Stuart, *St Petersburg: Portrait of an Imperial City* (London, 1990), pp. 42–3.
3. I. Vorres, *The Last Grand Duchess* (London, 1964), p. 29; D.N. Lyubimov, 'Russkaya smuta nachala devyatisokykh godov, 1902–1906. Po vospominaniyam, lichniyam zapiskam i dokumentam', Columbia University Bakhmetev Archive (New York: henceforth CUBA), Lyubimov Collection, pp. 89–93; and S. Harcave (ed.), *The Memoirs of Count Witte* (New York, 1990), pp. 157 and 174.
4. Manuscript Section of the Lenin Library (Moscow: henceforth RO), Fond 126, K12, p. 1, entry for 7 November 1894.
5. Vorres, *Last Grand Duchess*, p. 39.
6. S. Bradford, *George VI* (London, 1991), p. 20. See also V.N. Lamzdorf, *Dnevnik, 1894–1896* (Moscow, 1991), pp. 55–6.
7. Vorres, *Last Grand Duchess*, p. 52.
8. V.N. Lamzdorf, *Dnevnik, 1886–1890* (Moscow, 1926), pp. 7, 140 and 230–1; and Central State Historical Archive (Saint Petersburg: henceforth TsGIA), Fond 899, Opis 1, Ed. Khr. 32, pp. 40–1.
9. V.N. Lamzdorf, *Dnevnik, 1891–1892* (Moscow, 1934), p. 98.
10. Lamzdorf, *Dnevnik, 1891–1892*, for example, p. 251; and P.A. Zayonchkovsky (ed.), *Dnevnik P.A. Valueva 1861–1876* (Moscow, 1961), Vol. 1, p. 262, and Vol. 2, p. 151.
11. Central State Archive of the October Revolution (Moscow: henceforth TsGAOR), Fond 1,463, Opis 1, Ed. Khr. 1,115, p. 240; and Witte, *Memoirs*, pp. 156 and 170–8.
12. Anon., *Russian Court Memoirs* (2nd ed., Cambridge, 1992), pp. 17–18; and Princess Catherine Radziwill, *The Intimate Life of the Last Tsarina* (London, 1929), p. 68.
13. J. Pope-Hennessy, *Queen Mary, 1867–1953* (London, 1959), pp. 327–8; and Bradford, *George VI*, pp. 20–1.
14. Bradford, *George VI*, p. 185; Pope-Hennessy, *Queen Mary*, pp. 256–7; and K. Rose, *King George V* (London, 1983), pp. 19 and 26.
15. Vorres, *Last Grand Duchess*, pp. 53, 85–6 and 92–3; Grand Duke Alexander Mikhailovich, *Once a Grand Duke* (London, 1932), pp. 146–7; Baroness Sophia Buxhoeveden, *The Life and Tragedy of Alexandra Feodorovna, Empress of Russia* (London, 1928), p. 110; and G.A. Lensen (ed.), *Revelations of a Russian Diplomat: The Memoirs of Dimitri I. Abrikossow* (Seattle, 1964), p. 233.
16. Rose, *George V*, p. 10.
17. I. Surguchev, *Detstvo imperatora Nikolaya vtorogo* (Paris, 1952), pp. 45, 78 and 151; Witte, *Memoirs*, p. 125; and D. Duff, *Hessian Tapestry* (London, 1967), p. 250, quoting Princess Victoria of Hesse.
18. See, in particular, M. Zonis, *Majestic Failure: The Fall of the Shah* (Chicago, 1991), Ch. 2; and A. Taheri, *The Unknown Life of the Shah* (London, 1991), p. 225 for the quotation. Alexander Mikhailovich, *Once a Grand Duke*, p. 201.
19. Zonis, *Majestic Failure*, p. 30; and Surguchev, *Detstvo*, p. 68.
20. D. Mack Smith, *Italy and Its Monarchy* (London, 1989), p. 71.
21. Mack Smith, *Italy*, p. 147.
22. Surguchev, *Detstvo*, pp. 78, 79, 88–9, 108–9 and 132.
23. Surguchev, *Detstvo*, p. 82; and Vorres, *Last Grand Duchess*, pp. 26 and 32.

24. Surguchev, *Detstvo*, pp. 138–41; and Vorres, *Last Grand Duchess*, p. 48.
25. G. Botkin, *The Real Romanovs* (London, 1932), p. 32.
26. A.M. Verner, *The Crisis of Russian Autocracy: Nicholas II and the 1905 Revolution* (Princeton, 1990), pp. 20–1; and J.C. Trewin, *Tutor to the Tsarevich* (London, 1975), pp. 83–6.
27. Surguchev, *Detstvo*, p. 81; P. Popov (P. Knyazhnin), *Shest' let v Imperatorskom Aleksandrovskom Litsee (1870–75)* (St Petersburg, 1911), pp. 29–31; E.J. Bing (ed.), *The Letters of Tsar Nicholas and Empress Marie* (London, 1937), p. 85 (27 June 1894); Vorres, *Last Grand Duchess*, p. 34; A. Izvolsky, *The Memoirs of Alexander Iswolsky* (London, n.d.), p. 248; and V.N. Voeykov, *S tsarem i bez tsarya* (Helsingfors, 1936), p. 337.
28. P.L. Bark, 'Glava iz vospominaniy', *Vozrozhdenie*, Vol. 43, 1955, Paris, pp. 5–27: the quotation is from p. 7.
29. Much the best English-language study of Pobedonostsev is by R.F. Byrnes, *Pobedonostsev* (Indiana, 1968).
30. B.V. Ananich, 'The Economic Policy of the Tsarist Government and Enterprise in Russia from the End of the Nineteenth through the Beginning of the Twentieth Century', in G. Guroff and F.V. Carstensen (eds.), *Entrepreneurship in Imperial Russia and the Soviet Union* (Princeton, 1983), pp. 125–39: the quotation is from p. 136. *The Letters of the Tsar to the Tsaritsa* (London, 1929), p. 266, letter of 20 September 1916.
31. On the aristocratic Guards officer in general, see D.C.B. Lieven, *The Aristocracy in Europe, 1815–1914* (London, 1992), p. 189.
32. For a record of the journey in English, see R. Goodlet's translation of Prince E. Ukhtomsky, *Travels in the East of Nicholas II Emperor of Russia when Cesarewitch* (2 vols., London, 1896). Alexander Mikhailovich, *Once a Grand Duke*, pp. 188–9.
33. Ukhtomsky, *Travels*, Vol. 2, pp. 101, 143 and 419; and Bing (ed.), *Letters*, pp. 46–7.
34. Verner, *Crisis*, pp. 28–9; and Alexander Mikhailovich, *Once a Grand Duke*, p. 190.
35. Vorres, *Last Grand Duchess*, p. 67.
36. Witte, *Memoirs*, p. 126; V.I. Mamantov, *Na gosudarevoy sluzhbe* (Tallinn, 1926), pp. 168–70; and Bark, 'Glava', p. 7.
37. Marion Countess Dönhoff, *Before the Storm* (New York, 1990), pp. 39–40: I try to expand on this theme in Lieven, *Aristocracy*, especially in Chs. 7, 8 and 10; and Izvolsky, *Memoirs*, p. 247.
38. P. Gilliard (Zhil'yar), *Trinadtsat' let pri russkom dvore* (Paris, n.d.), pp. 69–70.
39. On the childhood and education of George V and Wilhelm II, see, for example, respectively Rose, *George V*, Ch. 1, and L. Cecil, *Wilhelm II, Prince and Emperor, 1859–1900* (Chapel Hill, 1989), Ch. 2. On Emperor Hirohito, see, for example, T. Crump, *The Death of an Emperor* (Oxford, 1989), pp. 75–7.
40. For Wilhelm II see, for example, Cecil, *Wilhelm*, Chs. 2 and 3. On Edward VII, see P. Magnus, *King Edward VII* (London, 1964), Chs. 1 and 2.
41. Lamzdorf, *Dnevnik, 1894–96*, p. 85; and A. Alam, *The Shah and I: The Confidential Diary of Iran's Royal Court, 1969–1977* (London, 1991), p. 478. Admittedly, Crown Prince Reza was only 16 when the Shah made this comment. Nicholas II was 26 when his father died. Still, the Shah's point is relevant.
42. As the paragraph indicates, I have my doubts about parts of Verner's argument in Chapter 1 of his *Crisis of Russian Autocracy*.

Chapter 3: Tsar and Family Man

1. *Dnevnik Imperatora Nikolaya II* (Paris, 1980; reprint of 1923 Berlin edition), pp. 12–48, conveys a sense of the heir's daily life before his marriage and accession.
2. Quoted in Verner, *Crisis*, p. 30.
3. *Dnevnik*, p. 49.
4. *Dnevnik*, p. 50.
5. Spiteful voices said that Alix had enjoyed being 'Queen' of Hesse and loathed being displaced by her brother's bride. Radzivill, *Intimate Life*, p. 6.
6. Duff, *Hessian Tapestry*, pp. 165 and 172; and Buxhoeveden, *Life*, pp. 29 and 80–1.
7. Duff, *Hessian Tapestry*, pp. 165–6; Buxhoeveden, *Life*, pp. 45 and 91–2; and L. Dehn, *The Real Tsaritsa* (London, 1922), p. 67. On Alix's mother, see G. Noel, *Princess Alice* (London, 1974).
8. Duff, *Hessian Tapestry*, pp. 103, 148 and 173–4; and Buxhoeveden, *Life*, for example, pp. 79–81.
9. Duff, *Hessian Tapestry*, pp. 168–9; Buxhoeveden, *Life*, p. 87; and S.S. Fabritsky, *Iz proshlogo* (Berlin, 1926), p. 118.
10. Buxhoeveden, *Life*, pp. 7–14; and Dehn, *Real Tsaritsa*, pp. 59–60, 94, 103, 185 and 197.
11. Buxhoeveden, *Life*, pp. 1–15.
12. G. Noel, *Ena: Spain's English Queen*, pp. 54–8 and 135–49; and L. Connors, *The Emperor's Adviser: Saionji Kinmochi and Pre-War Japanese Politics* (London, 1987), pp. 77–86.
13. *Dnevnik*, pp. 58 ff.
14. RO, Fond 126, K11, p. 307; Lamzdorf, *Dnevnik, 1894–6*, pp. 24–5 and 44; and *Dnevnik*, pp. 75–84.
15. *Dnevnik*, pp. 89–99.
16. Radzivill, *Intimate Life*, p. 92; and Lamzdorf, *Dnevnik, 1894–6*, pp. 85, 123, 376 and 404.
17. Verner, *Crisis*, pp. 39–43; and *Dnevnik*, p. 83.
18. Radzivill, *Intimate Life*, p. 70; Rose, *George V*, p. 77; and Pope-Hennessy, *Queen Mary*, pp. 422–3.
19. A. Bogdanovich, *Tri poslednikh samoderzhavtsa* (Moscow, 1990), p. 79.
20. Lieven, *Aristocracy in Europe*, tries to illustrate some of these points by comparisons between Russian, German and English aristocracy. Radzivill, *Intimate Life*, for example p. 48; see, also, Count P. Vasili, *La Société de St. Petersburg* (Paris, 1886); and Carl Graf Moy, *Als Diplomat am Zarenhof* (Munich, 1971).
21. Prince S. Volkonsky, *My Reminiscences* (2 vols., London, 1922), Vol. 2, pp. 83–4 and 104.
22. Noel, *Ena*, p. 104; Radzivill, *Intimate Life*, p. 111; and Gibbes, *Tutor*, p. 54
23. Lamzdorf, *Dnevnik, 1894–6*, pp. 339–40, 344 and 357–8; and Radzivill, *Intimate Life*, pp. 80–2.
24. Mamantov, *Na gosudarevoy sluzhbe*, pp. 136–7.
25. Lamzdorf, *Dnevnik, 1894–6*, p. 376; and RO, Fond 126, K11, p. 314i; K12, p. 46i; and K13, p. 57i.
26. Abrikossow, *Revelations*, pp. 231–6; and Bing (ed.), *Letters*, pp. 283–5. For the entourages of Wilhelm II and Prince Regent Luitpold see I. Hull, *The Entourage of Kaiser Wilhelm II, 1888–1918* (Cambridge, 1982); J.C.G. Röhl, *Kaiser, Hof und Staat. Wilhelm II und die deutsche Politik* (Munich, 1987); and K. Möckl, 'Hof und

Hofgesellschaft in Bayern in der Prinzregentenzeit', in K.F. Werner (ed.), *Akten des 18 deutsch-französischen Historiokerkolloquiums Darmstadt von 27–30 September 1982* (Bonn, 1985). See also, for example, Magnus, *Edward*, pp. 68–76.

27. Bing (ed.), *Letters*, p. 84; and G. Botkin, *The Real Romanovs* (London, 1932), p. 31.
28. Grand Duke Gavriil Konstantinovich, *V Mramornom Dvortse* (New York, 1955), p. 60.
29. Bing (ed.), *Letters*, p. 103.
30. Dehn, *Real Tsaritsa*, p. 70; and Buxhoeveden, *Life*, p. 51.
31. Fabritsky, *Iz Proshlogo*, pp. 87–8.
32. On hunting see, for example, A. Spiridovitch, *Les Dernières Années de la Cour à Tsarskoie Selo* (2 vols., Paris, 1928), Vol. 1, pp. 224–9. Fabritsky, *Iz proshlogo*, p. 116; and Gavriil, *V Mramornom*, pp. 36–41, which describes one such festival.
33. For a description of these balls and entertainments see, for example, V.N. Voeykov, *S tsarem i bez tsarya* (Helsingfors, 1936), pp. 36–40. Radzivill, *Intimate Life*, p. 124; *Russian Court Memoirs*, pp. 12–13; and G. Dobson, H.M. Grove and H. Stewart, *Russia* (London, 1915), pp. 103–6.
34. Spiridovitch, *Dernières Années*, Vol. 1, pp. 61–5.
35. Spiridovitch, *Dernières Années*, Vol. 1, pp. 357–9 and 374–5; Vol. 2, pp. 138–9; Mamantov, *Na gosudarevoy*, pp. 132 ff.; and RO, Fond 126, K13, p. 260.
36. Spiridovitch, *Dernières Années*, Vol. 1, pp. 187–93, and Fabritsky, *Iz proshlogo*, pp. 57–68 and 70–81.
37. Baron R.R. Rosen, *Forty Years of Diplomacy* (2 vols., London, 1922), Vol. 2, p. 26; A.A. Mosolov, *At the Court of the Last Tsar* (London, 1935), p. 11; and E. Elchaninov, *The Tsar and His People* (London, n.d.), pp. 1–2. The quotation's significance is underlined by the fact that Nicholas II himself approved, read and authorized Elchaninov's work. See a letter from the Grand Duke Paul of 29 May 1913 in V.P. Semennikov (ed.), *Nikolay II i velikie knyazya* (Leningrad-Moscow, 1925), p. 58.
38. Gavriil, *V Mramornom*, pp. 31–5.
39. Vorres, *Last Grand Duchess*, pp. 78–9; and *Krasnyy Arkhiv*, Vol. 76, 1936, pp. 31–48, which contains documents on the tragedy, including part of the report of the Special Judicial Investigator, Keyser.
40. Radzivill, *Intimate Life*, pp. 95–7; and Witte, *Memoirs*, pp. 240–1.
41. RO, Fond 126, K12, p. 55 ii; Witte, *Memoirs*, pp. 239–42; Vorres, *Last Grand Duchess*, p. 78; and Alexander, *Once a Grand Duke*, pp. 158–9 and 191–4.

Chapter 4: Ruling Russia, 1894–1904

1. Cecil, *Wilhelm II*, especially pp. 63–8; and Röhl, *Germany without Bismarck, passim.*
2. 'Iz dnevnika A.A. Polovtsova', *Krasnyy Arkhiv*, Vol. 67, 1934, p. 174. On Nicholas's elusiveness see, for example, Mossolov, *At the Court*, p. 28; and Mamantov, *Na gosudarevoy*, pp. 58, 131 and 158.
3. Spiridovitch, *Dernières Années*, Vol. 1, pp. 178 and 286; and Fabritsky, *Iz proshlogo*, p. 53.
4. The best source on office-holding is E. Amburger, *Geschichte der Behörden-organisation Russlands von Peter dem Grossen bis 1917* (Leyden, 1966).
5. *Dnevnik*, pp. 105–6; and S. Yu. Witte, *Samoderzhavie i zemstvo*, first published in Stuttgart in 1903 with an introduction by P.B. Struve.

6. Fabritsky, *Iz proshlogo*, p. 105.
7. 'Iz dnevnika A.A. Polovtsova', *Krasnyy Arkhiv*, Vol. 67, 1934, p. 170.
8. Ibid., p. 171.
9. Witte's autobiography, edited and translated by Sidney Harcave, is the best source on the man and his career. D.C.B. Lieven, *Russia's Rulers under the Old Regime*, (London, 1989), is a study of Witte's peers, in other words Russia's senior officials in the last decades of the empire. Anyone wanting a detailed statistical breakdown of social origins, education, career patterns and so on might look at Lieven, 'The Russian Civil Service under Nicholas II: Some Variations on the Bureaucratic Theme', *Jahrbücher für Geschichte Osteuropas*, Vol. 29, No. 3, 1981, pp. 366–403.
10. Bogdanovich, *Tri poslednikh*, p. 102; and A.N. Kuropatkin, *Dnevnik* (Nizhniy Novgorod, 1923), pp. 29–30.
11. V.I. Gurko, *Features and Figures of the Past* (Stanford, 1939), p. 67; and 'Iz dnevnika A.A. Polovtsova', *Krasnyy Arkhiv*, Vol. 67, 1934, p. 172.
12. The expression, ministry of 'national development' is used by Olga Crisp on p. 24 of *Studies in the Russian Economy before 1914* (London, 1976). Coming from her, the phrase has particular resonance because she is not at all inclined to exaggerate the state's role in economic affairs. The English-speaking reader can best appreciate Witte's programme by reading 'A Secret Memorandum of Sergei Witte on the Industrialization of Imperial Russia', *Journal of Modern History*, Vol. 26, 1954, pp. 64–73. Theodore von Laue, the memorandum's translator and the author of *Sergei Witte and the Industrialization of Russia*, is the doyen of Western studies of Witte and his policies.
13. Two relatively recent comments on Witte's policies are a highly critical piece by H. Barkai, 'The Macro-Economics of Tsarist Russia in the Industrialization Era: Monetary Developments, the Balance of Payments and the Gold Standard', *Journal of Economic History*, Vol. 33, No. 2, 1973, pp. 339–71; and the survey article by P.R. Gregory, 'Russian Industrialization and Economic Growth: Results and Perspectives of Western Research', *Jarhbücher für Geschichte Osteuropas*, Vol. 25, No. 2, 1977, pp. 200–18.
14. George Yaney is the leading Western apostle of the view that inter-ministerial conflict, and above all the battle between the ministries of finance and internal affairs, provides the key to Russian domestic politics in the late imperial era. See, above all, Ch. 8 of Yaney, *The Systematization of Russian Government* (Urbana, 1973). Kuropatkin, *Dnevnik*, p. 73, has a nice self-description of Pleske.
15. For a scholarly but very readable portrait of the provincial governors, see R.J. Robbins, *The Tsar's Viceroys* (Ithaca, 1987). There is now a large literature on provincial government even in English. One book which brings out the limits of the Ministry of Internal Affairs' power at this level is N.B. Weissman, *Reform in Tsarist Russia* (New Brunswick, 1981). I tried to provide a survey of the organization, functions and operations of the security police in, 'The Security Police, Civil Rights, and the Fate of the Russian Empire', in O. Crisp and L. Edmondson (eds.), *Civil Rights in Imperial Russia* (Oxford, 1989), pp. 235–62.
16. J. Schneiderman, *Sergei Zubatov and Revolutionary Marxism* (Ithaca, 1970), pp. 40–1, quotes Panteleev. An old, but still very interesting work on the debate on industrial development in radical circles is A.P. Mendel, *Dilemmas of Progress in Tsarist Russia: Legal Marxism and Legal Populism* (Cambridge, 1961).
17. The quotes are from Bogdanovich, *Tri poslednikh*, pp. 302 and 423. Gurko, *Features*, pp. 190–2.

18. The quote is from 'Iz dnevnika A.A. Polovtsova', *Krasnyy Arkhiv*, Vol. 46, 1931, p. 109.
19. 'Iz dnevnika A.A. Polovtsova', *Krasnyy Arkhiv*, Vol. 3, 1923, p. 96; TsGIA, Fond 1,642, Opis 1, Ed. Khr. 220, pp. 71–2, Letter of 13 April 1902; and RO, Fond 126, K13, p. 173i.
20. 'Iz dnevnika A.A. Polovtsova', *Krasnyy Arkhiv*, Vol. 46, 1931, p. 128.
21. S.E. Kryzhanovsky, *Vospominaniya* (Berlin, n.d.), p. 201.
22. TsGIA, Fond 1,044, Opis 1, Ed. Khr. 224, pp. 7 and 10.
23. 'Iz dnevnika A.A. Polovtsova', *Krasnyy Arkhiv*, Vol. 3, 1923, p. 114; and TsGIA, Fond 1,044, Opis 1, Ed. Khr. 269, pp. 1 and 29: a letter from Kokovtsov to Saburov dated 17 April 1903. On Nicholas and attempts at limitation of armaments, see D.C. Morrill, 'Nicholas II and the Call for the First Hague Conference', *Journal of Modern History*, Vol. 46, 1974, pp. 296–313.
24. TsGIA, Fond 1,642, Opis 1, Ed. Khr. 172, p. 53.
25. 'Iz dnevnika A.A. Polovtsova', *Krasnyy Arkhiv*, Vol. 3, 1923, p. 98.
26. 'Iz dnevnika A.A. Polovtsova', *Krasnyy Arkhiv*, Vol. 67, 1934, pp. 184–5, and Vol. 3, 1923, p. 103; and Gurko, *Features*, Ch. XI.
27. RO, Fond 126, K13, p. 218.
28. RO, Fond 126, K13, p. 36; and Bing (ed.), *Letters*, pp. 162–8.
29. A very good modern study of Russian university life is S.D. Kassow, *Students, Professors, and the State in Tsarist Russia* (Berkeley, 1989). A much older but still very valuable book was written by Thomas Darlington and published by the British Board of Education as *Special Reports on Educational Subjects. Vol. 23: Education in Russia* (London, 1909).
30. The quote is from Schwartz's, 'Moi vospominaniya o gosudare', in RO, Fond 338, Opis 1, Delo 3.4, p. 2. Schwartz's voluminous correspondence and memoranda in Fond 338 and TsGIA, Fond 1,672, are full of useful comments by a conservative professor about officials of the ministry, teachers, students and the problems of Russian education. A short article by C. Ruane and B. Eklof, 'Cultural Pioneers and Professionals: The Teacher in Society', in Clowes *et al.* (eds.), *Between Tsar and People*, pp. 199–214, well repays reading. So does S.J. Seregny, *Russian Teachers and Peasant Revolution: The Politics of Education in 1905* (Bloomington, 1989). See RO, Fond 126, K13, p. 243 for Saenger's views of Nicholas.
31. RO, Fond 126, K13, p. 313.
32. RO, Fond 126, K13, pp. 51 and 100.
33. The literature on the socialist parties is colossal. One of the best books on the early years of the Social Democrats remains J.H.L. Keep, *The Rise of Social Democracy in Russia* (Oxford, 1963). On the Socialist Revolutionaries there is no adequate work in English. One must turn to M. Hildermeier, *Die Sozialrevolutionäre Partei Russlands: Agrarsozialismus und Modernisierung im Zarenreich (1900–1914)* (Cologne, 1978).
34. S. Galai, *The Liberation Movement in Russia, 1900–1905* (Cambridge, 1973), is the best history of liberalism in the run-up to the 1905 revolution.
35. Lamzdorf, *Dnevnik, 1886–90*, p. 36.
36. The key documents surrounding the signing of the treaty of alliance are reproduced in the appendices of G.F. Kennan, *The Fateful Alliance* (Manchester, 1984). This volume, together with Kennan's earlier *The Decline of Bismarck's European Order* (Princeton, 1970), provides a detailed and finely written account of the origins of the

Franco-Russian alliance by twentieth-century America's most distinguished expert on Russia.

37. Lamzdorf, *Dnevnik, 1894–96*, p. 265.
38. There is no English-language general survey of Russian foreign policy in the reign of Nicholas II. On Russia's role in the Balkans, however, there is Barbara Jelavich, *Russia's Balkan Entanglements, 1806–1914* (Cambridge, 1991). F.R. Bridge, *From Sadowa to Sarajevo: The Foreign Policy of Austria-Hungary, 1866–1914* (London, 1972), provides a useful view of Russian policy from a Viennese perspective.
39. A. Iswolsky, *Au Service de la Russie. Alexandre Iswolsky. Correspondance Diplomatique* (2 vols., Paris, 1937 and 1939), Vol. 1, pp. 41–2; and Oldenburg, *Last Tsar*, Vol. 1, p. 131.
40. Kuropatkin's statement in 1900 is cited by David M. McDonald, *Autocracy, Bureaucracy and Change in the Formation of Russia's Foreign Policy, 1895–1914* (Columbia University Ph.D., 1988), p. 87. McDonald's book, entitled *United Government and Foreign Policy in Russia, 1900–1914* (Cambridge, Mass., 1992), has a very interesting discussion of the making of Russian foreign policy in this era. Kuropatkin, *Dnevnik*, pp. 19, 22 and 29. For plans to seize the Turkish Straits see 'Proekkt zakhvata Bosfora v 1896 g', *Krasnyy Arkhiv*, Vol. 47–8, 1931, pp. 50–70. Oldenburg, *Last Tsar*, Vol. 1, Ch. 5, discusses Nicholas's views on Asia. Useful background to this issue is M. Hauner, *What Is Asia to Us?* (London, 1992).
41. There is a large literature on the origins of the Russo-Japanese War. An excellent and very fair recent work is by Ian Nish, *The Origins of the Russo-Japanese War* (London, 1985).
42. Quoted in McDonald, *Autocracy*, p. 137.
43. 'Iz dnevnika A.A. Polovtsova', *Krasnyy Arkhiv*, Vol. 3. 1923, p. 99.
44. Kuropatkin, *Dnevnik*, p. 114; and McDonald, *Autocracy*, p. 217.

Chapter 5: Autocratic Government

1. Lamzdorf, *Dnevnik, 1894–96*, p. 401; and RO, Fond 338, Opis 1, Delo 3.4, p. 2.
2. RO, ibid. See, for example, Peter Bark's comments in 'Glava', *Vozrozhdenie*, 1955, pp. 11 and 24–5.
3. Kuropatkin, *Dnevnik*, p. 55.
4. RO, Fond 126, K 13, pp. 142 and 242; and 'Iz dnevnika A.A. Polovtsova', *Krasnyy Arkhiv*, Vol. 3, 1923, p. 87.
5. RO, Fond 126, K 13, pp. 100 and 252; and 'Iz dnevnika A. A. Polovtsova', *Krasnyy Arkhiv*, Vol. 3, 1923, p. 131.
6. Buxhoeveden, *Life*, pp. 108–10; and RO, Fond 126, K 13, p. 303.
7. Bark, 'Glava', *Vozrozhdenie*, 1955, p. 5.
8. Fabritsky, *Iz proshlogo*, p. 73; Bogdanovich, *Tri poslednikh*, pp. 217–18; A. N. Naumov, *Iz utselevshikh vospominaniy* (2 vols., New York, 1955), Vol. 2, p. 217; and Dehn, *Real Tsaritsa*, p. 86.
9. P.A. Zayonchkovsky (ed.), *Dnevnik Gosudarstvennogo Sekretarya A.A. Polovtsova* (2 vols., Moscow, 1966), Vol. 1, p. 213; and Vol. 2, pp. 109 and 246.
10. RO, Fond 126, K 11, pp. 39, 47, 99, 214, 233, 249, 295, 313 and 317.
11. Kuropatkin, *Dnevnik*, p. 53.
12. Izvolsky, *Memoirs*, p. 127.

13. TsGIA, Fond 1,650, Opis 1, Ed. Khr. 243, p. 28; and TsGIA, Fond 899, Opis 1, Ed. Khr. 50, p. 12.
14. TsGIA, Fond 1,650, Opis 1, Ed. Khr. 227, p. 90; and Ed. Khr. 234, pp. 62 and 73.
15. Prince B.A. Vasil'chikov, *Vospominaniya*, MSS; see in particular Ch. 7, pp. 55–60; S. Yu. Witte, *Vospominaniya*, (3 vols., Moscow, 1960), Vol. 3, p. 366; and Gurko, *Features*, p. 500n.
16. Bark, 'Glava', *Vozrozhdenie*, 1955, pp. 22–3.
17. Mamantov, *Na Gosudarevoy*, pp. 12–13, 35–7 and 165–76.
18. Fabritsky, *Iz proshlogo*, p. 89.
19. On the Third Section see P.S. Squire, *The Third Department: The Political Police in the Russia of Nicholas I* (Cambridge, 1968), and S. Monas, *The Third Section: Police and Society in Russia under Nicholas I* (Cambridge, Mass., 1961).
20. Rohl, *Germany*, pp. 273 ff.
21. On Stalin's private secretariat the basic essential reading is N.E. Rosenfeldt, *Knowledge and Power: The Role of Stalin's Secret Chancellery in the Soviet System of Government* (Copenhagen, 1978).
22. Mamantov, *Na gosudarevoy*, p. 145.
23. Bing (ed.), *Letters*, p. 212.
24. The letter from Nicholas to Trepov is dated 16/29 October 1905 and is quoted in Verner, *Crisis*, p. 238.
25. Verner, *Crisis*, p. 255.
26. Witte, *Memoirs*, pp. 514–15 and 518.
27. F. Millar, *The Emperor in the Roman World* (Ithaca, 1992), p. 6; and C.M. MacLachlan, *Spain's Empire in the New World* (Berkeley, 1991), p. 47.
28. B. Pares (ed.), *Letters of the Tsaritsa to the Tsar* (London, 1923), p. 455; and RO, Fond 126, K 13, p. 335.
29. Holstein is quoted by Cecil, *Wilhelm II*, p. 233. For William's own statement see K.A. Lerman, *The Chancellor as Courtier: Bernhard von Bulow and the Governance of Germany, 1900–1909* (Cambridge, 1990), p. 63. Apart from these two works and Rohl, *Germany without Bismarck*, I found I. Hull, *The Entourage of Kaiser William II, 1888–1918* (Cambridge, 1982), and J.C.G. Rohl and N. Sombart (eds.), *Kaiser Wilhelm II: New Interpretations* (Cambridge, 1982), of great interest when attempting to make comparisons between German and Russian monarchy. The debate about how much power the Kaiser actually wielded is by now an old one. A good introduction to this debate is an article by G. Eley, 'The View from the Throne: The Personal Rule of Kaiser Wilhelm II', *Historical Journal*, Vol. 28, No. 2, 1985, pp. 469–86.
30. The quote is from D.A. Titus, *Palace and Politics in Prewar Japan* (Columbia, 1973), p. 24. Apart from this excellent book, Connors, *Emperor's Adviser*, Crump, *Death of an Emperor*, and B.A. Shillony, *Politics and Culture in Wartime Japan* (Oxford, 1981), helped to shape my understanding of the monarchy's role in post-restoration Japan. On the earlier era I read H. Webb, *The Japanese Imperial Institution in the Tokugawa Period* (Columbia, 1968). M.B. Jansen, 'Monarchy and Modernisation in Japan', *Journal of Asian Studies*, August 1977, pp. 611–22, is a good short introduction to this topic and to the immense controversy it has aroused in post-war Japan and elsewhere.
31. Naumov, *Iz utselevshikh*, Vol. 2, pp. 216–17.
32. RO, Fond 126, K 13, pp. 367–9.
33. Bark, 'Glava', *Vozrozhdenie*, 1955, p. 11; and Vorres, *Last Grand Duchess*, p. 62.

34. K. Takeda, *The Dual Image of the Japanese Emperor* (London, 1988), is an interesting study of the Allied wartime debate on the fate of the Japanese monarchy.
35. Alam, *The Shah and I*, p. 190.
36. Ibid., p. 213.

Chapter 6: The Years of Revolution, 1904–1907

1. *Dnevnik*, p. 161.
2. TsGIA, Fond 1,650, Opis 1, Ed. Khr. 234, p. 70, letter to Princess Anna Obolensky dated 16 July 1904; and TsGIA, Fond 1,642, Opis 1, Ed. Khr. 220, p. 59, letter to Kulomzin's wife dated 5 April 1902.
3. The most recent study of the Kishinev pogrom is by S. Lambroza, 'The pogroms of 1903–1906', in John Klier and Shlomo Lambroza (eds.), *Pogroms: Anti-Jewish Violence in Modern Russian History* (Cambridge, 1992), pp. 195–247. This is an excellent collection of essays. Two older works on this issue repay reading: H. Rogger, *Jewish Policies and Right-Wing Politics in Imperial Russia* (Oxford, 1986), and H-D. Löwe, *Antisemitismus und reaktionäre Utopie* (Hamburg, 1978).
4. See, for instance, the diary entries for 29 May and 26 July 1903 in RO, Fond 126, K 13, pp. 235 and 252.
5. Kireev's diary is a useful source on Plehve's views. So too are the unpublished memoirs of D.N. Lyubimov, 'Russkaya smuta nachala devyatisotykh godov, 1902–1906', especially his record of a conversation between Plehve and Witte on pp. 48ff.
6. The letter, dated 31 August/13 September 1904, No. 2,703, was in the private collection of Mrs Nathalie Brooke, the ambassador's granddaughter. The whole collection is now in the Bakhmetev Archive of Columbia University.
7. 'Dnevnik E.A. Svyatopolk-Mirskoy', *Istoricheskie Zapiski*, Vol. 77, 1965, pp. 236–92: here pp. 241–2.
8. 'Iz dnevnika Konstantina Romanova' *Krasnyy Arkhiv*, Vol. 43, 1930, p. 96; Brooke, letter dated 3/16 December 1904; and 'Dnevnik . . . Svyatopolk-Mirskoy', p. 258.
9. Witte, *Memoirs*, p. 399; and TsGIA, Fond 1,650, Opis 1, Ed. Khr. 227, p. 88.
10. 'Dnevnik . . . Svyatopolk-Mirskoy', pp. 242, 248, 249, 251, 260–2, 266, 269, 271 and 277.
11. Buxhoeveden, *Life*, p. 108.
12. *Grazhdanin*, No. 73, 12 September 1904, pp. 17–20.
13. 'Dnevnik . . . Svyatopolk-Mirskoy', pp. 248, 257 and 261; Brooke, letter dated 3/16 December 1904 from Paul Benckendorff; and Gurko, *Features*, pp. 294–6.
14. M.K. Palat, 'Police Socialism', p. 125.
15. Lyubimov, *Smuta*, CUBA, p. 96. The fullest description of Bloody Sunday and the events which led to it is in W. Sablinsky, *The Road to Bloody Sunday: Father Gapon and the St Petersburg Massacre of 1905* (Princeton, 1976).
16. *Dnevnik*, 9 January 1905.
17. A. Ya. Avrekh, *P.A. Stolypin i sud'by reform v Rossii* (Moscow, 1991), p. 12; and Takeda, *The Dual Image of the Japanese Emperor*, pp. 84–5.
18. The quotes are from Verner, *Crisis*, pp. 172 and 177.
19. 'Dnevnik . . . Svyatopolk-Mirskoy', p. 247; and Brooke, letter dated 7/20 June 1905, No. 1, 926.

20. From a dispatch to Berlin written by Bismarck on 10 November 1861: See L. Raschau (ed.), *Die politischen Berichte des Fürsten Bismarck aus Petersburg und Paris* (Berlin, 1920), Vol. 2, pp. 129–30. I am grateful to Professor W. E. Mosse for guiding me to this report.

21. Ibid., p. 131; and Sir J. Hanbury-Williams, *The Emperor Nicholas II As I Knew Him* (London, 1922), pp. 75–6.

22. Brooke, letter dated 7/20 June 1905, No. 1,926.

23. Brooke, letters dated 16/29 December 1903, 25 December 1903/7 January 1904, and 12/25 March 1905.

24. The English-speaking reader has a choice between two good recent books on the war: J.N. Westwood, *Russia against Japan* (London, 1986), and R. Connaughton, *The War of the Rising Sun and the Tumbling Bear* (London, 1988).

25. Public Record Office (London: henceforth PRO), FO 371, 1467, No. 8,229, Knox to Buchanan, 22 February 1912, p. 489; and Kuropatkin, *Dnevnik*, p. 129.

26. A recent English-language study of the peace negotiations is R.A. Esthus, *Double Eagle and Rising Sun* (London, 1988).

27. An English translation of the manifesto can be found in G. Vernadsky (ed.), *A Source Book for Russian History from Early Times to 1917* (New Haven, 1972), Vol. 3, p. 705.

28. Quoted by Kassow, *Students*, p. 269.

29. H. Reichman, *Railwaymen and Revolution: Russia 1905* (Berkeley, 1987), p. 200.

30. Bing (ed.), *Letters*, pp. 186–7.

31. Brooke, letter dated 26 September/8 October 1905, Bing (ed.), *Letters*, p. 184.

32. Bing (ed.), *Letters*, pp. 187–8.

33. Brooke, letter dated 18/31 October 1905; and RO, Fond 126, K 14, p. 155.

34. Lyubimov, *Smuta*, CUBA, pp. 296–7; and Gurko, *Features*, pp. 439–41 and 449. On Durnovo, see Lieven, *Russia's Rulers*, Ch. 6.

35. Brooke, letter dated 20 December 1905/2 January 1906; and Bing (ed.), *Letters*, pp. 197 and 200–1.

36. *Byloe*, No. 4, October 1917, p. 204.

37. Witte, *Memoirs*, pp. 531 and 549; and *Sovet Ministrov Rossiyskoy Imperii 1905–1906. Dokumenty i materialy* (Leningrad, 1990), pp. 144–51.

38. On this issue see Avrekh, *Stolypin*, pp. 14–15, and the debate in the United Nobility, *Trudy pervogo s'yezda upol'nomochennykh dvoryanskikh obshchestv 29 guberniy* (St Petersburg (SPB), 1906).

39. Bing (ed.), *Letters*, pp. 191, 194–5 and 212.

40. Brooke, letter dated 27 November/10 December 1905. The quotations are from S.V. Tyutyukhin, *Yul'skiy politicheskiy krizis 1906 g v Rossii* (Moscow, 1991), pp. 23 and 24. On Witte and Nicholas in 1905 see, for example, H.D. Mehlinger and J.M. Thompson, *Count Witte and the Tsarist Government in the 1905 Revolution* (Bloomington, 1971).

41. 'Russko-Germanskiy dogovor 1905 goda', *Krasnyy Arkhiv*, Vol. 5, 1924, pp. 5–49: the quotations are from pp. 6 and 33. For Wilhelm's comment see T.A. Kohut, *Wilhelm II and the Germans* (Oxford, 1991), p. 146.

42. *Krasnyy Arkhiv*, Vol. 5, 1924, p. 35. The second quotation is from A.V. Ignatev, *Vneshnyaya politika Rossii v 1905–1907gg* (Moscow, 1986), p. 50.

43. Izvolsky, *Au Service de la Russie*, Vol. 1, p. 337.

44. 'Iz dnevnika Konstantina Romanova', *Krasnyy Arkhiv*, Vol. 45, 1931, pp. 118–19.

45. Dehn, *Real Tsaritsa*, pp. 134–5.

Chapter 7: Constitutional Monarch? 1907-1914

1. · *Dnevnik*, 30 July 1904; and *Stenograficheskiy otchot Gosudarstvennogo Soveta*, Session 6, col. 596: the words are those of P.N. Durnovo.
2. Pares, *Letters*, 11 June 1915, p. 88.
3. The story of Aleksei's illness and his mother's suffering is a familiar one and has, for instance, been recounted movingly by Robert Massie, *Nicholas and Alexandra* (London, 1968). Noel, *Ena*, is a much less familiar tale and an indirect commentary on Alexandra's devotion, see, for example, pp. 197-8; and Vorres, *Last Grand Duchess*, p. 125.
4. Brooke, letter dated 28 May/11 June 1904; Pares, *Letters*, 16 June 1915, p. 98; and Oldenburg, *Last Tsar*, Vol. 2, p. 50.
5. RO, Fond 126, K 13, p. 309; K 14, pp. 271, 279 and 324; K15, pp. 43, 69 and 85.
6. Fabritsky, *Iz proshlogo*, p. 54. There is an interesting short piece on Russian popular religion by M. Lewin in Eklof and Frank (eds.), *The World of the Russian Peasant*, pp. 155-68.
7. Vorres, *Last Grand Duchess*, p. 143.
8. Ibid., pp. 142-3.
9. Pares, *Letters*, p. 98.
10. There is an enormous literature on these themes. R. Pipes, 'Narodnichestvo: A Semantic Enquiry', *Slavic Review*, Vol. 3, 1964, pp. 441-58, discusses the term 'populism' in the Russian context. R. Wortman, *The Crisis of Russian Populism* (Cambridge, 1967), and A. Gleason, *Young Russia: The Genesis of Russian Radicalism in the 1860s* (Chicago, 1983), are good introductions to aspects of radical populism in the reign of Alexander II. A. Walicki, *A History of Russian Thought*, and a series of 'Slavophile biographies' by P.K. Christoff are the place to start as regards conservative populism. See also K.V. Mochulsky, *Dostoevsky: His Life and Work* (Princeton, 1967).
11. Vorres, *Last Grand Duchess*, p. 89.
12. French Military Archive (Vincennes), Service Historique, 7 N 1,535, Attachés militaires: Russie, 1906-1911: Report of Colonel Matton, 3/16 July 1909, No. 47, p. 5.
13. Durnovo's comment is from *Stenograficheskiy otchot gosudarstvennogo Soveta*, Session 6, 17 December 1910, col. 595. Rasputin's is from J.T. Fuhrmann, *Rasputin, A Life* (New York, 1990), p. 103. Rodzianko's is in M.V. Rodzianko, *Le Règne de Raspoutine* (Paris, 1928), p. 88. On the Tsarist myth the two standard works in English are M. Cherniavsky, *Tsar and People* (New Haven, 1960), and D. Field, *Rebels in the Name of the Tsar* (Boston, 1976). The latter in particular is quirky, well documented and interesting. The impact of the tsarist political tradition on Soviet politics is a big and complicated question. Two ways into the discussion of this theme are N. Tumarkin, *Lenin Lives! The Lenin Cult in Soviet Russia* (Cambridge, Mass., 1983), and R. Tucker, *The Soviet Political Mind: Stalinism and Post-Stalin Change* (New York, 1971).
14. More rubbish has probably been written about Rasputin than about any other figure in Russian history. A relatively sensible recent book on the subject is J.T. Fuhrmann, *Rasputin: A Life* (New York, 1990). The doctoral thesis of Mark Kulikowski, *Rasputin and the Fall of the Romanovs* (State University of New York, 1982), is useful. The standard English-language history of Orthodoxy at this time is N. Zernov, *The Russian Religious Renaissance of the Twentieth Century* (London, 1963). There is no

full-length biography of Guchkov. L. Menashe, ' "A Liberal with Spurs."
Alexander Guchkov, A Russian Bourgeois in Politics', *Russian Review*, Vol. 26,
1967, pp. 38–53, is a good short portrait. C. Ferenczi, 'Freedom of the Press Under
the Old Regime, 1905–1914', in O. Crisp and L. Edmondson (eds.), *Civil Rights
in Imperial Russia* (Oxford, 1989), pp. 191–214, is a succinct guide to the growth
of a largely free press. Isabel Hull, 'Kaiser Wilhelm II and the "Liebenberg Circle" ', in Rohl and Sombart (eds.), *Kaiser Wilhelm II*, is the best shorthand guide
in English to Harden and the Eulenberg affair. Anyone with Russian who wishes
to go more deeply into the Rasputin affair should look at the protocols of interro-
gations of imperial senior officials by a committee of enquiry of the Provisional
Government: *Padenie tsarskogo rezhima*, (7 vols., Moscow and Leningrad, 1924–7).
Some care needs to be shown in taking all this material at face value. In certain cases
prisoners showed an understandable tendency to ingratiate themselves with the new
regime.

15. For anyone who wishes to understand the detail of the new constitution there is one
bible: M. Szeftel, *The Russian Constitution of April 23, 1906: Political Institutions of the
Duma Monarchy* (Brussels, 1976). In the West historians have generally been divided
into optimists and pessimists as regards the viability of the constitutional system.
G.A. Hosking, *The Russian Constitutional Experiment: Government and Duma,
1907–1914* (Cambridge, 1973), on the whole belongs to the former camp and con-
centrates, as its title suggests, on relations between the executive and the legislature. In the more optimistic camp, the best recent work is M. Hagen, *Die Entfaltung
politischer Öffentlichkeit in Russland 1906–1914* (Wiesbaden, 1982), who looks at
the development of civil society in Russia at this time. Both books well repay study.
The leading Soviet historians on the political history of the constitutional era, none
of whose works are translated into Western languages, are the late A. Ya. Avrekh
and E.D. Chermensky, together with V.S. Dyakin and Yu. B. Solov'yov.

16. V.N. Kokovtsov, *Out of My Past* (Stanford, 1935), pp. 159 and 164; and Bing (ed.),
Letters, pp. 216 and 220.

17. RO, Fond 126, K 14, pp. 210–11 and 333.

18. D.C.B. Lieven, *The Aristocracy in Europe*, is an attempt to compare aristocratic
strategies to defend landowning interests in Russia, Germany and England.
L.H. Haimson (ed.), *The Politics of Rural Russia, 1905–1914* (Bloomington, 1979),
is above all a study of the rural nobility in the constitutional era. His chapters on the
United Nobility, the *zemstvo* and the Octobrists are of particular value in the
context of this discussion.

19. RO, Fond 126, K 15, p. 39.

20. Nicholas's note to Stolypin on the Jewish question is in *Krasnyy Arkhiv*, Vol. 5,
No. 13, 1925, 10 December 1906. See also, for example, Bing (ed.), *Letters*,
pp. 190–1, for his attitude to pogroms. Chapter 2 of Rogger, *Jewish Policies*, is a
good survey of the views of high officialdom on this matter. On the navy see Fuller,
Strategy, pp. 408–12, and D.C.B. Lieven, *Russia and the Origins of the First World
War* (London, 1983), pp. 101–18. Specifically on the Council for State Defence
there is an article by M. Perrins, 'The Council for State Defence, 1905–1909: A
Study in Russian Bureaucratic Politics', *Slavonic and East European Review*, Vol. 58,
No. 3, 1980, pp. 370–99. A Russian speaker should read K.F. Shatsillo, *Russkiy
imperializm i razvitie flota* (Moscow, 1968). Another major source of irritation to
Schwartz was the Emperor's intervention on the issue of girls who were enrolled in
courses of higher education. Nicholas was right on this issue but Schwartz, con-

vinced that his authority had been undermined, wrote in his memoirs that he decided to resign immediately: see RO, Fond 338, Opis 1, Delo 3.2, 'Zametki. Moya perepiska s Stolypinym', pp. 7–10.

21. Vorres, *Last Grand Duchess*, p. 126; and *Krasnyy Arkhiv*, Vol. 5, No. 51, 25 April 1909.

22. *Stenograficheskiy otchot Gosudarstvennogo Soveta*, Session 4, col. 1,350. RO, Fond 126, K15, p. 32. The two essential works on the army and civil and military relations for the English-speaking reader are N. Stone, *The Eastern Front, 1914–1917* (London, 1975), and D.R. Jones, 'Imperial Russia's Forces at War', in A.R. Millett and W. Murray (eds.), *Military Effectiveness: Vol. 1, The First World War* (Boston, 1988), pp. 249–328.

23. RO, Fond 126, K 14, pp. 92, 142, 156, 226 and 253; and Moy, *Diplomat*, pp. 111–12.

24. Lieven, *Russia's Rulers*, pp. 207–30 and 296–308, discusses Durnovo's views and personality. Durnovo's 'Memorandum to Nicholas II' of February 1914, translated into English and published in T. Riha (ed.), *Readings in Russian Civilisation* (Chicago, 1964), pp. 465–78, is essential reading for anyone interested in this period.

25. RO, Fond 126, K 14, pp. 157 and 342; Vasil'chikov, MS, *Vospominaniya*, Ch. 7, p. 82; and Kryzhanovksy, *Vospominaniya*, p. 75.

26. Lieven, *Russia's Rulers*, pp. 224–5.

27. The major study in English of the Kadets in the era of revolution is by W.G. Rosenberg, *Liberals in the Russian Revolution: The Constitutional Democratic Party, 1917–1921* (Princeton, 1974).

28. Quoted in Hosking, *Russian Constitutional Experiment*, p. 137; and V.N. Kokovtsov, *Iz moego Proshlogo* (2 vols., Paris, 1933), Vol. 1, p. 455.

29. Kokovtsov, *Iz moego Proshlogo*, Vol. 2, pp. 7–8.

30. *Grazhdanin*, No. 10, 13 March 1911, p. 12; and No. 8, 23 February 1913, p. 12; and *Padenie tsarskogo rezhima. Stenograficheskie otchoty doprosov i pokazanii* (7 vols., Leningrad, 1925), Vol. 3, pp. 85–6.

31. There is no balanced survey of the Stolypin reforms in English which makes use of the interesting research done in recent years on peasant society and agriculture. The reader will get a sense of both the complexity of the issues and the disagreements that exist between scholars by reading J. Pallot, 'Modernization from Above: The Stolypin Land Reform', in J. Pallot and D.J.B. Shaw (eds.), *Landscape and Settlement in Romanov Russia, 1613–1917* (Oxford, 1990), pp. 165–94; and D.A.J. Macey, 'The Peasant Commune and the Stolypin Reforms: Peasant Attitudes, 1906–14', in R. Bartlett (ed.), *Land Commune and Peasant Community in Russia* (London, 1990), pp. 219–36.

32. Gurko, *Features*, p. 195; V.S. Dyakin, *Burzhuaziya, dvoryanstvo i tsarizm v 1911–1914gg* (Leningrad, 1988), p. 112; and Brooke, letter dated 5/18 January 1914, No. 480.

33. L. Tikhomirov, *K reforme obnovlennoy Rossii* (Moscow, 1912), p. 282; and *Padenie tsarskogo rezhima*, Vol. 5, p. 196.

34. Anyone interested in pursuing this question should read Chapter 10 of R.B. McKean, *St Petersburg between the Revolutions* (New Haven, 1990).

35. Quoted in V.V. Shelokhaev, *Ideologiya i politicheskaya organizatsiya Rossiyskoy liberal'noy burzhuazii. 1907–1914* (Moscow, 1991), p. 63. A useful little example of the frustrations of the Russian middle classes is provided by M.F. Hamm, 'Kharkov's

Progressive Duma, 1910–1914: A Study in Russian Municipal Reform', *Slavic Review*, Vol. XL, 1981.

36. - The best way to get some sense of this issue is to read 'Was there a Russian Fascism?' (Ch. 8) and 'The Formation of the Russian Right' (Ch. 7) in Rogger, *Jewish Policies*. Then look at M. Blinkhorn (ed.), *Fascists and Conservatives* (London, 1990).

37. The student of modern Russian history anxious to learn about Spain could begin with A. Shubert, *A Social History of Modern Spain* (London, 1990), and R. Carr, *Spain, 1808–1975* (Oxford, 1989). Some of my arguments are owed to chapters in F. Lannon and P. Preston (eds.), *Elites and Power in Twentieth-Century Spain* (Oxford, 1990), in particular Chs. 3, 5, 6, 1 1 and 13. R. Carr and J.P. Fusi, *Spain: Dictatorship to Democracy* (London, 1979), and J.P. Fusi, *Franco* (London, 1987), were also valuable. On the Church see F. Lannon, *Privilege, Persecution and Prophecy: The Catholic Church in Spain, 1875–1975* (Oxford, 1987). On the army the essays in R.B. Martinez and T.M. Barker (eds.), *Armed Forces and Society in Spain Past and Present* (New York, 1988)), are of varying quality. See also P. Preston, *The Politics of Revenge, Fascism and the Military in 20th Century Spain* (London, 1990). Two contrasting essays on landowners in northern and southern Spain by M. Blinkhorn and T. Rees are also worth reading: see R. Gibson and M. Blinkhorn (eds.), *Landownership and Power in Modern Europe* (London, 1991), Chs. 11 and 12.

38. I discuss these issues in Lieven, *Russia and the Origins of the First World War*. An interesting comment on attitudes to war comes in the diary of Baroness Spitzenberg, an intelligent and sensitive lady close to the court of Wilhelm II. *Inter alia*, she stresses the need to look on war in a manly way, as Luther had done. R. Vierhaus (ed.), *Das Tagebuch der Baronin Spitzenberg* (Gottingen, 1960), p. 376.

39. PRO, FO 371, 514, 3,643, 29 January 1908, No. 104, p. 12.

40. PRO, FO 371, 512, 30,901, 4 September 1908, p. 4.

41. I discussed this in my *Russia and the Origins*, particularly in Ch. 4. C. Ferenczi, *Aussenpolitik und Offentlichkeit in Russland 1906–12* (Husum, 1982), and 'Nationalismus und Neoslawismus in Russland vor dem Ersten Weltkrieg', *Forschungen zur Osteuropaischen Geschichte* (Band 34, Berlin, 1984), are the most detailed studies of this issue. German literature on the connection between domestic and foreign policy in Russia must, however, be read with some caution. German historians are inclined to impose rather rigid and unproven 'scientific' theories about this relationship drawn from Germany's own experience before 1914. They do not necessarily fit Russian circumstances. In addition, the combination of obsession with 'scientific' theories and the ferocious warfare between German historical camps can lead to intolerance and dogmatism. On the making of Russian foreign policy before 1914 there is a good recent work by D.M. McDonald, *United Government and Foreign Policy in Russia, 1900–1914* (Cambridge, Mass., 1992).

42. PRO, FO 371, 517, 23,176, 12 June 1908.

43. Bing (ed.), *Letters*, p. 236.

44. Bing (ed.) *Letters*, pp. 240–1. The literature on international relations in the run-up to 1914 is vast. The introduction to D. Stevenson, *The First World War and International Politics* (Oxford, 1988), is a good survey of the issues involved. See also J. Joll, *The Origins of the First World War* (London, 1984).

45. Chapter 5 of Jelavich, *Russia's Balkan Entanglements*, fills in some of the details. S.R. Williamson, *Austria-Hungary and the Origins of the First World War* (London, 1991), is an interesting study of these issues as seen from the Austrian angle. Anyone

interested in a sample of Russian official thinking in the winter of 1913–14 would be well advised to read a report by Prince G.N. Trubetskoy in *Un Livre Noir: Diplomatie d'Avant-Guerre d'après les Documents des Archives Russe* (2 vols., Paris, n.d.), Vol. 2, pp. 373ff.

46. PRO, FO 371, 1,466, 8,486, 12 October 1912, p. 504; and 2,092, No. 15,087, 31 March 1914, pp. 215–16.

47. A.S. Avetyan, *Russko-Germansky Diplomaticheskie Otnosheniya 1910–1914* (Moscow, 1985), p. 159.

48. PRO, FO 371, 2,092, 15,312, 3 April 1914, pp. 292–6.

49. Brooke, letter dated 5/18 February 1914; and *Materialy po istorii franko-russkikh otnosheniy za 1910–1914gg* (Moscow, 1922), pp. 289–91.

50. Spiridovitch, *Dernières Années*, Vol. 2, p. 451; and Brooke, letter dated 29 May/11 June 1914.

51. *Mezhdunarodnye otnosheniya v epokhu imperializma* [MO] (3rd series, Moscow, 1931–40), Vol. V, No. 32, pp. 59–61, Shebeko to Sazonov, 30/17 June 1914.

52. Bark's memoirs are published in *Vozrozhdenie* and a rather fuller manuscript (in English) is held by the Bakhmetev Archive of Colombia University (CUBA). The quotes come from Ch. 7, pp. 1–6, and from the Daily Record of the Foreign Ministry: MO, 3rd series, Vol. V, No. 45, 24/11 July 1914, p. 45.

53. MO, 3rd series, Vol. V, No. 276, letter to Wilhelm II, p. 251; and *Documents Diplomatiques Françaises*, 3rd series, Vol. 9, No. 189.

54. Bark, CUBA, Ch. 7, pp. 7–23.

55. P. Gilliard, *Trinadtsat' let*, p. 83; and *Krasnyy Arkhiv*, Vol. 64, No. 3, 1934, pp. 130–9.

56. MO, 3rd series, Vol. V, No. 284, pp. 256–8.

57. Gilliard, *Trinadtsat' let*, pp. 85–6.

Chapter 8: The War, 1914–1917

1. TsGIA, Fond 1,650, Opis 1, Ed. Khr. 238, p. 48; and Gilliard, *Trinadtsat' let*, pp. 92–3.

2. Brooke, letter dated 12/25 August 1914.

3. Riha, *Readings*, pp. 465–78.

4. M. Cherniavsky (ed.), *Prologue to Revolution* (Englewood Cliffs, 1967), p. 22; and Pares, *Letters*, p. 86. On the army's morale during the war, in addition to Stone and Jones, see A. Wildman, *The End of the Russian Imperial Army* (Princeton, 1980). On peasant education and nationalism the best places to start are B. Eklof, *Russian Peasant Schools: Officialdom, Village Culture, and Popular Pedagogy, 1861–1914* (Berkeley, 1987), and J. Brooks, *When Russia Learned to Read* (Princeton, 1985), Ch. VI. Two recently published books in English on the Soviet home front are J. Barber and M. Harrison, *The Soviet Home Front, 1941–1945* (London, 1991), and W. Moskoff, *The Bread of Affliction* (Cambridge, 1990). See also S.J. Linz (ed.), *The Impact of World War II on the Soviet Union* (Ottowa, 1985). On the German occupation see A. Dallin, *German Rule in Russia, 1941–1945* (New York, 1957).

5. Pares, *Letters*, p. 304; and RO, Fond 70, Opis 3, Delo 7, p. 12, Letter to V.I. Guerrier dated 6 September 1915.

6. Brooke, letter dated 13/26 October 1914; Buxhoeveden, *Life*, pp. 190–6; Pares, *Letters*, p. 9; and Nicholas II, *The Letters of the Tsar to the Tsaritsa, 1914–1917* (London, 1929), p. 17.

7. Cherniavsky, *Prologue*, p. 37. Those interested in further discussion of the Myasoedov affair should read G. Katkov, *Russia 1917: The February Revolution* (London, 1967), Ch. 6.
8. Brooke, letter dated 10/23 July 1915.
9. Bark, 'Vospominaniya', *Vozrozhdenie*, No. 169, January 1966, pp. 80–1.
10. E.D. Chermensky, *IV Gosudarstvennaya Duma i sverzhenie tsarizma v Rossii* (Moscow, 1976), p. 99. The fullest account in English of domestic politics during the war is T. Hasegawa, *The February Revolution: Petrograd 1917* (Seattle, 1981). Another quite recent work is R. Pearson, *The Russian Moderates and the Crisis of Tsarism* (London, 1977).
11. Cherniavsky, *Prologue*, pp. 159 and 214–15.
12. Ibid., pp. 161, 217 and 219.
13. V.P. Semennikov (ed.), *Nikolay II i Velikie Knyaz'ya* (Moscow, 1925), pp. 68–9. This letter was actually written in April 1916. Even so it sums up many of the attacks made on the Grand Duke.
14. Anyone interested in pursuing this idea should read an article by H. Rogger, 'The Skobelev Phenomenon', *Oxford Slavonic Papers*, Vol. IX, 1976, pp. 46–77.
15. A good discussion of Nicholas's assumption of the supreme command is to be found in D.R. Jones, 'Nicholas II and the Supreme Command. An Investigation of Motives', Study Group on the Russian Revolution, *Sbornik*, Vol. II, 1985, pp. 47–83.
16. CUBA, Bark Collection, letter to A.N. Yakhontov, 9 September 1922, p. 9; and Cherniavsky, *Prologue*, p. 79.
17. Nicholas II, *Letters*, p. 90.
18. Ibid., pp. 85–6.
19. Ibid., pp. 57–8; and Pares, *Letters*, p. 86.
20. Pares, *Letters*, p. 114.
21. Voeykov, *S tsarem*, p. 255.
22. Cherniavsky, *Prologue*, pp. 164 and 226.
23. Nicholas II, *Letters*, pp. 137 and 219.
24. Ibid., p. 157.
25. Tsentrarkhiv, *Burzhuaziya nakanune fevral'skoy revolyutsii. 1917 god v dokumentakh i materialakh* (Moscow, 1927), pp. 127–35 and 136–9.
26. For an introduction to this issue see L.T. Lih, *Bread and Authority in Russia, 1914–1921* (Berkeley, 1990). I am also grateful to Professor K. Matsuzato of Hokkaido University, who sent me two interesting articles in manuscript on the food supply issue from which I learned a great deal.
27. Nicholas II, *Letters*, p. 266.
28. Fabritsky, *Iz proshlogo*, pp. 140 and 149; and Botkin, *Real Romanovs*, p. 125.
29. Nicholas II, *Letters*, p. 207; and Naumov, *Iz utselevshikh*, Vol. 2, pp. 514–15.
30. Bark, 'Vospominaniya', *Vozrozhdenie*, No. 175, July 1966, pp. 71–2.
31. Brooke, letters dated 30 August 1915, No. 2,136 and 6/19 March 1916, No. 1,089.
32. V.S. Dyakin, *Russkaya burzhuaziya i tsarizm v gody pervoy mirovoy voyny 1914–1917* (Leningrad, 1967), p. 77; and Bark, 'Vospominaniya', *Vozrozhdenie*, No. 174, June 1966, p. 96. V.I. Gurko (see *Features*, pp. 185–8) and S.E. Kryzhanovsky (*Vospominaniya*, pp. 193–6) served with Sturmer for many years in the Ministry of Internal Affairs and knew him well. Kryzhanovsky was one of the tough experienced officials whose appointment to head the ministry would have enraged public opinion.

33. Pares, *Letters*, pp. 170 and 175; Brooke, letters dated 11/24 October 1915, No. 2,527, 14/27 January 1916, No. 232, and 25 February/9 March 1916.
34. Dyakin, *Russkaya*, p. 228; and Nicholas II, *Letters*, p. 233.
35. Bark, 'Vospominaniya', *Vozrozhdenie*, No. 179, November 1966, pp. 102–3.
36. Nicholas II, *Letters*, p. 297; and Pares, *Letters*, p. 442.
37. Nicholas II, *Letters*, pp. 70–2; and Brooke, letters dated 15/28 November 1915, No. 2,840, and 6/19 March 1916, No. 1,089. On 13/26 September 1915 Benckendorff commented to his brother that, with Nicholas at Headquarters and ministers no longer coming to Tsarskoe, he was reduced to town gossip for much of his information. Even so, in permanant residence at the Alexander Palace in Tsarskoe Selo, he was very well placed to judge Alexandra's influence.
38. Bark, 'Vospominaniya', *Vozrozhdenie*, No. 175, July 1966, p. 78.
39. Pares, *Letters*, p. 93.
40. Brooke, letters dated 15/28 November 1915, No. 2,840, 26 August/8 September 1915, and 28 March/10 April 1916, No. 1,443; and Pares, *Letters*, pp. 433 and 445.
41. Bark, 'Vospominaniya', *Vozrozhdenie*, No. 180, December 1966, pp. 73–4.
42. Semennikov (ed.), *Nikolay II*, pp. 118–20 and 123.
43. Mosolov, *Pri dvore*, p. 99.
44. Hasegawa, *February Revolution*, p. 48; and V.S. Vasyukov, *Vneshnyaya politika Rossii nakanune Fevral'skoy revolyutsii. 1916-fevral' 1917g* (Moscow, 1989), p. 283. The question of food supply is a very complicated one and continues to cause disagreements among historians. Anyone interested in an alternative view to Hasegawa and Lih could usefully read T. Fallows, 'Politics and the War Effort in Russia: The Union of the Zemstvos and the Organization of the Food Supply, 1914–1916', *Slavic Review*, Vol. 37, No. 1, 1978.
45. Voeykov, *S tsarem*, p. 207.
46. P.E. Shchegolev (ed.), *Otrechenie Nikolaya II* (Leningrad, 1927), p. 147.
47. Voeykov, *S tsarem*, p. 229. For a fuller description of the revolution see either Hasegawa, *The February Revolution*, or R. Pipes, *The Russian Revolution, 1899–1919* (London, 1990), Ch. 8.

Chapter 9: After the Revolution, 1917–1918

1. Vernadsky (ed.), *Source Book*, Vol. 3, p. 884, has a full translation of the appeal.
2. Dehn, *Real Tsaritsa*, pp. 189–91.
3. Gilliard, *Trinadtsat' let*, pp. 203 and 209.
4. Dehn, *Real Tsaritsa*, p. 244; and Buxhoeveden, *Life*, p. 320.
5. Dehn, *Real Tsaritsa*, pp. 244–6.
6. Rose, *George V*, pp. 208–18.
7. Count P. Benckendorff, *Last Days at Tsarskoe Selo: Being the Personal Notes and Memories of Count Paul Benckendorff* (London, 1927), p. 103.
8. Botkin, *Real Romanovs*, p. 157.
9. Botkin, *Real Romanovs*, p. 158; and Gilliard, *Trinadtsat' let*, pp. 223–4.
10. A good recent history of the civil war is E. Mawdsley, *The Russian Civil War* (Boston, 1987).
11. *Literaturnaya Rossiya*, Vol. 39, 28 September 1990, pp. 19–20, contains biographies of the key Bolshevik leaders in the Urals in 1918. See also E. Radzinsky, *The Last*

Tsar (New York, 1992), for, rather confusingly presented, information on these men.

12. *Literaturnaya Rossiya*, Vol. 39, 28 September 1990, p. 19; and M.B. Olcott, *The Kazakhs* (Stanford, 1987), pp. 185 and 212–19.

13. Pipes, *Russian Revolution*, p. 758. The whole of Chapter 17 of Pipes's book is an excellent and very thorough study of the Romanovs' imprisonment and murder.

14. The extract from Trotsky's diary is in L. Trotsky, *Dnevniki i pis'ma* (New York, 1990), pp. 100–1. T. Emmons (ed.), *Time of Troubles: The Diary of Yu. V. Got'e* (Princeton, 1988), p. 179. Nos. 38, 39, 41 and 42 of *Literaturnaya Rossiya*, 21 and 28 September, and 12 and 19 October 1990, are devoted to the murder of the Romanovs. Apart from Radzinsky's book, now translated into English, these articles are the most detailed contemporary Russian source on the murders. They are also the easiest to follow. The most professional Soviet authority on the murders is G. Ryabov, whose articles in *Rodina*, Nos. 4 and 5, 1989, pp. 85–95 and 79–92, were full of new information when they first appeared. I discussed the murders with Mr Ryabov, to whom I owe a debt of gratitude.

15. *Literaturnaya Rossiya*, Vol. 39, 28 September 1990, p. 18.

16. An article in the *Sunday Times* of 10 May 1992 gives a description of the excavation. As I handed in my manuscript the bodies excavated near Ekaterinburg were being flown to Britain for identification.

17. Pipes, *Russian Revolution*, p. 788.

Chapter 10: Then and Now

1. See, for instance, *Literaturnaya gazeta*, 3 June 1992, p. 11.

2. In recent years there has been a great deal of Western scholarship on the Russian revolution, most of it sympathetic to the 'forces of the left'. Edward Acton, *Rethinking the Russian Revolution* (London, 1990), surveys this literature. A recent collection of articles by authorities in the field is E. Rogovin Frankel, J. Frankel and B. Knei-Paz (eds.), *Revolution in Russia* (Cambridge, 1992). Much of the work on the revolution has been written by first-rate scholars and is of a high standard. It will, however, be surprising if we do not witness a contrary trend in the next few years, much of it written by Russian historians using previously closed archival deposits. R. Pipes, *Russian Revolution*, and E. Mawdsley, *Russian Civil War*, are, to differing degrees, exceptions to the basic trend of Western literature in the 1970s and 1980s.

3. A short introduction in English to this issue is an article by Oxana Antic, 'Canonization of Last Tsar under Consideration', *RFE/RL Research Report*, Vol. 1, No. 28, 10 July 1992, pp. 90–2. Another source is V. Shlapentokh, *Soviet Intellectuals and Political Power* (London, 1990), pp. 206–9. A sense of the bitterness aroused by the issue of canonization can be felt from, for example, *Moscow News*, No. 27, 5–12 July 1992, p. 2.

4. G. Guroff and F. Carstensen (eds.), *Entrepreneurship in Imperial Russia and the Soviet Union* (Princeton, 1983), contains some thought-provoking essays and looks at this theme from many different angles.

5. Bill Fuller comments that 'Nicholas's practice of trying to bully and intimidate his neighbours with his military might often backfired, much as similar Soviet efforts did under Brezhnev in the 1970s and early 1980s': *Strategy and Power*, p. 250.

6. W.B. Lincoln, *In the Vanguard of Reform: Russia's Enlightened Bureaucrats, 1825–1861* (De Kalb, 1982).

7. Amidst the vast literature on the Gorbachev era A. Dallin and G.A. Lapidus (eds.), *The Soviet System in Crisis* (Boulder, 1991), has the great merit of presenting a large number of varied views with a brevity that nevertheless allows the reader to grasp the essence of their arguments. M. Perrie, *Alexander II* (London, 1990), is a very good short introduction to the Tsar's reign.

8. It is impossible to provide end-notes to back these comments. The bibliography would be vast, not least because my main job for the last seven years has been to teach and study the Gorbachev era. Some clue as to how my own ideas on this era developed can be found in Lieven, *Gorbachev and the Nationalities: Conflict Studies, No. 216* (London, 1988), and *The Soviet Crisis: Conflict Studies, No. 241* (London, 1991).

9. G. Shavel'sky, *Vospominaniya poslednego protopresvitera russkoy armii i flota* (2 vols., New York, 1954), Vol. 1, p. 52; and Kohut, *Wilhelm II*, p. 128.

10. H. Dollinger, 'Das Leitbild der Burgerkonigtums in der europaischen Monarchie des 19 Jahrhunderts', in K.F. Werner (ed.), *Hof, Kultur und Politik im 19 Jahrhundert* (Bonn, 1985), pp. 325–64, has some useful comments on possible royal strategies for survival in the Victorian era. Most of these strategies were impossible in Russia. S.R. Large, *Emperor Hirohito and Showa Japan* (London, 1992), was published after I had completed my manuscript. For anyone wishing to make comparisons between the Russian and the Japanese monarchy it is of great value.

Index